▶▶▶ Rave Reviews for *The Golden Highway*

"...accurate information, well illustrated and also fun and entertaining to read . . . "The Golden Highway, Volume I," . . .

. . . To report accurately, one must . . . go directly to the . . . actual words of those who were there and experienced what happened. That is what Jody and Ric Hornor have done in "The Golden Highway Volume I" . . .

. . . you will become involved and actually feel the joy, anguish and determination of the brave people who settled this land. . ."

Mountain Democrat, Placerville

"This is **a collection of incredible stories** found in actual historic documents and journals as well as **hundreds of restored photographs** taken by some of the first photographers to document the settling of California. Indexed, with a photo on every page, **a must have** for the local history buff."

The Union, Nevada County

. . . the Hornors have done a wonderful job of putting this book together."

Mountain Democrat

A 2007 Bronze Medal winner from the
Independent Publishers Association

▶▶▶Rave Reviews for *The Golden Corridor*◀◀◀

"... lots of authentic, historical pictures.... a wonderful job of putting this book together.

...you will actually feel the joy, anguish and determination of the brave people who settled this land...

"*The Golden Corridor*" is beautifully organized . . .

. . . **this is the one book you need to have.** You will spend hours reading the writings of those who were here and delight in the restored pictures of that era."

Mountain Democrat, Placerville

"Fans of old photographs . . .will love "The Golden Corridor." The book is **filled with amazing black and white photos** that bring early Northern California to life. Sidebars on each page give **fascinating quotes from diaries, journals and newspapers**, as well as anecdotes . . . **well worth checking out**."

The Union, Nevada County

"This is **an interesting read** . . . I especially enjoyed it because most of the book's dialogue comes from letters and journals of the pioneers themselves. These **firsthand accounts give the reader insight** into what it was like to travel through and settle these then wild lands. . . **the photos of the California Gold Rush are so marvelous** . . ."

True West Magazine

. . . a captivating study of 19th century people who helped shape the times.

Sacramento Bee

". . . this amazing collection of firsthand testimony . . . Sidebars offer amusing quick vignettes from the era! **Enthusiastically recomended reading . . .**"

Midwest Book Reviews

"**. . . educational and entertaining.** Profusely illustrated . . ."

Auburn Journal

Awards from:

The Independent Publishers Association

Sacramento County Historical Society

THE GOLDEN HIGHWAY
Highway 49

Volume II: 19th Century California including Amador, Calaveras, Tuolumne, Mariposa (including Yosemite) and Madera Counties

Including Jackson, Sutter Creek, San Andreas, Angels Camp, Sonora, Murphys, Jamestown, Mariposa, Coulterville, Oakhurst and smaller communities in between.

Written and photographed by the people who lived and made California's history.

Acknowledgements

This book is dedicated to the thousands of pioneers who wrote California's history, the early photographers who captured the scenes and the hundreds of historians who have preserved it over the years.

This work would not have been possible without the help of dozens of libraries, librarians and archivists including:

Amador County Archives

Bancroft Library

Calaveras County Archives

Calaveras County Historical Society

Fresno Flat Museum

Library of Congress

Mariposa County Historical Society

Tuolumne County Historical Society

Wells Fargo Bank

As we searched the vast libraries for the appropriate photographs, we found many of the same photos in different archives. The attributions are based on the archive from which we actually obtained the image. Any corrections or suggestions are welcome. Our apologies for any real or perceived errors.

We'd also like to thank our fact checkers and experts who helped assure the accuracy of this publication.

Deborah Cook, Amador County Historical Society

Shannon VanZant, Calaveras County Archives

Cate Culver, Calaveras County Historical Society

Leonard Ruoff, Tuolumne County Historical Society

Judy Sheets, Mariposa County Historical Society

Roger Mitchell, Fresno Flats Museum

GOLDEN HIGHWAY
Highway 49

Written by:
California pioneers and 19th century historians.

Researched and compiled by Jody and Ric Hornor
Photo restoration by Ric Hornor
Edited by Paula Bowden

Copyright © 2007

Ric and Jody Hornor

ISBN # 0-9766976-7-X

First printing: June 2007

Published by:

An Imprint of Electric Canvas™
1001 Art Road
Pilot Hill, CA 95664
916.933.4490

www.19thCentury.us

Table of Contents

Introduction — IX

Chapter 1: Amador County — 15
    Jackson, Plymouth, Ione, Sutter Creek, Volcano, and vicinity

Chapter 2: Calaveras County — 87
    San Andreas, Mokelumne Hill, Murphys, Copperopolis, and vicinity

Chapter 3: Tuolumne County — 145
    Sonora, Columbia, Jamestown and vicinity

Chapter 4: Mariposa County — 235
    Mariposa, Coulterville, Hornitos, Yosemite and vicinity

Chapter 5: Madera County — 275
    Oakhurst [Fresno Flats], Coarse Gold, and vicinity

Bibliography — 283

Index — 287

Additional Exhibits (when available) at — online
    www.19thCentury.us/Gold

James Lumsden, the man who cut the hole through the tree at Big Trees of Tuolumne, on Oak Flat Road on the way to Yosemite. This picture was taken right after he finished the job.

Introduction

Before the Gold Rush there was a trickle of hardy, adventurous and tenacious people who began to settle California. With the discovery of gold in 1848, thousands of people from the "States" and around the world came to pursue their hopes and dreams. For a few, those hopes and dreams came true. Most, however, battled bitter elements, a lawless society, disease and famine. Thousands suffered immeasurable hardships. Hundreds died. And a few — a lucky few, made their "pile."

It's on the labors and hardships of these early pioneers that California developed into what it is today.

Culled from roughly 5,000 pages of primary source documents, you witness their monumental accomplishments, brave deeds, and the exciting times that they experienced.

Feel the joy, anguish and determination of the brave people who settled this land. Enjoy their humor, admire their flair.

As you read their tales, you'll be amazed by their ingenuity, resiliency, and stamina. You'll feel their heartbreak and pain. You'll laugh at their antics. And you'll marvel at their accomplishments.

This is their story, in their words with their photographs.

With the exception of the photo captions and introduction, this book was written in the 19th century in the colorful language of the time.

Because of the many contributors and their individual writing styles, you'll find some that are challenging to read. Words were often spelled differently and punctuation and sentence structure were different as well. But they're well worth your effort. Our goal is to preserve these styles for you to enjoy, so we have intentionally done nothing that will make the chapters consistent in their presentation, punctuation, spelling or format, as it would eliminate each contributor's personal style and flavor in doing so.

There were huge cultural biases that are reflected in the text. As ingenious as these brave pioneers were, they had yet to invent "political correctness." As degrading and disheartening as some of the terms and stories are, they do reflect history.

Keep in mind that history, as it was recorded in the 19th century, was often done so subjectively. Many of the early history books (from which most of the core text is taken) were underwritten with the support of the people whose lives were chronicled within them. Thus the poor or not so vain may have been omitted unless they were truly newsworthy.

We're fortunate that there were a number of photographers, especially after 1860, who traveled extensively through the area and took hundreds, if not thousands, of photographs. Even so, finding the one image that exactly illustrates a point in the text is often impossible. We must sometimes go out of the specific geography or era to give you the best illustrations of the places and events being discussed.

Many of the original photographs are so damaged that it's nearly impossible to see the detail in them. They are carefully restored to uncover details that have faded over the years. Sometimes we make amazing discoveries in the restoration process. Other times there's a tinge of disappointment that we

> Our goal is to preserve these styles for you to enjoy, so we have intentionally done nothing that will make the chapters consistent in their presentation, punctuation, spelling or format as it would eliminate each contributor's personal style and flavor in doing so.

See page 113

See page 195

Photo restoration examples. These are the originals. See the noted pages for the restored version.

can't fix the many years of degradation. Even so, some of those images are included because they illustrate important points of our history.

Hundreds of hours of restoration have gone into the photographs used in *The Golden Highway*. Many of the original photos are in the public domain and available through the organizations noted with each image. Some are from private collections. In all cases, the restoration work is copyrighted. If you'd like copies of these images for your own use, you must contact the libraries or archives noted and obtain them directly from the respective institution.

Unique challenges and situations were encountered in the development of this particular book.

First, county boundaries changed over the years on most of the counties documented here. Calaveras was once part of Amador. Mariposa County, referred to as "the Mother Counties," first spun off Fresno County, which in turn spun off Madera County. Consequently, you'll read references under one county that refers to a location that is now in a different county.

Secondly, after all the splits occurred, records and archives were divided up and not all the records that we like to reference have been located. Thus more unique approaches were taken to compile the histories of those areas.

So have fun wandering *The Golden Highway* in the 19th century. Get a taste of the rich history. And, if this book has whet your appetite for more, pick up a copy of *The Golden Corridor,* which covers the area from San Francisco to Lake Tahoe, or *The Golden Quest* that covers Lake Tahoe and Northern Nevada. Have fun with your studies!

Side Bar Legend

Most of the side bars provide new information that is not contained in the main body of text. The nature of the information is denoted by the following icons:

Text from personal letters will appear in this script font with the quill pen.

Stories about crime will appear with the hangman's noose in this font.

Quotes from diaries or journals will appear with this image of President Taft's personal journal.

Call outs, text that appears in the main body of content, highlighted for emphasis, appears with this magnifying glass.

You'll also occasionally find direct quotes from old newspaper articles which are in this font and quoted and sourced.

Drytown Exchange Hotel around 1890, with George Worley Lemoin's name on the sign outside. The McWayne store is next door.

Chapter 1: Amador County — Jackson, Plymouth, Ione, Sutter Creek, Volcano, and vicinity

It is probable that some trappers occasionally visited the lower portions of Mokelumne river, though not often, for the Indians, who inhabited that portion of the country, watched with jealous eye the intrusion of strangers for any purpose whatever. The Hudson's Bay Company had a trail from French Camp to Oregon, which was most of the way through the tules, and of course far to the west of the present limits. As early as 1840, all attempts to raise cattle on the east side of the San Joaquin, had been an utter failure, the Indians invariably driving off the stock and destroying the ranches.

DISCOVERY OF GOLD IN AMADOR COUNTY. In the latter part of March, 1848, a man arrived in Stockton, then called

> It does not appear that any number of men wintered here in 1848, though some of Stevenson's soldiers wintered at Mokelumne Hill. The first permanent white resident of which any account can be found is Louis Tellier. [His] first house was a log cabin covered with rawhides; he also had a large army tent which had been used in Mexico.

Joaquin commenced his career in this county. His exploits are notorious, and like all events of that kind, are multiplied and exaggerated until the clearest sight can no longer distinguish the true from the fabulous. His first operations were to mount himself and party with the best horses in the country. Judge Carter, in 1852, had a valuable and favorite horse which for safety and frequent use was usually kept staked a short distance from the house. One morning the horse was missing. Cochran, a partner in the farming business, started in pursuit of the horse and thief. The horse was easily tracked. Coming to a public house kept by one Clark, he saw the horse, hitched at the door. Going in he inquired for the party who rode his horse, saying that it had been stolen. He was told he was a Mexican, and was then at dinner with several others. Clark, who was a powerful and daring man, offered to arrest him, and suiting the action to the word, entered the dining-room in company with Cochran, and, placing his hand on Joaquin's shoulder—for it was he—said: "You are my prisoner." "I think not," said Joaquin; at the same time shooting Clark through the head, who fell dead. A general fusillade ensued, in which one of the Mexicans was shot by the cook, who took part in the affair, Cochran receiving a slight wound. The Mexicans mounted their horses and escaped, leaving Carter's horse hitched to the fence.

Placer Mining at Volcano. Cleaning up the dump box, mid 1860s.

Tuleburgh, bringing with him specimens of scale-gold, from Sutter's mill. He informed the people there of the recent discoveries on the American river, the specimens confirming his report; whereupon, Captain Weber, catching a spark from the flame, fitted out a prospecting party. The fever was on them; haste and nuggets their watchwords; inexperience their companion, and failure the result, until they had reached Mokelumne river, where the Captain decided to make a more deliberate search, the result of which was the discovery of the first gold found in the section of country, that was afterwards known as the Southern mines. Owing to their more careful search and added experience gold was found north from this river, in every gulch and stream to the American river. Arriving at Sutter's mill, it was decided to commence mining at what was called afterward Weber's creek, near Placerville. As soon as he had got work on Weber creek well under way, he returned to Stockton and organized a party to explore the country south of the Mokelumne river. In a short time they returned with finer specimens than had been found at Coloma. A mining company was formed, which afterwards gave name to Woods creek, Murphy's creek, Angel's Camp, and other places. Then commenced the general working of the "Southern mines," the rush of miners, the immigration which built up the flourishing counties of Amador, San Joaquin, Calaveras, Tuolumne, and the changing of the world's commerce.

The Mokelumne river, the gulches at Drytown, Volcano, and Ione, were mined extensively in 1848. General Sutter and party tried it near the town of Sutter, but he was disgusted with the opening of a saloon near his works, and left the mines, never to return.

MOKELUMNE HILL IN EARLY DAYS. In early days Mokelumne Hill was reputed one of the liveliest places in the mines. It had the misfortune to be settled by a heterogeneous population— Yankees, Westerners, and Southerners, from the United States; and French, German, and Spanish, from Europe; and Chilenos and Mexicans. Death by violence seemed to be the rule. For seventeen successive weeks, according to Dr. Soher, of San Francisco, a man was killed between Saturday night and Sunday morning. Five men were once killed within a week. The condition of things became so desperate that a vigilance committee was resolved upon, which, however, did not continue in existence long. One man who was hung for stealing, confessed, just before his death, to having committed eight murders between Mokelumne Hill and Sonora. He was a Mexican, of powerful physique and desperate character. Shooting was resorted to on the most trivial occasions. Two strangers sat quietly taking a dinner at a restaurant, and talking with each other. A gambler

In the Winter of 1850-51 a party of four or five men were hunting deer in the mountains a few miles above Volcano. Venison being worth fifty cents a pound they could afford to take some risks. One day, while following a wounded deer, Askey discovered a party of Indians, whom, by their dress, he judged to be Washoes, who had the reputation of being much better fighters than the California Indians. They saw him about the same time, and, coming up, professed to be very friendly, wanting to shake hands, which he prudently declined. A conference, mostly by signs, ensued, in which both parties agreed to pursue the deer, Askey taking one side of the hill, the Indians the other. He did not follow the deer far, but made the very best time to the camp that his short legs would admit of. In the morning, reinforced by his companions, he made a reconnaissance in force, and, as he expected, found that the Indians had made an effort to cut him off, the tracks in the snow showing that they had followed him until they sighted the camp. The following day an old Indian came peering about, and, by signs, intimated that the bark and wood set around the hut would keep out arrows. Suspecting him of being a spy, they thought best to detain him until morning, when he was dismissed with an application of a number ten boot to his rear that accelerated his departure.

Placer mining in Volcano, the mine, mid 1860s.

Courtesy Library of Congress

Jack Sutherland had a ranch on Dry creek. Billy Sutherland, then seventeen or eighteen, who had charge of the place in the absence of his father, sold a band of cattle for several thousand dollars in gold. He took a notion to count the money before putting it away in the safe, a hole in a log. While piling it up, a shadow darkened the door. Looking up, who should he see but Joaquin, the famous bandit. Resistance was out of the question; for he was alone. He politely invited Joaquin to alight, and in answer to the question whether he could stay all night with his party, replied in the affirmative. Joaquin called to his party telling them to unsaddle. They were fierce and sullen looking follows. He pretended not to know his guests, and set about getting their suppers. After eating, the leader asked young Sutherland if he was not afraid to stay alone with so much money in the house; and inquired what he would do if Joaquin should come around? Sutherland replied that Joaquin was a gentleman; that he and his father were acquainted, and referred to some transactions in which his father had benefited Joaquin. Are you Jack Sutherland's son?" says Joaquin. "I am," says Sutherland. After some further conversation, they laid down on their saddle blankets, and slept until morning. At parting, Joaquin paid his bill, remarking that it would be as well for him to remember nothing about their having been there.

Miners' headquarters along a river — rarely did the miners relax except on the sabbath when, if they weren't seduced by gambling and drinking at the saloons, they'd often spend it doing their readin', writin', laundry and other personal chores.

seated near, fancying that he heard his name mentioned, drew his revolver and shot one man dead. The conversation proved to be about a mining matter which did not concern the gambler. A year after, to a day, the surviving man, who was talking with the person slain, had occasion to pass through the town, and remembering the former shooting of his partner, concluded not to stop, but a roysterer saw him, and disliking something in his appearance, drew a bead on him and fired; the aim was spoiled by some one throwing up the pistol at the moment of the explosion. The stranger thought it a curious country; his partner was killed a year before for some harmless talk; he was shot at while quietly passing along the streets.

The gulches around the hill were very rich, and in the Winter of 1850-51 the leads were traced into the hills. The yield was enormous, even fabulous. The hill is supposed to be a continuation of the same wash that made Tunnel Hill rich.

STAGING—GREEN AND VOGAN'S LINES. Charles Green and John Vogan commenced the business in 1833, running from Jackson, through Drytown, to Sacramento in one day. The line proving profitable, it was extended through Mokelumne Hill to Sonora making the whole distance in one day, through fare being twenty dollars. The cost of stocking a line was enormous. None of the horses cost less than three hundred dollars each, and some of them twice that. Concord wagons cost from six hundred to one thousand dollars, and Troy coaches twenty-five hundred to three thousand dollars. A good driver was worth one hundred and fifty dollars per month; hostlers one hundred dollars. Hay and barley were also high, sometimes one hundred dollars per ton. Notwithstanding these expenses, the line was profitable, the coaches generally being loaded to their utmost capacity. Staging then and now were quite different affairs. Then there were no roads, the coaches following the trails, or zigzagging around the dust-holes in Summer, and mud-holes in Winter. There were no bridges, and sometimes driver and horses were lost. During the Summer season the trip was rather pleasant, but when the coach stuck in a raging stream of water four or five feet deep, the situation made a timid man pray and a wicked one swear. The highwaymen occasionally levied tribute on the passengers, who, though armed, would find themselves unexpectedly confronted with a pistol in such close proximity that it was useless to resist.

MYSTERIOUS SICKNESS. In early days N. W. Spaulding, since Mayor of Oakland, and Judge Thompson, of Mokelumne Hill, were living in the same cabin, and both had a kind of rash

A party of Frenchmen opened a hole in the richest part of the hill. Some Americans mining near them conceived the plan of driving them out. The Frenchmen resisted, and the Americans raised the cry that the French had hoisted a French flag. The Frenchmen lost their claim. During the time of the difficulty, hundreds of persons jumped into the hole and carried away dirt which would pay from fifty to one hundred dollars per sack. The Frenchmen had camped in the hole, cooking, eating, and sleeping there, to prevent other parties stealing the dirt or jumping the claim. Though the people generally united to drive the original holders out, none can now be found to justify the expulsion, which is now looked upon as a downright robbery.

This four-horse stage owned by the Ione and Eastern Railroad served towns like Sutter Creek and Amador from the Martell station. This shot in front of Amador Livery Stable was taken after the railroad was built in 1904.

A genuine grizzly was discovered in a ravine a mile or two from town [Volcano], and a valiant party, armed with axes, knives, pistols, and a few guns, started after him. When the huge fellow, curious to see what all the fuss was about, raised himself up on his quarters to look around, all wisely ran but one man, who had faith in his rifle. He fired and hit the bear, only to enrage him however. He soon came up with the man, caught his head in his mouth, tearing off nearly the whole scalp, and otherwise lacerating the man. By remaining entirely passive, the man induced his bearship, Ursa, the terrible, to suspend farther punishment. After the bear left, the man contrived to crawl towards his home. A short time after a party better armed pursued the bear and killed him. The bear was a monster. When loaded into an ordinary wagon-bed, eleven feet long, his legs stuck out behind fully three feet, making his total length not far from fourteen feet. He was poor and tough, and was not considered fit for food.

"Sutter Creek Brewery, J Raddatz, proprietor about 1891. The men in front include John Raddatz and Albert Ludwig. Beer became a popular beverage in Europe when the Little Ice Age which ended in 1850 killed most of the grape vines and thus curtailed the wine industry for many years. Even though the climate changed for the better, the taste for beer was developed and has been a huge industry since.

or breaking out on the skin, which was very annoying, causing an intolerable itching. Dr. Sober, an eminent physician, was consulted in the matter, he said it was produced by a feverish condition of the blood, induced by a change from the cool air on an ocean voyage to the dry atmosphere of California, and recommended laxative medicines, which they took for several weeks without any beneficial effects. The matter became rather serious. A closer inspection revealed the cause of the sickness to be an army of grey-backs, who had taken up all the available ground on their bodies, and were doing their best to work it out, their operations being, happily, on the surface, however, tunnel mining not having been discovered. The clothing and cabin, even, were swarming with the vermin. A three days' campaign with boiling water, supplemented with a little unguentim, expelled the trespassers. The matter was considered too disgraceful to speak of publicly, and they paid the doctor's bill, sixty-five dollars each, without grumbling. Thirty years' silence over so good a thing having become painful, mutual threats of exposure brought out the story at a recent meeting of the San Francisco Pioneer Society, amid shouts of laughter. They were not the first or last persons thoroughly astonished at the unexpected presence of grey-backs in overwhelming numbers.

BULL AND BEAR FIGHT. In the days when Calaveras and Amador were one, the population of the ancient capital were went to amuse themselves with bull and bear fights. Sunday was the day set apart for these exhibitions, for, on that day, everybody came to town. A large portion of the population was Spanish, and anything pertaining to the fighting of bulls would draw out the full Mexican population, señors, señoras, and señoritas. Spanish cattle were plentiful, and there were plenty of men who had been trained to handle them; but bears, real grizzlies, were not to be easily caught and handled. They were valued all the way from one to four thousand dollars; consequently, when a real grizzly was caught and caged, he was generally given an unfair advantage. The bull was lassoed just before the fight, his horns sawed off, and the fight pretty well taken out of him before he was turned into the ring. On one occasion, the miners, and other spectators, got rampant over the way in which a steer was sacrificed, "without any fight at all worth speaking of. "Unfortunately, for the exhibitors, the bull-pen close by had several fierce, untamed, and undaunted steers, any one of which felt amply able to avenge their slaughtered companion. One of them especially attracted the notice of the spectators. He would have filled the old Mosaic requirements, being perfect in all his parts. Lithe as a cat, his horns long and slender, he commenced bounding around his limited arena as soon as he heard the bel-

We were sitting in the cool side of a porch of a road-side inn when two men rode up and called for dinner and they were riding bare-back. After they came out we questioned them pretty closely and they said that the horses belonged to their uncle and the reason they were riding bare-back was that their uncle had driven the horses up with a carriage and they were taking the horses back. They were two fine looking American horses and we well knew that it was almost a sure thing that a Spaniard was not the possessor of an American horse. We let them depart, but after came to the conclusion that they were riding stolen horses and we agreed that we would follow them up and take them. We told them in Spanish, it was no use for them to make any fuss about it, they would have to go back [to prison in Stockton] and that ended it. Just before we entered Stockton, we put the horses' necks together and tied the men's feet together under the horse's bellies, so we were sure they could not break away from us. As we were going up one of the principal streets, a man rushed out of a livery stable and hailed, or rather tried to hail us, but we only put spurs to our horses the more and rushed them through to the jail. They hadn't much more than gotten them in jail, till here came a man just puffing and blowing and pretty mad too because we wouldn't stop. He proved to be the Sheriff of Amador County and was after these same horses and wanted the men turned over to him.

Lorenzo Dow Stephens, 1849

It wasn't just gold that was mined in the area. The Gold Rush brought thousands of people with needs for many things. This fire brick clay mine in Ione provided a vital commodity for the hundreds of homes and businesses that were built in the area.

Courtesy Amador County Archives

In 1855, two Mexicans tried to rob a China camp about four miles below Jackson. They met with unexpected resistance; one being stunned with a blow from a hatchet, the other making his escape. The Chinamen wound their prisoner with ropes from head to foot, so tightly that he could not bend, and then guyed him up liked a smokestack to a steam saw-mill, and sent to town for help to arrest him. When the whites got there they found him standing in the middle of the camp with ropes reaching out from him, all around, holding him to his place. He was brought to town and hung.

Knight Foundry is a water-powered foundry and machine shop, established in 1873. Originally the Campbell, Hall and Co., Samuel Knight, a partner, bought them out. They established their business to supply heavy equipment and repair facilities to the mines and logging industry of the Mother Lode. Samuel N. Knight developed a high speed, cast iron water wheel which cornered the market until Pelton designed what some thought was a better design. Heavy competition between the two led to comparative tests in Grass Valley in 1883. Pelton's design proved the most efficient, winning the contract to supply wheels to the Idaho mine in Grass Valley.

lowings of his less able companero, that was being chawed and clawed in the hug of the grizzly.

The vaqueros were ordered to turn the anxious steer into the pen, a hundred revolvers being drawn to enforce the request. The proprietors knew that business was on hand, unless the request was acceded to, as the grizzly was sure to be shot, and, perhaps, some of their own number, too. There was no alternative, and they turned the anxious fellow in, though they expected the bear would be slain in a short time. The bull came in, proud and defiant, gave a snort of contempt, whirled his tail high in the air, lowered his head, and made a charge. His majesty seemed not to be aware of any unusual company, and looked as placid and serene as though he had just made an ample dinner of young and tender pig, and was going to take his daily afternoon nap. He received the bull with his usual affectionate hug, the bull's horns passing each side of his body. He caught the bull by the back of the neck with his mouth, and with the aid of his forepaws, held him firmly to his bosom, using his hind foot with terrible effect on the bull's neck and sides. One ear was stripped off in a twinkling. Every dig of those terrible claws left gaping wounds, while the bull seemed utterly powerless to inflict any damage on the bear. About five minutes of this kind of one sided fighting, served to convince the bull that he was not so invincible after all. His bellowings of defiance changed to notes of rage, and then to terror, and finally to cries for mercy; the last howls being so loud as to be heard a mile away. After punishing the bull for a while, the bear, entertaining no malice, magnanimously let the bull loose, which, blinded by blood and rage, made a charge at the picket-fence, which separated him from the spectators, and went through it, scattering the crowd in every direction, like a whirlwind. A dozen vaqueros mounted their horses and started after him. Down through the town went the bull, charging with his bloody head at every gathering of men, until he got to the clothing stores, kept by the Jews. The bright red shirts attracting his attention, he demolished these places one after another, until the vaqueros succeeded in getting their lariats around his horns and legs, curbing the further exhibition of his varying moods of temper. It is unnecessary to say that the several acts of the exhibition were highly satisfactory to the crowd, the general verdict being, "That thar bar's some, you bet."

Domestic Habits of the Miners. Many exaggerated stories are in circulation concerning the habits and characters of our early settlers. Bret Harte, Joaquin Miller, and a score of other writers, have taken some odd sample of humanity, added some impossible qualities, and set him up to be laughed at or

Some Frenchmen in 1852, during a time of scarcity, killed and eat a coyote, but their account of his good qualities was not such as to induce others to try the experiment.

Miners working in Jackson's Argonaut mine at the 3900 foot level.

This stagecoach with its six-horse team was on Ione Street in Ione. On February 13, 1899, the stage was held up at Cyclone Station. A monument, in honor of the driver who was killed (Michael Tougy) stands on Highway 88 near where this stage was robbed and Tougy lost his life.

"Stockton is celebrated for its mosquitoes, Sacramento for its bed-bugs, San Francisco for its rats, and Oakland for its fleas. They are larger and there are more of them; they can jump further and higher, bite oftener and deeper, than any fleas in the world. They are more persistent than a book agent, and hold with a tighter grip than a money-lender. Everybody 'has 'em bad.' The young and the old, the tender and the tough, alike are meat for them.

"Even the sanctuary is invaded by them; in fact, the church flea is the most ravenous of all. Starved during the week, he has an extraordinary appetite when the Sabbath comes.

"The fleas are not without their benefits, however. Half of the success of our business men is supposed to be due to the irritation of the fleas, who never let them rest, day nor night. No bed-bugs can live where such a race of fleas has taken the land. To use the words of a noted housekeeper, ''the fleas eat 'em up." Not a bed-bug is known in all Oakland. What a blessing these fleas would be in our interior towns, where the bed-bugs have had possession for a quarter of a century.

"If our country neighbors want some of these fleas, I think the Oaklanders would be willing to spare them. Though usually anxious to drive a good bargain, in the sale of fleas they would be generous. They will help you catch them. You have only to sleep a night or two in the churches, and you will have enough. Negotiations may be opened with our Mayor or any of the city officers."

Oakland Times

perhaps admired; when the fact is, the caricature is about as near the original as the Indian maiden of romance is to the filthy squaw that would eat the raw entrails of a horse or bullock without adding anything to the dirt, that already ornamented her hands and face. The '49er is represented as having pounds of dust loose in his pockets, which he passed out by the handful for whisky or whatever struck his fancy; as carrying an arsenal of knives and revolvers which he was wont to use on the slightest provocation—"rough but generous, bravo, and kind." The fact is, that the mass of the people had no resemblance to the ideals of Bret Harte or Joaquin Miller. They were sober, industrious, and energetic men, who toiled as men with ambition and strength can toil. The exceptions, which have given such a false character to the '49er, were unprincipled adventurers from every State and nation, gamblers in bad repute, even among their own kind, frontiersmen who acknowledged no law, and fugitives from justice everywhere. The description of this class is not the object of this chapter. The substantial, honorable, and industrious must now claim our attention.

When the lucky prospector had found a paying claim, the next thing was to set up his household. From two to four was the usual number of the mess. The summers were long and dry, and there was no discomfort in sleeping out of doors. But even in summer a house, though humble it might be, had many advantages over a tent for comfort and security. A stray horse or ox would sometimes get into the flour-sack or bread-sack, upset the sugar, or make a mess of the table-ware. Wandering Indians would pilfer small things, or take away clothing which might be left within reach; but in a cabin things were tolerably secure from depredation. A site for a cabin was selected where wood and water were abundant. These things, as well as the presence of gold, often determined the location of a future town. Bottle Spring (Jackson), Double Springs, Mud Springs, Diamond Springs, and Cold Springs, at once suggest their origin.

In the western settlements a floor made of hewn timbers (puncheons) was usual, but the ground served for a floor, and was considered good enough for a man. Generally, bunks were made by putting a second log in the cabin at a proper elevation and distance from the sides, and nailing potato or gunny sacks across from one to the other. Some fern leaves or coarse hay on these sacks, with blankets, made a comfortable bed. A good fireplace was necessary. Most of the mining was in water, necessarily involving wet clothes. A rousing fire, especially in Winter, was necessary to "get dried out." Some of those fireplaces would be six feet across, and built of granite or slate rocks, as each abounded. A shelf or two of shakes, or sometimes an open box in which pickles or candles had come around the Horn, would serve for a cupboard to keep a few tin plates, and cups, and two or three cans containing salt, pepper, and soda. A table of moderate size was also made of shakes, sometimes movable, but oftener nailed fast to the side of the house. Those who crossed the plains would often take the tail-gate of the Wilson for this purpose. A frying-pan, coffee-pot, Dutch-oven, and water-bucket completed the list of household utensils.

Not much attempt was made at neatness, and oftentimes one had to console himself with eating only his own dirt, for there were camps where the dishes were not washed for months.

Amador City, 1870s.

Courtesy Amador County Archives

> We left Volcano and came on up a new road just built, or rather building, across the mountains near the route of the old emigrant road. Soon after leaving Volcano we struck a table mountain of lava and followed it for two days, up a very gentle grade. Deep valleys lay on both sides, and from many points we had wide views of the foothills and the great valley, all bathed in a blue haze of smoke and dust, like our Indian summer intensified, in which all objects faded in the distance and those on the horizon were shut out entirely.
>
> The next day, still following up the table, we got partially above the sea of dust and haze and at times we could even see the coast ranges. At Tragedy Springs we were up over seven thousand feet. This place took its name from a fearful tragedy. Four men were killed here by the Indians and their bodies burned. Their names are carved on a large tree by the spring, their only monument.
>
> William Henry Brewer,
> August 14, 1863

"I had been mining on the South fork, in the Summer of '52, and came down to Dry creek in the Fall. About that time two or three families had settled on Dead Man's creek. I had seen a slender, willowy form flitting in and out of a cabin. I worked like a Trojan 'panning-out.' to get money enough to buy raiment fit to appear in her presence. At length the task was performed, and I hung the suit up by my bed and slept. I was awakened in the night by a scratching on the logs above my head, which I supposed was by the rats. They had annoyed me so often, that I resolved to fix 'em.' A gun was standing by my side. From the scratching I concluded there must be a dozen or two, at least. I succeeded in getting the rod out and did my best to kill the whole of them. There were three other persons sleeping in the cabin. Hearing the racket, they all roused up. Hastily stirring the coals in the fire-place, we raised light enough to see our friend crawling out of a hole in the unfinished gable of the cabin. Clothing, blankets, provisions, boots and shoes, and even the very logs of the cabin, were saturated with the essence of all that is villainous. Months afterwards when the scent had become so diffused that we could no longer perceive it, I made a visit to Fiddletown. There was a ball going on, and I stepped into the ball-room to get a glimpse once more of a woman's face. Several persons made the remark that somebody must have killed a skunk. I quietly retired. Somebody else got that girl."

A young and romantic miner

Fiddletown in the 1850s, probably the west side of Main Street. The Belle Creole Baths, a barber and a blacksmith shop provide some of the necessary services of the early settlers.

Sometimes a little hot coffee turned on a plate would take off the last-formed dirt; but washing dishes— the everlasting bane of woman's housekeeping—was, if possible, more repugnant to man, and was frequently omitted; it made the gold-pan greasy (the miner's prospecting-pan served for washing dishes as well as gold, also as a bread-pan, and wash-tub on Sunday). The cooking was a simple matter, boiling potatoes, making coffee, frying slap-jacks and meat, being the usual routine.

Practice made many of the miners expert cooks. New methods of cooking were sought out, and new dishes invented. Think of using a dry-goods box for an oven, and baking a pig or shoulder of pork in it! No trick at all. Drive down a stake or two, and on them make a small scaffold, on which to place your roast; now build a very small fire of hard wood, at such a distance away that a moderate sized dry-goods box will cover it all, and your arrangements are complete.

The Winter of 1852-53, was perhaps the roughest time ever seen in California. The long spell of high water utterly prevented the transportation of provisions from the cities, and there was much want, though no actual cases of starvation. Many men lived for weeks on boiled barley. Beans, without even a ham-bone to season them, furnished, in some cases, the only food for weeks. At one camp, a pork rind was borrowed from one house to another, to grease the frying-pan for slap-jacks.

A narrative of personal experience of one who lived on the south branch of Dry creek, in 1852, will give an idea of the troubles of that year:—

"At the head of Indian gulch we found some paying dirt. We went to work, and by dint of ground sluicing, rocking and panning, about four o'clock we had probably, an ounce of dust. With this I started to Fiddletown to buy a supper for the boys. The creeks were now nearly waist deep. The log on which I crossed in the morning was gone, and the water was running high over the banks. Two or three hundred yards away was the cabin, and I knew, by the bright light shining through the cracks of the door, that a big fire had been built to cook our suppers. The creek was nowhere fordable. After an hour's hard work, the bridge was found. It was a cedar tree. I could feel it swaying to the movement of the water. But the submerged part had limbs standing up out of the stream, and a charge in force across the bridge was ordered, with this caution, 'My boy, if you go overboard, the boys will go without their suppers.' The opposite bank was gained in safety, by feeling the way and holding to the limbs; and, an hour later, some bread and fried pork, and a roaring fire, brought us to a comfortable condition, and gave us the spirit to laugh at all our troubles."

A tax gatherer from Coloma, the county seat of El Dorado, put in an appearance one day and expressed the determination to collect poll-tax from every one in the place. He stopped long enough to take a drink or two, and was sped on his way by numerous threats, backed by revolvers, with his purse no heavier for poll-taxes.

This freight wagon had an unusual-looking load of mine machinery. On the back: "Podesta, close view of hoist drum."

William O. Clark, the famous temperance orator, recuperates his exhausted energies by ploughing the hill sides and harvesting the tall oats, as a recreation. Robert Cosner, a successful politician, several times elected to the office of Sheriff, and now a prominent man in San Francisco, commenced his career here as a clerk for J. C. Williams. Doctor Fox, a stock broker in the city, also resided here in early days, as did W. F. Curtis, a lawyer, afterwards a noted man in the Union army. D. W. Seaton, successful as a lawyer, politician, and miner, was also resident here from his first coming to California to the day of his death (soon after his election to the State Senate) by the explosion of the steamer Yo Semite. He gave his name to the Seaton mine.

Amador City view c. 1870 with the Amador Hotel prominent.

LAUNDRY AFFAIRS. The matter of having clean shirts and beds, though quite necessity, was not forcibly called for, and the washing was postponed from one Sunday to another until the traditional washing-day, in many camps, was well-nigh forgotten. A clean shirt was hauled over a dirty one, until the accumulations of sweat and red clay would afford a study for a geologist. The blankets, too, were slept in for months, for no miner ever dreamed of having clean sheets, and as for pillows, his boots tucked under his blankets served as a support to his head. When a shirt was changed, the cast-off garment was laid aside, or left in his bunk to be washed at a more convenient time—which never came. No wonder then that the gray-backed lice, the genuine army vermin, colonized every blanket and shirt. For months respectable men, who would as soon have been accused of stealing as being lousy, went scratching around without a suspicion of the trouble. Poison oak, hives, change of climate, and a hundred other things were supposed to produce the intolerable, persistent itching. When the true cause became known, for sooner or later the discovery was sure to come, the conduct of the victims became amusing. Some would swear, some would cast their clothing away, or perhaps bury it, and purchase an entire new outfit—but the fact was the louse had taken possession of the whole country. A vigorous war with hot water, on everything that would scald, would exterminate him, though some lazy, and consequently lousy, miners contended that hot water would not kill them.

THE FIERCE SANGUINARY FLEA is still an open question. Between 1851 and '53, contemporaneous with the irruption of the rat, the flea fought his way into every camp, and held the fort, too, against all enemies. If unwashed shirts and blankets were favorable to the existence of myriads of gray-backs, not less so was the swarming lice for the flea, for he made meat and drink of them, hot water had no terrors for the flea; he was out and off before a garment would go into the water. During the day he made his home in the dust floor of the cabin, and at night sallied out of his lair, thirsting for blood. And he must be a good sleeper indeed, who could close his eyes in slumber, while hundreds of lancets were puncturing his cuticle. Sometimes a cabin was abandoned on account of them. A person happening to come in would have hundreds crawling on his pants in a few minutes.

These Jackson Brewery employees pose for a photo opportunity. The brewery was closed down during prohibition and the building was turned into a creamery.

Grizzlies hardly ever gave the road, though not apt to attack man unless provoked. It was Mr. Spaulding's good fortune to have one of the most thrilling adventures with one. He had occasion to visit Mokelumne Hill late in the day. The trail led through a deep, shadowy glen which the animals sometimes visited. As a matter of prudence he took his rifle. The daylight trip was well enough, no "bars" putting in an appearance, but on his return after night-fall, he heard the ominous cracking of the brush, and the sound of footfalls along the trail. Nearer and nearer came the animal that was never known to give the road.

With gun cocked and hair on end, he waited. As the outline of the animal came dimly into view he took as good aim as possible and fired. An unearthly growling was succeeded by the monster's tumbling, rolling, and tearing down the trail, it was evident the animal was severely wounded, and like all grizzlies, would be then most dangerous. He went back on the trail, and making a wide circuit, reached the camp at a late hour. After hearing his adventures the men made a visit to the ravine the next morning and finish the monster. The guns were loaded, and plans laid for approaching the animal. They found signs of the conflict—blood and broken brush. One, bolder than the rest, followed the trail, and—a great roar of laughter, with "Darned if it aint Dr. Herschner's old jackass." The poor, patient old fellow had packed many a load of grub to the miners, and would, when relieved of his burden, return home alone, but he had made his last trip.

Stage in front of the Ione Hotel. Anthony Caminetti, who served as a senator, is seated in front.

🔍 A young man living on the Slate-creek side of American hill, near Oleta, was bitten [by a rattlesnake] in [bed] without any warning on the part of the snake. He felt the sting, felt the deadly paralysis coming over him, and, in company with two or three companions, started for town, but sunk helplessly to the ground before getting there, dying shortly after. The following morning an examination of the bed revealed the presence of a young and vigorous rattlesnake, three foot or more in length.

Sometimes a man would leave his cabin and blankets and sleep on the naked ground on the outside to got rid of his persistent bed-fellows.

THE MINERS' FLEA-TRAP. If necessity is the mother of invention, the flea-trap was a sure corollary. It was a simple and effective affair. It was known that fleas would gather around a light; taking advantage of this habit, the miners would set a lighted candle on the floor, and around it set their pans with a small quantity of slippery soap-suds in each. The flea would fall in, struggle vigorously for awhile to get out, and finally drown. A tablespoonful of the rascals in the morning was considered a satisfactory catch. Later the bed-bugs drove out, to some extent, the flea, and still hold the land.

RATS AND OTHER VERMIN. Rats have been mentioned as coming in with the fleas. The mild climate, exposed condition of eatables, and absence of cats and dogs, the natural enemies of rats, caused them to multiply with extraordinary rapidity. They were as much at home in the country as in the town, and a miner, camping in the hills away from the town, soon received visits from the rats, who thenceforth managed to have a share of all he brought into his camp. After he had retired to his blankets, the rats in troops would run over his body, making it the jumping-off place in their playful gambols. They left their tracks on his butter, gnawed holes into his flour-sack, danced cotillions on his table, and kicked up a fuss generally. Rattlesnakes sometimes crawled into the interstices of the logs, and first made their presence known by the sharp rattle or perhaps the deadly thrust of their poisonous fangs into the sleeper's limbs.

JACKSON. During the Summer of 1848 this was a stopping place for persons traveling between Dry town and Mokelumne river, though some mining was done with batayas by the Mexicans, at the spring near the National Hotel. The number of bottles left around the spring by travelers, "gave it the name of Bottilleas, until it was changed to Jackson, in honor of Colonel Jackson, who afterwards settled there. In early days freight to Sacramento was as high as one thousand dollars per ton. In 1850 it was reduced to two hundred dollars per ton. To Volcano from Sacramento it was two hundred and fifty dollars. There were no bridges, and, even in Summer-time, both men and animals were sometimes drowned. Lumber was worth three dollars per foot, the floor of a small room costing six hundred to one thousand dollars. The roads were mere Indian trails, which were, in many instances, too narrow to let wagons through.

There were two roads to Sacramento; one by way of Rancheria and Drytown, the other by way of Buena Vista. Louis Tellier caused the latter trail to be cut wide enough for a wagon, at his own expense. Charles Boynton built the "Astor House," and also a bowling saloon. It was equal to any building in the city though it was built of logs, and daubed with mud. There was a cabin near where R.W. Palmer's house now stands; also one on the site of his stable, occupied by John Papac, a Chileno. Towards the Gate was a cabin, with the sign, "brandy and sugar," hence called the Brandy and Sugar Hotel, kept by a

In 1853, a party of Mexicans, said to have been Joaquin's band, robbed some Chinamen, killing two of them and tying the others on the creek below the town. Joe Lake, a butcher, in his rounds to sell his meat, rode up to the camp at the time the robbery was going on, and was killed by the Mexicans. One Chinaman escaping, came to the town and gave information of the tragedy. A party was made up and the Mexicans were pursued and overtaken; in the running fight which ensued one was severely wounded and was afterwards arrested in Lancha Plana, taken to Jackson and hanged.

Sutter Creek's American Exchange Hotel graces the west side of the street, with a stage waiting for passengers.

In 1851, two Frenchmen were murdered in Squaw gulch near the Gate. One was stabbed with a long bowie-knife thirteen times, dying immediately; the other, though cut five or six times, lived for several days. Suspicions were fixed upon a young Mexican, who was afterwards arrested by Waterman H. Nelson, Sheriff of Calaveras county at Sacramento, and brought to Jackson handcuffed. The examination was before Bruce Husband, Justice of the Peace. The testimony was so positive that there was no doubt of the guilt of the accused, and as the atrocious details of the murder came out the French portion of the population became excited beyond control. The Sheriff determined that the prisoner should be taken to Mokelumne Hill for trial. The French armed themselves with shot-guns, and the Americans with pistols, the latter with the intention of defending Nelson if he was assaulted.

Now commenced the exciting part of the affair. The Frenchmen had assured Nelson that they would not hurt him. The Americans looked on, admiring the pluck of the officer, caring little what became of the "greaser." Twice the rope was placed around the fellow's neck, and twice it was cut by the Sheriff. Nelson was finally overpowered and the Mexican was hanged.

A busy Main Street in Sutter Creek. A six-mule team rests while stage passengers and town residents pose for this photo. In the background is the bridge over Sutter Creek and the Hubble building around 1870.

man by the name of Kelley. He also sold bread and butter; a slice off a loaf baked in a Dutch oven, was sold for one dollar; if buttered, two dollars. He charged one dollar per night for room to spread the blankets on the ground floor.

A Dr. Elliot had a tent near the site of the Central House where he sold goods. During the Autumn an emigrant sold his tent for six dollars; the rains coming on soon after, he paid one dollar a night for the privilege of sleeping under it. Evans came in March, 1850, with some beef, slaughtered on the Cosumnes, packed on some animals. He hung his meat on a pole resting on two forked posts, and soon sold out and went after more. His business flourishing, he soon after opened a store at Secreto, another at Butte, and a larger one at Jackson, near the site of the National Hotel. His store was of logs, and, not being well chinked, he filled up the holes with hams, the shank bones sticking out all around. He soon associated with him D. C. White (who afterwards put up the soda works), and A. Askey, the latter having remained with him since.

Duncan & Gage (who afterwards kept a Chinese Bazar at San Francisco), Levinsky, Sloan, Stevens, Stockier, Captain Dunham, and others, came soon after Evans. Levinsky had a large store for many years, as also did Stockier. Stevens ran the Young America saloon; Sloan afterwards lighted Jackson with Aubin gas. Captain Dunham kept a meat market near the hanging tree. There were also the two Doctor Shields (called the big doctor and the little doctor).

FIRST GREAT EVENT IN JACKSON. This was no less than the capture of the county seat. This brilliant exploit seemed to have had its origin in the fertile brain of Charles Boynton. When Calaveras county was organized, Double Springs somehow obtained the county seat. It had but one house, which answered for Court House, saloon, store, and hotel. The place had not grown as was expected. The county seat, metaphorically speaking, was reaching out its arms for a more suitable home; and Jackson, with its less than a dozen houses, was willing to receive it, and nurse it to greater strength. Elections and Acts of the Legislature, means usually invoked in such matters, were set aside as involving too much time, altogether too slow for the lively town of Jackson. One morning, while Double Springs was resting quietly on its dignity as a shire town, the enemy appeared, smiling as usual. They (Charles Boynton and Theo. Mudge) walked up to the county seat's bar, and throwing down the coin, according to the custom of the country, invited all hands to imbibe. The population of the town, or at least the larger part, responded with alacrity, the larger part being Colonel Collyer, a rather pompous, portly Virginia gentleman, fond of telling good stories, and fonder still of good liquor, never refusing the opportunity for either. While one detachment of the enemy artfully engaged the attention of Colonel Collyer, who was county clerk, and in that capacity custodian of the archives,

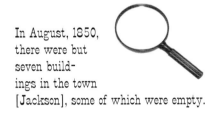

In August, 1850, there were but seven buildings in the town [Jackson], some of which were empty.

Fiddletown's U.S. Hotel, around 1852.

Courtesy Amador County Archives

Fred Iba's Bakery and Confectionery with the crew, probably all family, out front.

The Hanging Tree which has become noted wherever the name of California is known, formerly stood near Louis Tellier's saloon, and was a live-oak, with several branching trunks. It was never very beautiful, but was a source of so much pride to the citizens, on account of its history, that its likeness was engraved on the county seal, so that its appearance is not likely to be forgotten.

another detachment at the other end of the room gathered the archives under his arm, tumbled them into a buggy, and ran away with them to Jackson. When the Colonel found the county seat had vanished, he raised his portly form an inch or two higher, swung his cane furiously around his head, and swore that the army should be called out to vindicate the dignity of the court.

A shake shanty, at the foot of Court street, had been prepared for the bantling, and, on the arrival of Boynton and Mudge at Jackson, the archives were desposited with the proper ceremonies, the liquors being remarkably fine; and Jackson became the center of government for the great territory of Calaveras, which extended from Sacramento to the Rocky Mountains.

TRAGEDY—KILLING OF COLONEL COLLYER. At the election for county officers, held soon after the removal of the county seat, Joe Douglass, candidate for the clerkship against Colonel Collyer received the larger number of votes. The Colonel locked up the returns in his desk, in order to hold the office until his successor was qualified, which could not well be done without the counting of the votes, with his official signature to the result. Judge Smith broke open the desk in the absence of the Colonel, counted the returns, and issued the certificates of election to the successful candidates, Joe Douglass among the rest. This put a new face on the affair. The feud, occasioned by the removal of the county records, now grew into an open war. Threats to shoot Judge Smith on sight induced him to arm himself, and when they met, near the foot of the present Court street, Smith commenced firing, hitting Collyer, who does not seem to have been armed, two or three times. The shots were fatal, and Collyer fell at the foot of a large oak tree growing there, and shortly after expired. Smith was not tried for the homicide, but public indignation was so strong that he resigned.

EIGHTEEN HUNDRED AND FIFTY. In the Fall a great immigration came in, and by the 1st of December, Jackson had in the neighborhood of a hundred houses. Harnett built and kept a restaurant near the Astor House. Henry Mann and John Burke also had a restaurant, near the tree afterwards famous as the "hanging-tree." It was in this house that the Indian, Coyote Joe, was tried for killing the blacksmith near the Gate. The wife of Helmer Turner, present Deputy County Clerk, is a daughter of Henry Mann; a son is junior partner of the firm, Hutchinson, Mann & Co., engaged in insurance in San Francisco. Mr.

Placer mining in Volcano — working in the dump box in the mid-1860s.

"Doctor Marsh, who was murdered in Contra Costa county about 1856, was formerly owner of a ranch in this county. Being called upon in a professional capacity to visit a sick child, he got the mother to wash a shirt for him.

"On leaving he made out a bill for services amounting to fifty cows—the exact number of the woman's herd of cattle. She acknowledged the debt, but at the same time made out a bill to the same amount for washing his shirt. The doctor went off grumbling at the high rate for washing in California."

Ledger

A man, distrusting his companions, put his purse, containing several pounds of dust, under a flat rock some ways from the camp. In the morning it was gone. He was loud in his complaints of having been robbed by some one of the company. Instead of getting up a row, they were cool enough to inquire into the circumstances, and went with the loser to the defaulting bank. The depositor showed the line between two trees, where the gold was buried under the rock, which appeared to have been moved. A closer examination showed marks of a paw that had scratched around the stone. The purse, gnawed in holes and empty, was found not far away, the dust being scattered over considerable ground. It was mostly recovered, and good feelings in the family restored, though coyotes fared badly in the vicinity after that, all on account of "that thar blamed crittur that stole his puss."

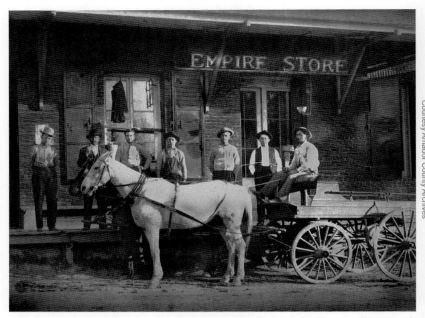

The Levaggi Store front, in Plymouth, later known as the Empire Store, with a two-horse wagon in front with a few of the locals.

Mann lost his life in a singular manner. A tame bear was kept tied to the famous tree near Mann's restaurant. One day he had been moved to a lot where some shoats were kept, which his bearship commenced killing. Mr. Mann, in trying to return the animal to the tree, angered the bear, which gave him a hug that proved fatal in two or three days.

SECOND REMOVAL OF THE COUNTY SEAT. Mokelumne Hill having outgrown Jackson, was hankering for the distribution of the public moneys among her own people. According to the law passed by the Legislature in 1849-50, the county seat might be moved every year if a majority petitioned for an election and two-thirds voted for the change. It was little trouble to get names on a petition of any kind, and, as events subsequently proved, not very much trouble to get votes in those days. An election being ordered, Jackson would make an effort to keep it. Though Mokelumne Hill had the votes, Jackson had the talent and daring, which, once before, had captured the county seat.

It was determined to gather a great multitude by means of a free bull-fight, hoping to out-vote Mokelumne Hill. Accordingly a corral was prepared, bulls engaged, and great inducements offered, or, as the play bills said, unparalleled attraction.

The bulls, some seven or eight in number, were brought in some day or two before, and fierce looking fellows they were, with their long slender horns and sleek hides, and the excitement was immense. It looked as if Jackson had got the bulge on the Mokelumne "Hellyons." Lest the cattle might be surreptitiously turned loose, a guard of three or four men with rifles, was stationed at the gate to insure the safe keeping of the animals. But the MokHillians were not asleep. They began to gather; they were not going to be beaten with a bullfight. They announced that the bull-fight was not coming off. A delegation of trusty men was sent to Jackson to watch the enemy. During the night they plied the guards so well with whisky that they slept at their posts, during which time the MokHillians quietly undid the fastenings without disturbing the sentinels. Getting on the opposite side of the corral they raised a great hullabalo, hearing which the guards sprang to their feet only to be tossed and trampled by the infuriated beasts, which charged at a run through the open gate and were gone in a moment.

The Spanish bulls having gone, an attempt was made to get up an entertainment with American cattle, but they would not entertain worth a cent, and the crowd programme was a failure. It was now learned what the horses at Mokelumne Hill were for. Bands of men were riding furiously all over the country voting at every precinct, but the horses of Jackson were few, and when the sun went down Jackson was beaten, because the other side had the most horses. An enormous vote was cast, out of all proportion to the population.

MINES. The gulches around Jackson were generally good, though no such strikes were made as in Mokelumne river. The

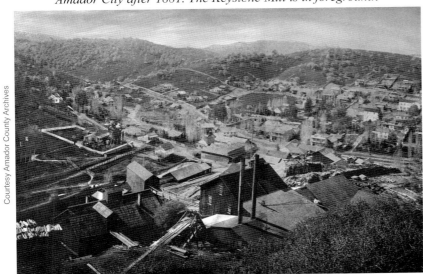

Amador City after 1881. The Keystone Mill is in foreground.

The invention or use of hydraulic pressure in mining, is generally accredited to Matthewson, of Mokelumne Hill. It is uncertain who first used it in Amador county. Some persons claim it for N. W. Spaulding, near Clinton. In the Winter of 1853-54, tin pipes were used as nozzles, with a pressure of twenty to thirty foot. It was thought impossible to use a hundred foot pressure, but experiments quickly taught the miners that no practical limit was probable; and we soon find the flow increased to seventy-five, one hundred, and even one hundred and fifty feet. The hose began to be made of the heaviest canvas, with two or three thicknesses. With a pressure of one hundred and twenty-five feet, the toughest clays around the camp would melt away like snow before a driving wind, and more gold was saved than before. Experience suggested improvements, and the way was pointed out which led to the Monitor, through which five hundred inches are hurled with force sufficient to move rocks tons in weight.

March 23, 1854, a Swede was hung at Jackson, for the stealing of a horse from Evans and Askey. The horse, a valuable and noticeable one, was taken from the stable on the night of the 17th. Suspicion immediately fixed itself on the person afterwards arrested, who had been camping in the vicinity. The camp was visited, but the man was gone. A blanket stolen at the same time, was found there, however, which served to confirm the suspicion with regard to the author of the theft. He was traced out of town. At the Cosumnes ferry, the man and horse crossed early in the morning, both man and horse being identified, as they were subsequently at Mud Springs (El Dorado). He was eventually captured near Bridgeport, in Nevada county. The chain of evidence establishing his possession of the horse from the time of the stealing to his capture, seemed perfect. He had a trial of only a few minutes, on the steps of the Louisiana House. A rope was put around his neck, and he was hurried to the tree, only a few people being present.

Public opinion was very much against the lynchers in this affair, and the next Grand Jury found bills for a high crime against several prominent citizens.

Jackson's "Colombo Saloon," with its proprietor and customers outside. Fletcher Alley or walkway is on the right, the Sanguinetti or bakery building is on the far right and the macaroni factory on the far left.

north fork of Jackson creek was good to its head; the south and middle forks were also good. The best spots were near the junction of the creeks, not far from the National House. A few men made as high as five hundred dollars per day at times. Thomas Jones had one of the best claims. Nuggets worth two hundred and fifty dollars were taken out near Dick Palmer's house. Hough also had a good claim near the same place. One day some immigrants inquired where they could find diggings, and a place was pointed out. In a few days they took out fourteen pounds each, and went home. The flats in the vicinity of Tunnel hill were also good. Jackson owed its prosperity more to being a convenient center than to any mines about the town. The different forks of the creeks came together at Jackson. The roads to Volcano, Mokelumne Hill, and the southern mines, passed through here, and all helped to make it a center for a large extent of country.

In 1854 the advent of the county seat gave Jackson a great lift. Several brick buildings were put up about this time, among which was the building at the bridge used as a Court House after the big fire, the house used by Ingalls as a drug store at the corner of Main and Water streets, and some others not recollected.

With the increase of population came also all kinds of mercantile institutions, where beauty and frailty had a market value. The sounds of music, the clinking of glasses, the chink of money as the gambler paid out his losses or raked in his winnings, were in time and tune with the other towns of California, neither better nor worse.

THE GREAT FRESHET. Eighteen hundred and sixty-one found Broadway built quite across the creek, the houses resting on posts, which were set in the ground but a little ways. It was nine years since the flood of fifty-two and three, and the people either had forgotten, or would not believe that the forks of Jackson creek would sometimes float a steamboat, and so they rested in security. The American Hotel, Young America Saloon, and other good houses, were built over the channel on Broadway. On the continuation of Main street, beyond the Louisiana Hotel (now National Hotel), was a row of barber-shops and saloons. The rains commenced about the first of December, and continued without much intermission for some weeks, until the ground was so full it could hold no more, each shower sending the streams, already full, over the banks. When the main rise occurred, bringing down trees, timber, fences, and mining machinery, the channel soon choked. The flood now turned into Water street, running along in front of the Louisiana Hotel, carrying off the wagon-shop to the west of the hotel, with its contents, and endangering the safety of all the buildings along the street. At this point the buildings began to give way. The American Hotel actually floated up stream a little. Slowly the mass of buildings, with the bridge, gave way and started, grinding along and tearing away the outbuildings which had been built from both sides into the creek. The row of barber-shops and saloons on the next crossing hardly checked

Chinese men parading down Main Street in Ione near the Thomas Bicknell Furniture Depot and A.A. Brunner Groceries.

On November 7, 1857, Martin Van Buren Griswold was murdered. Griswold was a daring, self-possessed, and powerful man, who crossed the plains to Oregon in 1848. He learned of the discovery of gold in California, and he immediately turned toward that place.

He finally settled down with Horace Kilham, an extensive mine and ditch owner near Jackson. Large quantities of gold-dust were bought and sold at this place, the safe having at times fifty thousand dollars or more in it, a great temptation to Chinamen (several worked about the place) who were in the habit of working for a mere pittance. One day he was missing; on examination the gold in the safe was also gone. Foul play was certain.

It was discovered that the China cook was also gone. A thorough search of the premises was now made when the body of Griswold was found under the Chinaman's bed. Death was produced by two fractures of the skull. Large rewards were offered for the apprehension of the China cook and his friends. The parties were arrested in Marysville through the assistance of the Chinese residents, there. The key of the safe, some jewelry, and other articles known to have been in the safe, were found on their persons. They received a fair trial and were found guilty. Three were executed [hung] on the sixteenth day of April, 1858. The fourth one committing suicide in his cell. Fou Seen, the cook who is supposed to have planned the murder was, in China, a desperado.

A man named Davis, answering exactly to the Colonel's description, had lived at San Andres, but whether really any relation to Senator Jefferson Davis might be doubted, although there was a resemblance in person and features.

While under the influence of liquor he went into a barber shop kept by a negro whose family occupied part of the same house. Going into the family room he insulted the barber's wife, and was ordered out. Not being inclined to go, the barber came to protect his wife, and very properly demanded, "Leave here, Sir, or I'll kick you out." The so-called Colonel deliberately turned to him and said, "No white man ever talked that way to me and lived"; and, presenting a pistol, shot the barber dead in the presence of his family.

The murderer, pursued by the indignant citizens, tried to make his escape, but in crossing a ravine filled with washings from the mines above, he sunk in the mire and was captured. He was neither shot, hanged, nor burned; but was handed over to the sheriff of Amador County and lodged in the jail at Jackson.

Of course there was great indignation against the murderer, and a few nights after his arrest a crowd appeared before the jail and demanded the prisoner. The sheriff, supposing they intended to kill him, made the jail as secure as possible, and tried to persuade them to let the law take its course.

continued in far right column

Woolsey's store, Ione, c. 1880.

the movement, and the mass went grinding and crashing into the cañon below, and the channel was cleared and the danger passed. Some twenty buildings went off in this burst, involving a loss of perhaps fifty thousand dollars.

GREAT FIRE AUGUST 23, 1862. Shortly after one o'clock the alarm of fire was raised, and smoke was seen issuing from an out-building in the rear of the assay office. The firemen were quickly at their posts, and for a few minutes it seemed that the firemen had the better of it.

The fire spread, and in a few minutes was beyond all control. The houses, mostly of pine, shriveling in the hot sun, caught like powder and flashed the fire from one to another, until the only question was to save life—property was not to be thought of. The Court House being some distance from the fire, permitted the saving of the records; but the house itself went like a pile of brush. In some instances people had to make their escape from besieged houses with wet blankets over their heads.

At night the town was a smoking ruin, the tall, ghostly chimneys keeping watch over the seething embers, while the inhabitants were camped on the surrounding hills, houseless and supperless.

There was no despair, however; no wringing of hands and shedding of tears. Before darkness came, lumber was engaged to rebuild some of the houses, and in the morning was actually awaiting the cooling of the hot ashes and cinders. Provisions came pouring in from the surrounding towns, and there was no suffering.

JACKSON FLOOD, FEBRUARY 17, 1878. A remarkable flood occurred in Jackson and vicinity, on the 17th of February, 1878. For some weeks the streams had been bank full; but, as sailors say, everything was made snug and tight, and no one anticipated any particular trouble, and were unprepared for a flood which had no precedent in the history of the State. Since the denudation of the hills of their wood, the country has become subject to extraordinary showers, the rain coming down in torrents.

Those who were watching the weather on that Sunday morning, noticed a dense bank of clouds to the south-east, with a line something like the colors seen in tempering steel, dividing this bank from a similar one in the north-west, both banks of clouds charged with water; both seemingly determined to "fight it on that line," the ominous line of precipitation being drawn just over Jackson. When its force seemed exhausted, and silence had come, a great roar of rushing waters, mingled with shouts and shrieks, was heard; the waters from the head of the north fork, and the other forks heading near the New York ranch, had come rolling in a wall or breast, variously estimated at five to ten feet high, carrying before it houses, barns, logs, fences, and uprooted trees.

In the meantime another small party came, privately assuring the sheriff that it would be impossible to keep the mob out and that the only way to save the prisoner and honor the law was to place him quietly in their hands, permitting them, without the knowledge of anyone in or about the jail, to remove him to another place, and after the mob had searched in vain, of course the sheriff would be honored for the wisdom of his strategy.

The plan was adopted, the prisoner delivered up, and under cover of the night conveyed to a place of safety. After a little more parley, the sheriff informed the mob that the prisoner had been removed and was entirely beyond their reach, and to verify his words invited them to come in and search the jail. Not finding him, they concluded that the public interests were safe in his hands.

But the sheriff never again saw his prisoner, he having been placed in the hands of his friends and associates, who not only wanted to get him away from the mob, but out of the hands of the sheriff, and they succeeded. Just how the sheriff settled with the county I am not certain, but I was told that he claimed his prisoner was finally taken by a mob, and whether put to death he did not know.

Rev John Steele, 1850

Sutter Creek Cornet Band, October 22, 1880. Before TV and radio entertainment often came in the form of parades and holiday festivals. Cornet bands were formed in many areas to perform at these events.

In 1854, a Mexican and a Frenchman, journeying together towards Oleta, drank to each other's health so frequently as to produce confused perceptions of passing events. On arriving at Oleta, the Frenchman missed his watch, and accused the Mexican of stealing it. The dispute coming to the knowledge of some of the "home rulers," they proposed to have a '49 trial. As they were ravenous for blood, they soon found the Mexican guilty, condemning him to be hung immediately, and set about executing the sentence. Henry Kutchenthall, E. M. Briggs, Ed. and Jonathan Palmer, expostulated with the crowd; told them they were not '49ers; that '49ers never acted in such an infamous manner, and much more of the same effect; to no purpose, however, until, led by Kutchenthall, they rushed in with drawn revolvers, and liberated the Mexican.

Three or four courageous men, backed by revolvers and a sense of right, were often able to subdue a cowardly mob of scores.

These six young ladies from Ione, sisters perhaps, pose in their finery around 1880.

It struck Chinatown (the north end of Jackson), carrying everything in its way. A few were able to take out some articles, but in five minutes the stream was full—struggling Chinamen, houses, shops, goods, all in a rolling mass. Most of the Chinamen escaped before the stream entered the cañon. Six of them went down the stream in the wreck, the bodies being afterwards found all the way from Jackson to Buena Vista. Some white men, assisting the Chinamen, were carried down the stream, but saved themselves before they entered the cañon. In half an hour or more after the flood had swept Chinatown away, the middle fork, which is longer than the north fork, came booming the same way, with a bulk-head of timber, fences, and trees. It struck the bridge across the creek near Genochio's store, forming a dam, and for a few minutes the stream turned through Jackson, in front of the National House; and at one time it seemed as if all that end of the town would be swept away in one wreck. Several persons narrowly escaped drowning in the streets. A foot-bridge, belonging to Mushet, lodged in the street in front of the National. The bridge finally gave way, and the channel cleared, carrying with it all the cut-houses and lumber in its course. The flood was over, and people could then estimate their losses.

BIG FROLIC. Thanksgiving day, 185-, the Bacchanalian press gang were out. They took possession of the Young America saloon and appointed a door-keeper who locked the door on the outside, opening only for the admittance of new victims, no egress being permitted. A press gang waylaid the Judge, who was expecting to hold court the next day. He resisted their importunities a long time on the grounds of public duty, but he had been known to take a spree and no excuse would answer now. "Good-bye, boys," said he; "it can't be helped." What took place on the inside can only be guessed. Some in their wild excitement were tossed like foot-balls over the tables. Speeches and songs, and shouts mingled in confusion dire. Fourteen dozen of champagne had their necks broken. Some were soon helpless on the floor; one or two escaped from an upper window, and some were able to keep up the orgies till midnight. When morning came those who were able had left. The Judge's pants were found on the steps of the Court House, other garments in other places. He, with a sense of public duty still uppermost, was delivering a charge to an imaginary jury. The officers of course took care of him until he was sufficiently sober to attend to business, which was not for some days. The Grand Jury found a Bill against him for misdemeanor and conduct unbecoming a magistrate. The Judge complimented the jury on having fearlessly done their duty, acknowledged the delinquency and promised that they should never have occasion to do so again, and with his silver tongue, which so often had charmed away opposition, turned aside the righteous indignation of his constituents.

Spring of '49. Very many came the following Spring. A company, consisting of J. S. Smythe; Michael and John O'Neal; Peter Jacobs, a German; Captain Rogers, from the Sandwich Islands; Godey and Perry Lake, the two latter of Stevenson's regiment, dammed the river near the mouth of Rich gulch. The claim did not equal their expectations; that is to say, it did not yield a bucketful of gold a day, and they abandoned it.

At night and sometimes during the day the dismal howl of the coyote would be heard in the adjacent hills, and chickens were thus warned to roost high. These predatory animals were very bold and would often approach within a few steps of the door of a ranch house to obtain food. While in the mines a friend of mine out alone prospecting placed his grub bag under his head for a pillow when camping for the night. Sleeping soundly after a hard day's tramp he gradually became aroused from his slumber by something tugging at his pillow, and before he fully awoke, his head dropped to the ground. Supposing himself to be attacked by nothing less than a grizzly he sat up in his fright and uttered a scream something in the nature of a warwhoop, or as he expressed it, more "like the bellowing of a frightened calf." It was, however, so sudden and pronounced a cry that the bag was dropped, and a moment later a coyote set up a howl not far distant that sounded like a whole pack mixing their discordant notes together. My friend passed the remainder of the night guarding his grub bag.

David Augustus Shaw, 1852

On back: Erected by C. W. Swain, over Sutter Creek in Ione. This is the property of Judge L.P. Gebhardt. A nine-horse team and wagons on bridge.

Courtesy Amador County Archives

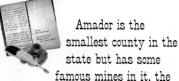 Amador is the smallest county in the state but has some famous mines in it, the most noted of which is the 'Hayward,' now incorporated with other mines, under the title of the Amador Mining Company. The history of this mine shows what pluck and perseverance will accomplish. About 1856 Alvinso Hayward commenced work on this lode, and for two years continued sinking shafts, erecting machinery, and following the course of the vein. The ore was poor, his funds were exhausted, but he was sure that he was on the right track, and would not be discouraged. He went to all his friends for he had many, and begged, borrowed, and scraped up all the money he could. All that went. His credit was exhausted. He could not even buy a pick. He had no money to pay his workmen, he was in arrear with them. One by one they withdrew, save one or two who were infected with their master's enthusiasm. He worked like one of them, suffered privations as they did, but still the mine yielded nothing. At length when worn out bodily and mentally, and almost on the point of giving up the mine in despair, he struck the main lode. Years had passed away in the meantime, but at length the reward had come. Of course all was now plain-sailing. Money is never wanting when money is in sight. In a short time Mr. Hayward's income was $50,000 a month. To-day he is worth millions, and has never forgotten those who stood by him in the dark days.

J.G. Player-Frowd, early 1870s

Cosmopolitan Hotel at Jackson Gate.

Colonel James gave his name to the bar. His partners were two brothers, Vanderslice, one a doctor, the other a gambler. Judge Smith, who afterwards killed Colonel Collyer at Jackson, and a man by the name of Haskell, kept a store there. Soon after the immigration got in it was estimated that a thousand men were mining on the river within a distance of two or three miles, mostly with pans and rockers.

The river in the vicinity of Rich gulch and Murphy's was very rich, men taking out with a rocker several thousand dollars in a day. In some places the gravel would be "lousy" with gold. It must not be supposed that all fared this way, however. As many men then were wandering around "broke" as now. When Winter came on most of the men left, some going up the gulches and others to Jackson and Mokelumne Hill, which now began to be permanent camps.

Sober & Parrish's Big Bar bridge has quite a history. The first ferry, a dug-out, was run by a Scotchman, the price of passage being one dollar. Getting tired of the business, he donated it to Dr. Sober, who in turn gave it to John Hasley, who sold it in 1850 to Pope & Burns for fifty dollars. They bought some lumber and built a small ferryboat, charging the same for crossing as formerly. Horses were made to swim by leading them beside the boat. Travel increasing, they began to make money rapidly, seeing which, Dr. Sober thought to buy it back; but the stock had now gone up, the parties asking twelve thousand dollars for it. The Goodwins, Soher, A. J. Houghtaling, and

Kenny bought it, the latter selling his share for six thousand dollars. The bridge was built in 1853, costing twelve thousand dollars—the road on the Amador side, twelve thousand dollars, and on the other, three thousand dollars.

TUNNEL HILL. This was the largest deposit of the drift, belonging to the north and south rivers of the county. Here it seemed to have spread out into a large body, most of which was swept away by the subsequent glacier erosion. The remains of the ancient plain may be easily see around the base of Butte mountain, also on all the hills around. The great wealth of the gulches around Tunnel hill, soon taught the miners to look for the source of the gravel; and we find that, as early as 1850, some of the miners had ascended the slope of the hill, until they had struck it sinking bed rock.

Daniel Haskell and Martin Love have the credit of being the first to work the dead river bed of gravel. They hauled the dirt to the south fork of Jackson creek about half a mile away. The dirt was rather hard to drift, but paid from one to two ounces to the cart-load. Madame Pantaloon, a woman dressed in man's clothing, and doing a man's work, made a large sum of money out of this hill; she drove a team and did light work at first, and for some time was supposed to be a boy.

The hill was first tunnelled in 1852, by Braxton Davenport, E. M. Johnston, and William McLeod, who, after one

Inside one of the Knight Foundry shops it's easy to see the magnitude of the work done there. Knight Foundry is the only water-powered foundry and machine shop in the US and has been in continuous operation in Sutter Creek since 1873.

Courtesy Amador County Archives

Wells, Fargo and Company had their agency at the United States Hotel, kept then by the Kendall brothers. One morning the safe was found robbed of the contents, some ten thousand dollars. A liberal reward was offered for the recovery of the money and the apprehension of the thief. Three strangers were suspected, arrested. Three masked men forcibly took one of the strangers and commenced taking testimony in a manner not laid down in modern works on evidence, but one in vogue a few centuries since. They told him that his partners, had confessed the crime and had been hung, and that they were going to serve him the same way unless he told them where he had hidden the money. The noose was fixed around his neck and he was drawn up and held suspended until he ceased struggling, when he was let down until he recovered. Denying any knowledge of the transaction, he was again "strung up," and again lot down. He was drawn up a third time by the baffled reward-hunters, who were getting enraged at the man who would not "own up." At this stage of the affair Dr. Phelps, who came up, interfered to save the man any further torture and with a Bowie knife cut the rope and the man fell to the ground.

Public opinion has fixed the robbery on one of the parties engaged in this hanging. As the men were masked, it is unsafe to attempt to name them. It is better that posterity should remain ignorant of the names of the parties, than have the doubtful honor fixed on the wrong person.

County officers on the steps of the courthouse in Jackson.

> Some of the men made fortunes and went home; others told their stories, all the better for a drink, which at last got the better of them, leaving them in a nameless grave.

year's labor of drifting, sold their interest to Peter A. Martin, who in the Spring of 1853, erected a trestle work, with a car track and chute, extending to the survey of the Cunningham ditch, which was soon after constructed along the western and southern side of the hill. The second tunnel was run by A. C. Loveridge, in the Spring of 1854, which year inaugurated a thorough prospecting of the hill, which was all claimed, and worked by the usual drifting system, until water was brought on the hill in 1858.

THE GATE. This place is on the north fork of Jackson creek, about one mile from Jackson. It takes its name from a fissure in a reef of rock, which crosses the creek, about twenty feet wide with nearly perpendicular walls on each side, through which the creek flows. The place was discovered in 1849 by a boy who ran away from Sacramento. It was not as rich as many other places, but uniformly good, paying eight to sixteen dollars a day to the man.

In 1850 as many as five hundred miners settled around the Gate. Diarrhea prevailed here as elsewhere at the time. The miners were shocked one day by seeing two boys carrying away, to bury, the corpse of their father, who, unknown to the minors, had died of the prevailing epidemic a day or two before. The boys were induced to suspend the interment, and in a short time several hundred men were collected together, to give him as decent a burial as the circumstances would permit.

Claims were fifteen feet square. This was the usual size of claims all over the country, until the Spring of 1851. Several of the Johnston family who came from Pennsylvania, were settled here. One of them being sick, a man called "Grizzly," jumped his claim. A meeting of the miners was called and it was decided that a sick man had no right to a claim. An appeal from the decision was made by a friend getting on the claim with a drawn revolver, and promising a quick passage to the happy hunting-grounds to anyone who should, attempt to work it. The decision was reversed and the claim respected until the owner was able to work. The largest lump of gold ever found at the Gate came out of this piece of ground. It weighed four ounces and was shaped like a bull's head.

Ohio Hill and Squaw gulch were rich places in the vicinity. From the former place one man by the name of Bodkin carried away some forty or fifty thousand dollars as the result of a Winter's work. Madame Pantaloon took out one hundred thousand dollars and then sold the claim for twenty-five thousand dollars more.

Clinton. This place, which is north-east from Jackson some six miles, was first worked by Mexicans, who drifted under

John Crouch found the hide of one of his missing cattle in a Mexican camp, at the forks of the Cosumnes. With the help of some friends, he gathered up five or six of the Mexicans, and took them to Jamison's ranch for a trial. Knowing the hasty manner of such trials, and the summary justice meted out, Beebee and other respectable persons at the Forks (Yeomet) sent an express to Coloma for the Sheriff, Buchanan, to be present at the meeting the next day. While the gathering was in progress, the Sheriff and deputies, two or three in number, with some friends and acquaintances of the Mexicans, came also. Some high words ensued, the Sheriff urging the citizens to give up the Mexicans for trial, the citizens insisting upon trying them then and there, as the courts were unreliable. While the angry colloquy was going on, several Mexicans, with arms in their hands, were discovered hanging around on the outskirts of the place. Several persons went with guns and pistols and drove them away. Several shots were fired at the Mexicans, and perhaps some were returned. They retired however without much delay.

Miners at the Argonaut Mine in Jackson descending to the depths for their day's work.

A sharp trade was driven in claims, a thousand dollars being frequently paid for a piece of ground thirty feet square. Moore Lerty was particularly successful in selling claims. His operations were bold, and perhaps original. He would open a claim in a good vicinity, down to good-looking dirt, and then would load an old musket with gold-dust, and shoot the ground full of gold. It is said that he has been known to punish a claim with two or three hundred dollars in this way. If he did not sell the claim, he could wash the dirt, and recover the dust. He sold a claim for one thousand dollars in this way to Henry Jones, notably the sharpest man in Volcano. Jones tried the claim for a day or two before purchasing, it is said, even going into the hole at night to get the dirt, so as to be sure that he was not imposed on. The dirt was all rich, so he bought it. The fun of the matter was in the fact that the place proved to be really rich, one of the best in the camp.

The Kennedy Mine, Jackson — The Kennedy Mine was one of the deepest gold mines in the world at 5912 feet. The Kennedy Mine was prospected in 1860 and continuously run until 1942. It produced approximately $34,280,000 in gold. One of the tallest head frames in existence today can be seen at the Kennedy Mine. The mine also had one of the largest stamp mills in the Mother Lode.

the red hills around the town, making moderate pay. After the introduction of water, by means of canals, quite a number of miners settled here.

N. W. Spaulding is the inventor of the famous circular shank saw tooth. He was a mill-wright by profession, and after mining a few years, returned to his trade, which became profitable in utilizing the vast forests of the Sierras. Movable teeth had been used before, but under such conditions as to cause them to be set aside. The improvement consisted in using a circular instead of a square shank. The continued vibration of the saw, incident to a high speed, caused a crystallization of the plate to take place, it being most intense at the corners of the cavity, causing a cracking and ultimate ruin of the plate; by distributing the crystallization evenly around the cavity, the plate would endure an indefinite amount of work. This little improvement became of so much value that it revolutionized the methods of sawing lumber, the circular saw being everywhere adopted, the improvement being appropriated by saw-mill men without leave or license. Four different lawsuits concerning this tooth were carried to the United States Supreme Court, one of which involved costs to the amount of twenty thousand dollars. An attempt was made to prove that this form of tooth had been in general use for years, and particularly in a mill owned by Tupper and others, in a certain town in Vermont, a man by the name of Percival, who was said to have been dead for some years, being the mill-wright who had made and used them. Mr. Spaulding, with his accustomed energy, set inquiries on foot, and found that Percival, though somewhat advanced in years, was still living, and among the pineries in Wisconsin; notwithstanding the distance, he was brought into court at San Francisco, before the close of the case. Every attempt to prove a previous use of the circular shank had failed, except in the case of the Tupper mill and, when Percival's name was called, a look of astonishment ran over the countenances of the opposing lawyers, one of them audibly remarking, "Rather a lively looking corpse," referring to the oft-repeated statement that Percival was dead. He had a vivid remembrance of the kind of tooth used in the Tupper mill, and, what was of much importance, had a veritable sample of the teeth then used, which he had kept in his tool chest for nearly a quarter of a century. When those were produced in court, behold, they had the square shank. This settled the matter, the defendants' lawyer remarking, "Well, Spaulding, you've beaten us. The saws now go to every quarter of the globe."

DRYTOWN is on Dry creek, in the northern part of the county, about twelve miles from Jackson. Dry creek, from which

Captain Stowers and his friend Slater, who lived in one of the shanties called by courtesy "hotels," came by one day, bandaged and bundled, terribly sick. Swellings all over them and indolent ulcers that would not heal, were symptoms of very bad cases of erysipelas! They were going to die; nothing would save them. Squire Yates was consulted as to settling their affairs. His good sense, or, perhaps, experience, solved the difficulty. "You dirty dogs," said he, after an examination, "you ought to be hung! You are rotten with lice, gray-backs"—which was the case. The lice were three deep, all gnawing away at the portly Captain, sucking the delicious juices out of his body. His feelings experienced a sudden revulsion, not exactly from mourning to joy, but wrath rather. Some few "cuss words," like scattering drops of rain before a shower, fell from his lips, and then the storm burst. ——— Better ring down the curtain.

This photo is clearly newer than the 19th century and the wheels were actually built in the early 1900s. But, the Kennedy Mine's wheels, several of which are still standing, show the grandeur of this and other mining operations in the Mother Lode. They were like a large conveyer belt and moved the mine tailings across the countryside for disposal.

Courtesy Amador County Archives

Chichizola Store building in Amador City with a branch of the Bank of Amador in the same building.

Perkins with his savings, about six thousand dollars, started for Sacramento, on his way home. While he was passing through a point of chaparral, he was shot and robbed by some concealed party. Though his body was discovered before it was quite cold, no clue to the murder was obtained for many years. It is now said that a big, one-eyed Indian, who formerly lived around Volcano, confessed to the murder of Perkins, and several other white men, some years since.

the town takes its name, runs through the place. It is the oldest town of any size in the county. As early as May in 1848, some fifty or more persons were working here, the most of whom were Mexicans from Monterey and vicinity. Isaac E. Eastman, now mining in the vicinity of Volcano, was here a few days at that time. Two ounces a day was the ordinary day's work, though occasionally, when a rich crevice was found, the ounces would become pounds. A hundred dollars to the pan was not an unusual occurrence. The tussocks, or bunches of grass along the ravines, would often have five or six dollars adhering to the roots. Mr. Thomas, who still lives in Drytown, thinks that in the Spring and Summer of '49, men averaged one hundred dollars per day. The town was very quiet, the Indians, Mexicans, and white population generally getting along without much trouble. The four or five white men began to think they were not having a fair show, considering they were the owners of the country, and posted up a notice ordering all foreigners to leave within a certain time, which, however, was not noticed. An Englishman by the name of Pilkinton, who had formerly lived in Mexico, and understood the Spanish language, kept a store in a brush shanty and got most of the Mexican trade. A man by the name of Williams, who had a store on Chile hill, got the Indian trade, his stock being mostly shirts and other cotton goods of gay colors, with which the Indians loved to decorate themselves. At this time there were but three or four log-cabins.

Pilkinton was the first Justice of the Peace, or the first elected rather, but as the election was carried by the residents of the town, who were mostly gamblers, it did not give satisfaction to the miners, who called a meeting in the evening to reconsider the matter. There was no town hall, but a big fire was built against a log, and the meeting was organized by the election of a man by the name of Beiterman as chairman—the chair being a portion of the log at a little distance from the fire. Mr. Beiterman was a portly, good-looking man, and had the only stovepipe hat in the country, and had the further distinction of having married a runaway wife of Brigham Young, hence was considered a suitable person for chairman. The fact that Pilkinton was an Englishman, and was chosen by the gamblers, was duly set forth, and the election was annulled.

During the Summer, when the "around the Horn men" began to arrive, there was a large accession to the white population. All the passengers, numbering thirty or forty, from the barks *Strafford* and *Anna Welch*, from New York, came in a body to the town, and a new impetus was given to affairs.

So far, the people had camped under trees or brush shanties, or in tents. The boots and hat often served for a pillow. Coyotes prowled around the camps at night, gathering up all that was eatable, or had the smell of human hands on it. One

A man by the name of Hunt was in Jackson he was informed by Evans, the gentlemanly proprietor of the Louisiana House, that a lady in the parlor wished to see him. The lady had arrived that morning, on her way to her husband, whose name was Steven Hunt, of Volcano. On inquiring she was much pleased to learn that he was in the house at the time. Evans was not aware that Hunt had no wife, and thought to give him an agreeable surprise. She clasped her arms around Hunt's neck, kissed him, and sunk her face, bathed with tears of joy, into his bosom. She took a second and better look at his face and starting back with a look of about equal parts of alarm and indignation, exclaimed, "You are not my husband!" "No," says he, "unfortunately for me, I am not." A little inquiry elicited the fact that the true Steven Hunt was in Volcano. As the interested parties were sensible persons, there was no shooting or other display of foolishness.

Blue Lake Belles, Washoe Indians, Alpine County. During the Gold Rush Amador County included what is now Calaveras and Alpine Counties. The natives adopted western clothing without delay. It's rare to find a photo of a California native in their traditional dress, or lack thereof as early descriptions depict.

Courtesy Amador County Archives

Post office and the office of Sutter Creek and Sacramento Stage, Butler and Talbot in Plymouth, September 22, 1906. Stagecoaches were a mainstay in transportation through the early 1900s until the automobile became more available and reliable.

> There was a terrible accident here yesterday afternoon. The premature explosion of a blast horribly burned two workmen; one died this morning, the other will perhaps follow. The poor fellows were brought into town last night and are horrible objects to look at.
>
> William Henry Brewer, 1863

morning, a minor missed one of his boots. He remembered that he put it under his head; why any one should steal one boot, he could not imagine. It was found some distance away, gnawed by a coyote, that had managed to pull it from under his head, without disturbing his slumbers.

CABINS. When the rains commenced there were few or no cabins; those who had been prudent enough to build them gave a place on the ground for a spread to those who were out of doors. It was found that the western man, either from having crossed the plains or from being accustomed to a rough life, was readiest to adapt himself to circumstances. He soon "knocked up" a log cabin, while the eastern man cursed the country and lamented his hard fate.

SCURVY. Nearly everybody was afflicted with what was called scurvy. The limbs and body would swell, the tongue crack and bleed, and the gums get so sore and ulcerated that the teeth would become loose, sometimes falling out. About thirty persons, one-fifth of the white population, died during the Winter, of this disease. Doctors charged eight dollars for a visit in town, and sixteen to fifty dollars per visit to the country. Dan Worley, who suffered from this disease for some time, employed a physician, who salivated and otherwise demoralized him, without doing him any good, for which he charged one thousand one hundred dollars. Dan thinks he could have got his teeth knocked out for a much less sum than that if he had set about it.

Until 1853, Drytown was a collection of log cabins and shake shanties, without much attempt at architectural display or even comfort, but the people caught the prevailing spirit of improvement, and commenced improving. A hall for general purposes was built. It was also used as a church and schoolhouse. In 1854 several brick buildings, supposed to be fireproof, were erected. In 1856-57 the town was at its best as far as numbers were concerned, though it was even then considered a "worked-out" place, the shallow gulches having been easily exhausted and no hill diggings taking their places.

GREAT FIRE. In the Autumn of 1857 a fire broke out near the creek, and, aided by the wind, situation of the town, and combustible nature of the buildings, in an hour it laid the whole place in ashes. Drytown never recovered from this misfortune.

DRY CREEK. From the crossing of the Mother Lode, down, this creek was probably the best in the county. It was the first to be extensively worked, having several hundred miners while there was yet but a house or two at Amador and Sutter Creek.

RATTLESNAKE GULCH. Was one of the richest gulches around Drytown. Its several branches start from the crest of the Black hills, (the rich quartz deposit heretofore described,) and empty into Dry creek, not far above the town.

MURDERER'S GULCH. An ominous name, was so called from its being the scene of several murders in 1849-50. It lies along the reef of Jurassic gravel, from which it probably derives

During the Winter, Rod Stowell, a Texas ranger, killed Sheldon, a Missourian, by stabbing him with a long knife. The statements concerning this transaction are very conflicting. Stowell claimed that on entering the cabin, which was a kind of public house, Sheldon shut and locked the doors, making him (Stowell) a prisoner, and then drew a knife to kill him, and that he acted in pure self-defense. Jim Gould, an eye-witness, states the house was not closed; that Sheldon drew a small knife and jocularly told Stowell he was going to kill him; that the killing of Sheldon was uncalled for and wanton. It may be observed that the habit of retributive justice was gradually adopted by early miners as a kind of necessity, and had not grown into a practice at this time, or Stowell might have fared hard at the hands of the miners, who were much shocked at the affair.

Knight Foundry machine shop in action. Knight's innovative water wheels were used in some of the first hydroelectric plants in California, Utah, and Oregon.

Dr. Flint of Flint, Bixby & Co., went into the mountains and purchased stock. In driving it down to Volcano some of it escaped, and was taken up by some miners at Fort Ann, who advertised the cattle as well as estrays. They refused to give them up to Flint on the proof of ownership, and a lawyer advised him to avoid the preliminary costs of a suit, a hundred dollars or more, by taking the cattle by force, so as to compel them to initiate the lawsuit if they wanted one. Flint took Rod Stowell along as the force element; but force was something that both sides could appeal to, and a row ensued, Rod getting a ball which made a cripple of him for life; and the two minors, wounds which were thought by the physician to be mortal. Stowell was arrested, and found guilty of murder by a jury of miners, and a resolution was passed to hang him when either of the victims should die. Unexpectedly, the two miners recovered, and Stowell escaped hanging.

Stagecoach in front of the two-story hotel, Mountain Spring Home, on the road between Ione and Jackson.

most of its gold. Blood gulch also was the scene of a murder in the same year. Some men seeing blood mingled with the water, went up the stream a few yards, and found a man who had been shot and robbed, hence the name.

FOREST HOME. This was the center of a mining district in the north-western part of the county, which was, perhaps, the poorest in gold of any portion that was extensively worked. The serpentine range here reached its largest development, some of the peaks forming landmarks for many miles around.

ARKANSAS CREEK, so called because no "Arkansas traveler" ever came that way, has its source near Forest Home, runs westerly several miles, and empties into the Cosumnes, near the county line. At the head of this creek were some deep diggings, called the "Yankee claim" and Wind hill.

Yankee Hill, was worked in 1850 by Griswold, Emerson, Purtham, Alexander, and others. Griswold is now an eminent composer of music in Boston. The lower part of the creek only paid moderately, three to five dollars being the usual result of a day's work.

BIG NUGGET. One day a Mexican, named Antone, struck a nugget with his crow-bar, which refused to give way. He enlarged the drift, and approached it two or three inches farther back, and struck his bar, as he thought, behind it. To his astonishment, the nugget still continued into the hill. A second enlargement produced a like result, and not until he enlarged and extended the drift a third time, did he get behind it. He began to be rather excited by this time, and when it came out, he thought he had about all the money he should ever want. He rushed to the nearest saloon, and treated all hands, depositing the chispa as security for payment. He continued to treat so many times, that the margin vanished, the nugget eventually falling into the hands of J. Elkins. The piece was seven and a half inches long, and worth three hundred dollars. The gold in this vicinity was mixed with silver, and was worth only thirteen dollars per ounce, forming a great contrast in appearance with the gold from Drytown, which was worth seventeen dollars and seventy-five cents per ounce.

WILLOW SPRINGS. This is the site of a glacial erosion, like Plymouth and other places. It was settled by —— Richardson and William Jonnings, who put up a first-class hotel, the place being on the line of the travel from Drytown, Fiddletown and other places to Sacramento.

THE CENTRAL HOUSE, two miles north of Drytown, is another place similar to Willow Springs in location and character. As before stated, the gold mining never attracted many persons to this vicinity. Soon after the breaking out of the copper excitement, several veins of copper were discovered, and for some years this "North-West Territory" bid fair to become a second El Dorado, or Copperopolis. This epoch of the history will receive more particular attention in the history of copper mining.

The Broadway Hotel in Jackson with boarders outside.

The murder of Beckman in 1853 was attended with such unmitigated atrocities that the community was thoroughly aroused. Beckman, a German, kept a store nearly in front of Mahoney Hall. One morning he did not open the store as usual. On examining the premises the rear door was found partly open, though not broken, and Beckman in his bunk alive, but speechless and insensible from a terrible cut with an ax, which had cleft his skull; the bloody ax, the broken safe or chest, in which he was known to keep his money, and other circumstances, revealing the details and motives of the minder. It was ascertained that Chris, a German, mining on Mokelumne river in company with Harry Fox, an Englishman, had been in the habit of sleeping in the store on his occasional visits to the town; that he had been there at a late hour the previous evening. Other circumstances also pointed towards Chris and Harry as the criminals.

It was learned that they had left the State. They were afterwards recognized on a Nicaragua steamer. [They were] apprehended and sent to California by a return vessel. On their way up, Chris threw himself overboard and was drowned, Fox was carried to Mokelumne Hill, and placed in jail to await his trial. He soon after escaped, the ten thousand dollars of which Beckman was robbed, being, possibly, a factor in the matter. The fugitives were [later] arrested.

Major Shipman was mining in a tunnel in Volcano. One day a piece of steel from his pick breaking off and cutting him severely over the eye. The wound was more frightful than dangerous, and it occurred to him to tell some of his friends. He first called on the Goodwin boys. They were alarmed at his appearance, the blood running freely over his face, and inquired how he got hurt. He told them he had a difficulty with a man by the name of Steel, whom he found in his tunnel; further inquiry elicited the fact that the man was still in the tunnel, and was likely to stay there until he was brought out. They went to Jim Farley, known to be a warm friend of the Major's. Farley immediately responded, and advised Shipman to leave the country, as the miners might lynch him, "if, as you say, every miner in the camp is a friend of Steel's." "Have you any money?" says Farley. "None to speak of," replies Shipman. "Well," says Parley, "I can get you two hundred dollars and a horse, and the sooner you are off the better." The Major's heart began to relent at the part he was playing was obliged to explain. "Few and short were the prayers" Farley said, as he turned on his heel. "Oh, h——ll"—nothing more.

H.C. Farnham's lumber warehouse in Plymouth.

PLYMOUTH. Is on the Mother Lode, near the northern boundary of the county, fifteen miles from the county seat. It has very little history separate from the history of its quartz veins. At the lower end of the flat, on which the town is built, there was formerly a small hamlet called Puckerville, or Pokerville. It might have had twenty or thirty miners in its best days. If the name was Pokerville, we may imagine the citizens playing poker, with beans for stakes, while waiting through the long Summer for water to come, or, through the Winter for the water to go down, so their claims could be worked, a practice quite common in early days in many a mining camp which has since made a town.

Plymouth proper was settled upon in an early day by Green Aden and others in search of quartz, but the commencement of its growth as a town, dates to the working of the mines by the Hoopers, father and son. About 1873 the town took a sudden start, occasioned by the purchase of the mines by Hayward, D. O. Mills and company. In the same year the precinct cast one hundred and seventy-five votes; in 1877, two hundred and seventy-five; in 1880, something over three hundred, showing a steady growth which is likely to be permanent.

The town is identified with the prosperity of the mines, though there is considerable farming land in the vicinity, which partially supplies the demand for hay and barley.

MINERAL SPRINGS. The White Sulphur Springs, about two miles north of Plymouth, possess relaxing qualities useful in cases of constipation and inflammatory diseases.

FIRES. The following letter from Plymouth to the *Dispatch* will explain itself:

> About three o'clock on Monday, the tenth of June, 1877, occurred the largest fire ever experienced in this town (Plymouth). The fire commenced in the rear of J. C. Williams' stable and spread over the upper part of the town in an incredible short space of time, reducing twenty or more buildings with their contents to ashes.
>
> The fire was said to have been started by some children who were playing with matches in some straw in the rear of the stable.

YEOMET. Is an Indian name signifying rocky falls, and was given to the forks of the Cosumnes river. Indian creek, north fork, middle fork, which received the south fork a mile or two above, all coming together here. Up to 1853, it had the appearance of becoming a town. Simpson, Beebee & Co., Bowman & Co., and others, had large stores, the latter persons also having a bridge across the river, and a hotel of considerable pretensions. Many of the settlers were from Pittsburg, Penn., perhaps induced to remain here by a fancied resemblance to the forks of the Ohio at that town. Some were steamboat captains, some merchants and clerks, some workmen from the great machine shops, that even then had learned to rival Birmingham and the Clyde in making ponderous machinery. Captain John King, who had steamed up and down the Mississippi a hundred times, told his stories, how he had entrapped a load of passengers once at New Orleans, by pretending that he had a famous French general on board, having arranged for a smart Frenchmen to

Some time in the fifties, a showman, traveling with a tame bear, gave an exhibition at Mahoney Hall. The bear escaped from its keepers, and started out in search of adventures. The bear made his way into a chamber occupied by a shoemaker, by the name of Poole, an odd, irascible character, who had been made the butt of many practical jokes, When he felt the bed-clothing being dragged off, he thought the boys were at their old tricks again. He made a grab for the intruder, and was lucky enough to catch him by the scalp. The supposed boy making no resistance, Poole's courage rose to the occasion, and he determined to light a match, and see who had so often disturbed his slumbers. When the German match flashed into a bright flame, revealing the parties to each other, their astonishment was mutual. If Poole was terrified, so was the bear, which gave a horrible howl, and tumbled out of the window with all possible dispatch.

Sutter Creek logging wagon.

Courtesy Amador County Archives

In the early part of 1853, H. C. Farnum and James McLeod built a steam saw-mill at Oleta. In the early part of April, the boiler collapsed a flue. The force of the steam, reacting against the bed in which the boiler was placed, threw it out of position, propelling it through the side of a building, also through the office or counting-room. McLeod, standing in the line of the movement, was caught on the end of the boiler, and forced along until the boiler stopped. Both legs and one arm were broken, and he was in addition thereto much burned, lacerated, and internally injured. He survived but a day or two, suffering intensely, and begging his friends to kill him. Farnum and another party were sitting on the opposite sides of a table in the counting-room, when the boiler, with McLeod on the end, came crashing through the building, passing between the two. Farnum had one arm broken; the man sitting opposite, inhaled the hot steam, which resulted fatally in a year or two.

Union Hotel, F. A. Charleville Proprietor, Fiddletown, about 1855. The "opposition line of stages" is advertised on the sign. Included with the photo was a short letter that J. C. Kemp sent to his aunt, "I send you the house I live in. The further window behind the sign up stairs is my room. It is 100 feet long. The picture is exactly correct, as it is a Photograph, your nephew, Send my letter (not this picture) to grandmother will you? Recollect I sent you a long letter by this mail." J. C. Kemp had "flying circus" photography in the 1870s in Sacramento.

play the part, which worked to a charm, his boat being crowded, while the boat having the real general was a few hours behind—empty!

VOLCANO AND VICINITY.

VOLCANO is situated on Sutter creek, twelve miles above the town of Sutter Creek, and about twelve miles north-east from the county seat. This place seems to have been discovered in 1848, as a party of Stevenson's soldiers were here about the time that another party was mining on the Mokelumne river. They built two huts on Soldiers' gulch, so named on that account. The party of Mexicans, who were first in the camp in the Spring of '49, found two dead bodies in the huts, and buried them on what was afterward called graveyard hill. How those came to their death, or what became of the balance of the party, is not known. They had been camping on Sutter creek near the present town, and represent that place at that time as entirely vacant; not a man, not a hole even sunk there, though the works of General Sutter and his party, who mined there in 1848, might have escaped their attention.

For untold ages the Indian had gathered acorns and pine-nuts, or captured the deer and other game with which the hills abounded. But there was gold in the hills, gold in the flat, in the gulches, everywhere; gold that opens the roads to influence, power, and happiness. The grassy plains have been torn up, the rich soil sluiced through the cañon, and are but unsightly piles of rock, holes of mud and stagnant water. It is not intended to find fault with the work done—it is probably well; for until the great balance sheet is made out, who shall say that the activity, the commercial life, the enlarging of man's powers by these operations, may not more than compensate the apparent destruction. The Illinois party, Green & Co., went to work on the ground staked off. They made about a hundred dollars a day to the man, some of which was coarse gold, one piece being worth over nine hundred dollars. At a depth of fifteen feet they struck a yellow clay, so tough that they could not wash it, and abandoned the claim as worked out. The same place was worked continually for thirty years. Probably a million of dollars in all was taken out of it, or in the immediate vicinity. It was afterwards known as the Georgia Claim.

GEORGIA CLAIM. A stout fellow was hired, for four dollars, to keep the water down during the night, which he did and had time to spare to dance away his wages at fifty cents a round, at a dance house in the vicinity. He afterwards found his way to the State prison for the theft of a watch, valued at fifty dollars, at a time that stealing fifty dollars was a capital offense.

Off to the mines in Volcano in the early 1850s.

The largest [stage] robbery occurred May 1, 1872. A suspicion that an attack was contemplated caused the agent of the express company to send through a corresponding weight of rocks for several days, which went without disturbance. One morning the bullion, worth about ten thousand dollars, was started. It was thought that no one had a knowledge of the affair, but when near the top of the hill the driver, Dick Hipkins, was confronted by two masked men with revolvers, who ordered him to dismount, which he did. One of the men mounted the box, took the lines and drove the team a short distance into the timber where the horses were unhitched from the coach. The men then proceeded to detach the treasure box from the wagon, after which it was broken open with an ax. After having taken out the treasure, the robbers told Hipkins to proceed on his way, the robbers taking the road to Volcano. John N. Boardman was arrested for the robbery, tried and acquitted. Several prominent men were suspected, but no other arrests were made.

Tome ill-feeling existed on the part of Captain Stowers, Carter, and Curtis, towards Unkles, in consequence of a misunderstanding in some commercial transaction. Captain Stowers went into the old man's drug-shop, gave the bottles a sweep with his cane, exclaiming, "This settles my account." Carter had his to settle also, and went, with some others, to the door of the cabin, and commenced abusing the Doctor. He met them and civilly requested them to stay out. This remonstrance not being heeded, he drew a small pocket-knife, and began thrusting and making passes at Carter, the foremost man in the crowd. Little attention was paid to his words or his thrusts. With an instinct born of his knowledge of anatomy, the little knife was a most deadly weapon. The first stroke laid bare the jugular vein; another penetrated his side, producing a sickening sensation, which compelled him to lie down, producing death in a few minutes. Carter's friends picked out a tree upon which to hang the Doctor; but when the circumstances that Unkles was physically insignificant, and that the parties pressing him were intent on serious mischief, became known, few were found willing to assist in his execution, and he was not molested.

Pope's Emporium on Main street in Sutter Creek around 1890. The group of unidentified boys and men outside likely includes Pope himself.

Besides the Green company, there were Dr. Kelsey, afterwards President of the First National Bank, Stockton, also Treasurer of San Joaquin county, who was afterwards found dead in a boat on the slough; Bunnel, from Ohio; Ballard, of Illinois; Kelley, from Ohio; Jacob Cook, now living at Pine Grove; Henry Hester; Jim Gould, now at Jackson; Philip Kyle, now of San Joaquin county; Mills, P. Fellinsbee, McDowell, Bod. Stowell, and other names not remembered, making a population of about fifty. Most of the mining was in Soldiers' gulch, the dirt being carried to the creek for washing. A number of men made hand-barrows, on which they carried the dirt. Finally a cart was rigged up, and, with a yoke of cattle to draw it, readily rented for eight dollars per day.

Cook & Co., got a barrel of syrup, one of whisky, and one of vinegar, from Sacramento, and started the first store. Syrup was worth five dollars per gallon, vinegar the same, and whisky was fifty cents a drink. They also kept a few boarders, at twenty-one dollars per week.

The Indians worked in Indian gulch, hence its name. A Misourian jumped an Indian's hole, throwing out his tools. The Indians came around and ordered him out. Upon his refusing to leave, they drew their bows, and prepared to enforce the command. He ran away, going to Soldiers' gulch, where a party was raised to pursue and chastise the Indians. When the party came in sight, the Indians ran, and the whites fired at them, Rod

Stowell, a Texas ranger, killing one. They followed them towards Russel hill, occasionally getting sight of them and firing, though no more were killed. The following day, one of a party of three or four men, traveling from Jackson to Volcano, stopped to let his horse eat grass at the flat where Armstrong afterwards built a saw-mill. When the others of the party had got out of sight, the Indians fell upon him and killed him; stripping off his clothes, they partially concealed the body by laying it by the side of a log, and burying it with brush. Being missed, search was made, and his body discovered, the Indians having left one foot sticking out. He was buried at the graveyard hill. This murder was supposed to have been in retaliation for the killing of the Indian by Stowell.

On the approach of Winter, Green's party, with others, numbering about twenty in all, built a log cabin containing several compartments, making it compact to avoid attacks of the Indians, who were evincing some signs of hostility, stealing all the stock they could. They got it all except a mule, which was saved by locking a chain, fastened to a log by a staple and ring, around its neck.

In the Autumn of 1850, many persons came in by the plains, and Volcano began to assume the appearance of a permanent settlement. At the opening of a saloon in 1851, the good-natured, but rough miners cut a hole in the lining of the

There were some prominent physicians, also Dr. Ayer, now of San Francisco, mined in Humbug gulch in an early day. Dr. Morgan, afterward of Sacramento, mined in the Soldiers' gulch, and also on the south branch. He was a wag of the first water, and generally kept some good thing in the way of fun traveling about the camp. He gave "Shirt-tail Bend" its felicitous name. It is related of him that he once sold a good claim for a very insignificant sum. When it proved a big thing, he was so mortified that he took himself out one side and chastised himself with a big hickory, exclaiming, between the blows, "Take that you d—n fool; sell a good claim for nothing, will you?"

The Grant House, Ione, circa 1870's. This group was enjoying a game of croquet, stopping long enough for this photo to be taken.

Courtesy Amador County Archives

George Woolsey Building, Ione, at the corner of Jackson and Buena Vista.

The shipment of gold through Wells, Fargo and Co.'s express will show the relatively prosperous years. No account was kept previous to 1870, though the annual amounts often reached one million dollars. Since then the amounts have been,—

1871	$412,853
1872	645,135
1873	530,112
1874	463,500
1875	517,569
1876	516,615
1877	517,548
1878	449,675
1879	185,194

roof, chucked the owner up through, and kept him there until he came to terms.

During the Winter, portions of the graveyard were found to be rich, and the gulches were worked much deeper. It now [was] learned, that the deposits of gold were enormously large, and that they extended to great depths. Henry Jones, L. McLaine, Fred Wallace, Dr. M. K. Boucher, Doctor Yeager, Ike West, ——— Thomas, Ellec Hayes, and others, had claims in Soldiers' gulch that were enormously rich. A cartload of dirt would have two hundred and fifty dollars in it. Sometimes a pan of dirt would contain five hundred dollars. Men who never in their lives had a hundred dollars, would make a thousand dollars a day. A company of Texans would make a hundred dollars each in a day, and gamble it away every night, and come to their claim in the morning broke. This was their way of having a good time, and gambling saloons came in for a large share of the profits. Clapboard gulch also paid good wages; though not so rich as Soldiers' gulch, the pay-dirt was easier washed and near the surface. Indian gulch was also found to be rich, especially at the head. The Welch claim had a mound of dirt a few feet across that had more than a hundred thousand dollars in it. Some of the gold was found in a tough clay that defied washing by any ordinary method. Boiling was found to disintegrate the clay, and boilers were erected in many places to steam it so that it would come to pieces. It was observed that when left in the sun to dry hard, the clay would fall to pieces, and drying yards were established where the rich dirt was dried and pounded.

SOCIETY. In 1852, Colonel Madeira, John Turner, Captain Richards, Story, Else, Oaf, Addison, Shultis, Wash. Lewis, Joe Lewis, Downs, Hartram, and Stevenson, settled in the place, and there began to be society. It was now possible to get up a respectable dance by pressing into service all mothers as well as children.

Perhaps few towns could boast of as much talent lying around loose as Volcano. On the flat, back of the town, was a number of cabins where a cluster of intellectual lights daily discussed and solved all the abstruse questions since modestly treated upon by Spencer, Huxley, Tyndal and others. Tom Boucher had edited a magazine in Cincinnati, and disliked to come to shoveling the tough mud in which gold was found in Volcano. Some half a dozen more of the same kind felt and thought the same way. The days were too hot for work, but the cool evenings were conducive to profound thoughts, so they wore their old broadcloth into dirty gloss, read all the books and newspapers that could be found, and trusted to heaven, or the generosity of the boys, for a square meal. This constellation of stars of the first magnitude finally became scattered. The country was not advanced enough in 1853, to sustain such a society.

THE NATURE OF THE GRAVEL DEPOSITS began to be studied. The fact that gulches crossing limestone ranges were generally rich below such junction, was observed, though the reasons were then, and are even now, little understood; a subsequent conclusion, that the hills adjoining must be rich, caused

A man by the name of West was arrested in Fiddletown for stealing a horse. Major Shipman, then residing there, was appointed Judge. He was familiar with law forms, having been a Magistrate, also County Clerk, in some of the older States. Witnesses were sworn, and the whole proceedings conducted in accordance with the form and spirit of the law, without its technicalities. The jury found him guilty and fixed his punishment at one hundred stripes. His fortitude gave way at this severe sentence, and he agreed if they would mitigate the punishment to thirty stripes he would make such statements as would expose the whole gang, enabling the people to convict them all. The thirty stripes were first administered by Abe DeHaven, a powerful man, after which he made a statement in private to E. Walker and Major Shipman, it being deemed best not to have the statement made in public, as being likely to interfere with the arrest of the gang.

An early school bus. This horse-drawn "bus" from Preston Castle is parked in front of Ione railroad depot after 1904.

The Sutter Creek Methodist Church sported a crop of lovely young ladies in their Sunday best. This shot was taken around 1900 when the street was still dirt.

In the Autumn of 1852, a man passing by the name of "one-armed Smith" turned out an old and worn-out horse, supposed to be worth about five dollars, to graze. A Mexican, seeing it apparently without an owner, put a saddle on it and rode a short distance, without attempting to take it out of the country, however. He was apprehended, and hung on a tree north-west of the town.

many good claims to be opened. The Mason & Foster claim was of this character. The point of rocks near the foot of the Boardman hill, was as unlikely a place to find gold, except for the theory referred to, as one could well find; yet the ground payed in places from the top down forty or fifty feet.

IN CHINA GULCH. The Chapline boys, Story & Co., A. J. Holmes, now owner of the Northern Belle mine in Nevada, had good claims in China gulch, on the same range. The south branch, which ran parallel with this range and touching it occasionally, was also immensely rich, though the gold was distributed through gravel in places sixty or seventy feet deep. Some places, like the Green claim in Soldiers' gulch, seemed to have no bottom.

The main branch of Sutter creek where Halsted, Bryant, and Henry W. Jones had their ranches, was also immensely rich in places. The Italians mostly worked this, some of whom carried away twenty-five thousand dollars each.

LYNCH LAW. The only execution in Volcano under this code occurred in 1854. A young man from Arkansas, by the name of Messer, had, during the Summer, evinced a very bloodthirsty spirit, evidently desirous of "getting away with his man" as soon as convenient. He wore a knife in a conspicuous manner, and often boasted of his ability to cut his way with it. He had already crippled for life a young man by the name of Byrne, in a trifling dispute over a game of cards, and, when the final offense was committed, there was no sympathy for him.

In the Autumn of that year a family by the name of McAllister had located in the town. The father and mother were ignorant, uncultivated people, and felt rather flattered with the numerous visits to their house, the chief attraction being a girl of perhaps fourteen years. One evening, Messer and his three or four companions were refused admission. By listening at the door they had ascertained that several men were already in the house, and Messer's companions urged him to clean them out, promising to "back him up." The door was fastened on the inside with a pin inserted in the doorpost, a usual method of securing doors in new countries. Messer, familiar with this kind of lock, succeeded in prying the pin out with the point of his knife, and, opening the door, entered with his companions. The old man expostulated with him, begged that he would make no disturbance, and it seemed, put his hand on Messer's shoulder, though without using any force, or trying to eject him. Messer drew his ever-ready knife, and, with a back-handed thrust, plunged it into the old man's bowels, completely severing the liver from the body. The wound was of course fatal, the pallor of death coming over his features in an instant. This seemed to have satisfied Messer and his companions, who left immediately. Several young men in the house witnessed the affair, which was so sudden and unexpected that they could offer no resistance. They were, apparently, too astonished to raise an alarm, and could hardly give a coherent account of the murder. Mrs. McAllister raised the neighbors by yelling at the top of her voice: " ——jiminy, send for a doctor" with a persistency that under less serious circumstances would have been quite laughable.

Two Mexicans were hung on a tree a few rods south of the Q dwelling-house, for stealing stock.

Another was hung on a tree by the roadside, about half-way between Dosh's store and the Alabama House, by the side of a little stream called the Wolverine.

A negro was tied up and whipped for stealing a horse. He stoutly objected to that mode of punishment on the ground that it would injure his character. These transactions took place after a trial and conviction of the parties before Judge Lynch.

Two men are perhaps enjoying the quiet of some down-time in the Balliol Mine mill around 1900. The noise level was horrendous when the mill was in operation.

In the fall of '50, it became known to the valley that the two Starkey brothers and a man named Haines, who lived at the lower end of Jackson valley, were engaged in stealing stock. One of the Starkeys, and a hired man by the name of Reed, were arrested and brought to Hicks' ranch, where forty or fifty men were awaiting their arrival. Starkey was immediately put on trial.

It was proved beyond a doubt that he had been in the habit of slaughtering cattle and selling the meat, though he put in a plea that the cattle seemed to be abandoned property and without owners. The crime of grand larceny had so far been considered greater than murder, the penalty prescribed by the statutes being death.

[Instead] a motion was made that he should receive one hundred and fifty lashes on his bare back, have his head shaved, and the letter R branded on his cheek, with the understanding that he might be hung if he preferred. On taking the vote, all but one present voted aye! The crowd demanded his reasons for voting against the sentence. He said that no man could live through such a punishment. It was finally agreed that Dr. Newton stop the whipping when necessary to save his life. He was tied to a log with his face down, and his back stripped. A Mexican, then doubled a rawhide riata, and commenced the work. Blow after blow... At the one hundred and twenty-fifth blow the doctor made a sign to suspend the whipping. He was untied and his shirt put on. He was able to step up to the bar and take a drink of whisky.

Knight Foundry interior, men pausing from work on the lathe.

A general pursuit of the parties commenced, and Messer was apprehended in a short time and taken past the scene of the murder. He was now bellowing like a baby, his courage having failed at the sight of danger. The crowd passed over the bridge toward the town. At the Miners' restaurant they halted a moment. In answer to the question—" What shall we do with him?" the cry was "Hang him! hang him!" A proposition was made to do something for the widow, but no response was made. Up through the main street, every house helping to swell the stream, no voices, no sound but the dull tramp, tramp of hundreds of feet, the crowd made their way. At Consolation street they turned toward the Methodist church. Up that street, no one knew whither, to the foot of the hill, thence to the left, halting in a ravine to the north of the church where there was a leaning oak tree, the top of which was broken off twenty or thirty feet from the ground.

There was no consultation, no form of a trial; every-thing seemed to be done by common consent. Here an unsuccessful attempt was made, by Constable Scott, to arrest the lynching. Messer seemed to have partially recovered his self-command, gave some directions as to the disposal of his property, and the payment of a few dollars he was owing in the town. His last words were to this effect: "If I was right in killing him, God will forgive me; if I am wrong, I hope God will punish him," evidently referring to himself. There was so little noise that persons sleeping in houses a little way off heard nothing of the affair, and were much astonished, when they awoke in the morning, at seeing a dead man hanging so near them. There was no frantic excitement or rage, usually manifested on such occasions. The hanging seemed a foregone conclusion.

Substantial justice had been done without the forms or delays of the law. No friends claiming the body for burial, it was taken by the doctors and skeletonized, some of the attending circumstances being revolting. Portions of the body were said to have been devoured by hogs, which had discovered the pool of water into which the remains were placed to disintegrate the flesh from the bones. The skeleton was used to illustrate public lectures on anatomy and physiology. All the circumstances were such as to strike those criminally inclined with terror, if such a thing were possible. Mark the result. Among the most prominent of the volunteer executioners were Dr. Goodwin, who was shot in a row at Snelling's ranch, Si Maynard, who was hanged by a mob for stealing cattle, and Johnson, who was hanged in Sierra county for murder. Mansur, who assisted, died shortly afterwards of consumption. These results are not related as retributive justice, but to show the frequent inutility of lynch law as a means of reform, or deterring others from committing crime.

NORTH-WESTERN PART OF THE COUNTY.

SUTTER CREEK. Though General Sutter and his party mined here in 1848, there was little done until the discovery of quartz in 1851. In October, 1849, persons passing through could see no evidence of any mining. There was a small, cloth tent at the crossing of the creek, owned by a man by the name of Jackson, from Oregon, where meat, whisky, and some provi-

In the early fifties two Mexicans getting into a difficulty, agreed to settle the matter in dispute with an exchange of pistol shots, the contest to be continued with knives, in case both parties survived the shooting, until one was slain, which was done. The wife of the party slain wished to continue the fight, but was not allowed. She remained faithful to his memory, and once every month, for years afterward, lighted twelve candles on his grave, and, alone, watched the whole night.

H.E. Potter, Undertaker store on Main Street in Plymouth. Men seemingly suspended in mid-air on wires.

The Balliol Mine head frame and mill around 1900.

> One evening of the previous winter a party of these roystering mountain blades were indulging in the bottle, when one of them unperceived emptied his canteen of pure alcohol on the head of another who was a famous bully, and seizing the candle, communicated the flame at the same moment. "Man on fire, man on fire, put him out, put him out," was the universal shout; and put him out they did with a vengeance, many embracing that opportunity to pay off old scores, and at the same time most effectually curing him of his bullying propensities.
>
> Theodore Taylor Johnson, 1849

sions, were sold. A few miners gathered here on Sundays when the weather did not permit them to go to Drytown or Jackson. After the discovery of the quartz mines on the north side of the creek, the gulches and flats began to be worked. The placers were only moderately rich. Perhaps the streams making off of Tucker hill were as good as any. A report is current that a twenty-five pound lump was found in the ravine below the Lincoln & Mahoney mills, but it cannot be traced to any reliable source. The gulch below the Hayward mine was only moderately rich. Indeed, it seems quite certain that a vein which has enriched many gulches has nothing left for milling purposes. Gopher flat, above the town, was worked mostly by Spaniards, by drifting from one hole to another, only a few feet below the surface.

The hills east of the town are gravel deposits of the pliocene period. Though worked in many places, they were only moderately rich. They are interesting as showing the course of the streams in past ages. One may still trace the directions by the bodies of gravel left in many places. The divide between Amador and Sutter is full of interesting points, showing a river running towards the west before the close of the volcanic period. Four or five miles west of Sutter this stream seems to have terminated in a precipitous fall, boulders of many tone in weight, some of granite and others of volcanic matter, being piled in a confused mass. Some few places along this line have been mined out, but, as in nearly all the rivers of the volcanic period, the irruptions of lava kept the stream from wearing away the beds of auriferous slates, the sources of the river gold. On the south side of Sutter creek is the largest stream of volcanic gravel in the county, which may be traced from Prospect Rock twenty-five miles east of Volcano, to some miles west of Ione, where it spread out into the ocean. This channel is remarkable as having at one time in the volcanic period a body of hot lava running from the summit to the sea. What a sight for the primeval man, which, according to Whitney, must have lived here at that time.

The mining here at first was of a primitive order, the rocker being the main reliance for separating the gold. In the Spring of 1850, a great improvement was introduced. Jim Wheeler, Boz. Goodrich, and Dick Moulton, brought a long tom, which was first used in the northern mines, from Sacramento. It was a daring innovation, and, like most new things, was unmercifully ridiculed by the conservative portion of the miners. It was only seven feet long, and sixteen inches wide. Small as it was, it effected a great saving of labor, and was soon brought into general use, though a year later it was displaced by the siring of sluices, which enabled men to make wages out of still poorer dirt. After the discovery of the quartz mines, the energy of the best men of the camp was turned in that direction, and placer mining became a minor interest. The development of quartz mining built up the most flourishing town in Amador county, that annually sent a million or more of dollars into the general circulation.

The first families in the place were those of McIntyre, Stewart, Jones, Tucker, Rice, and Hanford. E. B. McIntyre's family, as well as Levi Hanford's, came in 1832. Some of those

In September, 1852, a Mexican stabbed a Dutchman, for which he was whipped. The Dutchman dying sometime after the stabbing, the people reconsidered the whipping and hung the Mexican.

Twelve-mule team hauling heavy timbers and machinery for a mine. A "G. E. Gould, Palace Car." Notice the bells on each horse collar. They used to hear those bells long before the team came into view. The man on the wheel horse guided the team with a "jerk line."

"Some four or five miles took them to what they named Tragedy Springs. After turning out their stock and gathering around the spring to quench their thirst, some one picked up a blood-stained arrow, and after a little search other bloody arrows were also found, and near the spring the remains of a camp fire, and a place where two men had slept together and one alone. Blood on rocks was also discovered, and a leather purse with gold dust in it was picked up and recognized as having belonged to Brother Daniel Allen. The worst fears of the company: that the three missing pioneers had been murdered, were soon confirmed. A short distance from the spring was found a place about eight feet square, where the earth had lately been removed, and upon digging therein they found the dead bodies of their beloved brothers, Browett, Allen and Cox, who left them twenty days previously. These brethren had been surprised and killed by Indians. Their bodies were stripped naked, terribly mutilated and all buried in one shallow grave.

"The company buried them again, and built over their grave a large pile of rock, in a square form, as a monument to mark their last resting place, and shield them from the wolves. They also cut upon a large pine tree near by their names, ages, manner of death, etc. Hence the name of the springs."

William Henry Brewer,
August 14, 1863

A fanciful photo captures these "maids" with brooms. Next thing you know those young women will want real guns just like Annie Oakley!

families were from, the frontier, and others from the East, and the Yankees, and the extreme southerners and westerners, met here for the first time. Thirty years after, when these streams are flowing in the same channel, marriage and intermarriage having obliterated nearly every distinction, the aversion which they entertained towards each other has become the subject of much merriment.

Mrs. McInlyre tried to start a Sunday-school, but could get only three or four children to attend. Mr. Barlow, from Drytown, acted as Superintendent, Mr. Davidson and Mr. Glover, of the Amador quartz mines, preached occasionally, as did I. B. Fish, who was stationed at Mokelumne Hill. The preaching was usually in the school-room; sometimes in an unfinished room in Harding's Hotel. Money was raised to buy a Sunday-school library. Robert McLellan is remembered as having donated five dollars. "Dick's Works" were among the books bought.

FIRST FOUNDRY. Soon after the commencement of quartz mining, the want of a machine shop and foundry induced a small beginning in this way at the lower end of the town near the water-mill of the Lincoln mine. As it was a small affair and did not answer the purpose, it was removed to the present site, and enlarged so that the smaller parts of the quartz mills, such as dies, stamps, etc., could be cast, utilizing the worn-out castings. Frank Tibbetts was the proprietor for many years. The machine shops find melting capacity have been enlarged until now almost any required machinery can be put up, the cupola having a capacity of four tons.

KNIGHT'S FOUNDRY AND MACHINE SHOP. This was established in 1873 to construct water-wheels of a peculiar character, calculated to utilize small heads of water at a high pressure. Though no new principle was discovered, the adaptation of old ones to new conditions has all the merit of a discovery. A small wheel, seven or eight foot in diameter, looking much like a cart-wheel with a rim of tea-cups, drives a quartz mill of eighty stamps, with all the necessary shaking tables and amalgamators.

FIRES. Sutter Creek has had its share of the destructive element. The largest fire happened September 9, 1865.

This included all the business portion of the town. It was soon rebuilt better than before, and enjoyed a greater prosperity, in consequence of mining development, than ever. A smaller fire had occurred about the first of September, 1862, shortly after the big fire at Jackson, burning nearly all the buildings on Humbug hill, including Wildman's store, Birdsail's store, Rice's blacksmith shop and dwelling. This fire was at last stayed at the butcher shop at the foot of the hill.

INCORPORATION. Sutter Creek incorporated as early as 1856, under the general law for incorporation. The organization was found to be defective in many respects, and in 1873, it was re-incorporated by a special Act of the Legislature, an election for township officers being ordered, February 12th. The government was invested in a Board of Trustees, Town Marshal

In 1860, the sluices were often robbed. Some person would cut small creases in the bottoms of the boxes, and with a sharp, conical scraper, would clean several sets of sluices in a night. The act becoming common, Edward Evans, one of the miners, kept watch, and when the robber went at his work, gave him a load of shot. The culprit proved to be a Chinaman. The Chinese in the vicinity were compelled to bury him.

Evans received no punishment.

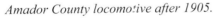

Amador County locomotive after 1905.

This mining group is at "tunnel 3" of either the Keystone, South Spring Hill, or Bunker Hill mine in Amador City. Notice the young girl with the buckets, perhaps bringing water or food to the miners.

> Dr. Ives, an eminent physician, helped for years to make the waters of Sutter creek a stream of mud and sand. In the chaos of social elements those men throw away the university gown and donned the hickory shirt and canvas pants of the miner.

and Clerk, to be elected annually. The Trustees were authorized to purchase the necessary real estate on which to erect a jail, and other necessary buildings; to assess taxes not exceeding one per cent, on the whole taxable property, no assessments, however, to be made on mines except the improvements which were above ground; to assess a poll-tax of not more than two dollars; to determine and abate nuisances; to prevent animals from running at large; to prevent and punish disorderly conduct; to license shows, theaters, hawkers, and peddlers; and to make all necessary regulations not inconsistent with the general law. The Marshal was to receive seventy-five dollars per year for collecting taxes, and to have a salary not exceeding one hundred dollars per month. The Town Recorder was to have the jurisdiction of a Justice of the Peace, and to pay all fines over to the Treasurer, who was to receive one-half of one per cent, for receiving and disbursing money. The Clerk was to receive no salary.

The effect of the organization was found to be salutary. A number of hoodlums, who had rendered night hideous and the streets disagreeable, dangerous even, to females especially, found themselves confronted with a lodging in a calabose, for any disorderly conduct. Nuisances were now removed at the expense of the authors. Boys were required to be at home at eight o'clock, and there was a marked improvement in the appearance of the town, especially after night-fall.

FUTURE PROSPECTS. At this writing (1881), the town is in a depressed condition, owing to the suspension of mining operations. It is by no means certain that Sutter creek is "worked out;" on the contrary, but little of the ground is even prospected, a few hundred feet of many thousands, only, having been explored. No one knows what chimneys of rich ore are slumbering "just below," waiting for the minor to lay bare its wealth.

AMADOR, situated on the Mother Lode, where it is intersected by Amador creek, about seven miles north of Jackson, was mined soon after the discovery of gold. Some Oregon men built two cabins, and stayed during the Winter. James T. Wheeler and four others built a large double cabin in the Fall of 1849, near where the Spring Hill mill was afterwards built. Some men from Virginia also built a cabin and kept a stock of goods, mining at the same time. W. H. Mitchell, William Lesaw, J. A. Tucker, Joseph Wright, Silas Reed, ———Ashloy, and Willson, are names remembered of the company who wintered here in 1849. Silas Rood was a famous hunter, and kept the camp supplied with game.

LOWER RANCHERIA. Is about two miles east from Drytown, and is about one mile east of the Mother Lode. Quartz mountain, and the other veins of the same formation, are supposed to have enriched the flats and gulches around this place, which were worked in 1848, and some years after, with great success. From all accounts, Deep gulch and Slate gulch were as rich as any places in Amador county, as much as ten thousand dollars being taken from a claim fifteen foot square and three feet deep.

> The Amador mine is a continuous vein, yielding a regular grade of ore of little more than twenty-one dollars to the ton. This is considered the best species of rock as it goes on in the same way for years. The mine is 1,850 feet long, and the vein of quartz is enclosed on the east by a wall of granite, and on the west by one of slate. The product for the year 1869-70 was $617,542, and the mill contains seventy-two stamps.
>
> J.G. Player-Frowd, 1870s

Keystone Mine miners posing by head frame in 1907.

Forest Home Inn.

Lumps were found at the foot of Deep gulch weighing twelve pounds. John Eagon, who mined here in an early day, picked up a piece which was worth about one thousand dollars.

OLETA - FIDDLETOWN. It may be well to give the origin of the first, as well as the last name. The place was settled in 1849 by a party from Missouri. The early records of the settlement, if kept, are lost, and only tradition is left to account for the musical name. It became necessary to name the young town. "They are always fiddling," says an old Missouri patriarch, "call it Fiddletown;" and Fiddletown it was, not only when it was a hamlet of three or four wagons and a tent, but when it was a town of large streets and a hundred houses, some of brick and stone.

The first settlers certainly manifested little taste in the selection of names. Poompoomatee they metamorphosed into Suckertown. Every Spring where the Indians camped had a name, generally sonorous and sweet, with a meaning sometimes full of poetry. What possessed men to baptize places Hogtown, Helltown, Shirt-tail, to say nothing of names which cannot be repeated, is a phenomenon to be explained. Oleta was settled in 1849, and had but a small growth until after the discovery of American flat, French flat, and American hill, in 1852. Previous to that the houses could be counted on one's fingers. Captain Stowers, in company with Carter and Curtis, kept the hotel which had the eminent distinction of having a real glass window. The bar-room was also sitting-room, dining-room and bed-room, the beds being potato sacks stretched across poles,

> In removing a pile of tailings [along Dry creek] deposited by a "forty-niner" my shovel uncovered a nugget of gold weighing half an ounce, or eight dollars.
>
> David Augustus Shaw, 1850

furnished with blankets, but no pillows, a man's boots being expected to serve that purpose.

Oleta occupied an anomalous position with respect to county governments. El Dorado was bounded on the south by Dry creek and Calaveras, on the north by Dry creek. There were two forks about equal size, Fiddletown being between the two.

At one time, four stage-lines concentrated here, taking passengers to Indian Diggings, and other mining towns, also for the cities. The hill diggings, though not rich, furnished remunerative employment to a great many men. Soon after the discovery of the Nevada mines, the population began to decline in common with the other placer mining towns of Amador county.

MINING PROSPECTS. There is more placer mining around Oleta than in any other of the mining camps. The gulches were soon worked out, but the low-grade gravel hills remained unworked until smaller wages were satisfactory, or until improved methods of mining were adopted. The reduced price of water also has had much to do with the working of low-grade gravel mines. Loafer hill, as well as other hills in the vicinity, has many years of drifting. The ridge between Slate creek and Sucker creek is also paying ground. At the Brown claim, on Sucker hill, may be seen the most advanced methods of gravel mining.

COSUMNES RIVER. This, by Act of the Legislature, 1856-57, constitutes the northern boundary of the county. The south

Early Amador City.

Courtesy Amador County Archives

The bear was known to frequent a patch of thick chaparral. A party of ten or twelve persons, among whom were the Johnstons, Jim and Jack, started out to find him. They succeeded in getting a fatal shot at his majesty the bear, which contrary to all expectation, retreated into the thick brush. From the amount of blood along his trail they judged that he was too severely wounded to be dangerous, and they imprudently followed him. The infuriated animal charged upon the Johnstons and brought one of them to the ground, his gun during the encounter being thrown out of reach. Each endeavored to draw the bear away from the other by pounding him over the head with the gun, when the animal would get the other down and commence again gnawing and lacerating his arms, head and body. It was a desperate fight now to get away. The balance of the party had deserted them. Jack's arms were now so useless that he could no longer raise the gun to strike the bear. The creature was a monster in size, his back being nearly on a level with Jack's shoulder. The struggle seemed hopeless, but at the last moment the bear gave a kind of snarl and beat a retreat. One of the men was now utterly helpless and the other one not much better; he however, succeeded in dragging his brother out of the brush to the open ground. He was taken away in a wagon and cared for, and recovered after several months.

Freight team in Amador City.

> At 11 o'clock we stopped at a place called Arroyo Seco, which the fire had not reached and where there was some water.
>
> About an hour after noon the heat became such that one felt uncomfortable even in the shade. This day turned out to be cruelest of all that we had had up to that time.
>
> Before we saddled our horses the idea occurred to me of having a test made, in order to determine whether this stream bore any gold. We had our bateas, a sort of large, shallow wooden dish of from 12 to 14 inches in diameter, which serve to wash gold-bearing soil. I had one filled with earth taken from the streambed. The operation of washing the earth. In less than half an hour, to our great astonishment, he showed us some gold which had remained in the bottom with a little black sand.
>
> Jacques Antoine Moerenhout,
> July 13, 1848

fork was probably the poorest in gold of all the rivers in the mines; though around Fairplay, Cedarville, and Indian Diggings, a range corresponding with Volcano and Murphy's, there were some very rich placers. Near the lower end of the flat, above the falls, were some deposits of fine gold where the miners made from two to six ounces a day.

Ione Valley and Vicinity.

Ione Valley is situated about twelve miles west of the county seat, and is formed by the junction of Dry creek, Sutter creek, and Jackson creek, soon after they leave the mountains.

Who has not heard of Ione valley. Whether one rides over the dusty plains from Sacramento, or descends from the pine-clad hills of the Sierras, Ione comes on his view like the realization of a dream. None ever saw but to admire. The Indians relate that, at the time Sutter settled in Sacramento, numbers of them went to see the man with a white skin; that afterwards they were captured (corralled would be a proper term), and driven to Sacramento and made to work for Sutter, though they soon after went voluntarily.

The name Arroyo Seco being given the Drytown branch of the creek by the miners who went there soon after the discovery of gold. Some of the Weber party in prospecting from the Stanislaus, might have passed through the valley, as it is recorded that they found gold on the Mokelumne river first, and at every place until they reached Weber Creek, in El Dorado county. Sutter, in an early day, 1846, got out timbers for a ferry-boat on the divide between Sutter and Amador, about three miles above the towns, but it is said that his wagons passed up on the north side of Dry creek, this route being the one over which wagons passed to and fro in the earliest days, Lower Rancheria being one of the way places. The pit where the sawing was done is still visible. J. T. Wheeler of Pine Grove, saw this in 1849, some of the partly-finished timbers being still on the blocks.

The first mining of which any knowledge can be obtained, was by a Mexican early in 1848, before Hicks had pastured cattle here. The Mexican told Indian Tom that the oro (gold) would buy beef and sugar, which induced the Indians to go to work.

FIRST WHITE MEN IN IONE VALLEY. About the last of August, 1848, two men then mining at Mormon Island, at the head of the American river, imbued with that restless spirit which characterized all early Californians, started out on a prospecting tour, and headed directly for this valley, reports having already reached them of its existence and its great fertility. Those two men were William Hicks and Moses Childers, who crossed the plains in 1843 in company with J. P. Martin. There were then living here (1848) in an adobe house, on the ranch

Main Street, Jackson, looking north. The Globe Hotel is on right. Photo around 1900.

Cool morning, & chill took hold of me in the morning & lasted untill noon, & I was unfit for work during the day. The wild Indians came round our tent & stole two Mules. They were tied at the tent door. They took one off a few rods & shot an arrow through him & cut out some meat. The other they drove off. They were barefoot & go naked, notwithstanding the Snow is knee deep where they come from. The Yankies are verry much enraged, & will shoot them sooner than they would a Deer.

Hiram Dwight Pierce,
Thursday, December 6th, 1849

National Hotel and stage office in Jackson.

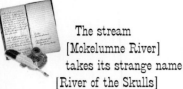

The stream [Mokelumne River] takes its strange name [River of the Skulls] from a war of extermination which the San José Mission had waged in 1818 against the Moquelome Indians, who had stopped near this stream to defend themselves. The Spaniards, about sixty in number, mounted and well armed, left between two and three hundred Indians dead on the field and carried away many prisoners. Although these poor Indians had only bows and arrows, they defended themselves well. Four Spanish soldiers lost their lives there and several were wounded. The crime of which these poor people were accused was of trying to entice away the Mission Indians, that is to say, they were trying to persuade their seduced or abducted children, brothers and relatives to come home.

Jacques Antoine Moerenhout,
July 13, 1848

now owned by the Winters brothers, the Patterson family, and a man named Edward Robinson. Soon after the arrival of Hicks and Childers, General Sutter, who was then living at Sutter's Fort in Sacramento, came through here with a retinue of Indians on an excursion to the mountains, and camped on the spot where Sutter Creek now stands, which event gave that town its name, and also the creek on which it is situated.

FIRST HOUSE. Hicks built his first house, with poles covered with hides. He and Martin engaged in the stock business, buying cattle in southern California and driving them here to fatten for market, the valley being then covered with a luxuriant growth of grass, "high as a man's head." The business proved to be lucrative. In the Spring of '49 Hicks converted his house on the knoll into a store, the first in the valley, with Childers as manager. His first goods were hauled from Sacramento in a cart. They sold all sorts of trinkets to the Indians, such as beads, jews harps, calicoes, and—whisky. They received gold-dust in exchange. Extravagant prices ruled. A bottle of whisky would often bring its "weight in gold-dust." It was estimated that there were five thousand Indians within a radius of ten miles around the valley at that time. Previous to its settlement by the whites, they disposed of their dead by raising them into the tops of the trees and fastening them with withes. Robert Ludgate, who came to the valley in 1851, relates that as he was walking one day down the lower side of the valley, he saw something in the crotch of a tree which attracted his curiosity, and climbing up to look at it, was startled to see the grim skeleton of an Indian.

The Q ranch was bought in 1853 by Charles Green, who, in company with John Vogan, established a line of stages between Sacramento and Sonora, via, the Q ranch, Jackson and Mokelumne Hill; and the Q became quite a noted place, having a post-office, blacksmith shop, and race track.

Origin of the Name Ione. The valley was named Ione before a town was started here, by Thomas Brown, who was a great reader. He was reading a historical romance of Bulwer, entitled "Herculaneum; or the last days of Pompeii," one of whose heroines was a very beautiful young girl named "Ione." By one of those happy thoughts which sometimes come to us like a revelation, it occurred to him that "Ione" was a most appropriate name for this valley, and he accordingly gave it that name.

Railroad. Previous to 1876, Ione was connected with the outside world with only the poorest kinds of wagon roads. Many persons had advocated and others had opposed a railroad. But the desire for a railroad yearly grew stronger. A ride over the abominated stage road between Ione and Galt was sure to convert one to the railroad system. About 1872 things began to shape themselves in this direction. The discovery of extensive beds of lignite, which made a very good substitute for coal, which had not then been found in quantities that it since has, turned attention to the valley.

Stockton Narrow Gauge. The design at that time was to build a branch road from Linden to Ione, but the embarrass-

> Rained all day. Tinkerd for myself. Our Log cabbin furnishes comfortable quarters. Two men were attacked by 3 Grisley Bears just below us. One of them got into a tree, the other shot one of the bears. The man pursued him & in backing off he fell down & the bear comeing up he stuck the musel of his gun in his mouth, when the bear turned & left him.
>
> Hiram Dwight Pierce,
> Thursday, [December] 13th, 1849

Amador freight wagon on the road between Jackson Gate and Martell.

Henry Koehler's store in Amador City, circa 1893.

> At daybreak all was astir. Men were leaving on foot and on horseback, loaded with pickaxes, picks and shovels, some going to loosen and dig out the dirt, others to cart it. Hardly a soul remained in camp. My traveling companions, likewise impatient to begin work, came to ask if I would lend them the pack horses to carry the dirt which must be brought from three or four miles away. I promised them the horses for three or four days and they set out immediately after some dirt.
>
> Jacques Antoine Moerenhout,
> July 17, 1848

ment of the company caused by the failure of the copper mines and the inability to complete or maintain possession of the road, induced them to re-organize and attempt the building of a narrow-gauge direct from Ione to tide-water at Stockton. Considerable money was paid in on the subscriptions, which seemed to be wasted in mere show, and finally the project fell through. The engines were soon removed and put upon the Nevada Narrow-Gauge, and the half-finished cars upon which a hundred or two dollars were expended is all to show for the fifty thousand dollars or more paid in by the citizens of Stockton.

OVERFLOWS. The same agency which has deposited the fertile soil of the valley, occasionally becomes a means of destruction. A large water-shed is at the head of Dry and Sutter creeks. In early days when no tailings or slickens burdened the water, the overflows were comparatively harmless, but not so when the streams are taxed to their utmost capacity to precipitate on the valleys the mud, sand, and rocks, from a thousand mining claims. The most disastrous overflow occurred in 1861-62. The piles of tailings—the accumulations of years—were forced through the canon, and, though pulverized by the constant attrition, lodged soon after reaching the valley, filling the channel, nearly to the surface; consequently the great mass of water either eroded new channels, or carried great quantities of sterile sand over the farms, destroying orchards, vineyards, and gardens—the work of years of industry—leaving only a waste producing willows and malaria. At the lower part of the valley, the waters from Mule creek had already buried some of the land with tailings. This freshet piled on new horrors, adding several feet more of slickens, and covering a still larger area.

BUENA VISTA. This is the center of a farming region, and, as its name implies, is perhaps one of the most beautiful places in the State. Jackson creek here comes out of the mountains, and the valley spreads out from one to two miles in width, maintaining this character until Dry creek comes into it, some five or six miles below. The long sweep of hills around the valley have the effect of a fine setting, and the Buena Vista mountain, with bold castellated peaks, varying their outlines with every change of view, bring to mind some of the ruins of the older world, and make one feel that he is on the ground of ancient civilization. The rich, black soil, covered with grass as high as a man's head, early attracted the attention of settlers, though it is impossible to learn who first visited it. It forms part of the tract of land granted to Teodosia Yerba in 1840, by Governor Juan B. Alvarado.

Cattle were grazed here as early as 1848, whether by some of Hick's and Martin's vaqueros, is not known; but the land was claimed by a man by the name of Diggs, who kept a trading post, ranched cattle and sold beef, in 1849. In 1850, it was purchased by Charles Stone, Warren Nimms, and Fletcher Baker, all from the eastern part of New York. Stone seemed to have been the business man of the firm, and, under his management, the valley had quite a princely look. They run a log fence around a thousand acres or more of land, put up buildings, costing, with the then high price of lumber and labor,

> Ten months since I left home, & have not made a dollar but am in debt for my board, & my health seems insufficient for the task. After the opperation of my Phisic I felt some better. Oh the loneliness of this desolate region. No Meeting, No Society, nought but drinking & card playing & hunting on the Sabbath
>
> Hiram Dwight Pierce, Sunday [January] 6th, 1850

Old Wildman store, formerly the Handford store, in Sutter Creek.

This six-horse stage is in front of the Louisiana House in Jackson which burned and was replaced by the National Hotel. Noted on the back: "Monna? Serran; stable for Volcano stages which burned in 1895; Palmer stable, blacksmith shop, stage stable, Jackson Ione line. On the porch - Evans, proprietor, Sam Parker, pioneer; on ground, Ray Parker and ?; driver Lee Hendricks, guard Eli Fisher at horses' heads Bunker, passengers, Lola Parker and Dave Kerr.

> Being present when an American, who had no other tool than his knife, found a rather large piece, I proposed that he sell it to me, to which he immediately agreed. I had neither scales nor money, but he told me to take it with me, to weigh it and send him whatever it came to.
>
> Jacques Antoine Moerenhout, July, 1848

several thousand dollars. They purchased large herds of cattle in southern California at low figures, kept them on the place until the condition of the market or the cattle was favorable, and sold them at a great advance. They also went into farming, and raised large quantities of barley, when it readily brought from one hundred and fifty to two hundred and fifty dollars per ton, hay being sold on the place for fifty dollars per ton. It is said that the yield of barley was sometimes one hundred and twenty bushels to the acre, and seven tons of weighed hay were sold from an acre at fifty dollars per ton, though, says the narrator, it was not quite cured. They were not suffered to enjoy such abundance in peace, however. The Johnston family, as well as others, laid hold of a quarter section, here and there, and expensive lawsuits resulted.

MULETOWN. This place was about two miles north of Ione, and in the fifties was a very lively camp. It belonged to the foot-hill diggings, the gold in the gulches and hills having been liberated from the quartz veins by a wash of the sea, all the gravel having a peculiar, polished appearance without the rounded form usually seen in river deposits. The ravines were very rich. Yancy, a native of the Argentine Republic, often made a hundred dollars a day with a pan alone. Others made nearly as much. A Chinaman picked up a piece weighing thirty-six ounces. He was so elated that he immediately left for home. After the ravines were worked, the hills were attacked with hydraulic power, and paid better than the ravines had ever done. The peculiarities of the Irish had full sweep. Most of those who could afford to, purchased horses, and on Sunday would ride out in quest of fun and adventure. They were not skillful or graceful horsemen at first, and a Muletown crowd could be distinguished at a long distance by the flopping limbs and furious riding. The pranks and funny affairs of Muletown would fill a book. A few only will be related.

MINERS' COURT. In 1860 the miners had got tired of being taken from their work to testify in cases of disputed mining titles, and a public meeting was called to consider the situation. It was finally resolved that all such cases should be settled by arbitration; that no appeal should be taken; that any party that should feel aggrieved should fight his opponent a fist fight, according to the rules of the ring, the best man taking the ground. It was also agreed, that in case of a great disparity in size or strength, the weaker person might substitute a friend to do his fighting. In order not to interfere with the work, the fights were to come off on the first Sunday after the dispute. It happened that the first trial of this kind fell on a Sunday on which there was to be a Catholic service. How to proceed so as to keep the priest in ignorance of the matter, so that he might not interfere, was the question. At a meeting held the evening before to make arrangements, it was determined to commence the fight at daylight at a spot a little distance from the town. It was thought that by conducting the matter quietly the Father might not hear of it. There were several parties to the affair, involving several fights, but it was hoped that they might be

After the mules were found we packed off up the river 3 miles & crossed it in a canoo with our packs swimming our mules. $1.25 each. We then went down the river one mile & encamped on what is called Washington flat, then containing 5 or 6 tents. My house was readdy prepared, it beeing an oak tree. Got my supper & lay down in the big tent, haveing the broad canopy over me.

Hiram Dwight Pierce,
Wensday, [March] 3d, 1850

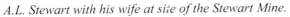
A.L. Stewart with his wife at site of the Stewart Mine.

This four-horse freight wagon was owned and operated by Louis Monteverde, who is shown here hauling freight from Ione to Sutter Creek stores around 1900.

"Coyote Joe," an Indian, charged with killing a blacksmith at the Gate, for the purpose of getting his money. He was tried by a jury of miners, Dr. Pitt acting as foreman, and found guilty, as some of the specimens the blacksmith was known to have, were found on the Indian's person. The trial was in a restaurant, not far from the tree, and he was soon hanging.

finished before the women and children should awake, as the custom was to sleep late on Sunday.

The morning came and nearly all the male population were present. The ring was marked out, the bottle-holders and seconds appointed, and the fight commenced. The contest proved longer than was expected. The litigants were both plucky. Round after round was fought, still no sign of yielding. The sun was getting well up and the women and children would soon be moving. So far there had been no cheering. The blows had fallen thick and fast, taken and given. It is not strange then that the friends of each party began to cheer the combatants, until the noise aroused the women and the priest, who came rushing to the ground, about the time each side thought the other side was about whipped. "How dare you desecrate the Sabbath this way?" says the priest, addressing one of the seconds, whose shirt, from sponging his principal's face, was quite bloody. The second, answering for the meeting, replied that it was much better to settle a difficulty by a fist fight than with knives and pistols, as had been recently done at Volcano, where the priest lived; that it was sometimes necessary to choose the least of two evils. The priest turned away, mounted his horse and left the place, without saying a word. There was no service that day. It was expected that he would give them a fearful admonition the next time, but the subject was never mentioned. This method of settling disputes involved so many inconveniences that it was not tried again.

THE FUNNY MAN. Muletown had a philanthropist by the name of Cunningham, who had very original ways of benefiting mankind. He had been very successful in trade, also in mining, and wanted to use his money for the benefit of the community. "He was rough, but generous and brave," as the poet would have it, a good deal addicted to drink, fully conscious of his importance, and inclined to be dictatorial when-in his cups. He built a hall which was free to all churches, public meetings, and respectable parties, which was dedicated with a dancing party, with the following schedule for tickets:

Tickets to gentlemen without ladies......$6.00
Tickets to gentlemen with one lady.........3.00
Tickets to gentlemen with two ladies.......free.

The entertainment was magnificent, and gave satisfaction to his numerous guests. The hall was used also as a schoolhouse, the old man contributing liberally to the support of the school.

While the camp was still flourishing, his wife died. She was buried without the usual funeral ceremonies, which were postponed to a more convenient season, that he might get them up in a style becoming his wealth. Sometime after, he stipulated with Elder Sharp, the Methodist preacher at Ione, to preach two sermons at twenty dollars each. He gave notice of a free

A verry hot day. Dug $4. In the afternoon prospected beeing verry sore & lame. Find gold all about but a job to get it. A bear fight occurd just below us a few days since. 3 men were attackted by one, & after he had recieved 3 balls in the hed & one in the shoulder, he retreated & they got into a tree.

Hiram Dwight Pierce,
Saturday March 13th, 1850

Amador Reduction Works.

Men posing in front of the Livery Stable, next to the Farmer's Exchange in Ione around 1900.

Kept the bed most of the day. I was verry sore. Our flat was visited by a grisley in the night & the next night he went into a tent below & helped himself. Some Thunder was heard yesterday. It is reported that the Senorians have Murderd the collector in that place, & that parties are arming.

Hiram Dwight Pierce,
Friday [April] 24th, 1850

dinner to all who would attend, and as the style of his entertainments was well known, the attendance was numerous. As the old man was somewhat wanting in reverence for the cloth, and apt to make disparaging remarks, the Elder thought it best to take along Father Rickey, and some of the elder members of his church, to overawe the old man, which did not succeed, however, as he was quite ready to applaud or condemn, when anything pleased or displeased him. "That's good," said he, "that's bully, that's first rate," looking around in triumph. "The next sermon will be better than this" the Elder continued his remarks without being disturbed by the applause. During the sermon, Mr. Cunningham felt a call from nature, and asked Elder Sharp to wait a few minutes till he could go out; but the preacher, not being used to such interruptions, continued his sermon. Cunningham commenced raising his bulky form, some of Sharp's friends trying to hold him down in his seat. He shook them off, however, for his strength was immense, and balanced himself in front of the preacher, wrath oozing out of every inch of his bloated face, his bulky form and baggy cheeks quivering with rage. "By G—, sir, I would like to know who is running this funeral!" The Elder heaved a sigh and subsided, waiting for the old man to come back.

Cunningham died, and was buried near his wife, nearly a score of years since, and the sheep and goats feed where once stood his hall and the surrounding town, but the memory of his many benevolent deeds will last until the pioneers have gone to their final rest.

Ore carts being pulled by a small electric engine making work more efficient at the Penn Mining Company in Campo Seco at the turn of the century. There were hundreds of mines in Calaveras County in the 19th century with barely a trace of them left today. When steel was needed for WWI and WWII, most Calaveras mines were "scrapped out" to serve the war effort.

Chapter 2: Calaveras County — San Andreas, Mokelumne Hill, Murphys, Valley Springs, Copperopolis, and vicinity

Calaveras County, to which a large proportion of the miners in halcyon days of '49 and '50 betook themselves and from whose hills and gulches million upon millions of gold have been poured into the treasury of the world, has an area of 622,000 acres. Here are found some of the best mines in this State, and the entire county may, in fact, be regarded as a bed of mineral deposits. The baser metals, copper, iron, cinnabar, etc., are found in abundance, and ledges of marble, limestone, and granite, and undeveloped deposits of coal are known to exist.

Calaveras is now attracting attention as a fruit and vineyard country, and its foot-hills are being occupied and covered

> Where one disappointed miner would leave the Mukelumne for the Tuolumne, or any other place about which he had heard fair report, perhaps a dozen unsuccessful Tuolumne diggers would pour into the Mukelumne. And so it ever was.
>
> Leonard Kip, 1850

These men were washing dirt in tubs of water. It was common practice when the water flow was low or stopped during the dry season to load bags with "pay dirt" and wash it elsewhere.

After having been held in snowy fetters so long, the residents were only too glad to visit the town, where they could spend a few hours' in the drinking-saloons and stores in talking over the prospects of the coming season, or visit the gambling-house and indulge their passion for gaming - a passion that existed in the breast of nearly every miner in California during the five years following the advent of the mining population.

The gamblers, those who dealt faro, monte, and other games of chance, and who followed no other occupation, were delighted with the change. For weeks it had been "dog eat dog" with them, and now the prospect of having a few outsiders to fleece was a source of great gratification. In order to celebrate the event they had clubbed together, raised a purse of a thousand dollars, and offered it as a prize to the person who could make the quickest time on snow-shoes over a track to be designated by a committe.

      Albert S. Evans, late 1860s

with fruit trees and vines that are yielding good return and promise well for the future.

    Calaveras is a wonder land, having more general and especial natural curiosities than any other county in the State. Among these we may mention the Big Trees, Natural Bridges, Hot Springs, Extensive Caves, Basaltic Cliffs, Table Mountain, and others world-wide in reputation.

    If a person would travel over the county he would find a never ending panorama of grand and pleasant scenes; the old abandoned mining grounds and towns going to decay; the present successful quartz and copper mines; extensive mining ditches bringing water long distances over hill and valley to supply the miner and the farmer; this canal winding its sinuous way on the top or around the sides of the ridge, or its sparkling contents rushing impetuously down the water-furrowed center of a ravine; here and there an aqueduct, a cabin, an abandoned mining claim, or a saw-mill, give variety to the landscape.

    There will unfold new sights of natural grandeur to the admiration of the tourist winding his way through a series of beautiful forests, valleys, and glens, where on either side towering mountains solemnly look down upon the placid silver streams beneath. Sunshine alternates with shadow in the secluded recesses of a quiet mountain ravine, where clear crystal brooks run like silver threads through the verdant landscape that they nourish.

Over the wide and open valley game wing their flight, seeming to be poised still in the clear mountain air. It is the real play-ground for the sportsman. Through the thicket springs the light-footed deer, and the footprint of the bear is stamped on the ground. Foxes, silver-gray squirrels, rabbits, hare, mountain and valley quail, are in abundance here, and the clear brook streams contain the red-spotted trout, the mountain brook, and the salmon trout.

In the agricultural view will be seen vast wheat fields; vineyards of the choicest grapes; the orange orchard; the largest fig-trees in the State. The valleys are rich with crops; there are cattle upon a thousand hills; the timber is of the finest kind, and the climate delightful. Its undeveloped resources now being opened up by new railroad connection are almost inexhaustible.

RAILWAY PUSHING EASTWARD. The San Joaquin and Sierra Nevada Railroad is pushing its way eastward through Calaveras County, opening up at least 300,000 acres of United States Government lands subject, to-day, tc entry, on which is found some of the best mineral lands in the States; besides, the foothills of Calaveras present the finest opening on the coast to men of small means, who desire to make homes for their fami-

The Central Pacific Railroad's engine 1003 with Mr. James and other workers in Calaveras.

At this point our camp life commenced and I took my first lesson in getting up a meal, thought I was doing splendidly and was congratulating myself on the extra style in which I cooked the steak, but my mode of seasoning with powdered sugar instead of salt, hardly suited the rest of the mess and they unanimously agreed that I had considerable to learn before they could class me as a good cook.

We had a five story gold washer, that is, five sets of sieves, one above the other, graded from very coarse to fine and warranted to catch all the gold, fine or coarse, for had it not been tested thoroughly in New York to the satisfaction of an admiring crowd with a bucket of sand and scraps of lead thrown in—not a particle of the lead escaping during the washing process. Then we had axes, picks and shovels and even a ten-pound crowbar, and last, but not least of all, a box containing various acids, duly bottled and labeled, so that no bogus gold could be played on us; for with our valuable box of acids we were not to be fooled.

Harvey Wood, 1849

Hanged. The day for the execution of George W. Cox arrived with the certainty of the rising sun. By ten o'clock the streets were crowded with men who had come to witness the execution, 250 invitations having been issued by Sheriff Thorn. The personal appearance of the prisoner had been improved by the barber's scissors, he looked decidedly genteel. He slept quietly during the night. He ate his breakfast with relish and was far from being low spirited and weak at the approach of death upon the gallows. At 10 o'clock the Sheriff read the death warrant, and the Sheriff and prisoner walked out to the scaffold; Cox walked with a quick and steady step. He looked over the sea of upturned faces and said, "Take a good observation, gentleman." He smiled blandly and laughed; in another second he said, "I'm not sorry for anything I've ever done." By this time the rope encircled his neck and the black cap was being adjusted over his face. Cox became slightly impatient and said to the Sheriff, "For Christ's sake give me a little air." In another moment the trap was sprung and Cox dropped 5 ½ feet with a heavy thud. He did not move a muscle, his neck was broken by the fall and death was instantaneous.

The crime for which George W. Cox was made to pay the extreme penalty was committed on the 3rd of last November at the Cox ranch, Table Mountain, near Sheep Ranch. Henry G. Cook, his victim, was his son-in-law. The young man

continued in far right column

The Mammoth Grove Hotel at Calaveras Big Trees in 1865.

lies and engage in either fruit or wine culture. "Valley Springs," the present terminus, is at a distance of forty-one miles from Brack's Landing on the Mokelumne.

We understand that the company intends to push the road through to the Big Trees at the earliest practicable moment. It will connect the foot-hill and mountain homes with the valleys, and will infuse new life and energy into every branch of industry. We confidently predict that within ten years the foot hills of Calaveras will be among the most populous and wealthy portion of our State.

MAMMOTH GROVE HOTEL. James L. Sperry Proprietor. The Grove Hotel having been enlarged can now accommodate one hundred guests. It has a laundry, hot and cold baths, a billiard table, bar, verandas, parlor, ball-room, the most pleasant sleeping apartments, and furnishes the best of fare at the table. It faces the grove, having the greater number of trees to the left, looking from the veranda, and the two "Sentinels" immediately in the front, about two hundred yards to the eastward.

The valley in which this grove is situated contains of the Sequoia trees, ninety-three, not including those of from one to ten years' growth. There are also hundreds of sugar and pitch pines of astonishing proportions, ranging to the height of 275 feet, and having not unfrequently a diameter of ten to eleven and a half feet. Anywhere else these pines would be regarded as vegetable monsters. Here, by the side of the Sequoia, they look like dwarfs.

There is good hunting ground in the vicinity, mountain quail are abundant near by, and on the Stanislaus, three miles distant, grouse and deer abound. The San Antonio contains trout of line size. Delightful horseback or buggy rides conduct the visitor to many interesting points of scenery, or objects of curiosity, among which, besides the Falls of San Antonio, may be mentioned the Basaltic Cliffs on the North Fork of the Stanislaus River, and the Cave at Cave City, fifteen miles to the west, and the Natural Bridges near Vallecito.

During the summer and spring months this valley is exempt from the heat of the lower country and from the cold of the snow range. Vegetation blooms early in May, remaining fresh and green until the middle of October. The water is always pure and cold, and the hotel is furnished with ice all through the summer and autumn. Snow falls usually about the middle of December, and disappears from the grove entirely by the middle of April.

The Big Trees have been heard of wherever the photographic art is known, or the English language is spoken. This

Even with all the equipment and innovation employed at the Penn Mining Company in Campo Seco, there was still lots of back-breaking work for the miners employed there. The Penn Mine was one of the major sources of copper in the Sierran foothill belt. Copper deposits in this area were discovered in 1861.

continued from far left column

had come home to his dinner from the woods where he was working. The noon day meal was eaten peaceably, Cox eating but sparingly of the victuals before him. Mrs. Cook had risen from the table and was outside the kitchen door. In the meantime Cox addressed Cook, and asked him, casually, how he was getting along chopping wood. Cook replied, "Very well." Cox then said, "Have you ever worked nights." To this fatal interrogation Cook replied that he had. "That lets me out _____ _____, " exclaimed Cox, and quickly went into an adjoining room, secured his gun, and before the family realized the terrible intention of the man, Cook was shot and instantly killed. The murderer took deadly aim and the ball pierced the young man's heart. The two affrighted women realizing their perilous position, attempted to disarm Cox who was now worked up to a mad frenzy. Mrs. Cook grasped the gun in her father's hands and with a desperation born of terror prevented him from reloading the weapon. Her hands were badly torn in the conflict and she was struck and kicked by her unnatural parent. Finally the heroic young woman got her father out of the house, and then locked the doors upon herself and her dead husband. After this fiendish outrage and murder Cox went to D.B. Reed's place and asked him to go to his (Cox's) house and get him his coat of mail and weapons; not mentioning

continued next page far left column

continued from last page far right column

one word of the black deed he had just committed. Mr. Reed got the articles for Cox, and although he saw the two women were in tears he refrained from asking questions. Cox went direct to Sheep Ranch and gave himself up to the authorities. He was brought to the County Jail the same night and incarcerated. He was tried before the Superior Court and the jury found him guilty of murder in the first degree and fixed the punishment of death. Some effort was made during the trial to save the prisoner's neck by introducing the insanity plea. Cox was undoubtedly weak, mentally, and of ungovernable temper. His imagination had been taxed by imaginary wrongs and he fancied any man in Calaveras with whom he had business dealings, had defrauded him and was his enemy. After an absence of many years, he returned to the home he had deserted, and found a cold and unwelcome reception from his family. His youngest daughter had married. He took a strong dislike to her young husband; believed him a shiftless and undesirable acquisition to his household. He was ready to believe Mrs. Cox guilty of infidelity, and young Cook was the suspected man. His insane mind resolved to do away with the innocent Cook, and the murder was committed. For his great crime he has suffered disgraceful death.

Calaveras Prospect,
Friday, August 31, 1888

Riding through the entrance of "Trapper Smith's Cabin" in the South Grove of the Calaveras Big Trees, 1908.

species of tree is known as the Sequoia gigantea, and was named in honor of Sequoia, a Cherokee Indian, who is supposed to have been born about 1770. The big tree is limited in its range, and is not so extensively found as the redwood. They are both a peculiarity of California, although a very few have been found across the border in Oregon. The big trees are found only in groves, while the redwoods cover extensive tracts.

Tourists, to visit these trees, leaving San Francisco, can take the Central Pacific Railroad to Stockton, and the Copperopolis Railroad to Milton, or the new [in 1885] narrow gauge railroad which connects with the Central at Lodi, thence to Valley Springs and San Andreas. Connection is made on either route with Matteson's daily line of stages, to the Big Trees. A daily coach leaves the Big Trees for Milton, connecting at Murphy's with a daily line to Yosemite Valley via Hutchings' new route, being the shortest and best.

THE CALAVERAS BIG TREES. The mammoth grove of big trees is situated in a small valley, near the head-waters of the San Antonio, one of the largest streams in central Calaveras, and five miles east of the falls of said stream, which are 150 feet in height, and surrounded by the grandest of scenery.

The grove is 4,585 feet above the sea, and contains 10 trees, each one 30 feet in diameter, and over 70 of which are between 15 and 30 feet. One of the trees which is down— The Father of the Forest — must have been 450 feet high, and 40 feet in diameter."

In 1853 one of the largest trees, 92 feet in circumference and over 300 feet high, was cut down. This tree employed five men for twenty-two days in felling it—not by chopping it down, but by boring it off with pump augers. After the stem was fairly severed from the stump, the uprightness of the tree, and the breadth of its base, sustained it in its position. To accomplish the feat of throwing it over, about two and a half days of the twenty-two were spent in inserting wedges, and driving them in with the butts of trees, until, at last, the noble monarch of the forest was forced to tremble, and then to fall, after braving "the battle and the breeze," for nearly three thousand years.

The stump of this tree has been smoothed off, and now easily accommodates thirty-two dancers. Theatrical performances have been held upon it, and in 1858 a newspaper, the *Big Tree Bulletin*, was printed there.

The timber of the redwood is very durable, and is so easily worked that a man needs but an ax, a betel, and a few wedges, to convert the largest of them, provided they are free from knots, into planks, rails, or clapboards, and I have seen Barnes fell a huge fellow, and in less than a fortnight he has carried it all away but the boughs and the bark. It is a fine sight to watch one of these trees fall to the ax; leaving the perpendicular at first so leisurely; then gathering impetus as it nears the ground, crushing all it meets, making the earth vibrate with its shock, and sending forth a booming echo, that startles the game far and wide.

Frank Marryat, 1850

This tree was one of the finest specimens in the North Grove of Calaveras Big Trees and was felled in the early 1850s. It took five men twenty days to cut through the trunk and three more days for it to fall. In 1856 Sperry and Perry constructed an elegant pavilion on the stump. It has been used over the years as a dance hall, so large that it accommodated 32 persons dancing four sets of cotillions with room for an orchestra and spectators.

Courtesy Bancroft Library

"Wallflowers" inside the dance hall in Calaveras Big Trees.

The bark of the redwood is perforated in every direction, and with great regularity, by a kind of starling, called, from this peculiarity, carpentaro, or carpenter. These birds form cells in the tree with great assiduity, and deposit therein acorns, which fit very tightly. They employ themselves continually, when not fighting, in depositing acorns in the redwoods. You may see a dozen of them clinging to the bark of one tree pecking away, each at a hole. But the carpentaros work for the more lazy portion of creation, and one of their enemies is the beautiful gray squirrel which abounds here.

The carpentaro has a more destructive enemy than even the squirrel or the bear, and a greater beast than either—the Digger Indian. These miserable specimens of humanity will light a fire at the root of a well-stocked redwood tree until it falls; they then extract the carpentaro's acorns and fill many baskets full.

Frank Marryat, 1850

Near the stump lies a section of the trunk; this is 25 feet in diameter and 20 feet long; beyond lies the immense trunk as it fell, measuring 302 feet from the base of the stump to its extremity. Upon this was situated a bar-room and ten-pin alley, stretching along its upper surface for a distance of 81 feet, affording ample space for two alley-beds, side by side.

About 80 feet from this stump stand the "Two Sentinels," each over 300 feet high, and the larger 23 feet in diameter. The carriage road approaching Sperry's Hotel passes directly between the "Two Sentinels," both very fine trees.

Another of these wonders, the largest tree now standing, which, from its immense size, two breast-like protuberances on one side, and the number of small trees of the same class adjacent, has been named the "Mother of the Forest." In the summer of 1854, the bark was stripped from this tree by Mr. George Gale, for purposes of exhibition in the East, to the height of 116 feet; and it now measures in circumference, without the bark, at the base, 84 feet; 20 feet from base, 69 feet; 70 feet from base, 43 feet 6 inches; 116 feet from base, and up to the bark, 39 feet 6 inches. The full circumference at the base, including bark, was 90 feet. Its height was 327 feet. The average thickness of bark was 11 inches, although in places it was about 2 feet. This tree is estimated to contain 537,000 feet of sound inch lumber. To the first branch it is 137 feet. The small black marks upon the tree indicate where auger holes were bored and rounds inserted by which to ascend the tree when removing the bark.

In the center of the grove is a tree 280 feet high, 17 feet in diameter, singularly hollowed out on one side by fire, and named "Pluto's Chimney." The "Chimney" made by the fire is on the north side, and extends from the ground 90 feet upward. One hundred feet north of the "Pioneer's Cabin," stand the "Quartette" cluster, the highest of which is 220 feet; and so yards east of this is a healthy young tree, 13 feet in diameter, and 250 feet high, and named in 1865 by a San Francisco lady, "America."

A few steps further bring us to the "Fallen Monarch," the base section of a huge trunk, which has to all appearances been down for centuries. It is still 18 feet in diameter, although the bark and much of the wood have been wasted away by time. What is left is perfectly sound; but the upper half or two-thirds, which struck the earth with greatest force in its fall, has all

There were thousands of Chinese all over California during the 19th century. Some were miners, many worked on railroads, and there were many Chinese merchants, laundries, and shops. Unfortunately this was another group that was underrepresented in both written and photographic media. Many Chinese returned to their homeland but Ah See Wahn lived out his days at Latimer's Gulch on the Calaveras River. He was popular with the young school children, giving them firecrackers and Chinese candies. He is shown here with a rocker working his claim.

Courtesy Calaveras County Historical Society

We crossed the [Stanislaus] river and encamped for the night. There we saw a fine specimen of California horsemanship and cattle driving. A Kentucky drover had employed a Spaniard, to assist him in driving forty or fifty head of cattle to the mines to slaughter for beef. A fierce, exasperated bullock, turned to attack the Spaniard driver, who, knowing that beef was wanted, suddenly resolved upon his slaughter. Raising himself in his stirrups, he threw a lasso over his horns, and adroitly bringing it to bear upon his legs, brought him to the ground. The admirably trained horse, the moment the lasso was ready for the pull, settled back, almost upon his haunches, to assist the rider.

William S. McCollum, 1849

We started at once in search of our bear—six in number—and accompanied by a small dog belonging to Sheldon.

Almost immediately I heard a crash and an angry roar, and then a shot was fired to the left. It was necessary for us to retrace our steps, to rejoin our party; which done, the bear was in view. I was astonished at his size; standing on his hind-legs with his mouth open.

A momentary uncertainty on his part gave me an opportunity of troubling him with one of my 1 1/2 oz. balls; but this only elicited a grunt and a rush in my direction.

Sheldon fired as the grizzly approached, but without effect; and the next moment poor Sheldon was down bathed in blood; one blow had carried away the flesh entirely from one side of his face, fracturing his jaw-bone in the most frightful manner.

The bear disappeared, and probably retired to die, while we carried Sheldon home, with what feelings of grief I need not say. We sent him on to Sonoma as soon as possible, and he afterward recovered, though dreadfully disfigured, and with the loss of an eye.

Frank Marryat, 1850

While there were many larger and more sophisticated mining operations all over the area by the mid 1850s, the lone prospector, wanting to keep his independence and his gold, did not vanish from the landscape.

disappeared, and trees nearly a century old are growing where it struck. This tree must have been over 300 feet high and 25 feet in diameter.

Further on standing near the uprooted base of the "Father of the Forest," the scene is grand and beautiful beyond description. The "Father" long since bowed his head in the dust, yet how stupendous even in his ruin! He measures 112 feet in circumference at the base, and can be traced 300 feet where the trunk was broken by falling against another tree; here it measures 16 feet in diameter, and according to the average taper of the other trees this venerable giant must have been 450 feet in height when standing. A hollow chamber or burnt cavity extends through the trunk 200 feet, large enough for a person to ride through. Near its base, a never-failing spring of water is found. Walking upon the trunk and looking from its uprooted base, the mind can scarce conceive its prodigious dimensions, while on the other hand tower his giant sons and daughters, forming the most impressive scene in the forest.

The burned-out tree in the grove called the "Pioneer's Cabin" has been cut through. The opening is now large enough to admit the passage of a loaded coach and horses. When it is taken into consideration that the tree is still alive and flourishing, it seems wonderful indeed.

SOUTH PARK GROVE OF BIG TREES. About six miles from the Calaveras Grove just mentioned is the South Grove. This grove has over 1,300 Sequoias and is nearly two miles in extent. There is only a trail leading to this grove, and the route is through a very wild and romantic country. For a mile is traveled a beautifully wooded hill. Green cells, open to the sunshine, divided the grove of pines. The sky is pure and cloudless, clasping the landscape with a belt of peace and silence. Out of these woods after crossing the turnpike is reached the Divide and a beautiful view bursts upon our sight. The steep Sierra uplifts its craggy summits, white with drifts of snow (August 1st). In the distance rises a sublime chain of granite peaks, soaring far out of the region of trees and lifting its rocky summits into the sky. And far beyond, filling up the magnificent vista—filling up the lower steeps, crowned with pines—were the shining snows of the Dardanelle peaks, while long ranges of dark hills fade away behind each other with a perspective that hinted of the hidden peaks between.

We would advise every lover of grand and beautiful scenes and sublime views to pay this grove a visit and judge for himself. It is well worth the trouble. One of the largest trees, called "New York," is over 400 feet high, 104 feet in circumference,

Hydraulic mining at Chili Gulch. The ravenous appetite of the Monitor washed hillsides clean of mud and debris and made gold more accessible in many areas. Unfortunately they also wreaked havoc on the environment, filling up rivers with silt and debris. As a result, hydraulic mining was banned in 1884 by the Sawyer Act, which prohibited the dumping of debris into rivers.

Terrible Mining Accident. Two men employed in the North Amador mine, at Sutter Creek, were instantly killed and another badly injured Sunday morning last. We take the following from a dispatch to the *Union*:

A fatal accident occurred here this morning about 5 o'clock, in which two men, named Patrick Collier and George Garadella, lost their lives, and one Patrick Grady was hurt, though not dangerously. The engineer, in hoisting, ran the bucket in the shives, breaking the chains and letting both buckets down the shaft, each bucket killing a man. Collier was mangled horribly, breaking nearly every bone in his body and tearing all the flesh off from the breast bone to the legs. After the accident, Patrick Grady, with another man, descended the shaft in search of Collier's missing arm. When within fifteen feet of the bottom they tied the bucket with a rotten rope and went to the bottom. Soon after they arrived there the rope holding the bucket broke, letting it down, striking Grady a glancing blow on the forehead and cutting a very ugly gash. Collier leaves a wife and three children.

Weekly Calaveras Chronicle, March 15, 1873

When the big trees fall their massive root structure is often exposed. This group poses on "Eagles Wings" exploring the vast openings at varying levels of this fallen giant.

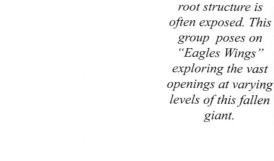

Instead of arriving in the mines with two mules each and three months' provisions as promised by the originator of the association, our mess of four owned one crooked neck horse and one mule.

Harvey Wood, 1849

and 34 feet in diameter. It surpasses all the standing trees in its size and its imposing grandeur.

"Smith's Cabin" is named after a hunter and guide, who lived in its burnt-out base for two years. The interior is 16 by 21 ½ feet. Its height is 340 feet. Here Smith weathered the terrible gale that was the downfall of "Old Goliah" his neighbor. During the progress of the hurricane he did not dare to venture out, as limbs and trees were constantly coming down. The fall of "Old Goliah" he compared to an earthquake. "Old Goliah" is the largest fallen tree in the grove; it measures, as it lies, 105 feet in circumference, and has a present length intact of 261 feet. A limb alone measures 12 feet in circumference. It required no stretch of the imagination to make it the deck of some long ship.

Sitting upon the upper part of the base of the tree we were 23 feet above ground. At 261 feet, where it is broken off, it measures 45 feet in circumference. It has also suffered from fire. Its base has been put to a highly practical use, being no less than a stable for horses. Scientific men of note pronounce the trees to be from two to four thousand years old, their age being judged by the number of circular woody rings they possess. That fire of one thousand years ago raged among the Sequoias alone. Nor does this seem incredible, when vast sugar pines 27 and 30 feet in circumference and 250 feet high, now growing side by side with these trees, show no sign of fire, proving conclusively that they had no existence at that time. All the Sequoias, wherever found, show marks of fire. There are no exceptions among the old trees, as they and they alone had no existence then.

To get some comparative idea of the size of one of these largest fallen trees, let us suppose it laid in the street of some town. It would fill the street the length of four ordinary blocks of one hundred feet. At its base it would reach from sidewalk to side walk (forty feet). Those living in the third story of houses could not see over its trunk.

If these old giants could only answer two questions, How old are you? and, What were the conditions under which you grew? how much speculation, and how many theories would vanish into space. Probably at one time this was a dense forest of Sequoias and time alone has seen its fall and ruin, only these few giants remaining to tell the story.

FAMOUS MINING COUNTY. Calaveras County is famous in the mining annals of the State. Abundant wealth, locked in the

Miner washing his dirt in a cradle on Lower Chili Gulch in 1880.

Emigrants Arrived – On Wednesday evening last, a train of five wagons arrived in this place, via the Big Tree route. The company contained, besides men, several women and children, all of whom have suffered the greatest inconveniences during the latter part of the journey. They were attacked by Indians near the head of the Humboldt and had all of their horses and a portion of their other stock stolen—leaving them scarcely enough to get into the country with, being compelled to leave two of the wagons by the way. At the same time they had two of their party killed, one of whom died immediately, and the other in a few days after. A third was severely wounded in the hip, and the ball has not yet been extracted, although the occurance took place near two months ago. The wounded man is a brother of Mr. Robert Epperson, who has long been a resident of this county.

Weekly Calaveras Chronicle

Copperopolis teamsters pass under a trestle that connected the Keystone and Union Copper mines to the concentrator just outside of Copperopolis, circa 1908.

Indian Diggings are so called from the Indians first discovering the Richest place which is a creek or large Gulch about two miles long from the Mocosme River or the south fork of the Mocosme or Cosumnes River to its head or where it branches into several small Gulches here is a large spring & here is situate the principle camp it is built along the Gulch from the spring down & consists of about 50 log cabins & two clapboard houses These two are Hotels Gambling houses & stores each containing a bar The Gulch is so narrow they have to dig into the hill side to build so the town or camp is in a string along the bank The waggon Road comes in from the North & stops at the Hotels at the spring the place being so narrow to permit waggons to go through or by the place The Gulch or creek is said to be verry Rich all the way to its Mouth

John Doble,
April 14th, 1852

arms of the earth, has inspired long lines of men to explore its depths for the precious metals. The tunnels, drifts, and other devices for mining operations, to be seen in many places in the county, sufficiently indicate the struggle and mighty endeavor to bear away the gold from its natural home.

Gold was discovered before and in the days of 1849-50, and the yield of bullion has been large ever since. Quartz veins crop out of every hill, and nearly every town was started by the discovery of a mine. Among the windings of every creek and river bed may be found old Mexican arastras, many of them almost obliterated by time.

"In 1853," says J. M. Hutchins, "we saw a large nugget of gold in a shape like the kidney of an ox, that was dug out here, which weighed twenty-six pounds. It would have been ours but for the trifling circumstance, we didn't have the money to buy it!"

At another time one weighing twelve pounds was taken out, and was purchased by Morris Cohen, who is now a resident of San Francisco. And in 1858, there were several pieces taken out, of various sizes, weighing from one to five pounds.

It may be stated as an interesting fact that when Mr. Murphy, after whom the camp was named, left this camp to take up his residence at San Jose, California, he had as much gold as six mules could haul from the camp. In those early days, under extraordinary conditions, when provisions were scarce, coffee, tea, sugar, and tobacco were put in the scale with gold to balance, and sold pound for pound.

Carson Hill is celebrated for its unparalleled yield of the precious metals; and the history of gold mining does not afford like examples of the enormous production of ponderous masses of gold in a short time—$2,800,000 worth of gold was extracted in seven months, and from contiguous pits not 100 feet deep; $14,000 worth was taken out of a shaft in a day; and $20,000 worth out of another only 60 feet deep. The weight of the masses of gold was expressed in pounds, not in ounces; one mass of gold weighed 6 ½ pounds and another 7 ½, pounds. But the most marvelous account of all is that of the blast in the Pacheco Shaft, which threw down a mass of rock so filled with gold that the masses held together when cracked by sledge hammers—one mass so broken out weighed 108 pounds and contained 104 pounds of gold. This is the largest mass of vein gold which has been found in the world, at least of which there is any record.

The mining resources of this section of country are too valuable to be ever neglected. Certainly they are too promising to be retarded because of lack of confidence in their outlook.

Hydraulic and channel mining meet with success if well managed. Marble, granite, limestone, iron, and coal have been

The McSorley Mine in Chili Gulch was an extremely rich hydraulic mine. Pictured are Barney McFadden (night watchman), Leslie Bastion, Jack McSorley (Superintendent), John Burton with $600 of gold in his hand, and Jack's brother Frankie relaxing in the hammock.

We found about fifty persons at the mine, two- thirds of them Mexicans. Occasionally, also, one or two of the overland teams came in and stopped among us. The huge canvass tops of the wagons would generally be taken off and pitched upon the ground, and thus made to serve for comfortable tents. The oxen were then tethered in a close herd in the middle, and, being sharply watched, were thus generally preserved from the thievishness of the Indians.

Leonard Kip, 1850

In front of the Union Hotel in Copperopolis, this stage was loaded and ready to go. The sign on the stage announces "Jos. DeShamps, Proprietor" and "Wells Fargo & Co. Express."

Within a year Mr. Marsh, made some two thousand dollars and the last I saw of him he was making good time for San Francisco, expecting to take the first steamer for his old home in New Hampshire.

Harvey Wood, 1849

discovered, and await capital and workmen for their development into new sources of prosperity.

TOWNS.

MILTON, in the southern part, is the terminus of the Stockton and Copperopolis Railroad. From the depot there provisions of all kinds are conveyed in large freight wagons to all parts, and this forms a profitable business to those engaged. From this point stage lines connect with all the principal towns and the counties above. Hundreds of tourists pass through every year, making the stage companies rich and the livery business a profitable one. The pursuits of sheep-raising and farming are engaged in, to which the residents look for their chief support. Population, 120. It is 340 feet above sea level.

SHEEP RANCH is the most modern town. It sprang up like a mushroom with the discovery of the American and Chavanne gold-quartz mines, and maintains its prosperity by their scientific development and permanent yield.

CARSON HILL is upon the great leading quartz vein of the State of California, known generally as the Mother Vein, which is believed to extend from Mariposa to Grass Valley, a distance of over 200 miles. The vein varies from a few feet to 20 and 30 feet in thickness, and stands boldly out on the crest of the hill.

WEST POINT is the extreme town on the northwest; Mokelumne Hill on the west center; Campo Seco, Comanche, Valley Springs, and Burson on the west; Jennie Lind and Milton on the southwest; Copperopolis and Telegraph City on the south; Altaville and Angel's Camp on the east center; Vallecito, Murphy's, and Sheep Ranch on the north-east of the county, where all supplies for the central and eastern portions of the county are received and distributed; stage lines diverge to San Andreas, Sheep Ranch, Copperopolis, Angel's, Murphy's, the Big Tree groves, and Sonora.

MURPHY'S CAMP. This was at one time one of the leading mining camps. It is situated at an elevation of 2,400 feet above the level of the sea and in a gold basin of extraordinary richness. It was named after Martin Murphy, its discoverer, who took out an immense amount of gold. The hills, gulches, gorges and small valleys in the vicinity of this camp have been tunneled, cut, scalped and literally torn to pieces by the energy of man seeking to wrestle from nature its coveted gold. The zeal of the miner appears to have been supported by the assurance that the metal was in the earth, and that only his want of energy kept him from its possession. "Terrific rich" is how the country folks express their idea of the district, and they have the obvious corroboration of their views upon all sides.

The Sheep Ranch Mine, circa 1885. This was the most productive gold mine of the Sierran East Gold Belt. By 1898 it had an output valued at four million dollars. The gold mined from this mine was prized by San Francisco jewelers because it was black quartz laced with gold instead of the typical white quartz.

Courtesy Calaveras County Archives

I proceeded to the new Art Union rooms last week to see the paintings, about which I had read so much in the papers during my recent three months' stay in the Big Tree region of Calaveras county; up there, you know, they read everything, because in most of those little camps they have no libraries, and no books to speak of, except now and then a patent-office report, or a prayer-book, or literature of that kind, in a general way, that will hang on and last a good while when people are careful with it, like miners; but as for novels, they pass them around and wear them out in a week or two. Now there was Coon, a nice bald-headed man at the hotel in Angel's Camp. I asked him to lend me a book, one rainy day: he was silent a moment, and a shade of melancholy flitted across his fine face, and then he said: "Well, I've got a mighty responsible old Webster-Unabridged, what there is left of it, but they started her sloshing around, and sloshing around, and sloshing around the camp before I ever got a chance to read her myself, and next she went to Murphy's, and from there she went to Jackass, and now, by G-d, she's gone to San Andreas, and I don't expect I'll ever see that book again; but what makes me mad, is that for all they're so handy about keeping her sashshaying around from shanty to shanty and from camp to camp, none of 'em's ever got a good word for her.

Mark Twain, March 18, 1865

Patrons at the Independent Saloon, J.H. Crail Proprietor, in Comanche.

Looked round in the forenoon & went to Curries and tried to buy a Mare off him but could not hit on the price   Came home to dinner & found Bill pretty tight & not able to cook or would not do it so I proposed a Division of the camp property which he excepted   I kept the tent & he moved into the house with Tom as they are better friends than ever   I am not sorry we are seperated as we never could have suited each other for Messmates although we never quarreled

John Doble,
May 6 1852

This part of the county, from Murphy's to San Andreas, a distance of about twenty-five miles, is well adapted to vine and fruit raising. The vine and fruit tree are in cultivation by a large number of the people, and the introduction of an abundant supply of water will give a marvelous impetus to this industry. There is plenty of room for active and honest workers here, and the future promise of this section of country from the fruit and vine growth cannot be overestimated. In fact there can be no exaggeration of the value of the vine and fruit interests.

The town is built in a forest of pine, and along the streets are planted ornamental trees. In Murphy's there are many magnificent orchards and vineyards; the fruit has a fine flavor and is of extraordinary size. Fruit trees are very thrifty, even young trees flourishing to a goodly degree the first year; apples, pears, quinces, figs, pomegranates, peaches, apricots, and other kinds of fruit do well. This section of the foot-hills might become the vast orchard of the State on account of the abundance of pure water and mountain climate. Also around this portion of the State in the vicinities of Copperopolis, Angel's, San Andreas, Murphy's, and, in fact, in almost every part of this county, there are good tracts of land to be pre-empted, and fit for raising hay, grain, vegetables and fruits, besides serving for pasture lands when uncultivated. Murphy's is one of the most lovely towns in the county. It is situated at such an altitude that the air is very pure and clear and invigorating.

MITCHLER'S HOTEL. This noted stopping place is situated at Murphy's, being on the Big Tree Stage Route. Passengers from Milton reach here the first day from San Francisco, which place the traveler leaves at 8 A. M., taking the Martinez line, changing cars at Stockton for Milton, which place is reached at 1:45 P. M. Here passengers take T. J. Matteson's stage for Murphy's where it arrives at 8 P. M. After a refreshing night's rest, tourists take the 7 A. M. stage for the Big Trees, having a beautiful view of the scenery along the line. The Big Trees being only sixteen miles distant from Murphy's, they are reached at an early hour.

The Mitchler Hotel is among the best of the country. The building was built by J. L. Sperry and John Perry, in 1855. In 1859 it was burned, the rear portion being constructed of wood. It was immediately rebuilt by the owners, the entire building being of stone, making it fire-proof. In September, 1882, Mr. Mitchler and his mother purchased the hotel. In 1884 Mr. Mitchler's brother, Frank A., also bought an interest, the partnership now being Mrs. Elizabeth Mitchler & Sons.

SUSPENSION FLUME AT MURPHYS One of the most superb pieces of useful mechanism ever constructed in this state

First called the Sperry and Perry Hotel, it was opened by James L. Sperry and John Perry on August 20, 1856 in Murphys. Thought to be fireproof due to its stone construction and iron shutters, the hotel was damaged in the fire of 1859 that destroyed most of downtown. However, it was restored and reopened in 1860. It was host to many famous people over the years including Mark Twain, John Jacob Astor, Ulysses S. Grant, John Bidwell, Charles Bolles (alias Black Bart), Henry Ward Beecher, Horatio Alger, J.P. Morgan and Thomas Lipton. Renamed the Mitchler Hotel in 1882, and the Murphys Hotel in 1945.

The sun was scalding hot—we were wearied—camped for the night. An early start the next morning, and a walk of fourteen miles, took us to Taylor's Ferry on the Stanislaus. There was at this spot a cantonment of two or three companies of U. S. dragoons. They were to be used in case of trouble among the miners, or with the native Californians; exigencies that were quite unlikely to occur; though it was well enough to quarter them there for it was a delightful, healthy spot, and it was necessary to adopt, to prevent a general desertion: the men in alternate detachments were allowed to work in the mines on their own account.

William S. McCollum, 1849

These miners sit in front of the Central Hill Mine near Murphys. Many have candles, some have tools. And the little boy has holes in the knees of his trousers, just like boys everywhere.

One of the caves can be entered to a depth of 150 feet, being on an incline of 45 degrees; here were 3 small but beautiful chambers in which lived a man for 6 weeks, escaping the sheriff's search in 1859.

From this point, descending 300 feet with rope, the whole mountain appears honeycombed with innumerable chambers which were not explored, from this point, and in the other caves no bottom could be found. This adventure, however, came near proving fatal to one of the party. While one remained below to steady the rope from swinging, it was not difficult for the others to climb out, but when the last man attempted to climb, the rope began swaying from side to side and he slid back many times. The blood of the whole party curdled at the thought of his situation. We tried pulling the rope; it would not move over the jagged edge of the rock on which it hung; the fear also of cutting the rope, as it made so many vibrations as he attempted to climb, filled every breast with horror. After two hours' rest, which seemed to us as many days, he at last succeeded in reaching the top, where two strong men with superhuman strength each grasped an arm, and landed him, apparently lifeless from exhaustion.

is the Suspension Flume Panning Murphy's Creek just below the Pluming Company's Works and within a good view of the town. The contract is just completed and in Wednesday the first water made its ariel voyage to the heights of Central Hill. The Plume is built on the Pen Stock plan or water tight box principle, and is held up with two wires or cables, inches in diameter, and 1000 feet long; with two guy wires to support the towers over which the cables are strung. The northern tower is 94 feet high—the southern 124 feet; from tower to tower the distance is 740 feet. The cables are firmly anchored at the ends, in the bed rock sufficiently secure to hold twice as much as the necessary force. From the flume down (perpendicularly) to the bed of the creek it is 290 feet, the entire length of the flume 1800 feet, the box will carry 50 inches of water forced by a fifteen foot heading. The sag of wire is 45 feet. The Flume was built by the Central Hill Mining Company-ten shares each man representing a share, all from the State of Maine.

There are several smaller canals receiving water from the Calaveras River and its tributaries and one of some importance is supplied from the Salt Spring Valley Reservoir, a beautiful sheet of water held in a natural depression of the valley by a strong earth dike extending several hundred feet. This vast water supply, if a reduction in its prices could be obtained, might be utilized by the horticulturist and manufacturer to such an extent as to become a source of immense wealth. Its fall, which is great from the east to the western border of the county, is utilized at present by some manufactories, but their operations are comparatively insignificant.

Mr. Matteson also owns a fine livery stable at Murphy's. A full livery outfit is kept, which affords ample opportunity for parties seeking pleasure in that section so abounding in interest.

MOKELUMNE HILL. This is a pretty little place of about 600 inhabitants, lying north of San Andreas, and near the line of Amador County. It has a number of stores and business places. The *Calaveras Chronicle* is published by Messrs. Burce & Day. It is one of the oldest established papers of the State, and is now in its thirty-fourth volume.

Rev. J. B. Fish was the first minister that preached in Mokelumne Hill. He was sent to Sacramento in 1851 by the Methodist Episcopal Conference in the East, and after preaching in that city one year, was sent to Mokelumne Hill in August, 1852. The first church in this place was a tent erected on Church Street, on the lot which is now the site of the residence of Mrs. Guy. The pioneer residents of this place will readily recall to memory the scenes and circumstances of those early times. The first parsonage was located where the Italian garden is now, and was a log cabin owned by a Mr. S. Newman, who generously donated the property to the church.

We found a colony of diggers in tents, small assortments of goods and provisions, booths, or places of refreshment; all that appertained to a central locality in the mining districts. Our tent was added to the colony, and we soon got ready to live after the fashion of our neighbors. The only thing appertaining to mining in which we were deficient, was a Rocker, and that we procured for the moderate sum of $55. We sallied out, prospecting; found squads of miners in all directions, which we took to be pretty good evidence of plenty of gold. After a day or two we pitched upon a spot and went to work in earnest; turned over rocks, delved and dug with pick-axe and shovel, opened a multitude of holes, tin-panned, and rocked the cradle; in fact, made a pretty faithful experiment in gold digging, and our success did not meet our expectations. Our earnings were, each of us, generally, from $3 to $6 a day; occasionally one of us would earn $12. Mr. Bradley, being an excellent house and sign painter, very rationally concluded that he could do quite as well at his trade, at San Francisco, with less of severe labor, falling in with a return train of mules, mounted one of them, and left the mines.

William S. McCollum, 1849

Dog and pony show, Main Street, Angel's Camp.

Courtesy Calaveras County Archives

The only interesting circumstance which occurred upon the route was when we passed through an Indian village. Several semicircles of brush-huts formed the town, in front of which the whole population was seated in two long rows; with the exception of a few who were pounding acorns, and of the papooses, which, strapped to their several boards, were carefully hung up overhead. The men were generally clothed in coarse blue shirts, but the women were seldom particular about having any clothes at all. One of the latter was adorned with a white pine stick, stuck through the nose, and projecting about two inches each side. This was the only display of ornament I ever saw among the natives. As we approached, the two lines of natives commenced waving their hands, twirling their fists, and beating their breasts; keeping up, in the mean time, a most unearthly howling. We at first thought that they were enacting a ceremony in honor of our arrival, but speedily discovered that the display was on account of the exit of one of their warriors, who had departed this life that morning.

The tribe being a friendly one, we stopped for a few minutes to witness the ceremony. None seemed to take any more notice of us if we had been so many standing trees, but all continued singing the same horrible strain without intermission. We moved on, but the song was not broken off.

Leonard Kip, 1850

Native Americans were under represented in historical writings and photographs. They possessed many extraordinary talents, as Susie Arnett, one of the last Washoe basket-makers, demonstrates here.

The first school in Mokelumne Hill was taught in the church tent, by the wife of Mr. Fish, the school numbering five pupils, two white children and three negroes. The daily session of the school was three hours, and the salary of the teacher was $75.00 per month. The pioneer preacher was a gentleman of excellent qualities of heart, charitable and kindly to all, and liked by all who knew him.

One of the oldest and most noted buildings in town is occupied by Mr. Frank W. Peek, a native of Mokelumne Hill, where he was born in 1857. He has always lived at his birthplace. When nineteen years of age he commenced the confectionery business in the Odd Fellows Building. Mr. Peek kept enlarging his business, keeping, besides confectionery, a general variety store. In 1880 he moved to the Hoerchner Building, one of the oldest buildings in town. It is constructed of stone quarried in the vicinity. It has stood the test of fire, resisting the flame when buildings close by were destroyed.

The father of Mr. Peek, Wm. P. Peek, was appointed postmaster in 1877. The post-office is still kept in the store.

COPPEROPOLIS, fifteen miles from Milton, is one of the most interesting mining towns extant. The opening of an immense copper mine called it into existence in 1861-62, and here were built the most extensive mining apparatus in the county. At one time there was a population of more than 5,000 inhabitants. At present it is a quiet place, full of deserted houses, with many bright, comfortable homes here and there among them. It has very commodious and well-kept hotels, a beautiful brick Congregational church, and a fine two-story schoolhouse. These two buildings are the best in the county devoted to such purposes. Many of the deserted houses have been moved away, but there remain still the gigantic work sheds, shops, and machine buildings, silent and unfrequented.

The copper ore lies in immense piles of grayish blue stone, glittering from summit to base with crystallized pyrites of the yellow metal, of which there are thousands of tons already above the surface.

At an early period it was a bustling town, and its future was full of bright promise. The population [in 1885] is placed at 150. It has a daily mail and express. It is situated 945 feet above sea level.

The widow [Fontana] is carrying on the business of general merchandising at Copperopolis. She has two good, substantial stores, a dwelling of six rooms, good stock of goods, and is doing a good business.

Penn Mining Company in Campo Seco had a sophisticated operation. This steam locomotive pushed large ore carts along the track for the next step in extracting the copper ore. This ore was transported to a concentrator where it was further processed.

We hitched a couple of farm horses to a spring wagon, filled it with provisions, tents and blankets, and struck out for the mountains, traveling from fifteen to twenty miles per day. The first place we reached of importance was the Big Trees of Calaveras County. I must admit that they staggered my imagination, and exceeded anything in the vegetable growth I had ever seen. In the stump of one of these trees a ball-room 33 feet across is built, and it requires a ladder of 18 steps to ascend to the top of the log, on which was built a ten-pin alley. It has been burnt up, but the old charred monarch of the forest still remains. Think of it ! a hollow log, through which one can ride on horseback 100 feet, and come out through a knot-hole! There are some 90 of these trees, measuring from 50 to 100 feet in circumference, and reaching up to the skies—from 300 to 450 feet.

From the rings that denote the annual growth of these trees, science has estimated some of them to be 4,000 years old, while they stand over the fallen bodies of a much older growth, covered over with earth and large-growing trees, as it is one of the peculiarities of this timber not to decay. It appears to be a species of redwood.

San Francisco Examiner

During the latter part of October, 1852, Joaquin was prowling around the northern part of Calaveras in the vicinity of Oleta (Fiddletown). One day, one of the Mexican women told an American that Joaquin was in the town. The presence of strangers caused no remark. His name, however, was sufficient to raise a storm, and in a few minutes he was being hunted. He was dressed in the usual Spanish style, with wide-brimmed hat, serape, white drawers, and pantaloons opening up the sides. When he found he was betrayed, he jumped on a table in a gambling room, flourished a pistol around his head, said he was Joaquin, and defied the town to take him. This bravado may have been necessary to ensure his retreat, for he and his party left immediately, with half the town in pursuit. As it was, he came near being surrounded, and had to force his way out. "Am Parks " had hold of his bridle, but was induced to let loose by a shot in his face. The party of three or four left, amid a shower of bullets from revolvers, none of them taking effect. In the pursuit which took place, the footmen kept well up, some Indians, who joined in the chase, being in the advance. Joaquin took the trail towards Slate creek, and thence across Dry creek towards Lower Rancheria. Fresh men joined the pursuers at every gulch. The Mexicans left their horses, and escaped in the thick chaparral on the divide between Rancheria and Dry creeks. That night they made their way into Lower Rancheria, accounting for their demoralization by saying they had been chased by Indians which was true.

Stone's Blacksmith shop. These Copperopolis blacksmiths performed a vital function in the community. They would fabricate and repair tools, horseshoes, farm implements, wagon wheel rims, and many other essential items well into the 1900s.

ANGEL'S CAMP AND ALTAVILLE. These places have been for a number of years noted mining towns, and quartz mining is yet extensively and profitably carried on there. The numerous quartz mills are industriously pounding and grinding the precious rock, which is found so abundantly in the vicinity. Active men are working with a fierce energy at the valuable deposits known to exist in this district, and a good deal of money has been invested in substantial mills.

The principal industry of this section of country is mining, yet its present agricultural resources, which are already vast and far advanced, will increase in extent and value when they are assisted by irrigation. The land is well adapted to vine and fruit raising. These important industries have already become popular with the people, and a great deal of land has recently been taken up and prepared for the growth of the fruit tree and the grape.

The vineyards, the orange, lemon, olive, apricot, prune, peach, apple, pear, gooseberry, blackberry, almond, English walnut, and other orchards, which are so immensely profitable in California, can be cultivated during all the winter. Rolling hills, with deep soil, and covered by a heavy growth of mountain shrubs, indicative of the richness of the earth, bend their winding way for many miles. All this land is of great value for the culture of fruit and grapes, for farming and stock raising. An adequate supply of water will give vitality and fresh vigor to this entire region.

Angel's—the Angel's Camp made famous by the writings of Bret Harte—is about fourteen miles south of San Andreas. It is a pleasant and prosperous place, the streets lined by neat cottages surrounded by small gardens. Here there is a marble-working establishment, and at Altaville, which is really a part of Angel's, being only a mile from it, there is an iron foundry doing a prosperous business. Silk culture has been attempted in Angel's and has met marked success. The *Mountain Echo* is published here by Myron Reed, and is a well-conducted journal.

The foundry was erected in 1881 by D. D. Demorest, together with his residence. He has a blacksmith shop in connection with the foundry, but will eventually change this business to another building.

This foundry is principally engaged in casting shoes and dies for quartz mills, but also does a general jobbing business in both iron and brass. The foundry is run by steam power. Mr. Demorest came to Calaveras County in 1849 and engaged in surface mining until 1860, when he acted as agent of the Union Ditch Company. In 1865 he entered upon proprietorship of the foundry, which he purchased in 1861, which had formerly been run by his brother. He has continued in the foundry business since that date.

At Angel's, J. C. Scribner keeps a general merchandise store, and a good line of drugs. He also acts as agent for Wells,

> This Morning a Circus came into Town which performs two nights here Circuses in this country perform altogather in the night as no inducements of that kind will draw the Miners from their work during the day During the afternoon a courier or runner came round among the Miners belonging to the Vigilance Committee warning them to meet at their Room in Town at night as a man had been shooting somebody or somebody else
>
> John Doble,
> Wednesday June 2nd 1852

Angel's Camp resident, Harry Barden playing with bear cubs.

Courtesy Calaveras County Archives

Thompson a Gambler from Mokelumne Hill was in an Italian gameing Room & was Bucking at Monte against the Italian who had the Bank after playing awhile they had a dispute about the ownership of a certain six dollars that Thompson had bet after disputing awhile Thompson left the house & the money saying no more about it

In passing up the Street he met Moore another Gambler of I know not where & Moore taking sides with the Italian renewed the quarrel and made some hostile demonstrations whereupon Thompson showed him he had no arms to defend himself this stopped Moore a short time but he soon again drew his revolver swearing he would shoot Thompson anyhow & immediately fired the ball [that] passed through Thompsons shirt just above the belt & some distance beyond went into a boys shirt sleeve where it lodged

They were then in front of the Union Hotel & next door is a Bakery Immediately after the pistol was fired Thompson run into the Bakery & seized on old Musket that was in the hands of an Indian & returned to the door to look out for Moore

Meanwhile Moore had run into the Union Hotel & had returned to the porch & taken refuge behind a large dry goods box that lay beside the door

continued in far right column

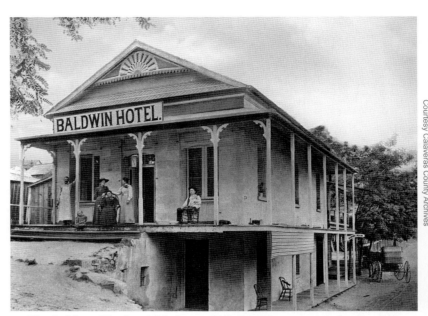

The Baldwin Hotel in Mokelumne Hill shared space with the Gardella Mortuary on the lower floor.

Fargo & Co.'s express. He came to Calaveras County as early as 1849, and purchased the business formerly conducted by Mr. Angel, the founder of this camp. The wooden building occupied first by Mr. Scribner was burned in 1855, and he replaced it by a very substantial stone building the following year. He has remained in business at this place ever since.

From Angel's the stage passes on to Murphy's, taking the toll road called the Grade, an excellent highway passing through a wooded canon.

ENTOMBED ALIVE! On last Monday [December 16, 1889] morning Dick Redmond, driver of the Angels stage, startled our quiet town by announcing that sixteen men were entombed alive in the [Utica] Lane Mine at Angels. Of course the news created great excitement and our people were all eager for the particulars. The high waters and muddy roads were reported impassible between this place and Angels, especially with vehicles, but the *Prospect*, ever on the alert for news, straddled the hurricane deck of a mustang and started for the ill-fated mine and in two hours after leaving here reached the scene of the terrible and appalling accident, notwithstanding the bad conditions of the roads and swollen streams.

At the scene of the disaster sturdy miners were at work endeavoring to reach the interior of the mine.

It is one of the most prominent gold mines in the county and owned by Messrs. Hobert & Hayward of San Francisco. The ore is extracted from the full 30 feet in width, and the openings thus left are braced by enormous timbers two and three feet in diameter, and were placed five feet apart. It was the pressure of the earth against the hanging wall of the worked out vein, increased by the heavy rains that caused the cave.

At the time of the cave, on Sunday, there were 19 or 20 timber-men at work.

Daniel Danielson [said] the following: "Myself and Anderson were working in the 400-foot level and were waiting for the timbers to come down the shaft. I went to the South shaft to get a shovel, and when returning I heard a fearful crash and explosion; the concussion of which threw me to the floor of the level on my face, and extinguishing the light. I crawled back toward the shaft and lit my candle; heard rocks and debris falling and timbers crushing above me and I knew that a cave had occurred. I found my partner, and as we started to run I heard a voice calling for help from one of the stopes. Going to the spot, I found Corwin grouping around in the dark with his face cut and bleeding and immediately hurried him along with me, and the three of us reached the Sickle shaft, through which we climbed the ladder 700 feet to the surface and gave the alarm."

[After several unsuccessful rescue attempts, the death toll was 18.]

Douglas Flat townspeople, 1898.

continued from far left column

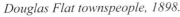

next to the Bakery with his pistol cocked & resting on the box Thompson being aware of what direction Moore was in was stooping forward with the Musket in his hand trying to get a sight of him when Moore again fired at his head & then ran up the stairs in the Hotel Thompson drew back & remained where he was A few doors below the Bakery was another Hotel with a porch in front on this porch stood a Dutch Drummer belonging to the Circus

The ball from Moores pistol passed through the corner of the crown of Thompsons hat & [went] on & struck the Dutchman in the side of the waist & passed through & lodged in his clothes on the opposite side

The Dutchman fell & was carried into the Hotel & his wound Examined by a Surgeon & pronounced Mortal though he supposed it possible be might recover One of The Officers of the place passing & hearing the firing but not seeing Moore & hearing of the wounded Dutchman etc took Thompson prisoner and put him in jail but afterwards coming to the truth Thompson was liberated & Moore put in his stead & now at 8-o clock Thompson is round telling how he tried to do & blowing considerable

John Doble,
Wednesday, June 2nd 1852

Calaveras County is a region rich in the history of the mining era of the State, it is too little heard of. We regard the county as one of the most promising fields for enterprise and investment and for humble home making.

The county has an area of 622,000 acres. Here are found some of the best mines in this State, and the entire county is exceedingly rich in mineral deposits. The baser metals, copper, iron, cinnabar, etc., are found, and ledges of marble, limestone, granite, and undeveloped deposits of coal, are known to exist.

Several most interesting natural wonders are also to be found here, among which are the world renowned Big Trees; the great cave, with its magnificent chambers and wonderful stalactites, and the wonderful bridge elicit the admiration of tourists from all parts of the world.

Among its other sources of wealth, Calaveras possesses one of the most valuable timber belts in the State, live-oak, sugar and nut-pine predominating. This county is one of the best watered sections of the State, and its undeveloped resources are almost inexhaustible. With the opening which is now made by the new railway, and the rapid extension of orchard and vineyard and poultry farming, the building up of the industries of the county may be expected.

The Rural Press

These big wheels, sometimes known as a Michigan log buggy, pulled the log by lifting one end and dragging it on the ground.

MOKELUMNE AND CAMPO SECO CANAL AND MINING COMPANY. The works of this company were begun in 1852, and completed to Mokelumne Hill in 1853, with a capacity of carrying 1,000 inches of water, miner's measure, and subsequently extended to Campo Seco, Comanche, and vicinities, a distance of 60 miles from the dam at the head of the canal.

The object of the enterprise was for the purpose of supplying water in washing out gold from the auriferous earth of this rich mineral region.

Like all enterprises of this character begun at an early day of our mining industry, the vicissitudes of the undertaking have been many, owing to inexperience of projectors in works of this kind, and the high price of labor and material during the construction.

But these difficulties have all been successfully overcome, and the company is now in a position to materially assist in the development of this section of the county in its mineral and agricultural wealth.

The works were originally constructed by building a wooden flume laid on the ground and carried across depressions on high tressel work. Owing to the enormous expense of repairs through the rapid decay of wooden structures, caused by the extremes of heat and cold, dry and wet, this has been changed by the substitution of gravel ditch and iron pipes.

This line of ditch has the prior right to the water of the South Fork and the Middle Fork of the Mokelumne River, streams fed by melting snow in summer, therefore always supplied with water.

The ditch system consists of a large storage reservoir in the mountains, distributing reservoirs where needed. A line of ditch, and branches, extends through Mokelumne Hill, supplying this place with water for town use, also Campo Seco, and Comanche, as leading points, besides Grain Mine, Pine Peak, Central Hill, Chili Camp, Poverty Ridge, and Cat Camp, and intermediate places, enabling residents along the line to wash either quartz or placer mines, to cultivate the soil successfully by irrigation, or to run machinery by having the necessary power brought to their doors.

In the building of the San Joaquin and Sierra Nevada Narrow Gauge Railroad through this section, the advantages and worth of this system of water supply will become more conspicuous and appreciated, as the agriculturist will have a ready means of transportation to market of his products, raised by successful irrigation of his trees, vines, and other crops, almost independent of the seasons.

The new stations of Valley Springs and Burson are within a short distance of this line of canal, and connections are now

Onita Ranch. Teams and wagon traveling what is now Highway 4.

Angels has enjoyed something of a ghost or spirit sensation. It seems that soon after the late accident in the Utica whereby a miner called "High-toned Charley," was literally blown to pieces by a blast, there has been a mysterious ringing of the bell or triangle, that regulated the hoisting of the tub. A number of mine-hands testify to the ringing of the triangle by some unknown cause. The clapper was seen to remain stationary yet the bell would ring as if human hands had pulled the clapper. The report soon found credency that the mine was being haunted by the spirit of "High-toned Charley." With the first occurrences of the bells there was a tendency to superstitious feelings among some of the employees but now all fears have been cast aside. Your reporter was informed that the position of the triangle was slightly changed in the hopes of subsiding the annoyance; but Sunday night there was another exhibition of bell force, according to the story of the engineer who experienced this strange delusion. If the bell rings at all, it is undoubtedly owing to some natural cause which can be readily ascertained by diligent investigation.

However, Angels has its sensation and is now besides being the banner mining town in the county, the center of spirit manifestations. The next thing in order is a séance.

The Calaveras Prospect, Friday, August 31, 1888

Main Street San Andreas — Late 1800s.

In California the different nationalities did not always harmonize. Those of different speech, not being able to understand each other, sometimes had serious quarrels.

Such we found to be the condition at the mining town of Mokelumne Hill. Reaching the place about dark, after supper we walked through the village to converse with the miners who had come in from their work. Passing into a large store, which seemed thronged, we were addressed in Spanish, to which I replied in the same tongue. Mr. Ford made some inquiry in English, when I heard some one exclaim with an oath, "¡ Es Americano, matele! ¡matele! (He is an American, kill him! kill him!).

At first I doubted my understanding of the words; but when a knife was flourished, and a rush made at Ford, knowing there was no mistake, I grasped the arm which held the knife, as it came down; and yet, in trying to parry the blow, Ford had his right hand severely cut. With a bound we were out of the store, and utterly bewildered at the unprovoked attack.

Rev. John Steele, 1850

being made by which the surrounding region can be supplied with water for any purpose desired, but principally irrigation.

SAN ANDREAS is situated centrally as to population. It was formerly a mining center, but now is a quiet, pleasant little place, the principal business clustering about the Court House and the neighboring ranches. The County Hospital is situated here, but has few occupants. It depends mainly upon its lodes for support, yet fruit-growing and stock-raising are important factors in the nourishment imparted to her growth. The altitude is 1,600 feet.

There are here two prosperous weekly newspapers, the *Calaveras Citizen*, established in 1870, and now published by C. R. Beal, and the *Calaveras Prospect*, now in its fourth volume, and published by Gitchell & Salcido.

The first paper issued in Calaveras County was the *Independent*, on Wednesday, September 24, 1856, by George Armor. In speaking of San Andreas, it says: "All places have had a beginning, and so had San Andreas. In the winter of 1848, a few Mexicans encamped at the forks of the gulch (since called San Andreas), about one-fourth of a mile above where the town now stands, and commenced working in the bed of the gulch by sinking holes, and washing out with "batteas." In the fall of 1849 their number considerably increased, but the place was not looked upon as worthy of any great note as a mining locality. But in the winter of 1849, or spring of 1850, a few Americans came in and commenced operations in the main gulch, which soon had a tendency to bring in others.

In the meantime the Spanish population continued to increase, until, in the fall and winter of 1850, they numbered 1,200 or 1,500. At this time the principal part were encamped on the hill-side, on which is now located the town of San Andreas, and on all sides were seen small tents, such as usually designated any important mining locality in the palmy, prosperous days of 1849-50. The mines were rich, every person was doing well, and of course gambling shops and fandango houses were in full blast, and dark and desperate deeds were committed.

In the spring of 1851 was erected the "Bella Union," the first frame building in San Andreas, which answered the purpose of court room, drinking saloon, gambling house, and dance house. About the time of its completion, rich diggings were discovered at Mokelumne Hill. A rush was made, everybody followed the rush, and San Andreas became nearly depopulated.

Early in the summer of 1851, Capt. Robert Pope came to this place, located the right of way, and surveyed the route of a ditch leading from Willow Creek to the foothills north of San Andreas. Shortly afterwards a company, calling themselves the Miner's Ditch Company, commenced a ditch along the same route, which was completed and water running through early in the spring of 1852. A suit was begun between Captain Pope and the Mining Company, which, in 1853, was decided

Once through the concentrator, the smelter takes over. This blast furnace was a part of the larger smelter erected in 1899. The smelter was equipped with a crushing and grinding plant, eight roasting furnaces, and a blast furnace.

Tired of a walk of many miles through the dusty soil, we were beginning to wish for any quiet place of rest and shelter, a light suddenly shone ahead, increasing in brightness as we advanced, and in a few minutes our lumbering vehicle drew up beside the first tent of the road.

These tents occurred at average distance along the route in such spots as would afford a moderate supply of water by digging; for in the whole sixty miles. They were generally large and well stocked with provisions, thus not only proving a source of wealth to their owners, but of accommodation to travelers. To say that sometimes over two hundred persons would stop in one day, would perhaps be a small estimate of the amount of business done in the most popular of these canvas restaurants.

At this first one, then, we stopped, loosed the oxen, refreshed ourselves with a slight supper, kindled a fire, and spreading our blankets upon the sand, lay down to sleep.

Hardly had we composed ourselves for rest, when the wild cattle which here abound, commenced a stampede, and every few minutes rushed over the neighboring ground in bodies of hundreds, shaking the earth as they passed along, produced an awful effect, more startling than the cries of more savage beasts. More fires were lighted to restrain them from making our bivouac their race-course and, as the sportive herd gradually became more quiet, we fell asleep.

Leonard Kip, 1849,
Along the Mokelumne River

The Metropolitan Hotel in San Andreas. This hotel was the scene of nearly all civic events and known as one of the finest hotels in the Mother Lode. The Stockton-Murphys stage is in the foreground.

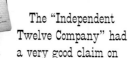

The "Independent Twelve Company" had a very good claim on the Bar. They had a way of mining without exerting themselves much that I suppose proved as beneficial to them financially, as to work steady ten hours a day. The Twelve men had one rocker, they managed to keep going until about ten o'clock a.m. with the assistance of from four to six bottles of brandy at $4 per bottle; by ten o'clock they would be so much fatigued that to work any more that day was too hard on their system, therefore after washing out the rocker and getting from 24 to 36 ounces of gold, and laying in a fresh supply of brandy they would rest the balance of the day by getting gloriously drunk.

Harvey Wood, 1849

in Pope's favor. In the fall of 1851, the miners began to return from the stampede they had taken in the direction of Mokelumne Hill, and the following winter San Andreas became again quite a flourishing camp. During the winter of 1851 another ditch company was formed, called the Union Company, for the purpose of bringing water from Murray's Creek. This was completed in 1852.

In the spring of 1852, the diggings on Gold Hill were discovered. During the years 1853 and 1854 the town made but small progress in the way of improvement, but in the spring and summer of 1855 it took a fresh start. That year, Kohlburg & Co. built the first stone house. The American Restaurant and Thomas Corcoran's, both stone buildings, were erected that year. In the winter of 1856 a fire swept away a good portion of the town, including the Bella Union, the first house built in town.

In 1856 the Odd Fellows' Building was built. It is of brick, with stone basement, two stories high, 30 feet above the basement, 50 by 30 feet, costing $8,000.

San Andreas can boast of one of the finest livery establishments outside of the cities that there is in the State. It is owned and managed by Mr. J. F. Washburn, and is complete in every particular. His arrangements are such that he can supply on short notice carriages and conveyances for any number of tourists, who may desire to visit any points of interest. The completion of the S. J. and S. N. Railroad to this place makes this now a favorite route of travel to the Big Trees and Yosemite.

The Metropolitan Hotel is located in San Andreas, and is the leading hotel of the county, and acknowledged by all travelers to be excellently managed and in all respects a first-class house. It was purchased by B. F. Hawes in 1879. He came to Calaveras County in 1852 and engaged in mining, and also in Placerville and Murphy's. At Campo Seco he mined twenty-two years, from 1853 to 1875, and is still interested in mining having a third ownership in the Campo Seco Copper Mine.

In 1875 he was elected Sheriff of Calaveras County, which office he held until 1880.

PHOENIX LIVERY STABLE, at San Andreas, is managed by P. Masterson, who makes a specialty of fitting out parties for the Big Trees or Yosemite or other resorts. Parties going to the mountains, Big Trees and Yosemite Falls, wishing teams, can be furnished with driver if desired, also suitable vehicles for drummers with large trunks. Carriages, buggies, wagons, and saddle horses for hire on reasonable terms. All telegrams answered free of cost.

Among the prominent merchants of San Andreas is Chancey R. Lloyd. He has a fine trade, and keeps a general stock of merchandise. He settled at San Andreas about the year

The pack saddle, or pannier, upon which our friend B. was seated, was as illy adapted to equestrian uses as the half section of a good sized forest tree, hollowed out, would have been. To accommodate himself to it, his legs were thrown out to a ludicrous extent; his stirrups, loops in the ends of a good sized rope, thrown across the huge saddle. When the Spaniard—conductor and owner—gave the word to start, B. pulled up the halter, the mule made a plunge, and mule and rider were soon floundering upon the ground, exposed to the stampede of the whole caravan.

William S. McCollum, 1849

This flag waving group was overflowing a stage at Murphys. Murphys was a popular stopping place for tourists en route to the Calaveras Big Trees.

Courtesy Calaveras County Archives

A man was detected about to steal some money from a tent. He had not yet fairly taken it, when seeing he was watched, he bolted out and took to flight. The hue and cry was raised, he was chased nearly a mile, and finally secured. The Alcalde immediately called a jury, and, after a hasty trial, the unhappy victim was adjudged to receive an hundred lashes, have his head shaved, and his ears cut off, and be drummed out of the mines; a sentence which was carried out on the spot. The sequel may be conceived. Driven from the ground without having time to take a few provisions with him, bearing the evidences of his guilt so plainly upon him, that no one would even sell him food, becoming consequently soon faint and famished, he stole a horse, hoping to ride beyond reach of his evil report. He was pursued, overtaken, and shot down like a dog.

Leonard Kip, 1850

Muckers working at the Lightner Mine in Angels. Muckers were responsible for loading the ore into carts after the ore had been blasted from the vein.

1865, and opened a store where the express office is now kept. About the year 1875 he opened the store now occupied by him.

Crime in San Andreas

Murdered by a Highway Man — San Andreas, April 30, 1892. —The regular stage left here at 7 o'clock this morning, bound for the great Sheep Ranch mine, owned by J. E. Haggle, Dave Raggio, a brother of the owner of the stage line, was the driver. He is only seventeen years of age, but is full of grit. With him on the front seat rode Mike Tovey, Wells, Fargo & Co.'s messenger, and Miss Johanna Rodersino of El Dorado. In the stage were Mrs. A. Lloyd and Miss Phillipini Rodersino.

There was a big box of treasure aboard, the money for the payment of the miners at Sheep Ranch. Tovey was sent along to guard this, and he sat with his short-barreled shotgun across his knee.

A light rain was falling and the side curtains of the stage were down to protect the lady occupants. The grade of the road is up hill and down dale, so the stage made slow progress.

Bang! Bang! Without a Word. Suddenly, just as it started to climb the grade after leaving Willow Creek, some four miles from here a man stepped from behind a tree, and, without a word of warning fired both barrels of a shotgun loaded with buckshot full at the stage.

"I'm shot" groaned Raggio, as he set his teeth to keep the blood from spurting out of his mouth.

The attack was so sudden that Tovey did not know whence it came. He felt the sting of a bullet in his right arm, but jumped from the seat, put the horses between himself and the robber, as is the custom of messengers, and trotted along a few yards while the wounded driver attempted to keep the frightened animals in the road.

" I'm about done" said Raggio.

Tovey saw the murderous robber scuttling away through the undergrowth, so he jumped to the box, strapped the fainting Raggio to the Seat, and whipped up the horses for Sperry's ranch, half a mile away.

SHOT TO DEATH. When the shot was fired Miss Johanna Rodersino, aged fifteen, had shrieked and fallen forward into the "boot" of the stage. It was supposed that she had fainted. At Sperry's it was found that she was dead. Evidently she had received nearly the full charge from one of the barrels of the highwayman's gun, for several bullets had entered her breast and two pierced her brain. Death was almost instantaneous. The other ladies were not injured.

The other barrel of the robber's gun had distributed its contents between Raggio and Tovey. The former is mortally wounded. He has four shots in his shoulder and breast, and his bleeding indicates that his lungs are pierced by two of the balls.

Utica Mining Company's Cross Shaft at Angels Camp. This mine was one of the largest and most prosperous deep lode mine, in Calaveras County.

The track was inclined at an angle of fortyfive degrees, and covered with loose sand. On the one side, the hill rose high above us, by a very steep descent sought the valley nearly half a mile below. As we looked down the abyss, we trembled for the fate of our groceries, and felt that no caution we could use would be thrown away.

Accordingly, stopping at the end of the passage, we waited until two more teams came up; borrowed their oxen, making a string of seven yoke; fastened to the upper side of the wagon a stout pole, upon which five men were to press to keep the wheels from flying up; passed over the top of the load two ropes, upon each of which three men were to pull for the same purpose; and then advanced. Vain efforts! At the very critical point, the wheels slipped in the soft sand, the pole broke, the ropes slid through our hands, and the wagon rolled over.

It is a question whether every member of the party did not for the moment secretly wish, that the unlucky wagon had taken one turn more and gone completely down the side of the mountain, so as to be irrecoverably lost, such an amount of vexation had already accrued from it. But as it only lay upside down in the road, there was no excuse for not attending to it further. So the rest of the day was occupied in taking out the goods, carrying them on our backs for half a mile, until we had passed the unlucky hill, setting up the vehicle, dragging it past the scene of trial, helping the two other teams safely through, in return for their courtesy to us.

Leonard Kip, 1849,
Along the Mokelumne River

Stickles Mine investors catch a ride down the shaft on a skip with a miner.

The Digger Indians burn the grass to enable them to get at roots and wasps' nests; young wasps being a luxury with them. These fires have the good effect of destroying immense quantities of snakes and vermin; and one can scarcely imagine the extent to which these might multiply were they not occasionally "burnt out." The wasps are so numerous here in summer, as to destroy with rapidity every thing they attack. Fleas not only abound in the skins of every beast you kill, but even live on the ground, like little herds of wild cattle.

Frank Marryat, 1850

Tovey received a flesh wound in the right arm between the shoulder and the elbow. It is not serious, though sufficient to disable him for some time. Notwithstanding his wound he brought his treasure through safely, though he bore with it a dead girl and a dying youth.

THE SHERIFF AND HIS POSSE. As soon as the news reached this place there was great excitement and mounting in hot haste. The sight of the dead girl and Raggio's ebbing life blood inflamed the people. Within two hours Sheriff Thorn, an *Examiner* correspondent and a posse of 150 men were in pursuit of the cowardly assassin, who had merely fired and fled, making no further effort to capture the treasure carried by the stage.

There is a rain falling, which makes tracking somewhat difficult. The stage itself was driven back to the shooting. From the bullet-holes piercing its sides and top the location of the footpad at the time of the shooting was ascertained to be behind a spreading buckeye, near and to the right of the road. From this point his trail was taken up and followed by eager men, skilled in woodcraft. If he is caught the law will not be bothered with him, unless Sheriff Thorn happens to be with the party apprehending him. In any event he will be kept from a mob with the greatest difficulty.

SUSPECTED MEN. Several men are under suspicion, and their comings and goings are being inquired into with the greatest care. A strict watch will be kept upon them, and they will be required to give a full account of their acts between last night and the time the murder and attempted robbery were committed.

Tovey's bravery is universally praised. He was taken by surprise, but was cool and collected in all his movements, and fulfilled the task set for him—the safe conveyance of the treasure intrusted to his care.

Bloodhounds maybe put upon the murderer's trail and every corner of the country will be searched with the diligence born of fierce anger and a desire for revenge.

At the time the *Examiner* correspondent left the pursuing posse the murderer's track had been followed for seven miles, but the rain was constantly making it more difficult to trace the footprints. The highwayman has two hours' start of the Sheriff and when last seen by Tovey he was making for Murray creek and Doak's old mill.

THE COUNTRYSIDE ALARMED. The entire country has received the alarm and more tragedies may mark the path of the escaping desperado before he is taken, dead or alive. Evidently he is an excitable man, quick on the trigger, but with little real courage, as he made no attempt to secure the treasure on the stage

Hydraulic mining was efficient for removing ore but devastated the environment.

Two miners who used to go to the neighboring village in the afternoon and return every night with household supplies. Part of the distance they traversed a trail, and nearly always sat down to rest on a great boulder that lay beside the path. In the course of thirteen years they had worn that boulder tolerably smooth, sitting on it. By and by two vagrant Mexicans came along and occupied the seat. They began to amuse themselves by chipping off flakes from the boulder with a sledge-hammer. They examined one of these flakes and found it rich with gold. That boulder paid them $800 afterward. But the aggravating circumstance was that these "Greasers" knew that there must be more gold where that boulder came from, and so they went panning up the hill and found what was probably the richest pocket that region has yet produced. It took three months to exhaust it, and it yielded $120,000. The two American miners who used to sit on the boulder are poor yet, and they take turn about in getting up early in the morning to curse those Mexicans—and when it comes down to pure ornamental cursing, the native American is gifted above the sons of men.

Mark Twain, 1872

Jim Smiley was the curiosest man about always betting on any thing that turned up you ever see, if he could get any body to bet on the other side; and if he couldn't, he'd change sides. But still he was lucky, uncommon lucky; he most always come out a winner. He was always ready and laying for a chance; there couldn't be no solitry thing mentioned but that feller'd offer to bet on it, and take any side you please, as I was telling you.

Well, thish-yer Smiley had rat-tarriers, and chicken cocks, and tom-cats, and all them kind of things, till you couldn't rest, and you couldn't fetch nothing for him to bet on but he'd match you. He ketched a frog one day, and took him home, and said he cal'klated to edercate him; and so he never done nothing for three months but set in his back yard and learn that frog to jump. And you bet you he did learn him, too. He'd give him a little punch behind, and the next minute you'd see that frog whirling in the air like a doughnut — see him turn one summerset, or may be a couple, if he got a good start, and come down flat-footed and all right, like a cat. He got him up so in the matter of catching flies, and kept him in practice so constant, that he'd nail a fly every time as far as he could see him. Why, I've seen him set Dan'l Webster down here on this floor — Dan'l Webster was the name of the frog — and sing out, "Flies, Dan'l, flies!" and quicker'n you could wink, he'd spring straight up, and snake a fly off'n the counter there, and flop down on the floor again as solid as a gob of mud, and fall to scratching the side of his head with his hind foot as

continued in far right column

Crew of unidentified miners at the Gold Cliff Mine in Angels around 1899. These men worked 10-12 hours shifts, seven days a week and earned between $2.50 and $3.50 a day for their efforts.

after firing his shot. He must have been someone who was fully informed of the movements of the money for the payment of the miners at the Sheep Ranch mine.

At last accounts Reggio was alive, but the doctors have small hopes of his recovery. Two wounds in the shoulder are not serious, but those in the breast are almost sure to result fatally. Miss Phillipini Rodersino narrowly escaped death, a bullet having embedded itself in the framework of the stage just on a range with her heart.

Late this evening some of the posse returned without finding the murderer. The others are sticking to the trail.

HE'S A FIGHTER. The news of the murder and attempted robbery was received at the San Francisco office of Wells, Fargo & Co. yesterday forenoon in a telegram from Michael Tovey, the "shotgun messenger" who was on the stage, but as the one daily train for that region goes at 7 o'clock in the morning detectives could not be sent to San Andreas until to-day. Tovey's dispatch was as follows:

San Andreas, April 30, 1892.

To Wells, Fargo & Co.: Sheep Ranch stage stopped by robber, who fired buckshot without warning, killing young lady passenger and mortally wounding the driver. I am shot through right arm. Not serious. Sheriff with posse left for scene. Nothing taken from stage.

M. Tovey.

HE WORE NUMBER SEVENS. Later dispatches containing secret information were received by the company in the afternoon. In one of these Tovey stated that he had a glimpse of the robber when the shot was fired, and he described him as being about five feet and eight inches tall, and of 150 pounds in weight. The measurement of a track in the sand showed that the man wore a No. 7 boot.

Tovey is confident that the robber can be captured. He says that all points of escape from where the murder was committed are guarded by Sheriff B. K. Thorn of San Andreas and a large posse of men. The trail of the murderer cannot well be followed as the the ground is covered with grass. A heavy growth of pine timber and underbrush affords opportunities for hiding, but all the country around there will be scoured by the Sheriff and large parties of citizens who are roused by the deed.

Special detectives will be sent from here this morning, and they will take charge of the search if the Sheriff does not capture the man by the time they arrive there.

McKay's Sawmill crew falling trees in the high country for the sawmill, late 1880s.

continued from far left column

indifferent as if he hadn't no idea he'd been doin' any more'n any frog might do.

Well, Smiley kept the beast in a little lattice box, and he used to fetch him down town sometimes and lay for a bet. One day a feller — a stranger in the camp, he was — come across him with his box, and says:

"What might it be that you've got in the box?"

And Smiley says, sorter indifferent like, "It might be a parrot, or it might be a canary, may be, but it an't — it's only just a frog."

And the feller took it, and looked at it careful, and turned it round this way and that, and says, "H'm — so 'tis. Well, what's he good for?"

"Well," Smiley says, easy and careless, "He's good enough for one thing, I should judge — he can outjump any frog in Calaveras county.

"I'll risk forty dollars that he can outjump any frog in Calaveras county."

And the feller studied a minute, and says, kinder sad like, "Well, I'm only a stranger here, and I an't got no frog; but if I had a frog, I'd bet you."

And then Smiley says, "That's all right — that's all right — if you'll hold my box a minute, I'll go and get you a frog." And so the feller took the box, and put up his forty dollars along with Smiley's, and set down to wait.

So he set there a good while thinking and thinking to hisself, and then he got the frog out and prized his mouth open and took a teaspoon and

cont'd next page far left column

continued from last page far right

 filled him full of quail shot — filled him pretty near up to his chin — and set him on the floor. Smiley he went to the swamp and slopped around in the mud for a long time, and finally he ketched a frog, and fetched him in, and give him to this feller, and says:

"Now, if you're ready, set him alongside of Dan'l, with his fore-paws just even with Dan'l, and I'll give the word." Then he says, "One — two — three — jump!" and him and the feller touched up the frogs from behind, and the new frog hopped off, but Dan'l give a heave, and hysted up his shoulders — so — like a Frenchman, but it wan't no use — he couldn't budge; he was planted as solid as an anvil.

The feller took the money and started away.

Smiley he stood scratching his head and looking down at Dan'l a long time, and at last he says, "I do wonder what in the nation that frog throw'd off for — I wonder if there an't something the matter with him — he 'pears to look mighty baggy, somehow." And he ketched Dan'l by the nap of the neck, and lifted him up and says, "Why, blame my cats, if he don't weigh five pound!" and turned him upside down, and he belched out a double handful of shot. And then he see how it was, and he was the maddest man — he set the frog down and took out after that feller, but he never ketched him.

Mark Twain,
Condensed from *The Celebrated Jumping Frog of Calaveras County*

Beer was always a popular drink among the miners. Most towns had their own brewery. The Angels Brewery was one of the larger and more successful of these operations.

Tovey's Bravery. Tovey is one of the oldest messengers on the road, and as a result of many years of vigilant and successful work in guarding the stages the company has the highest confidence in him.

Tovey began his career as a pony rider on Ben Holliday's line across the plains. He was intrepid in that work, and in 1871 he was engaged by the express company as a messenger to guard a stage running through a wild and very dangerous country from Helena, Mont., to Corinne, Utah. Several unsuccessful attempts have been made to rob his stages, and he has been shot in the same right arm three times in the past ten years.

That Midnight Duel. Tovey is the messenger who made himself famous in 1879 by holding a stage on the Carson City and Bodie line against those famous highwaymen, Sharp and Dowd. On that occasion the robbers stopped the stage in the middle of the night, but Tovey dropped behind a wheel of the coach and began to fire. Dowd was killed in the fight, but Sharp continued the battle, retreating after he had wounded Tovey in the arm. The injured messenger was taken to a farmhouse; and while he was there Sharp returned and robbed the stage. Some time afterward Sharp was caught in this city. He was tried and sentenced to twenty years' imprisonment at Carson City. Two years ago he escaped and he is still at large. There is a reward of $250 offered for his recapture.

The second shot in Tovey's arm was from the gun of Bill Withrow, another messenger, during a quarrel at Candelaria, Nev., in 1881.

MAY BE SHARP AGAIN. Sharp, the robber with whom Tovey fought in 1879, may be the man who did the shooting in Calaveras county yesterday morning. It is evident from the circumstances that the shot was intended for Tovey, as he and the driver and the young woman sat on the front seat together, and revenge may have been the motive. Tovey says in his telegrams that no warning cry given and in an ordinary attempt to rob the order to halt would be given before firing.

Wells, Fargo &' Co.'s detectives maintain, however, that they know about where Sharp is, and that he could hardly have been this robber.

THE CAPTURE OF BLACK BART — When the novelist of the future, anxious to imitate those writers who have secured fortune if not fame in telling of the bold deeds of Claude Duval and other noted robbers of days gone by, shall relate the history of "Black Bart" the mysterious highwayman of California, he will record, if he wishes truth to add force to his narrative, that his hero was at last taken into the toils of justice at 8 o'clock on the evening of Monday, November 12, 1883. For nearly a decade he had evaded the authorities of the law, had baffled detectives, who would have deemed it the proudest event of their lives to place him behind the bars of a dungeon.

But finally the fate that a criminal cannot avoid overtook him. He could conceal his identity no longer and his capture

> I got Supper & engaged lodging at Col. Coopers hopeing once more to sleep on a bed, & truely I had a bedstead & cords under me, but there was not enough in the tick to tell what it was filled with. The fleas literally cover a person, however I managed to pass the night.
>
> Hiram Dwight Pierce,
> September 9, 1849

Calaveras County Courthouse officials 1888.

Courtesy Calaveras County Archives

This 1883 photo is of the men who helped hunt down Black Bart. Seated left to right, San Joaquin County Sheriff Tom Cunningham, respected law enforcement officer and close friend of Calaveras County Sheriff Ben Thorn (holding the hatchet). Sheriff Thorn discovered evidence at the Funk Hill robbery scene which led to Black Bart's arrest. Former Alameda County Sheriff Harry Morse, a relentless man hunter was the man who actually collard Black Bart. Standing on the left is San Francisco Police Captain A.W. Stone, who at the request of Wells Fargo detectives, officially placed Black Bart under arrest. He accompanied Harry Morse to the Funk Hill robbery scene to recover Black Bart's hidden loot. Standing on the right is J.W. Thacker, a Wells Fargo special agent.

One of my associates in this locality, for two or three months, was a man who had had a university education; but now for eighteen years he had decayed there by inches, a bearded, rough-clad, clay-stained miner, and at times, among his sighings and soliloquizings, he unconsciously interjected vaguely remembered Latin and Greek sentences—dead and musty tongues, meet vehicles for the thoughts of one whose dreams were all of the past, whose life was a failure; a tired man, burdened with the present, and indifferent to the future; a man without ties, hopes, interests, waiting for rest and the end.

Mark Twain, 1872

was effected. The last robbery that he committed was the straw that broke the camel's back. He there left traces that gave the detectives a clue to discover his whereabouts. This deed of pillage, which like all others he committed, was done single-handed and occurred three miles this side of Copperopolis, early on the morning of November 3.

As the Sonora and Milton stage was rumbling over the mountain road, a man, whose face was concealed by a flour sack that had been ripped open and closed, jumped from behind the thicket that skirted the roadway and commanded a halt. He enforced his bidding with a present revolver. No passengers were in the stage at the time and the driver, McConnell, was compelled to get down from his seat, unhitch the horses and drive them behind the conveyance. The robber then broke open the treasure box of Wells, Fargo & Company with a celerity that only those who had been skilled by long experience in his profession could imitate, and took therefrom 228 ounces of amalgam valued at $4100, which had come from the Patterson Mine, at Tuttletown; three and a quarter ounces of gold and $550 in gold and silver coin. As McConnell drove the animals in the rear of the stage, he noticed an Italian boy on the foothills, a short distance away, who was carrying a Henry rifle. He beckoned to him and the lad came. The robber had secured his booty and was making off with it when McConnell seized the rifle from the boy's hands and fired at the despoiler. Black Bart, for it was undoubtedly, he ran. Mc.Connell pursued and discharged three more shots at him. In running, Black Bart lost his hat, a little round derby, and his handkerchief fell out of his pocket. He also threw away a package of papers that he had taken from the stage. These were red with blood and that fact induced McConnell to think that one of the shots at least had wounded the robber. The articles that Black Bart had left behind were picked up later when a posse of men from Copperopolis returned to the scene after McConnell had driven back to town.

THE TELL-TALE LAUNDRY MARK. Another piece of property, which was presumed to belong to Black Bart, was found behind some rocks near the spot where the stage was stopped. This was

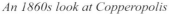

An 1860s look at Copperopolis

When I reached the Calaveras I was told that an American lady had just brought in a Frenchman who had died a few hours before, and I was asked to look into the matter. I went to the place where the carriage was, by which he had been brought in, and the lady told me that he had been sick in her house for five days, and that as she had to move, she had taken him in the carriage, but he had died on the way. She had not permitted anyone to search him until some witnesses should be present. The name that he had given in dying was Siniac.

I had the man's body taken out of the carriage, and although it was still warm, a surgeon whom I had called pronounced him dead. In the pockets of his trousers were found three keys and a small purse containing gold that I had weighed (27 1/8 ounces). The body being still warm, I thought it prudent not to bury it yet and had it kept through the night. The next day I had it buried on the slope of the hill near the river and drew up a report in English that the American surgeon and another of his compatriots signed. The lady called my attention to a person who had taken care of the sick man for five days. To this person I gave an ounce of gold and half an ounce to those who had watched over the body during the night and had dug the grave.

Jacques Antoine Moerenhout, 1848

Teamster Tom Moran hauls logs. Many teamsters made a living hauling logs to the mines to be used for timbering the underground shafts.

Still digging. Though my back is lame, I appear to be the nearest convalesent of anyone here of our party. Daniel Newcom has a verry sore hand caused by poison. Smith has a sort of felon on his hand caused by rubbing on the cradle, & Haskins hands & feet are sore from the Scurvey & Sunburnt. My back is lame but I carry dirt & Haskins rocks the cradle A great many are laid by about us, some with sore hands & feet caused by poison & some by disentary. As yet I have ben well.

Hiram Dwight Pierce,
Thursday, August 29th, 1849

the case of a pair of spyglasses, which it is thought he used to descry the stage from afar and note how many were in it. On the handkerchief was a laundry mark which ultimately [led to where it] had been purchased, and by whom. Captain Harry Morse, who had become interested in the capture of the robber of whose exploits all California, at least, was talking about, took the handkerchief.

"After a long search among the laundries of this city," says a *San Francisco Examiner* article of that time, "Hume finally found a Chinese washhouse on Valencia street where the mark on the handkerchief was recognized, the owner of it having his washing done there. From the Chinaman in the house, Morse learned that the person from whome he was looking was stopping at the Webb House, 27 Second street, his room being No. 40. Here was the clue so long desired. Anyway the man who occupied room No. 40 was 'spotted,' in the vernacular of the police, and kept under surveillance. Sheriff Thorn procured a warrant for his arrest on the charge of stage robbery from the Superior Court of Calaveras county, and armed with this terrible document, he came to this city. Black Bart, for the man who was arrested is the owner of that soubriquet, if the lynx-eyed Hume has not been deceived, was seemingly unconscious that the quiet in which he had hitherto been undisturbed, was about to be broken. He was taken to the central police station and there registered in the small book under the name of Spaulding. Tuesday morning he took a ride on the cars to

Stockton. Detective Mores, Johnny Thacker of Wells, Fargo & Co.'s force and Captain Stone of the regular police force accompanying him. At Stockton his photograph was taken. From the city of the insane asylum he resumed his journey to San Andreas in Calaveras county, where he was given quarters in the county jail and where he will be tried. On his person when arrested was found $160 in gold and $10 in silver."

CONFESSION IS MADE. "Since the above was in type," says the *Calaveras Weekly Citizen* of November 17, 1883, "we learn that on Thursday morning last the robber made a full confession to Sheriff Thorn, disclosing the hiding place of the treasure, and giving a full account of his travels from the time of the robbery to the time of his arrest. It seems that he took a wide circuit about the county, going to Sacramento via Mokelumne Hill. At Sacramento he took the overland train for Reno where he registered at the hotel and immediately returned to San Francisco. Thursday morning Sheriff Thorn and Wells Fargo & Co.'s detectives, accompanied by Black Bart, took a carriage to the scene of the robbery, where the treasure, $4500, was found concealed in a hollow tree, and brought to San Andreas by the officers."

After being away for several days, I returned to the cabin in company with Mr. Jeremiah Dobin. We had left our bunks with the blankets spread, it was about midnight, and tired and sleepy, we undressed and lay down, when Dobin remarked, "How does it happen that my blanket is wet?" and then, with a scream, sprang from the cot. Lighting a candle and examining his bed, we found that what he had taken for water was the cold coil of a large snake (colubrine) against his leg, and when it began to wriggle for more room, of course he at once surrendered the entire bunk. The harmless reptile was killed and cast out, and a thorough search satisfied us that no others were in the chinks, or about the cabin, before we could quietly yield ourselves to sleep.

Rev. John Steele, 1850

Courtesy Wells Fargo Bank

Charles Boles aka Charles Bolton, also known as Black Bart, robbed numerous Wells Fargo stagecoaches across northern California between 1875 and 1883. He was known as a gentleman bandit, always polite and never robbing passengers. He eventually began to leave poems at the sites of his crimes. Black Bart was very successful and stole thousands of dollars a year. During his last robbery in 1883, Black Bart was shot and forced to flee the scene. He left behind several personal items, including a pair of eyeglasses, food, and a handkerchief with a laundry mark. He was caught, convicted and sentenced to six years in San Quentin Prison for his final robbery and never charged for the other 27 robberies he supposedly committed. He was released for good behavior after serving four years. Released in January 1888 he disappeared without a trace. His San Francisco boarding house room was found vacated in February 1888 and the outlaw was never seen again.

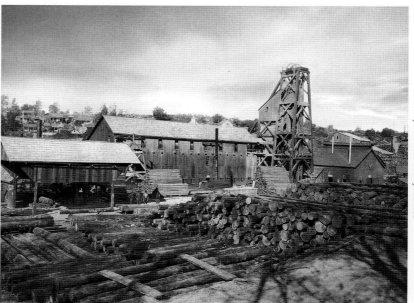

Utica Mine at Angels Camp. This mine was considered unlucky by townspeople. Fires, cave-ins, and broken hoist cables were among the causes of major disasters. The worst accident occurred a week before Christmas in 1889. A crew of 19 men were attempting a retimbering project to improve the mine's safety, when they were trapped by a massive cave-in. Only three men survived.

A Mexican having lost a mule, found one so similar in the color as well as the brand, that he supposed it was his own, and used it three days before the real owner came. The Mexican apologized for the mistake, but nothing would do but he must come before the Alcalde. "Pay me one hundred dollars or take fifty lashes," said that functionary, when he had heard the case. The defendant had no money, and slowly prepared himself for the alternative, when an Englishman, taking compassion on him, paid the fine. "And this is what they call a free country!" said the Englishman. "What is that you say?" roared the Alcalde, and immediately the speaker, being hauled up for treasonable expressions, was sentenced to pay fifty dollars or take twenty-five lashes.

Leonard Kip, 1850

DAILY EXPRESS NEWS October 3, 1857 Wm. M. Denig informs the public that he will from and after this date continue running a daily express from San Andreas, Calaveritas and Old Gulch starting from San Andreas immediately after the arrival of the Stockton stage, so as to deliver San Francisco letters and papers, and the *Sacramento Daily Union* and *State Journal* the same day the arrive at San Andreas.

On Saturday of each week the Express will be extended to Cave City and intervening Camps.

On the arrival of each Mail Steamer, an extra Express will be run for the distribution of Atlantic States papers, touching at Upper Calaveritas. Old Gulch, French Gulch, Mountain Ranch, Eldorado Mill, Cave City, O'Neil's Bar, Tunnel Hill, San Antonio Mill, Lower Calaveritas and Kentucky House.

Persons receiving letters or packages, forwarded per Mail or Wells, Fargo & Co., can have them delivered every day by leaving their orders at Morris Murphy's Store. Upper Calaveritas, or Osborn's Store, Old Gulch. And at Cave City, every Saturday, by leaving their orders at Burdick's Saloon.

Also—Collections of all kinds attended to, on reasonable terms. Office in Wells, Fargo & Co.'s Building, San Andreas where may be found San Francisco, Sacramento and Atlantic Papers.

VALLEY SPRINGS. This flourishing new town is growing rapidly. It is situated on the San Joaquin and Sierra Nevada Railroad, and a more beautiful, as well as favorable location for a village could not have been selected. The town has been well planned throughout. The streets are all named, and the work of grading them will commence immediately. The streets are all wide and regular.

Building lots are selling at a good figure, commanding a variety of prices according to location.

Every block has a row of trees around it that will make the town a mass of beautiful foliage as soon as they are grown. The water has been turned into the reservoir and the connection made with pipes so that the town is now supplied with water through them.

From the outset it was the intention of the management to make Valley Springs a desirable point of resort, for people who seek a healthy foot-hill climate and a desirable location accessible by rail. In point of beauty, scenery, climate, healthfulness, and hotel accommodations, the new town will rank second

I had a very comfortable time in Calaveras county, in spite of the rain, and if I had my way I would go back there, and argue the sewing machine question around Coon's bar-room stove again with the boys on rainy evenings. Calaveras possesses some of the grandest natural features that have ever fallen under the contemplation of the human mind- such as the Big Trees, the famous Morgan gold mine which is the richest in the world at the present time, perhaps, and "straight" whisky that will throw a man a double somerset and limber him up like boiled maccaroni before he can set his glass down. Marvelous and incomprehensible is the straight whisky of Angel's Camp!

Mark Twain, March 18, 1865

The Washoe Indian family of Joe Arnett, including his wife Susie and his mother, at their Dorrington domicile.

Pioneer Livery Stable in the town of Pioneer.

> [It] is a curious sight to look around at the end of the day and watch the different pursuits of the miners. As soon as evening closes, all commence straggling back from the golshes, at which they have been working during the day. Leaving their picks in the holes, they carefully bring back the pans, for the wash bowl is a valuable article, serving more uses than one; the least of which is the share it occupies in the preparation of the different meals. It is no uncommon thing to see the same pan used for washing gold, washing clothes, mixing flour cakes, and feeding the mule.
>
> Leonard Kip, 1850

to none in the mountains. It is backed by a good country, and is the distributing point for all parts of the county, and being connected by rail with Stockton, Sacramento, and San Francisco, will naturally become a busy business center. This alone suffices to mark its importance and give it a prestige.

Messrs. Paulk Bros. & Johnson have erected a large store for general merchandise, which is one of the best buildings in the county. This firm have a fine and varied assortment of goods, and are also engaged in real estate and insurance.

Messrs. Lamb & Cook have erected the "Pioneer Livery Stable." They have also built a restaurant and dwelling house, and, adjoining this, a saloon.

The railroad company have laid out eighteen blocks, each surrounded with walnut trees from one to two years old, and all boxed in good style. Every tree has a tube leading from above the surface of the ground to its roots, whereby they are irrigated without baking the ground or scalding the bark, as might be the case during the summer months.

Geo. Late is a pioneer of California, having arrived in San Francisco, August 22, 1849, after a trip around Cape Horn on the bark *Kirkland*. Mr. Late has been engaged in mining like all early comers, but now resides near Valley Springs, where he is engaged in farming and raising cattle.

MILTON. This is a post, express, and telegraph office. It is the terminus of the Stockton and Copperopolis Division of the Central Pacific Railroad, twenty-eight miles from Stockton, and where connections with the stage line for the Yosemite, Big Trees, and mountain resorts generally is made.

Milton Hotel is kept by J. C. Bund, and travelers will find it a desirable stopping place. Mr. Bund came to California in April, 1853, from Missouri, and settled first in San Joaquin County, and engaged in merchandising, and afterward came to Milton.

VALLECITO FLAT, which has often been the theme of scientific writers, is a basin, or depression, the lower portion of which when opened by a tunnel will be a natural outlet for the whole surrounding country. It has an average width of from two hundred to fifteen hundred feet; is from sixty to two hundred feet in depth, and extends in a northerly and easterly direction from the place of beginning for a distance of some three miles or more. In many places where it has been worked, the blue gravel part was found to be from fifteen to thirty feet in thickness, and very rich, having often paid as high as fifteen dollars per cubic yard.

Vallecito Flat has long ago engaged the attention of ambitious men. Its rich deposits have brought to its walls an army of toilers who have returned to their homes with the recompense of abundant gold. Practical mining has attested the wonderful

> During the night the clouds had blown away & after eating some grub this morning we divided into two companies & Bob Bill Black Jack & myself went west & the other 4 East taking with us our tools to see if we could find any of the Ore or a place to dig for it that suited... Just before dark the Mules & horses on the flat took a stampede The Alen that came with us thought it was Grizzly that had scared them as they had been verry plenty here lately
>
> John Doble,
> Thursday, April 15th 1852

The Late family bagging grain from the day's harvest. This was a successful ranch using steam power in its operation. Steam engines were commonly used in farming beginning in the late 1880s.

Stand and Deliver. Saturday morning the Ione Stage was stopped at the head of the Morrow Grade by one masked man, who used the persuasive eloquence of a double-barrelled shot-gun to enforce obedience to his command. There was but one passenger aboard. The driver handed out the two express boxes and four United States mail sacks, and drove on to Ione. After the stage had gone a little distance the highwayman fired off one barrel of his gun, it is presumed accidentally. The express boxes and mail sacks were taken a few feet from the road and broken open. Only $16 was in the Jackson express box, but the amount in the Sutter and Amador box swelled the haul on W.F. & Co. to $574. The registered mail packages were taken, one package from Sutter Creek contained $87, one from Mokelumne Hill contained 60.

The robber left an old hat, an old pair of pants, his mask, a piece of a woman's dress and an old ax by the demoralized boxes and bags. The ax is said to have been stolen from the Morrows. A man was seen the night before near Ione, at the Dog Ranch, who wore the hat and pants found and his

continued in far right column

Ditch tenders were vital to water companies supplying local town and the mines with water. They maintained the ditches, and as shown here, were responsible for measuring the amount of water being sent down the flumes to various locations. The box with the water flowing out was the measurement device used. The water was measured in order to collect fees for water usage.

richness of this region, and science has attempted to measure its extent, while the annals of California record its marvelous resources.

TELEGRAPH CITY. This place consists chiefly of the residence and farm of Edward Parks, who was born in South Carolina, in February, 1822. He was a veteran in the Mexican War. He came to California by way of Panama, where he remained nine months in business, and reached San Francisco in 1851.

He is now quite an extensive farmer, having 1,000 acres of grazing land, where he keeps about 70 head of cattle, 70 hogs, and 10 mules and other stock.

COLD SPRING RANCH. The timbered section of Calaveras County contains not only the largest trees in the world, but also extensive tracts of the largest and most valuable of California pine. Visitors to this section are surprised and delighted with the magnificence of these forests. Some experienced travelers even declare views which present themselves from various commanding points to be superior to any similar scene with which they are acquainted. In the midst of one of the noblest sections of this timber belt is situated the "Cold Spring Ranch." To reach the ranch it is necessary to travel either by the San Joaquin and Sierra Nevada Railroad, which connects at Lodi with the Central Pacific, and traveling to its terminus at Valley Springs, where connection is made with stage, or the more popular route by the way of Stockton, connecting with the Milton Branch, which connects at Milton with T. J. Matteson's excellently managed stage line, whence the tourist is conveyed to this mountain resort, which is situated two and one-half miles above the Calaveras Big Trees on the Big Tree and Carson Valley Toll Road. When purchased by the owner, Mr. John Gardner of Vallicito, California, it contained 320 acres, which have been increased by subsequent purchases until it reaches double that amount—an entire section.

The altitude of this ranch, about 4,800 feet, is too great for the production of many crops raised in the valleys, but makes it excellent grass and grazing land. The chief value of the ranch, however, is in its timber and its utility as a summer resort, and trading depot for herders and stock men who inhabit the mountains a goodly portion of the time. An excellent business is transacted with this class. The buildings on the place are substantial and commodious, the large two and a half story hotel being especially noticeable. The facilities for accommodating guests are so excellent that Mr. Gardner has had considerable

Calaveras Hotel, located in Angels Camp, was owned and operated by Italian immigrant Olivia Rolleri for 39 years. This hotel burned down in 1934 and was never rebuilt.

Courtesy Calaveras County Archives

continued from far left column

description given to the officers. Sheriff Murray and assistants at once started out to obtain a clue if possible. Detectives Hume and Thatcher arrived in town Monday night. They are confident they know the man, but as he is supposed to be the hero of twenty-two successful stage robberies, this knowledge is not of much use. It is said he has never been seen in town, always does his work in the identical manner that this last robbery was performed, is not supposed to be a drinking or gambling character. Eight hundred dollars is the reward on him, and he goes by the name of "Black Bart."

Three dollars was in a registered package from Rail Road Flat, and fifteen dollars in one from West Point, which swells the cash booty of the robberman to $759. As no trace has been found of the highwayman, it is probable that he is now safe from discovery.

Calaveras Weekly Citizen, June 30, 1883

Exodus—On Tuesday last; the Chinese Theatricals broke ups camp and departed this place, bound for Chinese Camp, in Tuolumne County, where they will stop for a "little session," and enliven the people of that place with their caustic performances, and make night hideous with their eternal hum-drum squeaking, squealing, caterwauling music. We can truly sympathize with the citizens of Chinese, for the suffering-and annoyance they have to undergo during the next month, but hope they will bear it with true fortitude, and endure the suffering with Christian patience. After they shall have sufficiently astonished the "natives" of Tuolumne, it is their intention to (oh! horror of horrors!) return, and again torment us with a monthly siege of their captivating performance and most fascinating musical accomplishments. The very thought of their return makes our nerves to tingle, our blood to chill, our brain to rack with pain, our bones to ache, and our flesh to quiver from the crown of our head to the sole of our feet. But, while we hold our breath, brace our nerves, grit our teeth, and our hair raises on end, still we feel truly grateful that they have given us a short season of peace and quite. They have gone—long may they remain.

San Andreas Independent, October 3, 1857

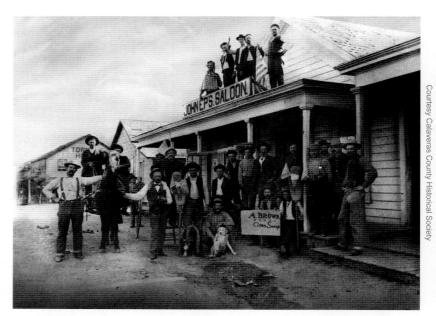

John Ep's saloon in Milton on November 8th, 1892. Proprietor John Eproson is standing on the chair. Charlie Vanciel holds a sign for A. Brown, clearly a favored candidate for these men.

patronage from tourists who find this such a charming resort. Opportunities are abundant for their enjoyment, hunting in the forests, or fishing in the San Antone, a splendid stream, running through the place, well stocked with trout, being among the most popular amusements. Mr. Gardner adds shake-making to his other industries, being the most extensive dealer in this class of building material in that section.

CAMPO SECO. This is one of the old settled points in the county.

FOOT-HILLS OF CALAVERAS. A drive among the foot-hills of Calaveras would, at this season of the year, amply repay the lover of nature. The lower ranges of gentle, smooth, rolling, treeless hills are covered with a complete mass of green vegetation, intercepted throughout with borders and beds of the loveliest of wild flowers of every hue, color, and shade of the rainbow. At this season of the year nature essays to deck our land in her loveliest attire, and nowhere under the sun is this more manifest than along the undulating hills of this county, Why it is that people of leisure will idle away hours of a brief life in the midst of grim, smoky, dusty towns, on the streets, sidewalks, in crowded saloons, halls, or theaters, when such a lovely panorama of nature can be seen at so little cost and trouble, is a mystery beyond comprehension.

To the discouraged, dyspeptic, indigo colored, thin lipped, liver discolored, constipated inhabitant of towns, we recommend a week among the foot-hills.

CAMP LIFE IN CALAVERAS. Calaveras is a great resort for campers who leave the dry, hot valleys with their families and live in the fragrance and grandeur of the pines and big trees. They seek to find rest and recreation away from the constant toil and pressure of business.

California offers special advantages for camp life. The rains will have generally ceased about the 1st of May, and for the six months thereafter everything has become so dry that no danger need ensue from sleeping out in the open air.

The mountain streams are alive with the speckled beauties that nip so charmingly at the treacherous bait. Hares of wonderful swiftness of foot and delicious eating abound on every side. Then the gentle dove furnishes a dish fit for a king. If you wish to try your gun on larger game, the coyote, beaver, wild cat, lynx, California lion and silver-gray fox will test the shooting abilities to the utmost. But it is the quail and deer that whet the appetite of the camper.

NATURAL BRIDGES OF CALAVERAS. The Upper Natural Bridge of Calaveras County is located 3 miles from Vallecito, and 500 yards from the stage road leading from Calaveras Big Trees to Yosemite. Unlike all the other natural bridges known in the world, the two of Calaveras County, California, are a gradual formation from crystal spring water, requiring countless

Debasing Gold Dust. A short time since, two Mexicans were arrested at or near West Point, in this County on the complaint of Mr. Benjamin of San Andreas, charging them with the debasement of sundry parcels of gold dust which they had sold to him, at the usual price per ounce; but which upon melting and refining at the Mint, did not realize to the purchaser as much as $12 per ounce. Suspicion tattled upon the party above named, and on their examination it appeared that they had been in the practice of this cheat for some time. We do not know the extent of their field of operations, but presume that it affected gold dust purchasers more or less, throughout the northern part of this county. Brass and copper filings were the substances they mixed with the dust.

San Andreas Independent,
October 3, 1857

Tom Moran's 12-horse team near Milton hauling logs to the mines.

Miwok Indians of the Murphys Rancheria. Lizzie Domingo with her children and Captain Yellowjacket, 1900.

Brutal Murder. A most atrocious murder was committed one day last week in Chinese Camp. A Mexican walked up the street with a bowie knife in each hand, and passed between two Americans who were standing in the street talking plunging a knife into each, inflicting severe wounds, one of which has since proved mortal. No cause is assigned for the murderous deed. The Mexican made his escape.

San Andreas Independent, October 3, 1857

ages to attain their present magnitude and grandeur, one writer estimating it 2,000,000 of years.

This bridge varies from 12 to 76 feet breadth of span, from 8 to 40 feet high, and 240 feet through underneath the arch. To see its beauty and magnificence, visitors must pass through underneath. Underneath the bridge, worn in the solid marble, are seven basins, or tanks, round, smooth, and true, as if measured with square and compass, and turned by rule. The two smaller ones, always in view, side by side, named the "Old Bach's and Old Maid's Wash Bowls," are one foot in diameter and one foot in depth; the others, in the center of the stream, are filled with water, rocks, and sand, varying from 4 feet diameter and 5 feet in depth to 23 feet diameter and 27 feet depth. Here is a study for scientific men. It is positive that the basins were worn before the flow of gold began.

As you go under this bridge, you first enter a large circular space 76 feet in diameter and from 8 to 16 feet high. In one corner, as it were, hangs what has been named the "Rock of Horeb," from which flows a living stream to refresh the thirsty visitor. Here the eye can feast for hours upon the overhanging wonders, never tiring. Passing the partition, which is 6 feet high, the span becomes narrower, the arch rising to a height of 40 feet, and hung in rich sparkling festoons, charms the vision of the beholder. Directly overhead is called the pulpit, where eight persons have sat at a time, singing for hours, listening to the echo of the voices resounding from wall to wall, charming the ear.

Passing on to the right is "Lover's Retreat," where many a tender pair have uttered tender words but could not be seen to blush.

A little further, and to the right hand, is the "Infant's Bath Tub," standing full of holy water, in which the Old Bach intends to immerse his first born. Still further on, also to the right, is the "Old Bachelor's Trap," where many a girl has paid toll for crawling through it.

Nearly opposite, and thirty feet high, is the "Bridal Chamber," which the Old Bach once entered alone; he remained but a short time, being so lonely; he descended and removed the ladder, resolving never to enter again until he was old enough to build a golden ladder, and enter in with his bride, pulling the ladder up after them. No pen can describe this vast arch so that one can realize it. No artist's pencil can portray its real beauty: it must be seen to be appreciated.

Passing on and to the left is a large cove called the "Miner's Cabin," in which lived for nine summers a company of miners while working in the creek. Passing out from under the bridge, and turning around, the eye meets a view that baffles all description. Unlike the upper bridge, this one in its formation rises and projects outward, overhanging the stream, having many small openings or caverns, some of which have been entered a distance of 30 feet. From this point can be taken one

Around each table could be seen a crowd of hardy fellows betting their hard-earned dust, and indulging in rude jests and boisterous laughter. The harsh oaths that would occasionally escape from the lips of some of the players, gave evidence that luck could not prevail against scientific attainments in the art of cheating, and that the gamblers were making hay while the sun shone.

Albert S. Evans, late 1860s

The C.M. Whitlock general mercantile business on Main Street in San Andreas served a big cross section of the public with everything from perfume to tobacco.

Henry A. Cavagnaro's Stanislaus Flour business was housed in the Letinois L. Garrat building, constructed in 1860. A barber shop was one of the other businesses sharing the site.

Worked on my cradle most of the day — This morning Charles Everbeck, my old partner of last spring, got himself into a small bit of a muss. David Keller went over into the North gulsh and there he found Everbeck stealing and washing out some of his (Kellers) dirt which was thrown up in one of the arroyas — Dave just rolled up his fist and hit Mr. Everbeck a chug in his larboard eye which sent him about 10 feet across the arroya — he then exercised his boot about his ribs and the lower part of his back and let him off at that, as he whined, promised and begged most piteously —

Leonard Wirthington,
February 19, 1852

of the finest stereoscopic views in the world. This bridge is 180 feet through underneath the arch, from 12 to 45 feet breadth of span, and from 6 to 15 feet high.

THE TIMBER BELT. About seven miles above Murphy's, the heavy timber belt commences, and spreads its flourishing growth widely and thickly, until the whole of this section is as dense as a tropical forest, with the sugar pine, the yellow pine, the spruce, fir, and cedar. The day is close at hand when this lumber region will be sought after and profitably utilized, and its valuable woods enjoy large sales in the valleys below and at Sacramento, Stockton, and San Francisco.

The timbered belt for grandeur, extent, diversity, and magnificent proportions, has no parallel in the entire timber belt of the western slope of the Sierras. Such is the opinion of all who have visited and traveled through this wonderfully profuse bounty of nature. This entire belt, during the summer and early fall months, is occupied by the pastoral population.

The San Joaquin and Sierra Nevada Railroad, now being rapidly constructed, has for one of its objects the reaching of this timber.

That immense timber belt extending along nearly the whole distance of the Sierra Nevada Mountains, on the western slope, here culminates (in the higher foot-hills) with that gigantic grove, the Big Trees of Calaveras, so famous for the wonderful size of its trees.

A Calaveras Home and Mine. The residence and grounds of Mr. S. S. Moser, represented in this work, are situated at Mokelumne Hill.

Mr. Moser has followed mining principally, having been strictly confined to that business for the past fifteen years.

The mine in which Mr. Moser is at present interested is a hydraulic mine, called the Bonanza. Mr. Moser owns a half-interest in the property, Mr. S. L. Prindle and Samuel Foorman being the other two proprietors.

This mine is situated about a mile southeast of Mokelumne Hill. The water supply is obtained from the Mokelumne Hill and Campo Seco Ditch and Mining Companies' Ditch.

The mine has been run on the hydraulic system for the past nine years, being a relocation of abandoned mines. A force of from eight to sixteen men are employed, according to the demand occasioned by circumstances. The mine has given good results, being considered the best in the vicinity.

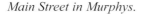

Main Street in Murphys.

A few days since an emigrant train crossed the Sierra Nevada mountains coming in by the Big Tree route. On the other side of "Uncle John's," some stock was lost or stolen. The train came down to the valley, where the owners, (Mr. Jasper J. Harroll, and his brother, Nathan Harroll) heard that some of the stolen cattle had been seen, and was no doubt in the hands of the thieves. He immediately returned to the Big Trees, he was most foully murdered by being shot through with three rifle balls. It is supposed the emigrant was killed to destroy certain information he possessed in reference to the stolen stock. Mr. Hendrickson and Hiram Allen, of Upper Calaveritas, found the body of the murdered man, seven miles this side of "Uncle John's" ranch. A party of men, headed by the murdered man's brother are now out in pursuit of the bandits and make every effort to trace them up and mete out justice to the aggressors in a summary manner.

San Andreas Independent,
October 3, 1857

On September 30, 1868, Mr. E. Said, the Superintendent of the Petticoat Mine at Rail Road Flat, was brutally murdered while on the way to Mokelumne Hill. Mr. Said was driving his own double team and accompanied by two of his men—a man named Meek and one named Kees. About two and one-half miles from Rail Road Flat, four men, masked and armed with shotguns arose from the brush that skirts the road, and without attempting to stop the horses or ordering a halt, fired two shots, one at Mr. Said, killing him instantly, and the other fired at the horses.

Immediately after the shots were fired, Meek leaped from the carriage and endeavored to escape, but was pursued, overtaken and robbed by the assassins. The horses broke into a run as the shots were fired and Kees with presence of mind and great courage, determined to prevent the anticipated robbery. Acting on the impulse, he sprang over the front seat, seized the reins from the hands of the dying man and holding the blood-stained corpse with one hand, urged the horses forward at the top of their speed. He succeeded in bringing the murdered remains of Mr. Said to Mokelumne Hill. Dr. Hoerschner of Mokelumne Hill found that three buckshots had taken effect upon Mr. Said.

Mr. Said was in the habit of taking the bullion from the mine to Mokelumne Hill, and apprehended an attack.

On Friday, June 7. 1873, Jose B. Coyado was executed in the jail yard at San Andreas, almost four years after the murder.

San Andreas Independent

Whisker Bill and his crew at his slaughterhouse in Angels. (The man on the right isn't missing his legs, but a sheep walked through the picture as it was shot.)

FINE SUPPLY OF WATER. There are three rivers in Calaveras, one from which the county takes its name, the Mokelumne and the Stanislaus, none of them very important, but all very useful.

The eastern border of the county is defined by the Stanislaus, while the Mokelumne River bounds the west, and the central portion is drained by the Calaveras River with its many tributaries. Water distributed by artificial means is used chiefly for mining purposes, the agricultural interests at present requiring only small quantities.

The largest aqueduct constructed at present is the Mokelumne Hill and Seco Canal, which receives its water from the Mokelumne River.

The Murphy Canal, or Union Ditch, receiving its water supply from the Stanislaus River, is nearly as important. Its waters are extremely fresh and pure, formed as they are from the melting snows of the mountains above drained by the Stanislaus; and its banks nearly the whole distance are embowered by alders, poplars, and vines, making the roadway between Murphy's and Big Trees, which is built upon its banks and between giant-wooded hills, one of the most picturesque and beautiful in the State.

Sonora's Bunnell and Coles, Carpenters and Builders, building, which is the site of the St. James Church built in 1860. The Empire Market is visible on the right.

Chapter 3: Tuolumne County — Sonora, Columbia, Jamestown and vicinity

The history of Tuolumne County properly commences with the date of its discovery by civilized men; a date which a careful comparison of accounts would show to have been in the early part of the summer of 1848, at which time a party of miners—Philadelphians, as is recorded—came to Woods' Creek. This very significant fact may, then, be regarded as the starting point of these records. It was at this time that the western slope had begun to resound with the blows of the hardy gold-seekers, whom the unprecedented wave of immigration had moved to California, bringing the throngs of adventurers from many lands to people the heretofore silent canons and gorges of the auriferous belt, and to do their wonderful works, for which the world stands indebted.

It has been poetically said, that, at the time of the first discovery by Americans, the country was one of the most pictur-

> The Sonoranian, who has been one of the most successful diggers in the ravine, besieged me to-day to sell him my pistols. They are an elegant pair, silver mounted and rifle bore, and good for duck or duelist—no matter which—for twenty or thirty paces. He offered me a pound of gold; so I determined to try the non-resistant principle, and let him have them. As he belted them about his waist, and strode off you would have advised even a California bear to get out of his way.
>
> Walter Colton,
> Friday, Nov. 10, 1849

Washington Street, Sonora, mid 1860s.

> The immense traffic carried on on the roads that lead to the mining regions affords an extensive field for the profitable management of houses of entertainment. These may be encountered at almost every mile throughout the whole country, and they vary in size from a wooden two-story house to the very smallest kind of canvas shanty.
>
> Frank Marryat, early 1850s

esque in the world. Noble forests existed, through which roamed the Indian and the deer. Streams of crystal clearness flowed, fish playing therein in all the freedom of security. The vast Sierra, bearing a diadem of snow, added grandeur to beauty. Pines and sequoias, the like of which can hardly elsewhere be found, tower heavenward. The oaks grew orchard-like in their regularity. Deer, antelope, wild fowl, in short, everything that was useful to man in his wild or unsophisticated state, here grew in profusion. This picture, though perhaps somewhat exaggerated, was not unfitted to the time and place.

Even now, after the lapse of a third of a century, and the desecration of land, the defilement of water-courses, and the annihilation of forests, the truth of those pictured lineaments may be seen, and one may lament the work of the pioneers that has destroyed so much of beauty while building up a great and glorious State—the brightest gem in Columbia's diadem.

The party of Philadelphians may, then, be regarded as the pioneers of Tuolumne County, for aught we know to the contrary. As mentioned above, they discovered Woods' Creek, naming it after their leader, the Rev. James Woods.

The next settlement was that of a party of Mexican miners. who, pushing up Woods' Creek beyond the Crossing, located Sonorian Camp—a name afterwards changed to Sonora—all the inhabitants of which were of Spanish extraction, until the arrival of the first Americans, who came most probably in the spring of 1849.

In August, 1848, Colonel James, a lawyer of San Francisco, located on Woods' Creek, and entered into mining speculations, in the course of which Jamestown was founded; but as this perhaps too enterprising gentleman assumed liabilities which he could not meet, thereby distinguishing himself as the very first of the long line of unsuccessful speculators in mines. Judge Tuttle, arriving on Mormon Gulch, built the first log cabin in the county, the previous structures having been cloth tents or Mexican remadas or brush houses. This cabin became the nucleus of a village, which, in compliance with the custom of the times, was named Tuttletown.

Among the more notable discoveries made during the summer of 1848, was that of Jackass Gulch, for which name the accidental loss of a long-eared animal contributed.

Jackass Gulch, despite its name, immediately took rank as among the very richest of the diggings yet struck. Its gold was

View of mining activities near Chinese Camp on the Tuolumne River, with Harvey Myron Sampson and Jeremiah Sampson.

A short time ago, Jim Hill, a man with a scar on his neck, went into a store at Camp Seco in the night and held pistols over the heads of the proprietors, while others of his gang stole the iron safe. Last night he was in Sonora. He went into a Spanish house of ill-fame, where Guadalupe, the keeper, is no doubt an accomplice. Hill took a pistol from a man, a stranger to him, struck him with it and then shot at him. The man ran out of the house, frightened, and gave the alarm, not knowing who had robbed and shot him. Hill then hid under a bed where he was found by the sheriff.

This morning a party of about a dozen of our most respectable citizens went to the jail and took Hill away to stand his trial at Camp Seco. His identity was proved and a fair and impartial trial was given before a jury of twelve men who rendered a verdict of guilty unanimously. It was then voted to hang the prisoner.

Enos Christman,
Saturday, June 28, 1851

Placer mining in Columbia, 1860s.

Two weeks from my departure south I returned to my cabin, and was surprised to find myself regarded by the Columbia Indians as a great medicine man. Most of those taken with smallpox had died, but after vaccination there were no new cases; and it was, no doubt, well for them that they burned their dead; thus, with them, consuming their infected clothing.

The Chief, Capitan Juan, accompanied by his son and the principal men of the village, made me a formal visit, thanking me for the benefits conferred in vaccinating them, and asking whether there was anything they could do for me. In reply I told them it was my wish that we might be friends, and that they would treat me as a brother.

Rev. John Steele, 1850

of a very coarse description, lumps of several ounces weight being of common occurrence; and it is stated that two of the earlier prospectors, Major Means and his brother Julius, took out from a claim of 100 square feet $10,000 worth of gold! Nor was the gulch limited to placer diggings. The same gentlemen discovered upon their claim a quartz vein which yielded two-thirds of its weight in gold! Mr. Carrington's vein paid from $100 to $300 per day for years, by simply pounding the rock in a mortar. Numerous discoveries of rich placers took place during the latter part of 1848, and the country rapidly filled up with seekers of hidden treasure, most of them, unfortunately, illy provided with means for comfortably existing through the ensuing winter. Exorbitant prices and much suffering were the consequence. From the annexed quotation of prices, it may be learned how scarce the comforts and necessities of life were. Flour during that time was $3 per pound. Hard bread, beans, coffee, sugar, saleratus, and indeed all the indispensable articles of culinary consumption, sold for the uniform price of $3 per pound. Salt pork, however, is quoted at the higher figure of $8. If so, it would seem that it was regarded in the light of a luxury. Merchants, it is said, no doubt truthfully, made speedy fortunes, both by reason of the high prices of their goods and the low price of gold dust, which was paid for at the rate of $8 per ounce, in coin, or $16 in trade. Merchandising, liquor-selling, and gambling stood nearly upon the same plane, if what has been written may be believed, and all three callings were undoubtedly immensely remunerative. Gambling was freely practiced by all classes; and the miner, after his day's work, betook himself to the monte or faro table, there to be relieved of his easily gotten ounces. Spirituous liquors found an abundant sale at the price of $1 per drink, and the consumption, then as now, seemed one of the great objects of human existence.

It has been often stated that the first women who arrived in Sonora were two sisters, Mariana and Jesus Ramirez; but the latter of the two, who is now the wife of J. M. Cabesut, Esq. of Sonora, disclaims the truth of the story, and says that the distinction belongs to other Mexican women, of the family of Leon, who arrived several months previous. Less unassuming was Ah Chi, a Chinese immigrant, who was the forerunner of the great and disastrous wave of his fellow-countrymen. This Celestial kept an eating house in Sonora, near the spot now (1882) occupied by O'Brien's store, and which was well patronized by the miners, being looked upon as the best kept restaurant of the town.

Placer mining, hoisting wheel of the Daley claim, 1860s.

Courtesy Library of Congress

During the last night there was a robbery in the settlement, which caused great excitement. A miner, formerly from Ohio, but who had been many years in Oregon, where he had a pleasant home, had been induced, by the hope of making a rapid fortune, to sell his valuable property, and, taking his large family, to remove to the mines. There, by hard labor and trading, he had laid up about $4000. Most of this sum was in a trunk at the foot of the bed in their tent. During the night this trunk was taken, and the next morning was found at some distance, broken open, and the money gone. A boarder was immediately arrested on suspicion, but, after a well-conducted trial, was released.

Daniel B. Woods,
January 2d, 1850

Teamsters Frank Simpson, Henry Hiniker, and George Stephenson, hauling pipe from Chinese Station to Gravel Range Mine and giving some campers a lift who were going to Yosemite Valley, 1898.

I left the Mokelumne River the afternoon following Election Day, and retraced my path to Jackson's Creek, which I reached at dark. Being unhorsed, I resumed my old plodding gait, "packing" my blankets and spurs. I was obliged to walk to the Upper Bar, in order to cross the Mokelumne, whose current was now very deep and rapid. A man named Bills, who kept a brush hotel with a canvas roof, had set up an impromptu ferry, made by nailing a few planks upon four empty barrels, lashed together. This clumsy float was put over by means of a rope stretched from bank to bank. The tendency of the barrels to roll in the swift current, made it very insecure for more than two persons. The same morning, four men who were crossing at once, overbore its delicate equilibrium and were tipped into the water, whence they were rescued with some difficulty. A load of freight met with the same luck just before I reached the ferry.

Bayard Taylor, 1849

Within the short space of half a year from the discovery of gold in California, extensive prospecting had been done, and the gold-bearing territory had been examined for hundreds of miles along the Sierras, and many extremely rich finds had been reported. Notably this was the case in Tuolumne County. News of this sort traveled fast, and this region, then called the Southern Mines, became the cynosure of all eyes looking for the fabled El Dorado. The reports sent by the earlier prospectors were probably not in excess of the truth; but there came an era of exaggeration, of wild misrepresentation, whose effects recoiled injuriously upon the new communities. One of the earlier writers said: "The main bulk of the immigration centered here. But so many gold seekers brought along with them some great drawbacks to the prosperity of the country. Hordes of gamblers kept in the wake of the industrious miners, accompanied by rum-sellers and abandoned females; and no sooner was a camp laid out by the miners, than a large rough tent was erected by the outcasts; a plank, resting on two empty barrels, served for a counter; and in lieu of the "fixins" of a regular bar, a barrel of whisky, with a tin cup or two, and we had a first-class hotel and gambling saloon, from which issued the din of cracked fiddles and the chink of money, from early-morn until late at night; and not infrequently would the sun find the gambling tables crowded and the game and the dance as lively as ever. "We are even yet reaping the fruit of these drones of society. It was the result, in a great measure, of the vast influx of Spanish population, and has been one of the chief hindrances to a better understanding between the American and Spanish peoples."

The author continues: "Hostility to everything American was originally engendered against us by the Mexicans during the war of 1846, and had not died out in 1849. Nor is it to be wondered that the Chiliens, Peruvians, and other Spanish immigrants who spoke the same language, had habits and religion identical, and who were daily regaled with stories of the brutality and injustice they had received at the hands of the American people. From the Spanish, the disaffection spread first to the French, then to the German and Italian portion, and lastly to the Australian immigrants, extensively known by the euphonious cognomen of "Sydney Ducks," a name very soon to become synonymous with all kinds of fraud and rascality. Accordingly, collisions became of daily occurrence. Murders soon followed, and became so frequent that at one time it was seriously mooted whether foreigners should not be expelled from the mines. It eventuated in bringing down upon them the heavy mining tax tantamount to expulsion from California."

[An] observing student of history is struck most forcibly with the apparent air of prodigality that pervaded all classes and

Lifiting wheel of the Columbia claim, c. 1865.

The miners prefer buying every thing at auction, and although I imagine the purchasers suffer in the long run by this principle, the "loafers" gain by it; for (supposing you are a loafer) you have only to mix with the crowd of bidders, and take out your clasp-knife; you can then make an excellent meal from the samples exposed to view, presuming always that your constitution will stand a mixture of salt butter, Chinese sugar, pickles, and bad brandy.

Frank Marryat, early 1850s

On Wednesday afternoon, July 3, after having worked off the first edition of the Sonora *Herald* in the Times office at Stockton, the proprietor solicited me to take a horse and start immediately for Sonora, seventy-five or eighty miles distant, in order that the papers might be distributed. I started about four o'clock, fully armed and with blankets and papers, on horse. After riding about 28 miles I stopped at Simmon's Tent, where I slept on a pile of boards, paying six and a half dollars for what my horse ate, and three dollars for my supper and breakfast. In the morning [I] rode on over the hills and plains under a scorching sun, and reached Sonora about three o'clock in the afternoon.

Great excitement existed along the road on account of the many horrid murders that had been committed. I had passed the bodies of three Americans who had been killed by the Mexicans when, in the distance, I saw coming towards me a figure on horse. I spurred my horse and he did likewise. We sped past each other, determined to escape death by the hand of a Mexican. But as we hurried past, each saw that the other was an American. We then turned, saluted, and continued on our journeys.

The day after my arrival I distributed copies of the first number of the *Herald* throughout the town. On the following day I bought lumber, borrowed a saw and hatchet, and fitted up some "stands" in a tent which we use for an office. I have known of printing offices in log cabins with the latchstring always hanging out, but here, I am seated at a table covered with papers in the middle of a "rag house," ten by fourteen feet.

Enos Christman,
Sunday, August 11, 1850

This gigantic log was shipped from West Side Lumber to St. Louis in 1905.

all doings of the time of which this section treats, and indeed of the subsequent years of rich strikes. He sees the spectacle of myriads of hardy, adventurous men daring every danger and hardship in the frantic pursuit of gold, which, after attaining, they flung recklessly away! ... With some, the fierce fight for wealth past, and the prize ungained, ambition loses her sway, and the once energetic miner settles into the narrow groove of a hanger-on of a whisky saloon, to clean the spittoons for a drink, to await the generous patron at whose expense the liquid stimulant passes his appreciative lips.

Charity to the unfortunate took the other hazardous, though hardly less praiseworthy, form of reliance upon the word and honor of strangers, so that, as is well known, an entire stranger could buy on credit, without introduction or reference, hundreds of dollars' worth of the necessaries of life, and this without exciting remark. Again, if a stranger became sick, it was not uncommon that the trader of the nearest camp assumed charge of the case, paid the bills, medical fees, etc., and in case of death, buried the unfortunate.

Early in the year 1849, two events occurred of which the narration will throw much light upon the primitive ways of administering what was thought to be justice. These events were two trials, for theft and murder, respectively. As is well known, neither written law, properly constituted officers, nor courts of law, existed. In lieu of the present machinery of the law, an officer, called by the Mexican term Alcalde, was selected from the inhabitants of a district, and to him were delegated the necessary powers for preserving the peace, settling disputes and trying offenders. The mode of choosing an Alcalde was as unsystematic as the powers that he assumed. Instances are on record of an Alcalde's assumption of his position without the form of a vote, or even a request from the surrounding inhabitants, as did R. S. Ham, the first Alcalde of Sonora, who was recognized in that capacity until a case which demanded more talent than he was supposed to possess, when he was summarily deposed and James Frazier, a store-keeper on Sonorita Gulch, was raised to the dignity.

As is the custom in all mining camps, the favorite day for trade and barter was Sunday; when her streets were thronged with miners from the surrounding claims, in town for their mail and for the purpose of purchasing supplies, and to seek the excitement of the gaming table. Still the memories of present inhabitants are recollections of the streets so densely thronged that locomotion was impeded; stores filled to overflowing with men seeking to spend their accumulations of the week; on such days the number of people in town could not have been less

Tiger claim, mid 1860s.

It has rained hard most of the day, and there was some thunder, a very unusual occurrence in California. Spent a part of the day and all the evening with Dr. R., singing, reading, &c. At the close of our pleasant interview, again we "lifted the heart and bent the knee" in prayer to Almighty God. In our visits to each other on these rainy days, like the ladies at home, we often take our sewing with us. To-day I took a pair of stockings to darn, one of my shoes to mend, and the "Democratic Review" to read. While we plied our needles, our tongues were equally busy speaking of mutual friends and hopes.

Daniel B. Woods,
Jan. 3d., 1850

A quarrel had arisen between one Atkins, an American gambler, and some Irishmen, at Big Bar, on Sullivan's Creek. Atkins, being roughly used, retired to his cabin, and, loading his rifle, fired at and killed a man whose name has been given as Boyd or Boyden, and who had been actively engaged in freeing Atkins from the assaults of the others. Then was seen the spectacle of a mob, clamoring for condign punishment upon the guilty man—a spectacle that has been witnessed many times since in Tuolumne, with all the added horrors of executions unauthorized and undeserved. In this case, however, the party of order triumphed. Atkins was taken away under guard and subjected to trial before Alcalde Frazier, when a verdict and sentence in the case were arrived at, "That Mr. Atkins be found guilty of murder and that he be fined five hundred dollars, and be ordered to leave the settlement, forthwith, under pain of death."

Using a donkey steam engine in a logging operation.

than ten thousand! And these vast crowds consisted almost wholly of men.

DISCOVERIES AT COLUMBIA. In March, 1850, the diggings at Columbia were found. This location, which has ever since been celebrated for the remarkable extent and richness of its gold deposits, is said by some to have been first discovered by a party of Mexicans from Santiago Hill, about a mile northwest of the new discovery. According to this account, these men were seen by a party of Americans, among whom were Dr. Thaddeus Hildreth, George, his brother, John Walker, William Jones and Alexander Carson. These, being informed that the place was rich, stayed to try their luck, and finding the result beyond expectations, they returned home for supplies and afterwards located permanently at the new discovery which [was] in March, 1850.

Their location is stated to have been four hundred feet above where a wooden suspension bridge was constructed about 1860. The new-comers took out fifteen pounds of gold dust daily for the first three days. The accounts of their success in the commencement disagree somewhat, but there is no occasion to doubt that it was immense. The immigration poured in from Sonora, Jamestown, Wood's Crossing, Jacksonville and other mining camps, as well as from Calaveras and Mokelumne Hill, all centering at Columbia. Wonderful stories were circulated, which spread into the remotest mining regions, causing a new impetus to be given to prospecting, with the result of abundant new discoveries. The trails were now crowded with men, in numbers before unknown, all traveling to the great centers of attraction, with their blankets on their backs, and if any diverged into side gulches or streams, they encountered the smoke of the pioneer or heard the rattle of the worker; or, below on the stream, they were surprised to behold the water muddied from the operations of some one who was before them, in a place where they thought no white man's foot had ever trod.

First of all who came to Columbia stands the name of Captain Avent. This gentleman had the good fortune to take out two and a half pounds of gold in his first day's work, and the second day secured to him one and a half pounds more. After this his average was twelve or fifteen ounces daily, until the failure of the water in July.

In the course of a few days, some thirty or forty remadas and cloth tents were erected in the immediate vicinity of the spot where the first strike was made, and lying along the south side of the creek. Among these occupants were Rochette, previously mentioned as having been at Yankee Hill, and then at Yorktown; James Letford, afterwards a resident of Sonora, and for many years Justice of the Peace; Major Farnsworth; Bonil-

Miner with a pan working in a hydraulic pit. Several black miners work behind him.

"The stabbing affair of yesterday caused a great excitement to prevail amongst the large concourse of miners and others assembled about the courthouse throughout the day.

When the officers brought out the prisoner for the purpose of conveying him to Sonora, people rushed upon them and carried off the object of their indignation, dragging him through the town to a tree, to a limb of which was already suspended the rope designed for his neck.

Without any preliminaries whatever, it was adjusted, and the next moment the prisoner was suspended in the air; but the limb broke, and it was then decided to give him a trial by jury.

While this was going on, the Sheriff of Sonora arrived, and attempted to rescue the prisoner from the hands of the populace, but was defeated.

Some five or six hours were occupied in the hearing the witnesses, &c. at the expiration of which time, the Sheriff succeeded in obtaining the malefactor, and carried him to Sonora."

Unknown San Francisco Newspaper

Crockett, appeared to keep him in a continual fever of irritation; for he was jealous, poor fellow and used to worry himself because there was ever a dozen or two of hairy miners gazing in a bewildered manner at Mrs. C.; but, if report speaks truly, the bonnet and boots of a "female" had been successfully exhibited in this region at a dollar a head (a glimpse of them being thought cheap even at that price), surely, therefore, Crockett might have excused the poor miners for regarding attentively the original article when presented gratis in the shape of a pretty woman.

Crockett carried a revolver of disproportionate size, he not being a large man, and this instrument he occasionally used upon provocation. A great number of miners had looked at Mrs. Crockett on the morning of our arrival, and her husband had not quite finished foaming at the mouth in consequence, when we entered the house. It was some time before he condescended to be civil; but having at length informed us that he was "so riled that his skin cracked," he added that he was a "devilish good fellow when he was 'right side up,'" and commanded us to drink with him. After this he procured us a most excellent breakfast, and, on the strength of our respectable appearance, allowed Mrs. Crockett to preside at this repast, which she did in a nervous manner, as if momentarily under the expectation of being shot.

Frank Marryat, early 1850s

Bradford's team with a load of 14,656 feet of lumber leaving the Empire Mill.

los, a Peruvian butcher. Charles Bassett came from Sonora and located on the north side of the creek, building there corrals for cows and sheep. He also opened a store, combining with it a restaurant, butcher shop and dairy. A part of his multifarious business was to peddle milk through the camp, it meeting a ready sale at one dollar per whisky bottle full. At such a price, he doubtless could afford to give the unwatered article.

By the middle of April following the discovery, not less than six thousand persons had located in the vicinity of Kennebec Hill—not all of whom were engaged in mining, but many in the dependent callings, as providers for those so engaged. A vast influx of gamblers had also arrived, and in a short time the number of faro banks in operation was reckoned at one hundred and forty-three, with capitals aggregating from one million to one and a half million of dollars! Gambling was the only amusement of the day, and was patronized accordingly. It was common to see sums reaching into the thousands staked on the turn of a card. As might be expected, with this sudden and great accession of population, with its great attendant twin evils of gambling and prostitution, much lawlessness was rife.

The honor of bestowing upon the new camp its present name, Columbia, is due to Majors Farnsworth and Sullivan and Mr. D. G. Alexander, who formally named the place on the 29th of April. The first tent put up on the present site of the town was occupied as a drinking and gambling saloon. Traveling musicians, a newly-found source of amusement, prospered beyond belief.

In the same month that witnessed the finding of Columbia, Springfield also took its rise. Its history is interesting, as evincing the energy and business talent that a woman displayed. In the latter part of March, Donna Josefa Valmaseda arrived from San Francisco. Previously she had been an influential resident of Guaymas, and in the war against the United States she had been a strong partisan of the latter country, giving aid and countenance to her country's enemies. Acting upon information furnished by her, the town of Guaymas was taken by the United States ships *"Cyane"* and *"Warren."* This course brought down upon her the vengeance of the Mexican Government, and she was compelled to fly to the protection of the American men-of-war, abandoning her property, which, according to usage, was confiscated. After the breaking out of the mining excitement she came to the mines, where she collected a number of her countrymen, whom she hired to mine at the place now known as Springfield—so called because of the remarkable spring which breaks out of the limestone at this place.

In a like manner, Donna Martinez settled at the camp which bore her name. Her location was in the midst of very rich deposits, and the camp increased rapidly, soon containing over

Among the mines in the Columbia Gulch, 1860s.

Several thefts had occurred, and the offending parties been severely punished after a fair trial. Some had been whipped and cropped, or maimed in some other way, and one or two of them hung. Two or three who had stolen largely had been shot down by the injured party, the general feeling among the miners justifying such a course when no other seemed available. We met near Livermore's Ranche, on the way to Stockton, [by] a man whose head had been shaved and his ears cut off, after receiving one hundred lashes, for stealing ninety-eight pounds of gold.

Bayard Taylor, 1849

Prospected with Captain Wadsworth at the Chilian diggings.

This is an open, level field, through which a stream formerly ran, but which now has so little water that many of the miners take the dirt to the river to be washed. Here was a large settlement of Chilinos, who have come from their own gold mines to try their fortune here. They often bring their families with them. I saw one family, the father of which, assisted by the older children, was "panning out" gold on a stream near his rude home made of hides. The mother was washing clothes, while the infant was swinging in a basket made fast to the branches overhead. An interesting girl of five years, with a tiny pick and spade, was digging in a hole, already sunk two feet, and putting the dirt in a pan, which she would take to the stream and wash, putting the scale or two of gold into a dipper a little larger than a thimble.

Daniel B. Woods,
January 7, 1850

Logging operation.

a thousand miners. Its downfall soon commenced, however, owing, in great part, to the Foreign Miners' Tax."

EFFECT OF THE MINERS' TAX. The Foreign Miners' Tax of twenty dollars per month went into operation on the 1st of June, 1850, by formal act of the Legislature. Its principal result was the almost immediate depopulation of certain camps, and the great injury of all, Sonora and Columbia suffered enormous losses, estimated, in the case of the former town, at four-fifths of the entire population; while the latter, whose growth had been so rapid, was reduced, through the Tax Law and the scarcity of water, to a community of only nine or ten persons. So it is credibly told. Of the seceding miners, some went to their homes in foreign lands, while others sought diggings in secluded places, where the obnoxious law would probably not be enforced. Others there were who resisted the collection of the tax by the officers appointed to collect it. The impression got about in Columbia that the foreigners meditated forcible reprisals on the Americans of that camp, resulting in a stampede from that town to Sonora of the whole American population, with the exception of Charles Bassett and a few others. A rumor having reached Sonora that Bassett was murdered, a band of armed men marched upon Columbia, headed by "Frenchy" Rochette, carrying the American flag. This statement is given upon the authority of Captain Stoddart, who further adds that the only destruction effected by this warlike band was upon the liquors and eatables of the said Bassett, who was nearly eaten out of house and home by his zealous friends.

Walter Murray, who subsequently became editor of the *Sonora Herald*, related graphically his impressions of the scenes consequent upon the first attempt to enforce the tax, and as a vivid picture of affairs at that time, it may be well to give it place in this work. He says: "It was a hot summer's day in June, when a man on horseback came tearing into the little encampment at Mormon Gulch, at full speed, evidently big with exciting intelligence. The miners, who happened to lie scattered in groups, talking over the events of the past week, eagerly rushed forward and gathered around the messenger, from whose broken exclamations they at length learned that there was something very like war approaching. It appeared that the Collector appointed by the State Government to receive the Foreign Miners' Tax had arrived at the county seat and issued his notice, calling upon all foreigners to come forward and pay their first month's assessment of twenty dollars. The attempt to collect this exorbitant impost put the immense foreign population, with whom the country was literally overrun, into a state of intense ferment. Meetings had been held upon the subject, inflammatory speeches had been made by Spanish and French

Machinery for pumping in Brown's Flat, 1860s.

We met a company of Californians about mid-day, on their return from the mines, and a more forlorn looking group never knocked at the gate of a pauper asylum. They were most of them dismounted, with rags fastened round their blistered feet, and with clubs in their hands, with which they were trying to force on their skeleton animals. They inquired for bread and meat: we had but little of either, but shared it with them. They took from one of their packs a large bag of gold, and began to shell out a pound or two in payment. We told them they were welcome; still they seemed anxious to pay, and we were obliged to be positive in our refusal. This company, as I afterwards ascertained, had with them over a hundred thousand dollars in grain gold. One of them had the largest lump that had yet been found; it weighed over twenty pounds; and he seemed almost ready to part with it for a mess of pottage. What is gold where there is nothing to eat?

Walter Colton,
Friday Sept. 29, 1849

On the afternoon of Wednesday, October 10, 1855, John H. Smith was shot dead by John S. Barclay, in the house on the corner of Main and Jackson streets, known as "Martha's Saloon." The house was of ill-fame, and Martha, the proprietress, of easy virtue. A few weeks before the murder occurred, she had, while on a business visit to Chinese Camp, there met and become enamored of young Barclay, marriage followed. Then returning to Columbia, the saloon was re-opened by the pair. Smith, a well-regarded sort of man, became embroiled in a quarrel with Martha, in consequence of having broken a pitcher. High words following, Barclay came to the rescue of his wife and shot Smith dead in the melee. Almost instantly the man was arrested and there placed in confinement.

A rush was made upon the jail, then held by Town Marshal Carder and a few police officers, who attempted to keep the mob back. A keg of powder was placed in position to blow the iron doors open, but fortunately it was not used. Crowbars, sledge-hammers and axes were applied instead, and the doors gave way. Simultaneously with their opening, the prisoner sprang out as if to make his escape by running; but he was instantly borne down and

continued in far right column

Wells Fargo & Company Express, Columbia, probably in the late 1800s. In the sidebar story on this page of the John H. Smith murder, it was in back of the Wells Fargo building above where "the prisoner was drawn up by his executioners overhead."

orators, and at length it appeared that some great demonstration had been made against the odious tax. The messenger averred that the county seat was in the hands of the excited foreign mob, numbering two or three thousand, all armed; that the safety of the place was menaced, and that the American citizens were fleeing from it. Furthermore, that the principal citizens had sent couriers to the surrounding camps asking for assistance.

"There had previously been so many rumors afloat of the expected insurrection of the Spanish-American population against the 'proprietors' of the country, and the 'boys' had in this way been kept in such a continual state of excitement, that the arrival of this intelligence operated at once like dropping a spark of fire in a tinder-box. Messengers were immediately dispatched hither and thither, calling upon the miners to assemble within an hour, at a given spot, on the way to the county seat, and the 'Gulch' was in a moment alive with busy, bustling men, getting out their rifles and pistols and preparing for the expected conflict.

"Being unarmed, and therefore forming no part of the expedition, I started, with a few others, ahead of the main body, which consisted of about one hundred and fifty-men; but all were so eager to get on, that it was with the utmost difficulty we could keep the smallest distance in advance. We met several persons on the way with later intelligence from the seat of war, but their accounts were all contradictory, some saying that the excitement was all over; others, that there was immediate need of our services. However, we pressed on, determined not to stop short of the place for which we set out. On arriving at a camp of Mexicans, one mile short of our destination, we were surprised to see its motley inhabitants very quietly seated in front of their brush hovels, playing monte and other games, as if nothing unusual had transpired. They, too, were none the less surprised to see the column of armed men advancing on them in close order—especially as they heard the general yell that was joined in by the American party as they advanced toward Sonora. Reassured by this apparent calm, I hurried on to the town, reaching it five or ten minutes in advance of the party. All appeared quiet and peaceful as ever. I waited to see the little procession enter town. Soon it came along, headed by fife and drum—which, by this time, had been scared up—and, first and foremost, by the glorious stars and stripes, borne aloft and waved very gracefully to and fro by an inhabitant of the big city. Thus, with music sounding and banners waving, the little band marched through the whole length of town, vociferously cheered

carried by the excited mass up-town.

Sheriff Stuart arrived. Reaching the ground, he, laying his hand upon him, demanded him in the name of the law. Some one immediately seized Stuart by the throat, while others rudely laid hold of him, throwing him back violently. Getting free after, he rushed towards the prisoner, who was then under the flume with a rope around his neck. He made ineffectual endeavors to cut the rope, but while so engaged he received a heavy blow on the head from the butt of a pistol, while others laid violent hands upon him. Barely was his life preserved.

The prisoner was drawn up by his executioners overhead, ascending with a savage yell from the multitude. No precautions had been taken to pinion the victim, and he, reaching upward, seized with desperate grip the rope, above his head, and held on. To break his hold, those above drew him up and let him down suddenly, several times, but still his powerful grasp held good. One of the executioners, leaning over the flume, called out, "Let go, you — fool, let go!" Finally his strength gave out. Drawing up his legs, he gave a few convulsive movements, and then hung straight. All was over, for body and soul had parted.

Columbia from the public school, 1860s.

Interior of the Golden Gate Mine hoist room.

On a Sabbath evening some of our best citizens sit down in front of a drinking house and sing such songs as "Dearest Mae," "O, Susanna," and "Uncle Ned." Sunday is a great day here. Business is more active and there is more frolic on this day than in the whole of the other six. In the morning we have public auctions, in the afternoon the bullfight and the circus, and in the evening the circus and Dr. Collier's troupe of Model Artists, together with numerous fandango rooms, dance houses, and scores of gambling halls.

Enos Christman,
Sunday, August 25, 1850

all the way by the American inhabitants, who turned out "en mass" to see them. On arriving at the other end of town, the word, 'Forward, by file left; march,' was given, when the foremost man found himself headed off by a well-stocked bar, whereat each one, as he arrived, was 'liquored up.' They were then countermarched through town again, the same hospitality being extended at several places on the route, and were at length halted in front of the principal hotel, where the Collector of Foreign Miners' Taxes made them a speech. After speaking for about ten minutes, he informed them they might rest that night and the morrow `to business.' Accordingly, all was soon bustle and scurry at the big hotel; waiters went hurrying to and fro, and all was busy preparation for a general meal. After an hour or so, which seemed an age to the hungry miners, the long tables were loaded down with eatables, and the word given to fall to; and fall to they did, in a manner only to be paralleled in California and in the mines.

"After supper, the arms were all stored away in a building temporarily devoted to the purpose of a guard-house. A watch was set during the night, with regular reliefs; patrols were organized, and the city speedily assumed the appearance of being under martial law.

"Many and various were the reports circulated on that eventful night. According to some, the town was to be attacked and set fire to at different points. Rumors of assassination and massacre were fearfully rife; but at length morning dawned, and the country was discovered to be safe. Breakfast was spread out for us at the same hospitable board, and then all were assembled on the main street, and divided into companies, headed each by its own captain and lieutenant. A column of some three hundred armed men, in all, was thus formed, which, headed by the Collector and Sheriff of the county, commenced its march through the disaffected camps.

"Alas, as we marched along, what a scene of confusion and terror marked our way! Mexicans, Chilenos, men, women and children—were all packed up and moving, bag and baggage. Tents were being pulled down, houses and hovels gutted of their contents; mules, horses and burros were being hastily packed, while crowds upon crowds were already in full retreat. What could have been the object of our assembly, except as a demonstration of power and determination, I know not; but if intended as an engine of terror, it certainly had its desired effect, for it could be seen painted upon every countenance and impelling every movement of the affrighted population. However, on we marched, through this dire confusion, peacefully pursuing our way, until we reached what was deemed to be the headquarters

Columbia, the reservoirs, 1860s.

Bargained with Mr Peyton to transport my freight to Sonora or Shaws Flat for 3 1/2 cts pr lb. Also settled with Capt Johnson paying $6. per ton freight, my passage free. Loaded my freight on a 4 mule team and started for Sonora at 3 P.M. Got stuck in a mudhole, but finally arrived at the 14 mile House where we put up for the night, although I slept on the load of goods.

Stephen Chapin Davis,
April 10, 1852

On Friday, December 8, 1854, Robert Bruce was hanged at Sonora, for the murder of a Mexican Indian boy, of sixteen. The murder took place in Sonora the previous year, and was committed during a brawl in a fandango-house. Bruce was immediately arrested, tried and convicted, but owing to the law's delays, more than a year passed before his execution. In the meanwhile the criminal, in company with another convicted felon, named Hayes, broke jail, and, aided by the darkness, got as far as the vicinity of Burns' Ferry, where they were discovered by the pursuing party. In the attempt to arrest them, Bruce was severely wounded. Being returned to the county jail, a day was set for the execution, on which Bruce was to suffer.

On Friday, the people from the surrounding camps began at an early hour to make their way to the place of execution, and by noon the largest assemblage thus far seen in Tuolumne County had gathered. Just at noon Bruce was taken from the jail, placed in a carriage, in which the Sheriff and other officers were seated, and escorted to the place of execution, by the two military companies of Tuolumne, the Sonora Grays and the Columbia Fusiliers. Arriving at the gallows, the doomed man alighted from the carriage and ascended the steps to the platform, with a firm and determined tread, exhibiting a stoical indifference to life, which he maintained throughout the whole proceedings. His hands and feet were tied, the rope adjusted around his neck, and at fifteen minutes before one o'clock the trapdoor fell, and all that remained of Robert Bruce was a corpse suspended from the gallows.

Mine hoist, probably at the Golden Gate Mine.

Courtesy Tuolumne County Museum

of malcontent—a camp containing some thousand Spanish Americans—about four miles from the county seat. Here we halted for the last time (liquored up, of course, for it was the month of June, and the roads were dry and dusty), and, after being paraded through the main street, and held for an hour or more in readiness, awaiting the report of certain officials dispatched to inquire into the truth of a rumor that a foreign flag had been hoisted somewhere in the vicinity, were finally discharged. Every man then fired his rifle in the air, reloaded his piece, and started homeward, each on his own particular way. I, too, started for the Gulch, and until I reached there never lost sight of the train of fugitives scattered along the roads in every direction. Some were going north, some south. The great body were probably bound for home; some by way of the sea, others by way of Los Angeles and the Great Desert. Others, again, were scattering themselves over the country, to commence the career of bloodshed and cold-blooded atrocity which for months afterward stained the pages of California history. Even those who were bound for home often left behind them, along the way, bloody traces of their deep-set hatred to Americans, or, perhaps, their natural thirst for massacre and pillage. When, however, the evil effects of the tax were clearly seen, even the most pronounced of its former advocates became dubious about the wisdom of the measure; and those who only tolerated it as a measure of political wisdom, finding it the precursor of serious evils.

Affairs are represented as remaining in a state of comparative inaction until the foreign element began to return to and work in the mines; and by the next spring a large number of those who left had come back and resumed operations. But neither of the two principal camps ever recovered the entire bulk of their population.

Martinez, lying a short distance east of Columbia, was a distinctively Spanish camp, named, as has been already said, in honor of Doña Martinez. It had been discovered previously, and up to the time of her arrival had been known as the "New" or "Spanish" camp. The lady seems to have been influential and wealthy, as she brought with her a large number of "peons" (Mexican servitors) and considerable money and jewelry. Apropos of the latter, the Mexicans attach great importance to the possession of jewelry. Indeed, the predominant characteristics of Mexican families are children, jewelry and dirt. Doña Martinez had very good success in her mining operations having taken up a considerable tract of ground, on which her bondmen were set to work.

SETTLEMENT OF COLUMBIA. Columbia, as already noted, sprang into existence in the month of March, 1850. New, and very rich deep diggings were struck there, together with

Columbia Gulch from the west, 1860s.

> Many of the Americans employed Sonorians and Indians to work for them, giving them half the gold and finding them in provisions. Notwithstanding the enormous prices of every article of food, these people could be kept for about a dollar daily—consequently those who hire them profited handsomely.
>
> Bayard Taylor, 1849

Parrott's Ferry which was in operation from the early 1850s to about 1900.

The year 1856 was the murder of Bond by McCauley. Bond resided at the Flat, where he followed the occupation of miner. His murderer, Edward McCauley, was a large, strong fellow, whose occupation, if he had any beyond quarreling and fighting, is not set down. Andrew J. Carr and Tom McCauley, his aiders and abettors in the murder, were of precisely similar type. In the course of a trial for larceny, Bond had been an important witness against the McCauleys, incurring their bitterest enmity.

Bond was sitting with friends in a saloon when Ed. McCauley entered, [he] was met at the door by Carr, who pushed him backward into the room, and a scuffle ensued. Bond shot Carr, Ed McCauley approached Bond from behind and stabbed him with a bowie-knife. Being released from his enemies, Bond started homewards, and reaching his cabin, died within ten minutes. Carr dying at nearly the same minute.

The trial ended in sentencing Tom McCauley to State's prison for ten years, while the more guilty Ed was consigned to the gallows, meeting that merited fate on December 11, 1857.

very extensive, though poorer, surface deposits; and the people from surrounding camps and elsewhere, flocked there in great numbers. At once the place (first called American Camp, and afterwards Columbia) contained several thousand inhabitants, and the greatest success was achieved in mining, although by the most primitive means. With the giving out of the water, however, the population as rapidly fell off to a score, more or less, who alone remained of all the vast multitude.

The winter of 1850-51 set in with the most sanguine expectations, but the miners left shared in the general disappointment at the insufficient fall of rain, scarcely enough falling to enable the ground to be prospected. Still, some made wages by carrying their dirt a long distance to water. The general success of these opened the eyes of the people of the surrounding camps to the possibilities thus indicated, and their attention was drawn also to the extent of these grounds. It was seen that there was not a foot of ground upon the immense flat, from Santiago Flat to Tim's Springs, and from Shaw's Flat to the hill overhanging the Stanislaus, but was rich enough to pay for working, if water could be obtained for that purpose; and that there were hundreds of ravines and gulches that contained gold.

These tremendous resources, richer in kind than elsewhere found upon the earth's surface, drew again the swarms of people who were to make Columbia the typical placer mining camp of the world.

From the latest date mentioned, the growth of the camp was steady and permanent. From the obscure location, containing perhaps half a hundred miners, who washed a limited amount of dirt in water brought in barrels, or laboriously carried the gravel to the distant springs, the town grew by successive additions from every camp and from every country. With them came artificial wants. The rude and primitive modes of mining would no longer answer. The winter rains could not be depended on, yet were taken advantage of to the utmost extent. At Christmas time in '51, a stream, fed only by the rains, was flowing through the streets of Columbia. Fifty "toms" intercepted its progress, and not a drop of the precious fluid but was made to do its work over and again, in separating the yellow particles from the gravel.

But such resources as the temporary streams, supplied from the clouds, were necessarily of small avail in the business of gold extraction, and so a move was made to speedily introduce an abundant and steady supply of water. The project was no less than turning a branch of the Stanislaus River into the table land in the vicinity of the town.

The boulder range at Krupps Ranch, 1860s.

The [Indian] men and boys were busy with their bows and arrows. A difficulty had arisen between this tribe and one not far remote, and they were expecting an attack. Though the less powerful tribe of the two, they seemed not the least dismayed. The old men looked stern and grave, but the boys were full of glee as if mustering for a deer-hunt.

Walter Colton,
Tuesday, Oct. 3, 1849

Unidentified blacksmith shop.

Prices current [1850], prepared expressly for Sonora, by Peter Mehen, merchant:

Flour, per cwt $17 to $18

Barley, per cwt. 16 to 18

Mess Pork, per cwt. 45 to 50

Prime Pork, per cwt 35 to 38

Bacon and Hams, per lb 55 to 60c.

Lard, per lb 60 to 75c.

Rice, per lb. 18 to 20c.

Brown Sugar, per lb 36 to 40c.

Coffee, green, per lb 60 to 75c.

Coffee, brown, per lb 80 to 90c.

Sperm Candles, per lb 95 to $ 1

Brandy, per gallon $ 2 to $ 4

Gin, per case 10 to 11

Whisky, per gallon 2 to 4

Claret, per box 10 to 11

With men of that day, to plan was to act, and the great work was commenced by the incorporation of the "Tuolumne County Water Company," and the construction of a suitable ditch, or race, was immediately begun.

Joseph Dance, Esq., was chosen President of the new company, and General Benard its Engineer. On July 1, 1851, the work was commenced at Summit Pass. Though financially embarrassed, the company persevered, and finally help was given by D. O. Mills & Co., bankers at Sacramento, who afterwards established a branch house at Columbia.

The company turned the water of Five Mile Creek into Columbia on the 1st day of May, 1852, and in August of that year the ditch was completed to the South Fork of the Stanislaus.

During the succeeding autumn, the town site was laid out, and building proceeded with great rapidity. Split boards were the favorite material used in the construction of the simple houses of that date, and their consequently easy and ready combustibility proved the ruin of the town on more than one subsequent occasion.

From the *Gazette*, of January 22, 1853, the following scraps of mining news are copied, in order to show the general status of that branch of industry at a time when Columbia and vicinity were at a high pitch of prosperity:

"Although we have not visited many of the camps this week, yet we are pleased to learn that the mines generally are doing better than at any time since last summer. Columbia Gulch is crowded with "toms," and the men in many of the claims are making wages."

"The Coyote Diggings, on the hill between Columbia and Gold Springs, are paying, in many places, as high as fifty and one hundred dollars per day to the man. New holes are sunk, and new strikes are made almost daily. Hundreds, however, sink holes and find nothing, as the course of the leads is as hard to find out as it is to discover the true feelings and sentiments of a heartless coquette; still the miners work ahead as if they expected to find thousands of dollars of the precious metal in every hole they sink."

"In Hatch's garden they are sinking holes in every direction, which in a few cases pay well."

"At Gold Springs, where thousands of dollars were carted and washed out previous to the rainy season, many of the miners are discovering better pay dirt under the claims that had been previously worked out."

"On Shaw's Flat, many of the miners are making good wages, and, as at every other place, hundreds are doing little or nothing."

Hydraulic mining in Columbia, 1860s.

"Big Strike.—Two Mexicans, Gregorio Contrares and his partner, commenced sinking a hole on Wednesday last, below Campo Seco, on the other side of Sullivan's Gulch, near Page's Ranch, and struck a pocket from which they took out, by 12 o'clock on Thursday, $5,700; one piece of which weighed eight pounds. In one hour they washed out two hundred ounces in their Mexican bateas. The lucky Mexicans have bought fine suits of clothes, and intend vamosing for home in a few days."

The Gazette

About this time a Mexican named Joaquin, a notorious desperado and leader of a gang, who, by murder and robbery, were a terror to the country, had been traced to the neighborhood of San Andres. One evening, while at supper in a hotel, he, being unknown to any about the place, seated himself at the supper table. Back of him was an open window, and some twenty feet below was a water ditch probably ten feet wide, and on the opposite side were piles of broken rock. He faced the door and windows, which opened upon the street, and as I sat nearly opposite to him at the table, my back was towards the door. He was a fine looking man and I had no idea who he was, but judged from his appearance that he was a Mexican, and wishing to improve every opportunity to practice my newly acquired Spanish, I gave him the usual salutation, "¿Como le va, Señor?" (How do you do, Sir?").

"Muy bien, ¿De donde V.?" (Very well, where are you from?).

"Del norte, cerca de Coloma" (From the north, near Coloma).

As neither he nor any of his gang had operated in that region, he was evidently sure that I had no suspicion as to who he was, and so the conversation ran on.

Suddenly he arose, turned to the window, and as several shots were

continued in far right column

Miners working at their flume.

"At Springfield, Santiago, Brown's Flat, Summit Pass, Yankee Hill, and the various gulches around Columbia, many of the claims are paying astonishingly, and the deeper the miners work down, in many cases, the richer they find the dirt."

"On Experimental Gulch, although it was supposed to have been worked out last season, many of the miners are making money. On a claim owned by Messrs. Beals & Hussey, one piece was taken out, last week, which weighed four and a half ounces; and another was found the same week weighing over two ounces. This claim pays ten dollars a day to the man."

"Although many of the miners are doing well, yet there are hundreds who work equally hard and live as frugal and economical as men can well live, that are not clearing expenses."

The *Gazette* concludes with the following sage remarks, which, by the way, have proved applicable through all the succeeding years since they were penned, and even now would prove worthy of consideration:

"If miners would content themselves and remain on a claim, even if it did not pay them more than four or five dollars per day, the chances are in favor of their doing better than by wandering from place to place and spending all they have made, prospecting. How many thousands would now have their piles, and be ready to leave the mines, had they contented themselves to work on the first claims they located. Every miner who came to this country in '49 or '50 can now look back and see hundreds of instances where he could have made a fortune, if he had contented himself to remain where he was, instead of going in search of 'Golden Lakes' and 'Golden Bluffs.'"

The New England Water Company, it seems, from the pages of the Gazette, had conveyed the waters of a spring, distant one mile from town, through wooden pipes underground, to a reservoir containing four thousand gallons. Thence it was taken in water-carts throughout the town, supplying families at the then cheap rate of five cents per bucketful.

The enterprise was said to pay extremely well, and later, iron pipes were laid down, capable of supplying a town of twenty thousand inhabitants. By the year 1856, hydrants connecting with these pipes had been put in position, from which streams could be thrown eighty feet high, affording a great safeguard against fire.

Additional matters relating to the progress of Columbia is to be gleaned from the advertising columns of the *Gazette*. There are to be seen the advertisements of Wells, Fargo & Co., who announce a daily express to and from San Francisco, Stockton, Jamestown, Sonora, Columbia, Murphy's, and Mokelumne Hill, connecting with a daily express from Mount Ophir, Mariposa and all other prominent places south. Also, to all parts of the Atlantic States and Europe, as well as the

fired, sprang out. Whether he was hit I do not know, but it was a desperate jump across the ditch upon those rocks; and although it was hardly dark, he disappeared in a large growth of chaparral just beyond and made his escape. The sheriff's posse had surrounded the house except on that side, not thinking it possible that anyone could pass in safety from that window.

Seated with my back toward the entrance, I had not seen the attacking party; but there were those who had observed me in conversation with Joaquin, and under suspicion, I was held until the pursuers returned, and then put through a rigid examination.

Mr. Ford explained whence, how, and when I came to San Andres; but his wounded hand excited distrust, and for awhile both of us were in serious danger; not from the sheriff and his posse, who were satisfied with our innocence, but from the unreasoning crowd, insisting that we belonged to Joaquin's gang and, of course, ought to be lynched. I am sure that one who has never faced such a condition can have no idea of the situation. However, we were both young; certainly not hardened criminals; and as I could refer to well known men in Coloma and Sacramento, we were at last entirely relieved from suspicion.

Rev John Steele, 1850

Miner working with a rocker.

George Palmer, a miner by profession, was eating his supper at the "Arkansas Hotel," in the northern part of Sonora, when John Thornley, otherwise called Wilson, a man of bad character, already the slayer of one man, entered the hotel, and approaching Palmer, revolver in hand, ordered him from the house. Palmer, begging him not to shoot, acquiesced, and leaving the hotel walked a dozen paces, when Thornley fired two shots at him, the second of which inflicted a death wound.

The murderer fled, and, aided by a dark night, made his escape to Green Springs, and was there taken by Sheriff Work and Deputy Sheriff Vyse, and lodged in jail at Sonora. As soon as it became known that he had been captured, a people's meeting was held and a feeble attempt made to get possession of the prisoner. Meanwhile the culprit was taken before Judge Tuttle, and his examination commenced. Six Deputy Constables were appointed to aid the Sheriff to maintain strict order. The prisoner was committed to jail to await his trial by the District Court.

The *Herald*, describing these occurrences, laments the insecure condition of the county jail at that time, a fear that proved well founded, for the miscreant broke jail shortly after, and escaped to Los Angeles. After several months he was recaptured, brought back to Sonora, tried and acquitted!

W. H. Barron and Sons Dry Goods and Groceries, Soulsbyville, c. 1895.

Northern Mines. Wm. Daegener was the agent at Columbia, and the office of the Company was at the American Hotel.

Adams & Co. announce at the same time (February, 1854) the removal of their office to the building occupied by C. P. M."

D. Brown, on Main street, where they had erected a fire and thief proof vault, "one of the best in California," and were prepared to receive gold dust and coin on deposit, paying also the highest rates for the former.

James Mills & Co., Bankers (Branch of D. O. Mills & Co., of Sacramento) did business on the corner of Main and Fulton streets, where they had "one of Herring's largest fire proof safes, enclosed in a commodious and secure vault." A peculiarity of this firm was that they were closed to business on Sundays, an additional evidence of the improvement in morality, before mentioned.

W. G. Vanarsdall, of the American Hotel, announces a new opening of his house, he having fitted it up in elegant style, incidentally mentioning that Kelty & Co.'s stages leave his doors four times a day, bound for Sonora.

The Trustees of the Tuolumne Water Company declared, at that time, a dividend of thirty-two dollars on each of their two hundred and seventy-five shares. This is signed by W. H. Clark, President, and R. A. Robinson, Secretary.

Others, whose business affairs appear in this and other issues of the *Gazette*, were T. R. Taylor, Counsellor at Law, office on Broadway, one door below old Court-room; J. T. Fish, Attorney and Notary Public, office corner of Broadway and Washington streets; H. Stone, tin shop; Andrew Hochmouth, meat market; Gischel & Hildeubrand, "Boston Bakery;" Fleming & Hedden, blacksmiths and wagon-makers; John Leary, auctioneer, Broadway, four doors north of Columbia Exchange; Dr. Fields' " Columbia Drug Store;" John A. Cardinell & Co., St. Charles Restaurant, corner of Broadway and Washington streets; John G. Sparks, law office, Broadway, near Court-room; Messrs. Sotrr & Marshall, butchers, Columbia market, corner Main and Fulton streets; Eagle Cottage (boarding house), William Odenheimer and Captain McLane; Columbia Brewery and Syrup Manufactory, P. Rocker & Co.

THE FIRE OF 1854. On July 10, 1854, Columbia was ravaged by the most serious and extensive conflagration that had ever occurred there, and with the exception of the burning of Sonora, the most serious fire that Tuolumne county had ever witnessed. It broke out near Clark's hotel, on Broadway, and consumed nearly every house on Broadway, Fulton, Washing-

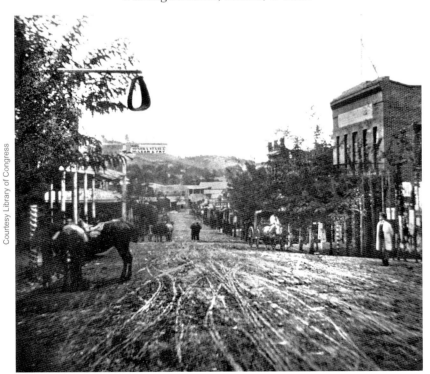

Washington Street, Sonora c. 1865.

At 6 A.M. the team started in company with 12 or 15 others, one of which was loaded with Chinese goods and followed by about 50 Celestials on their way to the mines. At 10 A.M. my team got into a mudhole, and in pulling out, broke the axle. So we were oblidged to unload and get another waggon which detained us 2 hours. At 7 P.M. arrived at the "Mountain Brow" 3 miles north of the Stanislaus where we remained for the night. I slept on the waggon, and as my money is getting short I subsist on my crackers & cheese, so that my expenses are little or nothing. The Chinese camp here also, and make night hideous by their uncivilized "powwow," which was kept up all night.

Stephen Chapin Davis,
April 11, 1852

Group of Digger Indians in front of store on Washington Street, Sonora, 1895.

A Texan whose name was Rose, was one day at the Indian camp, when words were exchanged between him and the chief, "Lotario," ending in the fatal stabbing of the latter. The Indians present immediately killed Rose, by shooting him with arrows. The whites in the neighborhood rushed to arms, and without inquiring into the cause of the trouble, attacked the natives with firearms, killing two and wounding several. This fracas resulted in the destruction of all relations between the whites and the aborigines for a considerable time. The red men were finally pacified, however, through the exertions of Mr. Savage.

ton, State and Main streets, the only notable exception being Donald & Parsons' fireproof building on the corner of Main and Washington streets, which escaped the general destruction.

The mails at the Post Office were saved, as also was the express matter of Adams & Co. and Wells, Fargo & Co.

Losses made up a sum total of half a million of dollars.

Although almost entirely obliterated by the devouring flames, the town did not remain extinct, but with true California enterprise, immediately began the work of rebuilding, while yet the smoke arose from the unconsumed fragments. By noon of the next day, thirty buildings were sufficiently far advanced to admit of occupancy, and many others were well under way. Quite a number of the new structures that were begun were intended to be fireproof, and were of a very substantial character.

COLUMBIA IN 1857. Columbia's second great fire occurred on August 25, 1857, and even exceeded the terrible conflagration of '54, in extent of damage. Breaking out in a Chinese dwelling on the north side of Jackson street, the flames could not be stayed, and within a very short time the whole northern part of the town was burned. Buildings which were supposed to have been fire-proof, disappeared like magic, shaking faith in brick walls.

During the fire a most fearful incident occurred: this was the explosion of a large quantity of gunpowder in the store of H. N. Brown, resulting in the instant death of five men.

The well organized and efficient fire companies of Columbia, together with assistance from Sonora, did excellent service in saving property, until the water in the hydrants gave out, rendering their services useless.

The total footed up a round half million of dollars.

It does not seem that the fire was an actual detriment. At least it did not detract from the enterprise of the citizens, but on the contrary stimulated it, for the newspapers of the succeeding months report a period of activity and energy far in excess of the two or three preceding years.

Shortly after the fire the Trustees took action against the Chinese element, debarring them from residing within the corporate limits of Columbia. [They were considered] dangerous to the safety of the town, and injurious to the good character and public name of the corporation.

One of the more pretentious structures which grew up after the fire was Cardinell's Theatre. It was two stories in height, the lower portion to be occupied by stores, saloons, etc., while the theatre was in the second story. It contained a dress circle or gallery running around three sides of the room, and was ar-

The Tuolumne County Courthouse in Sonora, c. 1865.

The action of vigilance committees and lynch law proceedings were less favorably looked upon, and when in 1851 a man named Thomas Jones was given fifty lashes on the bare back, with the added ignominy of being branded on the hip, and half his head shaved, public feeling took sides with the culprit, and his alleged offense—horse-stealing—although looked upon as a grave crime in those days, was thought to have been too severely expiated.

Loaded ore cart at the Golden Gate Mine, 1894.

The year 1855 was known as the grasshopper year. At times the light of the sun was obscured by clouds of "hoppers" filling the atmosphere. Their appearance continued for several weeks, and during the time nearly every green thing was eaten or destroyed by them. Grain fields and fruit trees in many instances were ruined. The course of their flight was westward and they finally disappeared in the ocean. One curious feature during their appearance was that they became the food supply of the Indians. The Indians would dig funnel shaped holes, to the depth of two or three feet in the earth, when bucks, women and children would form extended lines, and with willow bushes and old sacks drive the "hoppers" into the holes. Then they would fill their sacks and carry them to their rancheries for food. They were regarded as a great luxury, to be eaten raw, cooked, or dried.

David Augustus Shaw, 1850

ranged with nearly every advantage of a first-class theatre. The space between floor and ceiling was twenty feet, and the stage was thirty feet deep. The seats in the pit were removable, thus allowing the use of the auditorium as a ballroom on occasion, furnishing the largest dancing hall in the mines. The next modern improvement which the growing importance of the town suggested was the introduction of lighting by gas.

The gas-works were situated on Gold street, in the rear of the Broadway Hotel. The price of the illuminating material to consumers was fifteen cents per each burner for one evening; and in consideration of the privilege of laying mains through the streets, the Company agreed to furnish fifteen lights gratis to the city, besides lighting the churches, schools, and other public buildings. The street lamp-posts were to be of cedar, turned, and painted black.

Columbia was incorporated as a city on April 9, 1857.

Sonora

On the morning of July 4, 1850, appeared the first issue of the *Sonora Herald*, the first newspaper published in the California mines. It is interesting to observe the straits to which the publishers were put by reason of the scarcity of material. Wrapping paper was used in at least one case of necessity. The *Sonora Herald* existed until the year 1859, pursuing its course successfully. The price of a year's subscription is the rather startling figure of twenty dollars. In the first number of the *Herald* is to be seen an advertisement of the first stage line from Sonora to Stockton. The coaches were to leave the latter town on Monday and Thursday of each week. The fare was twenty dollars. Judge J.G. Marvin advertises his express line, which has started, connecting San Francisco with the southern mines. People who wish their letters collected and delivered once a week, are advised where to leave orders, and the following price is appended: $2 00 for each letter, when we pay postage; $1 50 when postage is prepaid; $1 00 for a drop letter; 25 cents for newspapers; 50 cents for mailing each letter in San Francisco; 30 cents for mailing each newspaper in San Francisco.

A RIOT IN SONORA. The deep feeling of jealousy and distrust that had, through one cause and another, been daily increasing, with its attendant ills of threats and violence, culminated in July of this year in a series of extraordinary outrages, and the lynching of certain parties, and the attempted execution of others. Nothing could exceed the state of excitement into which Sonora, and the Southern Mines in general, were thrown by certain events which took place near the county seat during the fortnight ending July 20. The circumstances which gave rise to such a condition of affairs were these: On the morning of Wednesday, July 10, four Americans arrived in Sonora, having in custody three Mexican Indians and a Mexican, named Pablo

Sonora around 1865.

"This world is all a fleeting show, For man's illusion given," for next day the rain poured down incessantly, the river rose rapidly, and by night the artificial dam was washed adrift, and the hard labor of weeks was destroyed in a few hours. oh, how delightful to a wayworn traveler to meet with even one person that exhibits a little of the milk of human kindness.

I breakfasted on fresh deer steaks, fresh mountain trout, hot rolls and excellent coffee, for which I paid $1.50. I observed a number of Indians loitering about, and was informed, that from them mine host procured his deer and trout.

Luther Melanchthon Schaeffer, 1849

Lunch with a view. This group of well-dressed ladies and gentlemen take advantage of the view from Bald Mountain in Sonora, mid 1890s.

Fuller and his victim were partners in mining, at the Flat. For awhile they lived together in harmony, but a difficulty arose in relation to Fuller's taking some of the partnership funds to gamble with. Later, the quarrel was augmented by a dispute concerning the possession of a fly-tent. Finally, these troubles culminated in a fist-fight, Fuller being decidedly worsted. Being thrown, he yet retained his hold on his stronger partner, who, in order to release himself, threw hot coals and ashes in his opponent's face as he lay upon him. Both arose, and Fuller procuring his rifle, shot at Newby, who was retreating, and gave him a mortal wound.

In spite of a plain case of murder being made out, the jury brought in a verdict of manslaughter, and fixed the penalty at nine months' imprisonment and a fine of one hundred dollars!

Martinez, Dionisio Ochoa, Gabino Jesus, and Ruiz Molina; and there Port immediately became circulated that a horrible murder, the third or fourth within a week, had been committed at Green Flat Diggings, about eight miles from town. Immediately the entire population of Sonora crowded in front of the house of Justice Barry, and demanded the particulars of the affair; and as some who possessed, or thought they possessed, the desired information, related the horrible details, the angry exclamations and flashing eyes of the mob told plainly of a deep determination to avenge the crime that their countrymen had suffered. The prisoners were arraigned before Justice Barry, and then commenced a scene of tumult and confusion then unparalleled. In the tumult the predominant cries were, "string them up!" "hang 'em!" "we'll have no mistake this time!" and a rope was produced and a knot tied in it, that there be no delay. The utmost efforts of the officers of the Court produced no impression on the crowd. George Work, the redoubtable Sheriff, a man of the steadiest courage and iron nerve, who never quailed in the discharge of his duty, was as one without influence on the reckless mob. Judge Marvin, Associate Justice of the Court of Sessions, addressed the people, but ineffectually. While these things were transpiring in front of the house, Justice Barry was engaged in taking the deposition of the four Americans who brought in the prisoners. They testified that on the previous evening a Mexican boy had informed them that two Americans had been murdered at the Green Flat Diggings, but they took no notice of the report. In the morning, however, another Mexican called and corroborated the boy's statement. Witnesses immediately proceeded to the spot indicated, and found there the four prisoners, in the act of burning the tent and the bodies of two men. They were immediately taken into custody, and brought to Sonora. There also appeared in evidence the shovel and pickax belonging to the prisoners. The defense set up by the prisoners was to the effect that it was a custom of their countrymen to burn the dead; that the bodies, having been dead several days, had become offensive through decomposition, and in order to remove the nuisance, they attempted to burn them. The prisoners, of whom the three Indians were described as uncouth, and the Mexican, on the contrary, of gentle and pleasing appearance, maintained a calm and becoming demeanor that aroused the sympathies of some in the audience. By this time it was resolved by the authorities, as the best that could be done, to immediately impanel a jury and proceed with the trial. But Mr. McAlpin and others who were drawn upon the jury, refused to serve, and the case became still more perplexing. While in consultation the officers had withdrawn, and the opportunity was taken by the people to elect a Judge from among themselves; and Peter Mehen was chosen for the office. A rope was then put around the neck of each of the supposed culprits, and they were led to a hill in the vicinity of the town, where the trial was commenced anew. A jury was impaneled, the trial concluded, and the prisoners sentenced to be hanged. The rope

Chinese miners in Columbia, c. 1865.

> The long bar of a saloon is always actively engaged, and the bar-keeper must be prepared for all demands in all languages. Here he serves a Mexican group with agua diente; now he allays a Frenchman's thirst with absinthe, in the pouring out of which he displays much art; again he attends with rapidity to the demands of four Americans, whose orders embrace respectively, a "gin-cocktail," a "brandy-straight," a "claret sangaree," and a "Queen Charlotte;" these supplied, he must respond with alacrity to the call of a cockney miner, whose demand is heard even above the surrounding din: "Hain't you got no hale nor porter?"
>
> Frank Marryat, early 1850s

Divall's Camp, 1895.

The colonel turned suddenly to me, his hands being occupied with his ribbons, with "I guess there's a flea on my neck;" and I perceived on the instant that there was a large, broad-shouldered insect, refreshing himself on the place indicated, in apparent oblivion of all around. As in duty bound as box seat, I pulled him off and put him to death, the colonel remarking, as he nodded his thanks, that he generally had three or four of the "darned cattle to put through" in that fashion during the journey.

Frank Marryat, early 1850s

was passed over the limb of a tree, and the Mexican, chosen as the first victim, was given a few moments in which to pray. He knelt down, prayed affectingly, kissed the cross he had in his bosom, and with the gentlest resignation gave himself into the hands of his executioners. Another moment, and Judges Marvin, Tuttle and Radcliffe, together with William Ford, County Clerk, and others arrived, and by flinging themselves boldly into the crowd, succeeded in effecting a diversion that enabled the proper officers to regain possession of the prisoners, and contrary to expectation they succeeded in lodging them in jail.

The prisoners remained in the jail, without any indication of an attempt at mob law, until the following Monday, which was the day on which it had been and understood their trial was to come off. On the morning of this day a mob of eighty men, armed with rifles and shotguns, and marching in military style, and presenting a most imposing appearance, arrived from Green Flat, intent on seeing justice done on the murderers of their neighbors. Besides this band, there poured in from Jamestown, Shaw's Flat, Columbia, Woods' Creek, from mountain, gulch and ravine, hundreds of miners, armed with rifles, shotguns, revolvers, knives, lances, etc. All were highly excited, and would not submit to delay. They halted opposite the Court House, when Judge Tuttle appeared and addressed the throng, urging them to be moderate, and assuring them that justice would be done.

In consequence of a rumor that the Mexican prisoners had colleagues in a camp several miles distant, Sheriff Work proceeded there with a posse of twenty men and arrested nearly the whole adult portion of the inhabitants, numbering one hundred and ten men; whom he brought to town and confined in a corral, under a strong guard.

During Monday evening several hundred men arrived in town, swelling the ranks of the mob to two thousand armed men. To oppose this force, of whom the greater part were bent on summarily executing the presumed offenders, the county officers stood alone.

When, in the order of business, the case of the four Mexicans was called and they were arraigned, a most exciting scene took place. 'When the plea of "not guilty" was heard, one of the guards, standing on a bench, dropped his gun, and the hammer, striking some object, exploded the weapon. Instantly numberless revolvers were drawn, bowie knives flashed forth and the tumult became indescribable. One man, in his haste to get out, accidentally fired his own gun and the terrific melee became tenfold fiercer. The struggle to quit the court-room became indescribably violent. Doors, windows, all means of egress were put in requisition. An alarm of fire added to the clamor and even the street was cleared instanter.

My Ellen: Camp life agrees with me first-rate. I can cook some splendid dishes but it is a part I don't relish much. I know you would laugh at some of our stews, and say our plates were dirty, but so the world wags.

*Enos Christman,
May 24, 1850*

Public school in Columbia, c. 1865.

On Tuesday, June 10, 1851, Captain George W. Snow, a native of Maine, aged thirty-one years, was murdered in Dragoon Gulch, near Shaw's Flat, by three Mexicans or Mexican Indians. The Mexicans had purchased a "long tom" from the Captain, and directed him to call the next morning at their encampment for his pay, this being, as afterwards appeared, but a ruse to secure the presence of their victim, the fact being well-known that he carried a considerable amount of money on his person. On entering their tent the next morning, he was assaulted and stabbed in two places. He hastily left the tent, calling out as he did so, and proceeding some fifteen yards fell from loss of blood. Help arriving, he was conveyed to his own quarters, where he died at the midnight following.

It was discovered that the murderers had dug a grave in their cabin to receive the body of their victim, concealing the cavity from view with a rawhide and a blanket, and removing the dirt so as to avoid suspicion.

Perhaps a more cold-blooded, premeditated, and cruel murder was never chronicled. The perpetrators had been in the employ of Captain Snow for a considerable time.

The neighboring miners turned out to search for the villains, but it was not until the following Sunday that two of the three were found in Sonora and arrested.

Immediately on their arrest, the two suspected men, Antonio Cruz and Patricio Janori, were removed by their

continued in far right column

Ox team working at Hale's Mill, 1894.

During the following evening the army went on a spree of such magnitude that it was seriously feared that grave disturbances would result; but such was not the case, however, and in the morning many of them left for their own camps, leaving Sonora in comparative quiet. The examination of the accused men was resumed, when, there being no evidence against them, they were acquitted. So ended this curious case, which is given mostly to illustrate the peculiar feeling shared by most Americans against the Spanish-speaking population. It seems as if the whole proceedings were merely an outgrowth from the jealousy and distrust which the one race bore the other.

BUSINESS AFFAIRS IN SONORA. The people of Tuolumne, and of Sonora in particular, felicitated themselves upon the improved prospect of business affairs, and argued from the look of things a permanent prosperity that future years has shown to be well founded. At the time of which these facts are noted, Sonora contained, according to trustworthy estimates, two thousand permanent inhabitants with which to begin the new era of things. There was invested in merchandising the sum of three hundred and fifty thousand dollars, with at least one hundred business houses of a substantial character, and a large and constantly increasing number of comfortable dwellings. Large stocks of goods were carried by the business houses, and even from the earliest times it has always been possible to purchase nearly every article of comfort or luxury that the fancy could dictate.

Among the more prominent business houses that existed at that time were E. Linoberg & Co., who kept a store commonly known as the "Tienda Mexicana," situated on the corner of Washington and Linoberg, streets, of which Mr. Morris officiated as head salesman. Their line was provisions and clothing. The firm employed a pack train which made constant and regular trips to and from Stockton, laden only with their own purchases. Dodge Co. dealt in beef, but added a stock of provisions, clothing, liquors and groceries, at their store on Washington street, fronting the plaza. Apothecaries' Hall, of which John E. Stothers was proprietor, was situated on Washington street, opposite the Court House. Then, Perkins & Co. did an extensive business in general merchandising. Reynolds & Co.'s express, as a portion of the legitimate business, engaged in the transmission of letters on a very considerable scale, if their advertisements of unclaimed missives are to be taken as a criterion. On some occasions the number thus advertised was not less than two hundred and fifty. Sullivan & Mehen, auctioneers and commission merchants, also wholesale and retail dealers in provisions and miners' tools, kept a store on Washington street, fronting the plaza. Green & Holden, another prominent firm, occupied quarters opposite E. Linoberg's store, on Washington street. Peter Mehen's original store, being vacated by him, was

Looking into the dump box at a Columbia mine, c. 1865.

Courtesy Library of Congress

captors to Shaw's Flat, there to be tried by a People's Court. A court was organized [and] the juries were then selected, one for each case, and the trial proceeded in what is described as a fair and impartial manner. Although every opportunity was given the accused to establish their innocence, the evidence was overwhelmingly against them, proving their complicity in the crime beyond a doubt. The deposition of the deceased showed that Antonio was at the table, pretending to weigh out the gold, at the time when the others stabbed him.

The verdicts of both juries were unanimous, and both prisoners were pronounced guilty. The Court then adjourned, leaving the disposition of the prisoners to the assembled multitude. By them it was put to vote, and the decision was to hang the murderers forthwith, at the precise spot where they had committed their crime, and to bury them in the grave they had dug for their victim! Swift and terrible retribution, this, and promptly and unflinchingly carried out.

After an hour, granted in order that a priest might administer the solemn rites of his office, ropes were adjusted about their necks and they were swung off.

Before their execution, the younger man made a partial confession, acknowledging that he knew the murder was to be committed, but denying complicity. He also said that his companions had been concerned in the murder of three other Americans, of which they had escaped suspicion.

Elijah [a slave] was at work, and doubtless when some of "Jeems" Georgia neighbors were ready to return, he would have earned enough to pay his fare and might go with them.

But he discovered a mine, and working on his own account, was soon in possession of considerable gold. Very industrious, he worked in his mine during the day and often in the evenings washed clothes for the miners.

My uncle had read to him the letters sent by his master, answered them, and assisted him in business matters; and after he left, Elijah came to me for such help, and so by reading and writing his letters and assisting in his business, I became familiar with all his affairs. He was intelligent and sociable, and related many incidents, some humorous, others exceedingly sad, all of which gave me an inside view of slavery.

Rev. John Steele, 1850

Donlin's Gravel Mine on Saw Mill Flat, 1894.

occupied next by Major Stewart, who carried on a similar business. Next, south of the Major's place, was the Sonora Restaurant, situated nearly opposite the town well. The establishment was kept by Louis Maris. Labetoure & Walsingham were auctioneers and commission merchants. At a somewhat later date, Bennett & Phillips opened a store in the northern end of town, which had been occupied by Street & Co., with an assortment of provisions, clothing and miscellaneous goods. The Eagle Restaurant, founded in 1851 by Sanderson & Co., upon the dissolution of their co-partnership, was afterwards carried on by Sylvester Harlow. Messrs. Street & Co. instituted the manufacture of syrups in Sonora, in the Spring or Summer of 1851. Yaney & Barabino kept a large stock of mixed goods and were the most prominent dealers in cigars, tobacco, etc. Other merchants doing business in Sonora were A. Elkins, P. McD. Collins, M. M. Steward, Terrence Clark, Louis Elordi, G. G. Belt, besides others, many Mexicans. W. O. Tripp was the first shoemaker to establish himself in town.

Messrs. Moore & Edmundson did an express business, running a passenger or saddle train to and from Stockton tri-weekly.

The mining operations conducted here were of a very extensive character for that day, being devoted to turning the course of the river. The Jacksonville Damming Company was organized on the 20th of January, 1850, with the object stated as follows: "To change the present course of Tuolumne River, above and below Wood's Creek, by digging a canal of 20 feet in width by 2,380 feet in length, requiring a depth of 2 feet in the first 200 feet, and an average depth of 18 inches throughout. "The company, comprising fifty members, went to work and constructed the race and also a stone dam across the river. After all this work, the race had to be deepened throughout from 10 to 20 feet, but before the work could be completed, a freshet destroyed the portion completed.

The company erected a wing dam, by which means they took out sixteen thousand dollars, in fifteen days, from two small holes, sunk to the bed-rock, and to keep these clear from water, twenty-eight men were employed in pumping.

Abandoning work for the rainy season, they increased the number of shares to one hundred, and resumed their attempts in the summer of 1851. This year they deepened the race and built a dam of logs, locked together, and supported by other logs pinned to them at right angles, with a backing of stone and dirt. This form of dam has always been found to give better results, as to its efficiency and durability, in withstanding the severe floods of winter, than stone structures, being also less difficult and costly of construction. The above-mentioned dam, which

There is to be found one incident of a partly personal, partly political vendetta, that made once a great stir. That was the killing of Davis, alias Keiger, by McCarthy. It does not matter what insignificant affair their quarrel began in; it is enough to say that, after a season of newspaper denunciation, Davis suddenly met his death at his enemy's hands, the tragedy occurring in Steinmetz's restaurant, where McCarthy found his man dining.

Interior of the dump box at a Columbia mine, c. 1865.

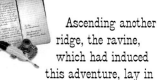
Ascending another ridge, the ravine, which had induced this adventure, lay in jagged wildness beneath. It was in uproarious life; an elk had been shot; and the miners were feasting on its fat ribs. The repast was hardly over, when the monté table, with its piles of gold, glimmered in the shade. It was the great camp of the Sonoranians, and hundreds were crowding around to reach the bank, and deposit their treasures on the turn of a card. They seemed to play for the excitement, and often doubled their stakes whether they won or lost.

Walter Colton,
Friday, Oct. 20, 1849

This is the head of the ditch at Lyons Lake Dam in 1895 and possibly taken during the opening ceremony. The gentleman was making sure the ladies had a safe look at the operations while a young boy looks on from below the fall.

occupied only seven weeks in its construction, replaced a stone structure which was eight months in building.

Hawkins' Bar, situated on the Tuolumne, below Jacksonville, was the site of the first river-bed workings on the Tuolumne. Its name was derived from one Hawkins, who kept a trading tent, the first in the place. In April, 1849, there were fifteen or twenty miners working on the banks, with pans and rockers, in the primitive mode of mining. By September of the same year, the population had increased to seven hundred men, who, at the first legislative election, cast five hundred votes. The hillsides were covered with tents, and all the bustle characteristic of some old market town was exhibited. Large operations were commenced, but the rise of the water interfered disastrously with them, as had been the case at Jacksonville. Consequent upon this, large numbers left the camp, while the remainder gave themselves to the digging of an immense canal for the complete drainage of the bar in the coming season. Again fortune frowned upon their efforts, for in the summer of 1850 a sudden rise of the water drove out of their respective claims the various companies, who had just commenced to extract gold. At that time the number of miners was six hundred. By the next year the number had dwindled to one hundred and fifty, with perhaps one hundred on the opposite side of the river, and half as many more scattered along the river, from Red Mountain Bar to Swett's Bar. The latter worked either alone, or with two or three in company. The average daily product of these river miners, in the year 1851, was stated at eight dollars per day.

Of the claims at Hawkins' Bar, that of Captain Lutter was worked by coffer damming, as was also that of Armstrong. These two claims employed fourteen men. The McAvoy Company consisted of sixty men, who, for a time, averaged twenty dollars per day each. The original company, consisting of one hundred and thirteen men, known as the Hawkins' Bar Company, after two years of persistent efforts, finally abandoned their attempts to work the bed of the river by damming.

Nearly the same was the experience at the several camps of Stevens' Bar, Indian, Texas, Morgan's, Don Pedro's, Rogers', Swett's, and many other "Bars" on the Tuolumne. In the beginning of November, 1849, the Swett's Bar Company, composed of seventy members, commenced operations by cutting a race, concluding their work just as the rise of the waters took place and caused an abandonment for the season of their contem-

The top of a dump box at a Columbia mine, c. 1865.

Hawkins' Bar, afterwards dignified by the appellation of Hawkinsville, was beautifully situated on the Tuolumne river, a narrow stream which gently flowed along, its course about as straight as a Virginia fence. Hawkinsville contained a population of about one thousand men; not a single woman or child within fifty miles of the place. The hardy miners "dwelt not in marble halls," but under the fragile covering of 10 cent muslin. Preachers, doctors, lawyers, mechanics and laboring-men cooked their provisions, mended and washed their clothing; and not unfrequently a man who had been classically educated, and perhaps had been professor of belles lettres in some college, might have been seen turning his "slap jacks" dexterously in the frying pan, or sitting on an old stump mending his breeches. All the citizens were on an equality; and not unlikely, the boisterous sailor was the most successful miner.

Luther Melanchthon Schaeffer, 1849

Sonora-Milton stage at Milton, 1890s.

> The sounds of the crowbar and pick, as they Shake or Shiver the rock, are echoed from a thousand cliffs; while the hum of human voices rolls off on the breeze to mingle with the barking of wolves, who regard with no friendly eyes this intrusion into their solitude. They resemble their great progenetrix, trembling in stone, as the Vandals broke into Rome. But little care the gold-diggers about the wolves, it is enough for them to know that this ravine contains gold; and it must he dug out, though an earthquake may slumber beneath. If you want to find men prepared to storm the burning threshold of the infernal prison, go among gold-diggers.
>
> Walter Colton,
> Wednesday, October 4, 1848

plated works. Such misfortunes have almost invariably befallen the river miners, but have never disheartened them.

On the 10th of August, 1850, the same company, then reduced to sixty men, resumed their labors, widening their race to twelve feet width at bottom. After fifty-nine days, they had completed the dam, only to have it washed away the same evening. Rebuilding it, it was again washed away, and the men laid aside their task for the year, it being then too late to effect anything.

In August, 1851, resuming work, the company, now consisting of but twenty-seven men, in a few weeks had completed a dam, which enabled them to engage in taking out gold, which they did at the rate of an ounce per day to the man, and continuing for some time very successfully.

The "Stony Point" Company abandoned their work under the pressure of difficulties, but another company, consisting of thirteen members, calling themselves the "Rum Blossom" Company, achieved a considerable reward.

The population of Swett's Bar was estimated, in 1851, at one hundred and thirty men.

Big Oak Flat, situated on the south side of the Tuolumne River, was first located and the diggings opened by James Savage, a white man, who had acquired influence over a large number of Digger Indians, whose labor he utilized in his mines, paying them with provisions, blankets, etc., and also protecting them—or pretending to protect them—from the encroachments of other whites.

In February, 1851, several milling companies of miners along the edge of Mr. Joshua Holden's garden, now the time-honored title of the low land lying above and to the north of the present City Waterworks, and bordering on Woods' Creek, the search for gold having proved successful, the various parties entered into an agreement to reimburse the proprietor of the soil for all damages accruing to the ground and the growing crops. After Mr. Holden's departure for San Francisco, a short time afterward, the Washington Company commenced encroaching upon the more valuable portions of the garden, in the course of their work finding considerable quantities of gold, to secure which they laid off an extensive mining claim.

On Mr. Holden's return, he proposed an arrangement by which he was to receive compensation for the additional damage to crops, etc., but at a meeting of those interested, at which the miners, but not Mr. Holden, were present, opposition was made to paying any damages whatever, and the meeting was broken up without any action on that point. On the following

> When the American company, only five or six in number, were away, some persons claiming ownership sold the American mine to the newly arrived Chilenos, and receiving the price, a considerable sum, left before the fraud was discovered and they identified. Having bought not only the mine, but the mining implements, the Chilenos immediately began work, and when Messrs. Burt and Grove, the real owners, returned on Monday morning they found that their claim had been "jumped."
>
> Rev. John Steele, 1850

The Friedenburr water wheel for raising the car, c. 1865.

This Post Office and Western Boot and Shoe store is believed to be Tuttletown in the 1890s.

Constable John Leary was murdered while in the discharge of his duty.

Mr. Leary, with Marshal Mullan, was watching some suspected characters, and while endeavoring to detect and arrest them on Waldo street, Mr. Leary was killed, having, it is supposed, come upon them while they were engaged in robbing a drunken man, and at the moment of seizing one, received a heavy blow upon the forehead, which fractured his skull, while another shot him through the body, the ball passing near the heart. The murderers escaped, though fired upon by Mullan.

The next day, two men, Harrison Morgan and Richard Wallace, were arrested. Morgan's life was short. Taken up Broadway and along the Gold Springs Road to the flume, a rope was put around his neck, and without a moment for prayer, he was run up.

At nightfall, a Chinaman, brought up against the lifeless form of Morgan. Looking up, the affrighted Celestial beheld with horror the pallid corpse. He started off at a pace that made his pigtail assume a nearly horizontal position, and it is a matter of conjecture whether he has yet stopped.

day a personal collision occurred between Mr. Holden and two of the members of the Washington Company, at which a number of bystanders, mostly gamblers and roughs, resisted, by the exhibition of pistols, the attempts of other individuals of that company to assist their fellow-members. By this interference, the gambling community became unwittingly identified with Mr. Holden's cause, a fact that proved of the greatest detriment to that gentleman subsequently.

Later in the day, this portion of the gambling fraternity, fourteen in number, "jumped" a portion of the ground claimed by the Washington Company, and prepared to hold it at all hazards. Whether or not Mr. Holden was a party to this action is not at all clear. It is highly probable, from the circumstances, that he was; but his standing as a business man and his well known character, would seem to contradict that theory. The Sonora Herald, the only paper published at the time, by the tenor of its remarks, would indicate that he had nothing to do with it; but the prevailing opinion was strongly against him, as will be seen in the conclusion of this narrative.

Being invited to go upon the ground to observe the boundaries of the Washington Company's claim, Mr. Holden accepted, but delayed going until the next morning.

In the meantime the jumping party organized, armed themselves, and determined to hold their claim at all hazards.

Proceeding to the ground, against the advice of Mr. Holden, they found there all the members of the Washington Company, prepared with firearms to receive them, but keeping quietly at work in their ditch. The aggressors arranged themselves on a hill, perhaps a hundred yards distant.

Major Barry (the celebrated Justice) was an eye-witness, and to him the following account is due. He said: "About eight o'clock in the morning I went to the garden, having understood that a difficulty was expected between two companies, each contending for rights in the same claim. When I had approached within about thirty feet of the claim I heard a shout behind, and, turning round, I saw a company of men, all armed, about three hundred yards off. One young man, named Alexander Saloschen, was running towards the Garden Company [Washington Company], with his rifle, against the remonstrances of his own party, who shouted to him not to shoot. As he came within hailing distance of me, I told him to go back, and he did so for a short distance, but turning again, he ran and fired on the Garden Company, which was quickly returned with a volley. All the arms on both sides were fired off, amounting, it is supposed, to from sixty to seventy-five shots. Only one man was killed —named Leven Davis. The young man who commenced the

On the 16th of January, 1878, the stage was stopped by three men, at a place on the Brown's Flat road one and a half miles from Sonora. Mr. Shine was the driver on this occasion, and Messrs. Caleb Dorsey, J. H. Condit and J. G. Divoll were passengers. The amount taken was somewhat over five thousand dollars. For the crime Pedro Ybarra, Richard Bolter and J. Thayer were arrested, and by the following May, Ybarra was sentenced to imprisonment for life; Thayer received eight years, while Bolter was set free in consideration of his turning State's evidence.

Columbia Gulch, c. 1865.

Butterfield's store in Jamestown, 1890s.

Lines of stages now traverse the country in every direction, and there is scarcely a canvas mining village that is debarred from communication in this way with the principal towns. The horses used by these lines are of the best quality; for a Yankee stage-driver knows wherein true economy lies; but the capital required to start a line is very considerable, and as soon as the profits begin to "tumble in pretty freely," as Colonel Reed remarked, up starts an opposition—for stage-driving is a favorite speculation!

Frank Marryat, early 1850s

attack was slightly wounded in the cheek. Of the Garden Company, three were wounded, but not dangerously. Thus the matter rested for a moment. The Garden Company shortly after held a meeting and appointed a committee to draft resolutions. I was called upon to address the assembly, which by this time amounted to about five or six hundred, and there was the most profound order and attention. They then adjourned, to meet again at three o'clock, at which time they convened, and all passed off in good order. An arrest was issued from my office, as Justice of the Peace, and handed to the High Sheriff, to bring on the originators of the riot. Several persons were brought in, but, not a witness appeared on the part of the State; and so, of course, there was no action. Mr. Holden was exculpated from all participation or blame, he himself having invited the most rigid investigation."

In this affray Leven Davis, a young man on the side of the gamblers, was shot in the head, dying immediately. The gambler, Saloscheu, who fired the first shot and received a slight wound in the face, was a former partner of Labetoure, a well known French resident, previously mentioned. At a later date he resided in Stockton, which place became too hot to hold him, in consequence of an unprovoked attack upon a citizen. After leaving that city, all traces of him were lost.

Of the men belonging to the Washington Company, whom Justice Barry described as "wounded, but not dangerously," two died of their wounds; showing that the gentleman was misinformed as to their true condition.

THE HOLDEN'S GARDEN CHISPA. "The largest lump of gold that has yet been found was taken from Holden's Garden last Saturday evening—weighing 28 pounds and 4 ounces, lacking 13 grains. It is mixed with quartz, but the gold is estimated at 20 pounds. As yet it has not been accurately weighed in water, and so we can not exactly state the relative proportions of gold and quartz. Mr. Peter Mehen offered four thousand five hundred dollars for the lump, at sight, but his offer was not accepted. The fortunate party consisted of eight men, and are known under the name of "Wheaton Company." This was the first party that undertook to work the spot known as Holden's Garden, some two months since, their claim being at the foot of the quartz mountain. Between them and Mr. Holden there has ever been, we believe, the most amicable feelings, and there is probably no person in town who is better pleased than Mr. Holden to hear that the company have been so successful. From the first they have been taking out gold by the pounds. Frequently their day's work has amounted to five pounds. For a week or two, however, the yield has been comparatively small, and some of the members, accustomed to heavy strikes, were

Miners among the boulders at the Columbia Claim, c. 1865.

I bought an interest in the Robinsons Ferry property, located on the Stanislaus River between Angels Camp in Calaveras county, and Sonora in Tuolumne county, where I have resided ever since.

Harvey Wood, 1856

On Sunday, November 13, 1853, an Austrian named Peter Nicholas, from Sawmill Flat, visited Columbia, and becoming intoxicated and quarelsome, sought a difficulty with Captain John Parrot, from Pine Log. Parrot strove to avoid his assailant. Stepping backward, he fell; upon which the Austrian sprang upon him and thrust his bowie knife into the neck of the prostrate man, making a wound which penetrated into the cavity of the chest, and from which recovery was impossible.

Immediately upon the conclusion of the bloody deed, Nicholas, still drunk, and with the bloody knife still in his grasp, was arrested by citizens and handed over to the authorities. A large crowd had assembled, among whom were miners from Pine Log. The prisoner was loudly demanded by the ever-growing mob, and active measures began to be taken to defeat their intentions. Constable Connor swore in a posse of special Constables, and the prisoner was chained to staples driven into the Court-room floor. But these precautions were absolutely of no avail, for, at a signal, the officers were secured, the staples drawn out by means of a pick, and the prisoner was thrown or dragged out of the house and passed along over the heads of the dense crowd, until a convenient pine tree was reached. A rope was speedily procured, and the prisoner would have immediately met his deserts had it not been for the timely interference of Mr. James Coffroth, who made appeals to the multitude to grant a fair trial, which, after much parley, was acceded

continued in far right column

Seven teams pulling a harvester in a wheat field at the Rosasco Ranch in 1890.

beginning to be discouraged. Two of the original party sold out to Mr. Rounds and Mr. Gore, who entered the company just in time to share the glory and the profits of the big lump.

[SONORA POLITICS.] "The first assemblage for political purposes occurred at Lytton's Exchange, Sonora. The chairman, General L. A. Besancon, explained the object of the meeting, and urged an immediate organization of the Democratic party.

"Up to this time there had been no decided advantage in either the Democratic or Whig parties, both seeming actuated by the same spirit of apathy; but a circumstance was about to occur by which the political proclivities of the miners of Tuolumne were to be unmistakably marked. Mr. Edward Marshall, brother of the celebrated Tom Marshall, of Kentucky, having come forward, and as he prefaced his remarks by saying he was glad to appear before the assemblage as a Democrat, having been born and raised on good Democratic soil, the Whigs who were present showed a disposition to hiss down his speech and disturb the meeting. This raised the high-spirited Kentuckian, and he paused for an instant, then throwing open his coat, he commenced such a burst of eloquence and determination as completely overawed his opponents. His exact words were: 'I have been in larger crowds than this, and a great deal more dangerous.' Throwing off his coat so as to expose his revolver, he added: 'And by God's will, I am going to make a Democratic speech.' The Democrats present cheered, and those who were on the fence going over to the Democrats, the Whigs were completely in the minority in Tuolumne county." This incident occurred in 1850.

SONORA'S ORGANIZATION OF TOWN COUNCIL, ETC. On May 26, 1851, the Common Council of the City of Sonora held their first meeting.

Among the more important business transacted by this Board was the passage of Ordinances numbers Fourteen and Fifteen, relating to gambling. The former of these provides that "The game known as 'French Monte' or 'Three-card Game,' or the game of 'Loop' or 'String Game,' or the game known as 'Thimbles,' or the game known as 'Lottery,' or the game known as 'Chinese Puzzle' or the 'Lock Game,' or any game having in its tendency deception or fraud, is hereby prohibited within the corporate limits of the Town of Sonora; and, on conviction of any person or persons of an infringement of this ordinance, the party so offending shall be fined in a sum not less than twenty-five or more than one hundred dollars, and imprisonment not more than ten days, or both fine and imprisonment, at the option of the Recorder.

THE VIGILANCE COMMITTEE. The formation of the first regularly organized and permanent Vigilance Committee in Tuolumne County took place in Sonora, Sunday noon, June 29, 1851. The immediate occasion was the attempt to burn

Henry Robinson's store sits in the shadow of Table Mountain. The river runs at what would be the bottom of the picture (out of frame) where Robinson's Ferry operated.

continued from far left column

to, and the multitude, now increased from hundreds to thousands, moved toward Gold Hill as a convenient spot for the proceedings.

On arriving at Gold Hill, Dan. Patterson was appointed Sheriff with several deputies, a jury was impaneled returning in a quarter of an hour with the following verdict:

"We the jury find the prisoner guilty of assault and battery with intent to kill Captain John Parrot; but as Parrot is not yet dead, they agree that the prisoner shall be given up to the civil authorities."

The wildest excitement followed. "Hang him!" "String him up!" "Give him to the Sheriff!" was heard issuing from hundreds of mouths. A vote was being taken to ratify the decision of the jury, when, deeming it a propitious moment, Messrs. Solomon, Randall and their backers charged upon the crowd, broke their way to the prisoner, hustled him out, mounted him upon a horse, all manacled as he was, and mounting their own animals rode rapidly toward Sonora.

Incarcerated in the jail at Sonora, the murderer awaited his trial; which coming, he was convicted of murder in the first degree and sentenced by the redoubtable Judge Creaner to death. Before the day set for execution, however, his sentence was commuted, by an over-indulgent Governor, to seven years' imprisonment.

Toward the last of November of the next year [1875] the Phoenix reservoirs, on Sullivan's creek, broke, from the overcharge of waters incident on the heavy rains. At first the creek began to swell gradually, but perceptibly, then move rapidly, until a great wall of water rolled down with thunderous roar, yellow with accumulated mud, and bearing upon its foaming crest huge logs and immense pieces of timber. On reaching Bergel's place, where the Summerville road crosses the creek, the waters hesitated an instant, owing to the narrow passage through which they had to pass. Then, with a mighty effort, it lifted the bridge as if it were a feather, carrying it away and dashing it to pieces in a twinkling. A number of Chinamen had formed a settlement on an island near where the road to Kincaid Flat crosses. When the waters of the creek began to rise, three of these men climbed a tall cottonwood growing on the banks of the creek, and were for the moment safe, but the wall of waters, rolling twenty feet high submerged them, drowning them where they clung.

the town, by some persons unknown. The attempt was unsuccessful, owing to the early discovery of the fire; but the recent terrible conflagrations in San Francisco and Stockton had so acted on the feelings of the Sonorans that an organization, similar in all respects to those of the larger cities, was effected. It was composed of the most orderly and respectable citizens, and the quality of zeal was certainly evidenced in the prosecution of its labors. For the first fortnight of its existence it administered upon six cases brought to its attention. An American thief was hunted up and banished from the Southern Mines, under penalty of death in case of return. A Frenchman, detected in passing counterfeit coin, was also banished. A Mexican, caught in the act of stealing, was whipped with twenty—five lashes on the bare back. Two other Mexicans—counterfeiters—were also given twenty-five lashes each. The sixth, a Mexican horse-thief, proved to have been a consummate villain, received the heavier sentence of one hundred lashes, his head was partially shaved, and he was banished, under penalty of death if returning. Later in the year, owing to the greater efficiency of the courts, the Committee executed but few judgments upon criminals, but among these few were two that are recorded. In the first of these, the criminal, an ex-convict from Sydney, arrested on suspicion of stealing a mule, received seventy-five lashes, had his head shaved, and was banished from the mines. A Mexican, for stealing a pistol, was sentenced to receive fifty lashes, a shaved head, and banishment from the mines.

Fire Captain Thomas Stoddard of the Washington Hose Company #1 in 1895.

In June an affair of considerable notoriety occurred in Sonora. This was a conflict which took place in a disreputable portion of the town, and threatened to precipitate a general war between the American and the Mexican population of the city. The circumstances were these: a row occurred in a Spanish dwelling-house, in which one Contreras took part, and was arrested, but the bystanders interfering, Marshal McFarlane was compelled to shoot one of them, a Chileno, who fell mortally wounded. Another of the same party was killed by Americans, who came up to assist the Marshal.

PROGRESS OF THE TOWN OF SONORA. At no time in its history were so many permanent structures being erected. Vacant lots were built upon, and the sound of the hammer and saw were heard in all parts of the city.

One of the most notable structures built this season (the spring of 1852), was a large and substantial frame building at the corner of Taney and Washington streets, in which Messrs. Yaney and Bertine established themselves as bankers. Within the building was a very large safe—an article so ponderous as to require a very considerable outlay of time and money to transport from San Francisco. This safe was regarded as a nine days' wonder by the hardy gold-seekers.

Previous to the establishment of the house of Taney & Bertine, three firms, Messrs. Reynolds, Todd & Co., Adams & Co., and Wm. Hammond & Co., existed. The former firm have the credit of being the original bankers and express men of Sonora, having commenced their operations in May, 1850, as Reynolds & Co. Their business had been very extensive as early as the fall of 1850, when the firms of Reynolds & Co. and Todd & Co. were consolidated, and in 1852 the special deposits reached the amount of one hundred and eighty thousand dol-

The LaGrange ferry across the Tuolumne River. This area is now under Don Pedro reservoir.

Dear Eliza,

do not look for me so much. When I get ready to start for home, I will write to you so that you may know when I am coming. You must write to me regularly until I return, and direct to Sacramento City

I thank you for those kisses you sent ma. Tell the Children to kiss you for Pa and you must also kiss them for me. Dear Eliza do not think that because I am staying so long here that I care but little about my Family. No one in this world can think more of his Wife and Children than I do of mine. The reason I have stayed so long here is because I thought it would be for our interest after spending so much time and money in coming to Cal. to make something before I return home.

Horace Root
written from Sonora on
April 5, 1852

In the latter part of 1852, the following business houses and places of entertainment existed [in Sonora]:

21 Produce and grocery stores.
30 Saloons, groceries & restaurants.
17 Dry goods and produce stores.
4 Hotels.
7 Boarding-houses.
4 Banking & exchange offices.
3 Express offices.
2 Book and stationery stores.
5 Doctors' offices.
5 Law offices.
3 Tobacconists.
7 Bakeries.
1 Tin shop.
2 Barber shops.
3 Meat markets.
3 Blacksmith shops.
8 Carpenter shops.
3 Silver-smith shops.
1 Printing office.
3 Drug stores.
2 Wagon-maker shops.
3 Laundries.
4 Livery stables.
1 Reading room.
1 Brewery.
1 Ground coffee depot.
1 Daguerreotype room.
1 Boot and shoe shop.
1 Wine and liquor store.
1 Fruit & confectionery store.
1 Mexican fandango house.
Total–150.

J. Curtis "Buchannan Mike" and team in from of Pat Burk's blacksmith stable and carriage shop on Washingon Street. Hidden by trees is Sears and Wenzel's blacksmith and carriage shop and the Stockton Street entrance to Sonora. The white pole to the rear of the last wagon marks the site of Ghirardelli's chocolate shop. This freight wagon is likely headed for the Buchannan Mine in the southeast of Tuolumne.

lars. The firm of Adams Co. occupied, at the latter date, a neat building on Washington street, in which was contained a large fire-proof vault, built of stone and cement, with double doors of boiler iron, and within this fire and thief-proof cavern were two large iron safes of the most approved construction. Dr. J. Steinberger remained as agent in charge until 1852, when he was succeeded in his duties by Mr. A. G. Richardson.

Wm. Hammond & Co. began business in Sonora in November or December, 1851, in general banking and the purchase of gold dust. Their office was in the first story of the adobe building known as Masonic Hall.

It may here be proper to remark that this building, celebrated in the annals of Sonora, was commenced on June 24, 1851, the Masonic Order laying the corner stone with appropriate ceremonies. The occasion was one long remembered in Tuolumne. Among the Masons who took part in the observances of that day were Charles M. Radcliff (Master of Ceremonies,) Judge Tuttle, E. Linoberg, Mayor Dodge, A. F. Chatfield, Captain Tormey, William Perkins (Orator of the Day,) W. Vyse, Major Sullivan and others.

After a considerable delay, the building was finally completed and occupied; but its life tenure was short. The inside was completely burned out by the fire of June 18. The rains of the following winter so acted upon the adobe walls remaining, that the whole structure became unsafe, and had to be propped up. After remaining in this empty and forlorn condition for some time, it finally fell in, and remained a wreck until the following July, when the county authorities gained control of it by lease, and entered into a contract with J. M. Huntington for its repair, at a cost not exceeding two thousand dollars. It was the intention to devote it to the use of the Courts, there being at that time no suitable rooms for that purpose. Whether the money was expended on the building does not appear, but shortly after the Supervisors are found to have made other arrangements, and the presumption is that the contract with Mr. Huntington was not fulfilled. The building stood on the northeast corner of Church and Washington streets.

GREAT FIRE IN '52. The fire of June 18 was one of the most serious calamities to which Sonora was ever exposed. It began at one o'clock in the morning, in a building called the "Hotel de France," situated on the plaza, and facing up Washington street. It was occupied by Mme. Landreau. From thence it spread northwards, destroying the block situated in the center of Washington street, and beginning at a point about midway between the present locations of O'Brien's store and Boyd's

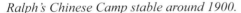

Ralph's Chinese Camp stable around 1900.

One of the more noticeable events of 1855, was the murder of Kittering at Algerine Camp. Previous to the account of this case it will be essential to introduce the story of another affair, notorious at the time, and which is intimately connected with the above murder. This was the bold murder of Judge Brunton at Yorktown, which occurred in the night of June 30, when a band of burglars, four in number, entered the sleeping apartment of that gentleman and abstracted twelve thousand dollars from a safe in the room, where most of the family were asleep, and accomplishing their object without awaking any one but the Judge. The account given by the latter was to the effect that upon his waking he saw a man standing over him with an axe in his hands, remarking to him to lie still, as money was all they wanted. Accordingly the Judge lay quiet until the burglars had left the room, when he arose, and taking a pistol, followed them into another room, where he had an encounter with the rearmost one, who knocked him senseless, besides inflicting a severe knife wound upon his neck. He was discovered the next morning by the family, who raised an alarm.

Team hauling sacks of grain to market.

The next sensation pertained to Columbia, and was the under eminently justifiable circumstances, of Adolf Parou, by Thomas Hayes. Parou met his deserved death through the lowest species of immorality, touching as it did the well-being and virtue of young school-girls; and probably no manslayer ever met with more general approbation than did Hayes.

livery stable. The streets separated by this block were known as East Washington and West Washington streets. The southernmost building which fell a prey to the flames was the Masonic Hall, already spoken of. The wind blowing northward, the fire steadily progressed in that direction, burning nearly every building on Washington street to its head and even here the flames were not stayed, but continued as far as the Barnum House, in the northern part of the city, and fully a half mile from the starting point.

Thus nearly every building in town was burned, only such scattered dwellings as were far removed from the fire having been saved. Many of the structures swept away cost from ten to twenty thousand dollars each, and the total loss was said to exceed three-quarters of a million dollars.

Brick became the favorite material for building, and the brickmakers began to ply their vocation actively. Real estate, it was said, had risen, within a few days, to a greater value than previous to the fire.

The *Herald*, by its respectable moral tone, by the fullness and completeness of its various departments, and by the vigor, energy and courage of its conductors, commanded success and achieved it. There was not at that time, nor has there since been, published in California a more respectable weekly newspaper. Its editorials were terse and vigorous, and always up with the times. They were such as to furnish an exponent of the feelings of society in general on all prominent topics. This is fully shown in the editor's comments on the Chinese question, in 1852, when that topic was for the first time agitated. It is surprising to the reader of the present day to observe how little progress has been made in considering that question. The subject remains, morally, in the same light in which it was then regarded. To prove this, let a few sentences be quoted: "They prove convincingly, if proof were needed, that the Chinese have been hardly and harshly treated. Coaxed and invited hither by one class of Americans, they have been driven about and maltreated by another class. Taxed by the Legislature, in return for that protection which it well knew it could not honestly guarantee, they have been driven back by miners, whose voices spoke out long ago against any competition with inferior labor. Who, then, are to blame in this matter, the miners, or their would-be masters, the merchants? The merchant clique of San Francisco thus writes: The immigration of the Chinese to this country is productive [and] of great profit to us, and we believe is of great benefit to the mining and agricultural interests of the State.' The merchant memorialists will pardon us poor miners if we presume to have our own ideas about our own peculiar interests. We have too long served as shuttlecocks, to be bandied about from side to side, the sport and prey of sharper legislators and reckless speculators; we have too long served as cat's paws, by which the merchants and bankers have drawn the golden store out of the fire.

Ah Mow, of Chinese descent, fell by the murderous hand of his fellow-countryman, Ah Bun, at Jamestown, in 1872, and his slayer, tried and convicted of the murder, received sentence of death; but to avoid the penalty, the crafty heathen, a week before the time set for his sudden taking off, hanged himself in his cell—a common trick of condemned Celestial murderers, and one which is said to have more than once cost certain well-known attorneys a fee contingent upon a legal hanging.

Sonora Railroad Depot just after 1900.

Courtesy Tuolumne County Museum

Early Bradford Street in Sonora.

I had been directed to a place called Holden's Hotel as a sleeping place. The lower floor formed the gambling-saloon, in which were the Ethiopian serenaders already alluded to; the upper being converted, as I had understood, into sleeping apartments. On applying at the bar for a bed, I was requested to pay a dollar and enter my name on a slate opposite a vacant number; 80 it was. I wished to go to bed, and was directed to mount the staircase and find No. 80 for myself. On reaching the second story, I found myself in a long and dimly-lighted room of the same dimensions as that below, and round and about which were ranged about a hundred wooden stretchers, covered with canvas, and furnished each with one dark-blue blanket, and a small bag of hay to represent a pillow.

Frank Marryat, early 1850s

"To say that the Chinese will permanently settle in, improve and populate this country, does not mend the matter. It is but a mere assertion, anyhow. That a country containing so immense a mass of human beings could speedily populate this country, none can doubt. But what we want is not mere population; this were worse than useless, if it were not a healthy increase. We want a permanent population; but we also want a free, intelligent, enlightened one. We want a population that speaks our language, understands and appreciates our laws, sympathizes with the expansive spirit of our people, harmonizes with and readily assimilates to us. We want a population each one of whom is capable of sitting on a jury, of depositing a ballot, of understanding the drift of a resolution, the prayer of a petition. Such a population the Chinese can not be. Why, then, should we commit political suicide, because our fathers made our country a refuge for the oppressed? In plainer and more unmistakable words, why should we ruin our rising country by diluting its already adulterated population with the admixture of a strange and an inferior race, merely because certain merchants find it productive of great profit to them?"

Never were more pointed words applied to this question, which has remained an unsettled problem to this day. The ideas above advanced contain all, or nearly all, of argument that has been promulgated on that side. Nor, on the other hand, have the supporters of Chinese immigration got beyond the idea of self-interest in their own arguments. So that the whole subject may be said to be in the same state in which it existed thirty years since.

LATER EVENTS IN SONORA. The latter years have not been prolific in history. On the contrary, there is a dearth of interesting matter strongly opposite to the times whose chronicles have already been set down.

In May, 1870, the "People's Accommodation and Express Company" was organized, as a move to secure cheaper fares to Stockton, the design being to run a line of stages from Sonora and Columbia to that city, the trips to be made in ten hours or less, and the price of a passage either way to be not over five dollars.

For one year, or thereabouts, the organization kept to its purpose of reducing the fare, and by the month of June, 1871, the Stockton and Copperopolis Railway having been completed to Milton, the People's Company was dissolved.

During this period it had been in competition with the stage-line of C.H. Sisson & Co.

Previously, three lines, those of Fisher, Dillon and McLeod, had run lines of stages between those places, but through the decline in travel Fisher and McLeod were compelled to retire, while Dooley succeeded Dillon in the conduct of his business, and subsequently the firm of Sisson & Co. conducted their traffic unhampered by competition. In later years Shine & Co. alone have run the transportation lines of this region.

On March 23, 1875, the mail stage was robbed near Reynolds' Ferry by three masked men. The passengers, eight in number, were unmolested, though some of them made offers of their money, but the treasure box of Wells, Fargo & Co. was taken, its contents being valued at six thousand dollars.

Looks like a tour of this mine. The ladies are holding candles and picks as if they to were going to work.

A peculiar instance of how thoroughly the placer diggings have been worked is evidenced in Shaw's Flat, an exceedingly rich plateau in the county of Tuolumne. In 1851 this was a beautiful level park, studded with trees, among them many noble cedars. In 1860 the whole plain, from four to five miles across, was one scene of gaunt desolation. The entire dirt had been washed away, not a single tree remained. Shaw's Flat, once proverbial for the richness of its mines, was silent and solitary. The bed rock was composed of limestone. The head-waters of the river Stanislaus had been brought to bear upon the soil, and had washed every grain of it through Dragoon gulch into the lowlands. Nothing remained but the white bare rocks that looked like tombstones, the more so as they were of all shapes, some of them flat, others peaked, others needle-shaped, and some arched. A small town had sprung up during the brief and brilliant prosperity of that place, but not a sign of life was now seen in the cluster of wooden houses. They will stand there until some drunken traveller, by negligence, will drop a lighted match against the dry walls and put the town out of its misery. A few ashes will mark the spot where the bar-room, the general store, the gambling-house and the Baptist chapel once stood. No one will miss them, and the fact of their destruction will hardly be mentioned in the local papers. Fortunes have been made here, but the face of the country is ruined for centuries.

J. G. Player-Frowd, 1870

The Alameda Mine was one mile from the Rawhide Mine on the right side of French Flat Road. The stamp mill is at the right in this 1898 photo.

FIRES IN SONORA. The City Hotel [in Sonora], escaping the flames, was a very prominent building in those days. It was erected by Messrs. Green & Lane (Alonzo Green and Judge James Lane) to take the place of the hotel of Captain Green, mentioned previously as having been destroyed in the great fire in 1852. The old pioneers spoke of this structure as "the finest building to be found in the mountains of California" Its dimensions were fifty by one hundred feet. It was built with thick adobe walls, and consisted of two lofty and spacious stories. It was fitted up as a family hotel, and was furnished throughout in what was then regarded as fine style. The lower story was taken up by the saloon, billiard and dining rooms. The saloon, being very capacious, was frequently used for the purpose of holding political meetings, etc. A spacious staircase, opening on the street, leads to the upper story, which contains twenty private rooms, parlors, etc., all carpeted and furnished. From the roof a most delightful view of the city and its environs could be obtained, the hotel being situated at an angle of the main street, from whence nearly the whole of the town, not less than a mile in length, could be seen.

The eating arrangements were on a par with the excellence of the hotel and its other appointments. The first proprietors were said to have been men who understood the business perfectly; and their enterprise and good judgment met its reward in the successful career of this house, which was for a long time regarded as one of the best hotels in California.

MONTEZUMA AND THE HYDRAULIC DITCH. Among other camps which had attracted attention previous to 1853, Montezuma was one of the most prominent.

Its mining interests were very important, although up to the last of 1852 the ground had hardly been more than prospected, as no streams passed through these flats, so they were only capable of being worked through a few weeks in the heaviest rains; yet during that period they proved at least ordinarily rich.

As might be expected, the enterprise of the various water companies led to the immediate construction of ditches to convey the valuable fluid to the anxious miner on the Flats. The Tuolumne County Water Company, by the 1st of December, 1852, had their canal completed to the desired spot, and constructed a large reservoir for use in the dry season. The Tuolumne Hydraulic Association, whose canal tapped the Tuolumne River some twenty-five miles east of Sonora, and at an elevation of five thousand feet, inaugurated even more extensive works, of which the main branch carried water to Montezuma.

The following description by Mr. Murray, of the *Sonora Herald*: "Being fairly fagged out with too much work, and having heard a great deal touching the mountain region of Tuolumne, we determined to shake the dust of Sonora from our feet and take to the hills for a day or two. Accordingly, one day

> On the 7th of October our election for state and county officers took place. Everything passed off quietly, but the clerks of the election got so drunk they could not count off the vote.
>
> Enos Christman,
> Tuesday, October 22, 1850

This accident on the Standart Lumber Company Railroad at Japs Camp (not referencing Japanese) in the early 1900s certainly derailed that day's profits!

A tour of the App Mine on Quartz Mountain in the late 1890s.

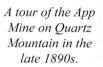

In December, 1865, occurred the burning of the County Jail, with the cremation of Tom Horn. This individual, represented as something of a rough, who hailed from Columbia, had entered Sonora in the progress of a drunken spree, and had been locked up. Shortly after, an alarm of fire was raised, and Mr. Mills, the Jailor, by the utmost exertions, was only enabled to remove the other prisoners from the burning building, leaving Horn, who was undoubtedly the incendiary, to perish in his own bonfire. The Jail, which was new, had cost the County thirteen thousand dollars, and was almost the only piece of property in her possession that was worth boasting of.

last week we procured ourself a good horse and started off up country, with the intention of seeing a little of the far-famed mountain range, as well as inspecting the works of the Tuolumne Hydraulic Association, of whose operations the public have heard so much.

"All the way along we met a constant succession of wagons, bringing shingles, lumber, etc., into Sonora.

"About twenty miles from Sonora we passed the last ranch and entered upon still higher ground, peculiarly fitted for shingle-making and timber cutting. The pines here are magnificent, and attract quite a large colony of shingle-makers, who camp out here in squads, and haul the results of their labor into Sonora for disposal.

"About twenty-five miles from Sonora we left the main road, called the Ice Trail, which continues on along the main ridge toward the Sierra Nevada, and descended a rather precipitous hillside to the store of Captain Puckett. This is beautifully situated, at the bottom of the ravine formed by Sugar Pine Creek. Although we had passed through many miles of a fine timber country, we were fairly surprised at the scene which here presents itself. Thick-set as are the pines on the summit and slopes of the ridge, below they are far more so. The whole bed of the creek is fairly choked up with vegetation. Pine and cedar trees, from the smallest size up to eight and ten feet in diameter, and of proportionate hight, spring up in serried ranks all around. No other shade is needed, for the rays of the sun can with difficulty find their way through the thick tops to the earth's surface. The ground is covered with a dense undergrowth of fern and other plants and bushes, and everything around is of a beautiful green, contrasting delightfully with the arid and dusty appearance of things nearer the plains.

"We found here some twenty or thirty men, who were at work upon the race of the Tuolumne Hydraulic Company. The race is intended to cross Sugar Pine Creek at this place, with a flume some forty or fifty feet from the ground, supported by ample pillars. We inspected the race on either side of the creek, and found it to be of large size, and well and securely constructed.

"We slept at Captain Puckett's one night, and early in the morning proceeded one fourth of a mile up the creek, to the house of Judge Ketchum, the contractor and engineer of the Company. Upon making ourselves known to this gentleman, he very kindly offered to show us over the works, and soon mounted his mule. We traveled on a few hundred yards along the left bank of the creek, until we struck a beautiful bottom, which the Judge has taken up for a ranch.

"The dam at the head of the race is, at the highest calculation, about thirty miles from Sonora. It is built of strong,

Our inside passengers consisted of a young Canadian woman, who traveled under the protection of an ill-looking dog, a kind of Irish Yankee, who was very quarrelsome and bumptious, and carried his revolver in a very prominent position. We had two or three miners, who, as a matter of course, brought their rifles and blankets with them into the coach, and who squirted their juice at passing objects on the road with astonishing accuracy. We had, however, one decided character. This was a man who, as he gratuitously informed us, was professionally a bear-hunter, bear-trapper, and bear-fighter; who, in fact, dealt generally in grizzly bears.

Frank Marryat, early 1850s

Frank Ralph driving his buggy with C.H. Burden and a friend on horseback.

Unknown Tuolumne County mine.

A bull and bear fight is, of all exhibitions of this description, the most cruel and senseless. The bear, cramped in his limbs by the strict confinement that his strength and ferocity have rendered necessary, is placed in the arena; and attached to him by a rope is a bull, generally of fine shape and courage, and fresh from the mountains. Neither animal has fair play, and, indeed, in most instances, each one avoids the other. The bull's power of attack is weakened by the shortness of the tether, while the bear, as above mentioned, has scarcely the free use of his muscles.

The bull invariably commences the attack, and the immense power of the bear's fore-arm is then exemplified; for, raising himself on his hams, he meets the coming shock by literally boxing the bull's ears; but this open-handed blow saves his entrails, and the bull swerves half stunned, while his horns graze Bruin's skin. But if the bull approaches in a snuffing, inquisitive kind of manner, the bear will very probably seize his enemy's nose, and half suffocate him in his grip. The fight generally ends without much damage on either side, for the simple reason that neither of the combatants means mischief.

Frank Marryat, early 1850s

stout logs, set into the bed of the river in a slanting Position, the upper ends resting upon a structure composed of logs, laid horizontally, one upon another, after the fashion of a log house. Other logs are planted so as to support the dam, being firmly braced upon the solid rock. The superincumbent water thus lies upon the dam, pressing it down and keeping it in its place. The winter freshets will pass over, leaving it undamaged.

"Much skill has been displayed by the engineer, in this department. Huge trees have been felled, and firmly propped in their places.

"Judge Ketchum assures us that there are now, in all, about eighty men employed on the race, and that the whole of the work will be completed in three months.

"We cannot convey to the reader any idea of the depth of solitude which reigns in this region, or of the extreme difficulty which exists in the way of progression. We were unable to divine how men could even have traveled along this route, much less construct the extent of grading and woodwork which has been accomplished.

"We regained our horse and spent some two hours in clambering out of the unpleasant position in which we had placed ourselves. It was then about four o'clock, and we were some twenty miles from Sonora. So we put spurs to our Bucephalus, managing to get in not long after nightfall; receiving solace for our wanderings in the shape of a long night's sleep."

SOCIAL PROGRESS. Under date of March 25th, 1854, the editor of the *Sonora Herald* wrote as follows: "We are gratified to see the marked improvement that has taken place in the society of our little city in the past year. As an evidence of this, witness how differently Sabbath is observed. In past years, on this sacred day, might be seen a fantastically dressed Mexican clown, preceded by a band of shockingly bad music, parading the streets and notifying the citizens of a bull and bear fight about to come off. Now, instead, at the same hour of the day, troops of rosy-faced, quiet, orderly children are seen returning from Sunday-school, and well-dressed men and women on their way to the house of worship. We can boast now of five churches of different denominations, and all of them well attended —good evidence of an advanced state of civilization.

"And what has caused this great change in public sentiment? To what else can it be attributed but to the presence of woman; virtuous, pure, sympathizing woman; whose influence is as effective in the formation of public character, as it is felt

"If you stay in Sonora two weeks, you'll come back; and if you come back you will stay all your life," they say; and it seems to be true. The town contains an astonishing number of bachelors and widowers; men who came here, many of them, so long ago as 1849, most of them before 1853, and who live on with but little purpose, apparently, in their lives, except to sun themselves and to enjoy the climate. The gold has gone. In the frenzy of the earlier days, when millions were taken out every week; when the jail was as full as the mines; when on Sunday the miners formed a cue half a mile long, waiting for their letters at the post-office; when every other house in the place was a bar-room or gambling-den; when Wells-Fargo's strong box went down to 'Frisco daily with the ransom of an emperor—in the frenzy of those exciting days these elderly men spent their energies.

Charles Nordhoff, 1872

This logging train belonged to the Hetch Hetchy Valley Railroad. It was pulling quite a load to serve the huge demands for a growing population.

Courtesy Calaveras County Archives

Jim Hill, a man of well known bad character, accompanied by others of the same stripe, entered a store at Campo Seco and drew his pistol, presenting it at the head of the proprietor, while his companions removed the iron safe with its contents. Going to Sonora a few days later, he entered a house, and meeting a man, a stranger to him, he snatched the latter's pistol from his belt and struck him with it, and then fired it at him. The man, frightened, ran from the house and gave the alarm, upon which the Sheriff arrived and found Hill concealed under a bed, from whence he was removed to the jail. It was in a Spanish house of ill-fame that this occurred. In the morning following, a dozen men, took the prisoner to Campo Seco, to stand his trial. It was a matter of course that the prisoner, accused of robbery, should meet the punishment due for the greater crime of murder.

Immediately hundreds drew their pistols, and a universal stampede resulted. In the excitement Hill was thrust into a carriage and it was driven off hastily toward Sonora. But short as the time was it had been long enough to enable the would-be lynchers to notify the people of Sonora. Gathering at the sound of the [gong] instrument, the assemblage was addressed by Mr. Edwards, who ended by proposing to take the expected malefactor as soon as he arrived with Work, and hang him. There was not a dissenting voice.

Work was seized and overpowered. Separated from him, the prisoner made no resistance. In fifteen minutes he was hanging by the neck on an oak tree behind the El Dorado Hotel.

Mr. Ralph and blacksmith Mr. Jose at the Ralph Blacksmith shop, Sonora.

in the domestic circle; the great controller of public opinion, without whom society is dull and existence a blank.

Another of the permanent institutions was a military company, the "Sonora Greys," which was organized in the Spring of '54. It numbers about fifty members, and was commanded by Captain H. W. Theall.

DIVERSIONS OF THE EARLY MINER. By this date, a noticeable progress in refinement over the rough and reckless previous years had become apparent. As already mentioned, Sonora had taken the initiative in establishing schools and places of worship. Contemporaneously with these came the institution of theatrical exhibitions, which at first were, as befitted the mixed tastes of the earlier inhabitants, not of the highest order. It has been seen that the Town Council of Sonora was impelled to prohibit, by ordinance, the lewd exhibitions called "model artist shows." Bull fights, introduced by the Mexican inhabitants, had previously been a recognized means of diversion—more particularly, it was the regular source of amusement for beguiling the time on Sunday. Good fortune has, notwithstanding, preserved this relation of a typical combat which occurred near the spot where Wolfling's slaughter-house now stands: In 1850, Captain Gridley had advertised himself as being in possession of two bears, which he proposed, on a certain day, to pit against a long-horned Mexican bull, or, more properly, a steer, that was owned by another party. This, of course, was not exactly a bull fight, but was a contest perhaps more to the taste of such as chose to pay their dollar to behold, than the real simon-pure bull fight would have been.

At the appointed hour, the corral was surrounded by an immense crowd, standing on tiptoe and craning their necks to view the promised sensation. The bears, being let into the enclosure, excited a feeling of disappointment from their diminutive size, and the outcome showed that they were utterly unable to cope with their active and powerful antagonist. On the first charge of the excited steer, goaded to desperation by the shouts of the bystanders, the smaller of his two antagonists was toppled over instantly, rolling under the legs of the steer. The other, daunted by the onset, sought to escape by climbing the fence, despite the chain by which he was fixed to a stake in the corral. The bystanders, giving ground before the array of teeth and claws, fell over each other in confusion. On order being restored, it was found that Bruin had been shot and partially disabled. Thereon a quarrel arose with the proprietor, who insisted that the crowd should pay him for the damage done to his property. This was not acceded to, but a collection of a few dollars was made up on his promise to let the fight go on.

Three times more the animals were brought or driven in contact, each time resulting in a victorious charge by the hoofed quadruped that scattered his enemies in utter demoralization, and then the fight was declared "off," the owner of the steer offering to match his animal against five grown-up grizzlies.

Dr. Gillette, Mr. James, Captain Tracy and several other of the miners entertained us with a hospitality as gratifying as it was unexpected. In the evening we sat down to a supper prepared by Baptiste and his partner, Mr. Fisher, which completed my astonishment at the resources of that wonderful land. There, in the rough depth of the hills, where three weeks before there was scarcely a tent, and where we expected to live on jerked beef and bread, we saw on the table green corn, green peas and beans, fresh oysters, roast turkey, fine Goshen butter and excellent coffee.

Bayard Taylor, 1849

Ralph Blacksmith Shop on what is now Washington Street in Sonora. The building was torn down in 1930.

Courtesy Tuolumne County Museum

Ed Doyle's saloon in Sonora.

At 9 o'clock in the evening of January 18, 1855, Mr. McBirnie, a member of the firm of Bell & McBirnie, the Court House contractors, having business to transact, entered Mr. Heslep's office through the closed but not fastened door. To his horrified gaze the form of Joseph Heslep, his blood—his very brains—oozing through half a score of wounds upon his head.

No words can do justice to the extreme excitement that arose in saloons, in stores and in hotels. Messengers mounted on fleet horses were immediately dispatched to each of the ferries in the county to stop the egress of suspected parties.

Dr. Manning, the examining surgeon, reported that the deceased had received eight wounds upon the head, with an axe; that the skull was crushed at the crown, and that some of the brains were scattered upon the floor.

Griffiths, who, it appeared, had been last seen in the office, conversing with Mr. Heslep. Examined and reexamined, no question had shaken his testimony nor disturbed his coolness. During, however, his second or third examination, and while still sitting within the room where the jury were, Deputy Sheriff Randall and Constable Phillips entered the room, the latter calling the attention

continued in far right column

As there were no takers, one must conclude that the doughty bovine had achieved a reputation as invincible, or that grizzly bears were not easily procurable in quantity.

To return to the subject of amusements: In 1852 Messrs. Richardson and Imbrie built a theater in Campo Seco, which was one of the earliest structures of the kind in the county. Like most buildings of that date, it was built of wood, boarded up at the sides, and covered with canvas. It was, in fact, hardly more than a tent. In the front portion of the building was the familiar bar. In this primitive structure the Chapman Family held forth for many nights, playing the initial engagement. These actors seem to have had an exceedingly successful season in the mines, playing in all the camps which contained any facilities for such performances, or men enough to compose an audience. Every man went to hear them, and very possibly no actors, "star" or otherwise, ever met the expectations of their audiences more fully; and certainly no audiences ever rose to the demands of the performers with such unanimity—such excess of satisfaction, and ebullition of feeling—as theirs. At Columbia the stage was covered with buckskin purses, each containing what the generous givers thought a proper testimonial of their appreciation. Discovering, however, that there was not noise enough about it to fully emphasize their feelings, the boys took to throwing silver pieces, and there was, it was said, an immediate scarcity of these coins, which, by the way, had not long been in circulation in the mines. Enthusiastic, red-shirted miners escorted the actors to and from the theater, and even intruded their effusive good wishes into the privacy of the strangers' apartments. The force of generous sympathy could go no further than it did here.

THE BANKS OF TUOLUMNE. The year 1855, however, marked an era of misfortune and peril to the banking houses of that date. As before mentioned, the house of Wells, Fargo & Co. had established themselves in the mines, having several offices in Tuolumne county. Besides this firm, there were Adams & Co., Page, Bacon & Co., D. O. Mills & Co., all of whom had the confidence of the public to a remarkable degree. That this confidence was abused, time has made evident, for in February, 1855, rumors of the forthcoming ruin of some of the firms began to be heard throughout all California, into nearly every mining camp of which State their branches had extended. A universal panic was created, which led shortly to the suspension of some of these houses and the total failure of Page, Bacon & Co., thereby rendering penniless hundreds of those whom the hard won accumulations of years had made comfortable. Still there remained some firms who came forth from the wreck honestly and well, more flourishing and prosperous than ever, passing safely through the ordeal, and coming to possess the esteem of the communities wherein they transacted business.

In Columbia, D. O. Mills & Co. stood the fight bravely, paying their claims as fast as presented, and going on without embarrassment. Their stability was hardly doubted from first to

Kelly's Stable, Sonora.

continued from far left column

of the officers and jury to a valise which he held in his hands. As soon as Griffith caught sight of the valise, recognizing it, he exclaimed, "Ask me no more questions; I am the guilty man!" Constable Phillips and Deputy Randall then related how they had visited the room of the accused at the United States Hotel, where, concealed within the blankets of his bunk, they found the blood-stained garments, fresh clots of gore still remaining undried upon them, and these pressed into a valise, the heavy overcoat alone being placed under the pillow. Within the pockets of the latter garment were over six thousand dollars in gold coin.

At this point resolutions were passed declaring that the prisoner should die at daybreak. The crowd at daybreak made preparations to hang him. Sheriff Solomon made an ineffectual attempt to gain possession of him, but without the slightest avail, as he was alone in the midst of a vast and determined assemblage, which had firmly resolved on the man's death.

This well-outfitted cook tent is quite an elaborate set up for this camp's cook.

"Yankee Hill—On Sunday last, three Frenchmen found a lump of gold weighing 249 ounces, and valued at $3,600. This claim is in a small gulch, about one mile from Columbia, and was offered for sale but three days before for one ounce."

"Every miner who wishes work can find it at from four to five dollars per day, wages."

The Gazette

last, although a considerable "run" was inaugurated upon their house, which compelled them to pay out largely.

Wells, Fargo & Co. remained in working order through out the State, with the exception of a few of their offices, which suspended for a short time.

Adams & Co. had remained for several years the most prominent express company in the gold region. Their enterprise had been remarkable, even for the time in which it was displayed. Their offices in Tuolumne county were on a par with the amount of business they transacted. Taking the lead in all matters of enterprise as they did, their house was regarded as one of the least likely to be affected. But the storm which had burst upon them was not to be resisted. Their doors in Columbia and Sonora closed February 23, their agents stating that the suspension was only temporary, and that business would immediately be resumed, they having ample funds to satisfy depositors. The firm, however, was insolvent, and by the next mail came advices that they had applied for a discharge from their liabilities, by assigning their property to their creditors, their express business remaining intact throughout.

Upon receipt of this news in Columbia, a high degree of excitement was occasioned, and the office of Adams & Co. was besieged by a crowd of men clamoring for their deposits. But Charles J. Brown, the agent, had removed the available funds, depositing them in the safe of the Tuolumne Water Company, where they remained until handed over to the proper receiver, A. A. Cohen, of San Francisco. R. A. Robinson, the Secretary of the Water Company, who had assumed the responsibility of secreting the money in the said safe, incurred great odium therefor, he being looked upon as particeps criminis, by the miners, who were disposed to hold every one guilty who had anything to do with the banking companies, who had so suddenly become objects of detestation. The funds that thus escaped the search of these unauthorized creditors amounted to seven thousand dollars, including two thousand held for Mr. Bullock, the Springfield agent. At Sonora a large number of persons who had money deposited with Adams & Co. met on the 4th of March and took possession of the express office, broke open the vault, and removed the funds therein contained. A committee of four respectable citizens was appointed to disburse the money to those who held certificates of deposit. This the committee proceeded to do, until all the funds, amounting to about forty thousand dollars, had been paid out to the depositors present.

An incident of the career of Messrs. Adams & Co. may be worth mentioning here. It is the robbery of the Sonora and Stockton stage, of the box containing the shipment of the above firm, amounting, this time, to more than twenty-five thousand dollars. The robbery took place at a point one mile out of Sonora, and was effected by cutting the straps which

Later in the year 1855 came the murder of Isgrigg by Bessey, and that of Sam Poole by McCarthy, two cases, both of which grew out of low quarrels in ginmills, or deadfalls, and which do not possess sufficient interest to warrant a narration in these pages. The year of their occurrence was an exceptional one in the matter of man-killings.

Look closely and you'll find an interesting group at this Columbia butcher shop. The well dressed men in back are displaying the horns to still bloody stumps. The boy at the right, probably the butcher's son, is dragging the head of their latest project.

Courtesy Tuolumne County Museum

This case was the shooting of Drake by Hunter in the streets of Sonora. The difficulties that arose between the miners of Shaw's Flat and the different companies tunneling into Table Mountain, particularly that portion who were drifting into ground thought to belong to Shaw's Flat Mining District. The operations of the "Lager Beer" Company infringing upon the "Virginia" Company, brought about this state of things, Mr. Hunter was a well-known attorney something of the browbeating, swaggering stamp. He was a little, fussy man. On the occasion of the hearing of the mining case, as counsel for the Table Mountain side, he took occasion to severely score Eugene B. Drake, a well-known and influential miner of the Shaw's Flat party.

The parties met in the "Palace" saloon and came into personal collision, resulting in Hunter's being thrown by Drake, who was much the larger of the two. Following this came another hostile meeting, in front of the Placer Hotel when Drake seized Hunter, and pushed or threw him from the sidewalk.

Hunter placed his right hand under his coat tail, on his right hip, then

continued in far right column

The Camp 8 Logging Train and the opening of the River Bridge in 1900. The event drew a crowd of 2,000 people. The timbers ultimately became part of the Pinecrest Lodge.

held the box on the rear of the stage when it slipped off by its own weight. The weight was such as to require two men to lift it. With characteristic decision the agent, Mr. Bancroft, offered a reward of two thousand five hundred dollars for the arrest of the parties who committed the robbery, and five thousand dollars to any one through whose agency the money should be recovered, and a proportion of that sum for any part of the lost bullion. The result was that about one-half of the stealings were recovered, being found in Wood's Creek, about two hundred yards from the scene of the robbery. The company immediately fulfilled its promise, paying to the finders the sum agreed.

THE MINERS' CONVENTION. Public opinion had by the year 1852 been aroused to such an extent upon the subject of the disposition of the mineral lands of California, that action was taken in many localities towards influencing Congress to pass acts relating thereto.

Nine-tenths of the population of the State was then either centered in or directly dependent upon the product of the mines, capital, enterprise and labor all concentrating themselves around the diggings as a focus, while the larger cities, San

Francisco, Sacramento and Stockton, all owed their activity, and their existence, to the great industry of gold extraction.

All the laws and regulations concerning the mineral lands of the various sections were the result of the miners' own action. Untouched by State or national laws, the gold seekers were left to their own devices as regarded the disposal of the ground in which they worked. But early in the history of this county it has been seen that leagues of miners existed. The want of systematic rules giving to each one his proper rights was felt immediately upon the first experience in mining; and with the true manly instincts of the pioneers to uphold the weak and helpless, they made such regulations within their own "districts" as served to restrain the strong and aggressive, while giving to each his right to profit by the riches so plentifully diffused.

INNER LIFE OF THE MINERS. The inhabitants of the Atlantic States and of the cities of California, and even the earlier immigrants to the mines first imagined that the rainy season, corresponding as it did to the cold, dreary winter of the East, was of necessity the most disagreeable and unremunerative portion of the year to those engaged in mining. In the earlier years in which this industry was prosecuted, a succession of severe winters, coupled to the added disadvantage of the total want of roads, rendered the mines at times totally inaccessible. Famine, in consequence, was seriously feared, and the fashion then become common of retiring to the towns near San Francisco Bay, in order to pass that portion of the year.

F. J. Ralph, wheelwright, and Fred Dambacher blacksmith, Sonora, 1902.

Courtesy Tuolumne County Museum

raised his hand, in which he held a pistol, which he cocked as he raised it. Drake was slower; at first his pistol caught in his clothes. When he [Hunter] fired, Drake said: 'Oh, Lord!' and partly doubled up. Hunter fired again, and Drake fired twice in quick succession. Then Hunter fired again.

It was found that three of the four shots discharged by Hunter had taken effect—one in Drake's left arm below the elbow, glancing up and cutting the main artery; the other two in the right thigh, about half way above the knee; one shot passing through, the other remaining. He was taken to the Placer Hotel and attended by Drs. Kendall and Brown, who did all in their power is save him, but it was only by resorting to amputation of the arm that they were able to do so. Several days later a second amputation of the injured member was made, and the patient slowly but steadily recovered.

Hunter was unhurt by his antagonist's bullets, but he was immediately arrested, [and] he escaped punishment.

George Brown's team hauling freight from Chinese Station to Big Oak Flat, Groveland and Yosemite.

A man by the name of Jewell entered the American Hotel in Sonora, kept by Charles Ashton, and engaged in a dispute with the proprietor. The latter attacked him with a knife, evidently intending to cut his head off, but only succeeded in inflicting several gashes across his throat, none of which were of a serious character. Both were taken before Judge Jenkins, who, after hearing the evidence, pronounced judgment as follows: "Charley, I have to fine you ten dollars and half the costs; and as for you, Jewell, you're a disgrace to any community, and I fine you ten dollars and the other half!"

The Sonora Herld

This erroneous custom became abandoned in the succeeding years, when the fact was demonstrated that a far greater portion of the mining ground was workable during the wet season than at any other time. During the dry season most of the land surface was above the influence of the running streams, around which were gathered the majority of the population. On the hillsides and elevated table-lands water was rarely to be found, the ground was baked to its hardest, and the labor of prospecting was found burden some and disagreeable. When winter came, a new direction was given to the exertions of every miner. They then forsook the river beds and the coyote diggings, and spreading themselves over the surface of the country, took advantage of every little pool of water and every running streamlet, to minister to the desired end. The most provident, not wandering aimlessly, had before prospected and found a deposit of "pay dirt," near which they had erected a cabin and provided themselves with a store of food sufficient to last through their winter labors. The situation of those whose wise foresight had dictated such a course was not only tolerable, but was far superior to that of the laboring class in the cities.

Winter and spring were, and are, preeminently the most favorable seasons for placer mining, and they were, in addition, the most pleasant in the life of the gold-digger.

During the long winter evenings the miner enjoyed, better than at other times, the opportunities for rational delights. If he has had the forethought and the good taste to have provided himself with books, papers, pens and ink, he then had the opportunities of passing the time with good and lasting effects, besides making himself comfortable through their agency. He then indited long letters home, or read such volumes as by accident found their way to this secluded region; or, if his lot happened to be cast among congenial spirits, he sat and whiled the time away with conversation and song, diversified, perhaps, with a friendly game of cards or similar amusement. Happy they who spent their leisure time in their own log cabin after this fashion, rather than at the drinking-house, the gambling table, or the dancing saloon!

Not for all was this happy fate reserved; many a one had left all the endearments of home, and, with a heart buoyant with expectations, sought the far-off land of gold. The clank of his pick had been heard in its rugged ravines, his merry laugh had rung upon the hills, and life went prosperously on until Death's unfeeling hand beckoned him from the busy ranks of life. Disease prostrated his manly form; upon a rude couch, within a narrow tent, without the gentle, pain-dispelling hand of woman about his sleepless couch, he wasted away. When the icy arms of Death were thrown around him, chilling life's warm current, no father or mother was there to smooth his rough passage with their prayers; no wife, sister nor brother stood by him as he contended with the fell monster. No sobbing mourners followed in his funeral train, no church bell tolled for his depar-

The road to Sonora, as indeed to most places in this country, has never been laid out by Government, but is, in fact, a natural trail or path marked out by the first pioneer wagons that passed that way, deviated from, from time to time, as experience indicated a shorter cut; receiving no assistance from the hand of man, and encountering a vast number of obstacles from the hand of nature.

For instance, we arrive at a part, that, skirting the base of a hill, presents a rapid declination to the left, which is a very hard and rocky-looking ravine. Colonel Reed exclaims, as he places his foot on the break, which works from the box, "Hard up to the right!" upon which the insiders loll their heads and bodies out on that side of the vehicle to preserve its equilibrium. We had to "hard up" a great many times either to one side or the other, during which time J. Bellow always considered it necessary to assist the fair Canadian; whereupon the Irishman looked fierce and talked large, but finally one of the miners told him, in a quiet but unmistakable manner, that "if he didn't 'dry up" he'd chuck him out of the stage.

Frank Marryat, early 1850s

Golden Gate Mine with Underground Superintendent Joe Francis on left and Louis Hofer.

My Dear Wife

On the 8th of May, while sinking still deeper on our Claim, we struck a lead which paid at first about 50 cts per pan, and before night 2 & 3 dollars, we were now offered 1000 dollars for our Claim, we did not know how extensive the lead was, but we prefered to keep our Claims, and the result has proved that we made a good choice, for in ten days we washed out from this lead, three thousand dollars. The last day we washed we took out 695 dollars. We have now at least 1200 dollars a piece in our pile of dirt that we have hauled ready to wash when the water comes in. Two weeks ago one of our men washed out 86 dollars in one pan of dirt, but you must know it does not all pay as well as that but we have frequently got from 5 to 10 dollars to the pan. As our sucess became known, we had thousands of visitors from the mines around us, and we were all weary in answering their numerous questions about our diggings. Our luck (as people are pleased to call it) received a passing notice in the Columns of the Sonora Herald. I could sell my share now for 1500 dollars, but think I can do better by staying and washing the dirt myself

*Horace Root,
Shaws Flat,
Saturday, July 10, 1852*

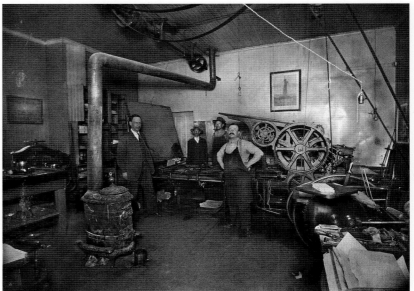

Interior of The Tuolumne Independent *that was located on the Northeast corner of Jackson and Washington Street, in Sonora.*

ture, or gray-haired pastor chanted the prayer for the departed; a few comrades bore him to the lonely spot where he now rests.

THE FANDANGO. The mining camps have furnished, and will continue to furnish, a limitless field for the exertions of the humorous writer. They were, and are, rich in pathetic incidents, and the names of those who have drawn upon this inexhaustible storehouse of wit, humor and pathos, are fresh in the minds of the English speaking world. But jokes, stories and pathetic scenes, it may be said, are not suitable materials for use in a book like this; nor is it the intention of the writer to include such in an undue degree, nor to give prominence to any subject outside the domain of the judicious narrator of facts. But there are subjects akin to the lighter walks of literature, of which a regard for the completeness of the historical picture compels mention.

Taking on importance from the reckless prodigal support of the burly, red-shirted American miner, to whom gold was but as the dust moved by the idle wind, the new importation waxed strong, furnishing an amusement not out of keeping with the men of that time. Its votaries were not alone the brutal and the ignorant, for many a son of pious training, many a respected grey-headed former resident of staid and moral Eastern communities, were found pursuing the lascivious pastime through the merry mazes of the dance, while even the cloth itself, as we are told, disclaimed not the seductive blandishments of the dark-hued syrens, daughters of Terpsichore, whose many twinkling feet and far-extending and lavishly displayed charms lent enchantment to the views of men in whom the hot blood of youth beat, untempered by any very severe asceticism.

Spreading wide their portals for the motley train, the Fandango house flourished, the arbiter of pleasure and of play. There the tinkling guitar, with soft, lascivious strain, kept time to the song from Italy, the step from France. The midnight orgy, the mazy dance, the smile of beauty and the flush of strong drink, for fools, gamesters and all, combined to energize the subject they pursued, giving both the devil and his dance their due, where fools' paradise might seem dull to what there passed through the fleeting hours of night.

Various were the different styles of Fandangoes; improving upon the unfastidiousness of their Mexican cousins. Sonora boasted among her five houses devoted to this species of entertainment, of a palatial center, wherein all that art and elegance might do was brought to their aid. In stylish and brilliantly lighted room, girt around and ornamented with priceless pictures, costly furniture, and lined with Venetian mirrors, to reflect back the scenes they witnessed, and provided with a bar, from whence the costliest liquors, the rarest wines, were dealt out with unsparing hand, grew the American edition of the Fandango in all its glory.

Tuolumne County family enjoying the day.

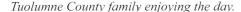

I had a fragmentary suit of clothes in which I had just crossed the desert. The shirt was mostly of earthen hue—and the collar was as stiff with sweat and dust as a piece of sheet-iron. The drawers had once been of woollen goods, and had a seat to them, but from contact with the saddle there was a frightful vacancy where the seat had been. The socks were pretty much of a piece with the shirt, and the cravat ditto. A fit of generosity came over me. I had donned a new suit of under-clothing, and the old one was worthless; I could afford to be liberal. Calling a young buck, I bade him strip himself, put the shirt, drawers—what there was left of them—socks and neck-tie upon him, turned the collar of the shirt up so that it reached nearly to the top of his head, and then turned him loose. I saw him going down to the rancheria with two buxom squaws following admiringly behind him, the condition of his drawers being no draw-back on his appearance in that society. I felt that I had done a noble thing and made a fellow-creature happy. I came back an hour later and found him stretched at full length on the dusty earth, playing cards for the various articles of clothing I had bestowed upon him. They had played everything off him but the neck-tie when I arrived, and, clad in that light and airy costume only, he was then gambling for that, with a fair chance of losing.

Albert S. Evans, 1860s

The Blakesleys, or Blakelys, were sitting at supper in company with one Verplank, Saturday, February 14, 1857, when they were fired upon from the outside of the window, and one of the brothers, John Blakely, was shot in the back. All instantly jumped to their feet, the light was blown out, and they fled for safety through the back door. John Blakely fell at the door; his brother William, lingering a moment to seize a rifle standing in the corner, saw a man, who entering the open front door, fired at him. William Blakely was shot in the arm at that discharge, a very severe wound being inflicted, which necessitated amputation. The three survivors escaping, brought the news to Sonora.

Sheriff Stuart proceeded to Lyons' residence and arrested Lyons, Poer, and a young man named Wallace.

Wallace was induced to confess the guilt of himself and of his accomplices. [He said] they left Lyons' residence on Friday night while it was storming, and traveled to the Blakeley's place and hid themselves in a cave. When night approached they approached the house. Lyons had planned that all three of the brothers should be killed, so as to leave no one to tell the tale.

The verdict of the Coroner's Jury was that John Blakeley was murdered by Lyons and Poer.

On the eleventh of December, 1857, the final sentence of the law was executed upon Lyons, Poer and McCauley. They were conveyed to the place of death followed by an immense concourse of people numbering perhaps five thousand.

Post Office and West's Store in Soulsbyville. Thomas West is on the left.

Upon the scene the tallow candles cast a feeble glare, and the smoke of cigaritos and cheap and bad cigars fills the room with a dim haziness. Through the murky gloom the dancers are moving with a perfect looseness, a crowd of men, spectators of the scene, line the sides of the apartment, while the perspiring guitarist and the catgut-torturing fiend of the violin lustily horrify the drowsy ear of night with uncouth sounds from their dyspeptic instruments.

Every race under the sun seems to have sent its representative to honor the Fandango. On either side sit swarthy, filthy, vermin-infested greasers, wrapped in dirty serape, and puffing cigaritos with imperturbable nonchalance. The Sydney convict, with under-hung jaw and furtive grimace, comes next, elbowing perfumed gentlemen in broadcloth, titled with Major, Colonel, Judge, or Alderman. In corners lounge handsomely dressed young gentlemen, having the appearance of clerks in mercantile houses. Sporting men are also there to assist in the display of animated nature; and physicians and lawyers, the victims of clients and patients, or of hereditary laziness. The senoras, of brown complexion, of scanty habiliments, of plumptitudinous figure, urge on the merry rounds until the wee small hours approaching tell of expiring night; then homeward, not unguarded, under the gleams of Venus' star, hasten, with not reluctant feet, to silence and repose.

The first Board of Trustees, in a formidable onslaught on the enemy, interdicted the use of drums and trombones, and the sweet sounds necessary for the measures of the giddy dance were prescribed to issue from the dulcet flute, the neighborly piano, the effeminate guitar, the agile violin. Thus did the first reform savor of peace and gentility. Died away the warlike roll of the drum, and the brassy voice of the trombone ceased from out the land. The law was triumphant; and save the wakeful cat, the hilarious he who runs amuck, and the watchful chanticleer, no sounds there were to break the dreams of the softly sleeping citizen.

Next, fandangoes were ordered and directed to go out of operation upon Sundays, that they might no longer offend the day devoted to quiet, to repose, and the discharge of grateful duties for the manifold blessings enjoyed by man.

NOTED ROBBERS AND ROBBERIES. Only authentic data which relate to the life of this desperado are only to be gathered by word of mouth from those living residents of the Southern Mines who knew Joaquin and watched his career. Of these, probably Hon. Caleb Dorsey, of Sonora, is best qualified to supply facts relating thereto, as he was, through a remarkable chain of events, brought into close relations with the noted robber and his band. Of all the mass of so-called recollections of the man who was at the time the terror of the mines, scarcely a thing has been said that does not partake of the grossest exaggeration. To begin with, the story of the outrage upon his wife by Americans,

I saw a man who came to the river three weeks before my visit, without money, to dig in the dry gulch. Being very lazy, he chose a spot under a shady tree, and dug leisurely for two days without making a cent. He then gave up the place, when a little German jumped into his tracks and after a day's hard work weighed out $800. The unlucky digger then borrowed five ounces and started a boarding-house. The town increased so fast that the night I arrived he sold out his share (one-third) of the concern for $1,200. Men were not troubled by the ordinary ups and downs of business, when it was so easy for one of any enterprise to recover his foothold. If a person lost his all, he was perfectly indifferent; two weeks of hard work gave him enough to start on, and two months, with the usual luck, quite reinstated him.

Bayard Taylor, 1849

A Porter engine moving car full of rocks at Relief. The sign on the engine reads "Union Construction Company."

With so many teams and wagons on so narrow a trail, there is occasionally much disputing for the right of way. Men carry arms on the road as a general rule; but very seldom use any worse weapon than their tongues in these disputes. In a very awkward descent we found the road entirely and unnecessarily blocked up by a wagon, drawn by eight yoke of oxen. The colonel at a glance recognized a teamster with whom he had previously had many words on the same subject, and he opened fire by ordering him to his own side of the road; to which the teamster sulkily acquiesced after some delay.

On either side were gambling-houses of large dimensions, but very fragile structure, built of a fashion to invite conflagration, though offering little of value to the devouring element when the invitation was accepted, which it was about every other night or so. In most of these booths and barns the internal decorations were very glittering; chandeliers threw a brilliant light on the heaps of gold that lay piled on each monte table, while the drinking-bars held forth inducements that nothing mortal is supposed to be able to resist. On a raised platform is a band of music, or perhaps some Ethiopian serenaders, or, if it is a Mexican saloon, a quartet of guitars; and in one house, and that the largest, is a piano, and a lady in black velvet who sings in Italian and accompanies herself, and who elicits great admiration and applause on account of the scarcity of the fair sex in this region.

Frank Marryat, early 1850s

Boarders at the Yo Semite House hotel, 1890s.

and Joaquin's consequent oath of undying hatred toward his enemies and all their race, is, most likely, untrue.

The definite and positive information which can now be gathered of Joaquin Murietta represents him to have been a resident of Martinez, near Saw Mill Flat, in the early part of 1852. Previous to this his history is not known in the least, unless it be so to his own countrymen, the Mexicans. At that time he had not commenced his career of open robbery, but was addicted to a more underhanded kind of thievery, that is to say, he was a monte dealer; and in company with a number of other scamps, engaged with him in the business of fleecing his fellow countrymen and such low trash of other nationalities whose tastes and ignorance led them into the sharpers' clutches. Graduating from this trivial occupation to the more exciting and probably more lucrative one of footpad, or in more magnificent language, highwayman, Joaquin and his band committed several outrages in that neighborhood, and being tacitly supported by the entire Mexican population, then very large, he easily evaded arrest.

The officers of the law were put in defiance, the authorities were powerless, and even a display of military force was insufficient to overawe the outlaws.

The lucid, plain and logical account of Mr. Dorsey, concerning the cause and results of the somewhat noted "Battle of Saw Mill Flat." Mr. D. was engaged in the summer of 1853 in lumbering on the Flat, being a partner in the firm of Dorsey, Jacobs and Smith, owners of a saw-mill. Ira McCrae, a prominent man, kept a store on the Flat, and was a buyer of gold-dust, as a part of his mercantile affairs. For several days Messrs. Dorsey, McCrae and others had been meditating the capture of Joaquin. Finally word was brought that the individual was at a fandango which was running. Mr. Dorsey fell into conversation with an ordinary looking Mexican [and] made that it did not matter how he was taken, alive or dead, for the Americans were bound to have him in some shape or other. The expedition were intensely surprised and a good deal discomfited when, on their return to the Flat, they were informed that the very man who held Mr. D. in conversation was Joaquin himself! Shortly after, an attempt was made to destroy the lives of many persons, by poisoning the waters of the spring which furnished a supply of water to a portion of the residents of Saw Mill, but this failed, owing to the extreme diffusion of the drug that was used.

Immediately after this episode, it became known that Messrs. Dorsey, McRae and Turner had become marked by the outlaws, and that their death had been resolved upon.

"About two o'clock on Monday morning a young man named William Bowen, from Providence, Rhode Island, was stabbed with a sword or knife, and died near daybreak. He appeared to be about 22 or 23 years of age. His name, together with an anchor, were pricked in Indian ink on his arm. As far as we can learn, he was flourishing a sword in a Spanish house just behind Justice Barry's office, where men were drunk and women were dancing, at a late hour of the night. The place, the company, and the hour, were all against him; and we trust the unhappy result will be a warning to others.

The Sonora Herald

Big Oak Flat Road to Yosemite National Park in the early 1900s. Buggies, stagecoaches and horseback transported thousands into Yosemite for many years. The waterfall on the right whets the traveler's appetite for the spectacular scenery yet to come.

On August 3, 1855, two Chilenos, Escobar and Sebada, were executed by due process of law for the murder of John Sheldon, a constable of Sonora.

Marshal J. F. McFarland, in endeavoring to convey a drunken Spaniard from the Tigre to the jail, was beset by several of the prisoner's friends, who tried to rescue him. Calling for assistance, several Americans responded, and in the brief combat that ensued, a Chilean, name not given, was shot with three bullets, any one of which was sufficient to have let out his life. The man died, but the officer was not forgotten by his friends, and for years thereafter the footsteps of John Sheldon were dogged by the unforgiving former intimates of the dead Chilean, until at last a fitting opportunity came, and accounts were squared by another violent death. Sheldon, who was night watchman, was perfectly aware that his enemies had determined to kill him. On one excessively dark night in May, 1855, three men sprang upon him from behind some obstructions, and seizing him, muffled as he was in his cloak, stabbed him fatally, and ran off in the darkness, leaving no trace save a hat which one of them dropped. The wounded man staggered to the United States Hotel, and within a few minutes expired. Fleeing to Tuttletown, two of the murderers were there taken on the very next day, the lost hat furnishing the sole clew by which they were identified. Proofs of their guilt being forthcoming at their trial, a verdict of guilty of murder in the first degree was rendered. August 3 they hanged in presence of a crowd of three thousand spectators.

Denny Guerin and his six-horse team of the Milton, Jamestown and Sonora stage.

The next sensation came from the report that McRae's store was to be robbed on that very night. A messenger rode to Columbia in haste, and the military company of that place was collected, and it immediately set out for the scene of the expected hostilities. Revolvers and rifles had been cleaned and loaded, their hats decorated with patriotic feathers, and the little brass cannon, used for doing service on great days in firing salutes, was brought along. Firing the little two-inch cannon about once in every hundred yards, the command finally arrived at their destination, Col. Tom Cazneau in command. It was soon seen that this imposing force would be of no use, for no attack was made, nor was any seriously meditated. The military, however, gave a good example of their destructive powers by charging upon the eatables and the drinkables, completely cleaning out the small supply of both that was then held at the Flat, and rendering it ever since a doubtful question whether it wouldn't have been better to be robbed by Joaquin's men than to be protected by Cazneau's.

While prospecting for gold on the North Fork of the Stanislaus in company with several friends, it became necessary for Mr. Dorsey to return suddenly to Sonora. Starting sufficiently early in the day, he would have got through to town on the same evening, had it not been that while crossing the hill above the South Fork, he became uncertain of his way, and fearing to descend the hill lest the ground become impassable, he dismounted and made preparations to camp at a spring near by. After getting comfortably fixed for the night, a gang of six Mexicans rode up and also made preparations to pass the night.

After cooking supper, they called Mr. Dorsey to share their repast, which, being concluded, songs were sung before the party retired to rest. In the singing, as their suspicious visitor noticed, a certain one-eyed man took the lead. This observation, it will be seen, has an important bearing on what followed. Retiring to his own ground, Mr. Dorsey slept the sleep of the tired, even in the midst of danger; for it was well known to him that he was regarded as an especial enemy by the Mexicans; but he had reason to hope that these people did not know him, even if they were of the outlaws, as he surmised. His intuitions were correct; for, when morning dawned, the Mexicans arose, prepared breakfast, and again invited their neighbor to partake with them, and this invitation, as the other, was accepted, as the guest did not think it prudent to decline. After doing justice to the viands, all were about to ride off, when the leader of the band, calling Mr. Dorsey aside, demanded sternly of him, under pain of death, that he give his word of honor not to divulge the fact that he had met them. Under the circumstances, it is no wonder that the gentleman did as requested. Subsequently he learned that his entertainers were indeed a portion of Joaquin's band, and their mission on that trip had been to steal horses.

This novel experience was followed by an equally novel one, but one in which the element of danger was lacking. A Mexican charged with stealing horses was incarcerated in jail in Sonora. Demanding counsel, Mr. Dorsey was sent for by the attendants. Upon entering the jail, the prisoner proved to be no other than the one-eyed musician of the previous paragraph. He, perhaps even more surprised than Mr. Dorsey, explained the estimation in which the latter was held by his compatriots,

September, 1849, was not a handsome place, but money was plentiful and the gamblers were reaping a harvest from the miners who had been fortunate in finding good claims, made money fast and spent it still faster. Monte was the favorite game with the Mexicans. Often bags of gold dust would be staked on the turning of a card with apparent indifference as to the result. No steamboat had yet been put on between Stockton and San Francisco so we were obliged to take passage on a schooner paying $16 passage. We made the trip in six days, tying up in the tules at night at the mercy of millions of mosquitoes, was anything but pleasant

Harvey Wood, 1851

Crew of the Eagle Shawmut Mine, 1898.

Courtesy Tuolumne County Museum

Shawmut Mine, April 1898.

> Our company had a few members who advised organizing in military style to insure our safe arrival in California. They managed to have themselves chosen as officers, then commenced the drilling of us raw recruits. We actually had guards stationed out day and night, going through all the forms of a soldier-life. The trouble was we had too many officers for the number of privates. Playing soldier did not last long
>
> Harvey Wood, 1849

and solemnly announced that if they had known him on the night of the meeting at South Fork, they would have shot him to strings. Now, however, the case was reversed; and Mr. Dorsey, while agreeing to defend the criminal and use his utmost exertions to free him, received in turn a promise that he should not in future receive harm from the outlaws. This, the prisoner said he would prevail on Joaquin to sanction. The result was, that, while Mr. Dorsey lived unmolested by the bandits, the prisoner—through the representations made to the Grand Jury in regard to the situation of Messrs. Dorsey and McRae with reference to the gang, and their promise not to carry out their threats of vengeance—escaped indictment.

Later on, an affray occurred at Sawmill Flat, which resulted in the wounding of Claudio, Joaquin's lieutenant. It seems that a Mexican had been detected in stealing a pistol, and while Constable John Leary of Columbia was attempting to make his arrest, several Mexicans rushed to their companion's assistance. Joaquin himself took a hand in the fight, and, although shot at repeatedly, made his escape. Not so fortunate was Claudio. This person, who was a mere youth of eighteen or so, was very badly wounded. Lying upon the top of a hill up which his pursuers had to advance, he emptied his two six-shooters at them before they could reach the spot. Advancing with cocked pistol, the Constable was about to blow the youth's brains out, when Mr. Dorsey interfered, saving his life. Badly wounded, Claudio was borne to the hospital, there to re-main until his naturally strong constitution enabled him to recover from his dreadful injuries. While convalescent, he, in an interview with his preserver, corroborated what the one-eyed man had told concerning the oaths of vengeance taken by the band, but said that as the former culprit had got free, if they would undertake to secure his safety, he would see that those promises were carried out; at the same time promising Mr. Dorsey that the whole band should leave the county and go to Mexico, never to return.

When asked on what security these promises were to be fulfilled, he answered proudly: "Sir, you have the word of honor of a highwayman!" which was pretty lofty language, considering the speaker.

On sending for Joaquin to come in and sanction the treaty, that individual refused to honor Sonora by his presence, but assented to the arrangements which Claudio had made. And the Grand Jury proving facile, the young criminal escaped.

Once again it was Mr. Dorsey's fortune to come in contact with the gang. This was while on his way to a session of Court in Mariposa County, when he fell in with and took dinner with Claudio and other members, at Moccasin Creek, where he found them encamped by the roadside. Claudio then represent-

"H.N. Brown and Co. Wholesale and Retail Dealers in groceries, provisions & hardware" at corner of Washington and Main Streets, Columbia, California, 1858.

Recently our town [Sonora] was thrown into excitement by the discovery of two murdered men, named Burke and Dolf, about one mile from this place. A jury went out and held an inquest and the bodies were brought in in a wagon and placed in the hospital where they were bathed and dressed, and buried the next morning. Their bodies were most horribly cut and mutilated, one with his head nearly cut off, from behind, a heavy gash in the face, and several deadly stabs in the breast. The other had a single cut across the head and face, which severed it in two pieces. They were horrible pictures to look upon. During the day they had been to an auction and purchased some clothing, and in the evening left for Sullivan's with a small piece of beef for their supper. About eight o'clock they were found murdered, with their pockets turned inside out, evidently for plunder. The citizens offered a reward of $2,500 for the murderers but no clue has yet been found.

Enos Christman,
October 22, 1850

Robinson's Ferry on the Stanislaus River. Sometimes called cable crossings, ferries like this were usually the first step toward a bridge. There were literally hundreds of these crossings on rivers all over California. The remnants of many can still be found along riverbanks..

My Ellen:—A year has passed since I held thy hand and bid thee a sad adieu. What a short time! Yet how many trials, difficulties and dangers have we passed through during that time! How many midnight hours have we spent upon a sleepless pillow, thinking of each other.

You say you cherish a letter from me. Then how much more must I cherish a letter from you? You are surrounded by old associations. I am in a strange land among strangers, battling hard to climb the mountain now before me.

Enos Christman to Ellen Apple, Sonora Herald Office, Sonora, California, Wednesday, July 24,

ed that they were on their way to Mexico, and he took occasion to renew his promise of the present of a splendid horse and trappings to his guest in return for the favors done him. Leaving the camping place, Mr. D. proceeded up a steep hill, and on the way met a horseman magnificently mounted, whom he soon recognized as the redoubtable Joaquin himself. Both drew their pistols, and a conflict seemed imminent, when the Mexican, holding up his hand, cried out: "We keep our word; you are safe, sir!" And, re-assured, the traveler passed on, having met the scourge of the mines for the last time. It was not long after that the notorious brigand fell by the hand of Captain Harry Love; and his head, which was exhibited in Sonora, was inspected by Mr. Dorsey, who knew him so well in life, and who, to silence the doubt which has been expressed as to the certainty of Joaquin's death, says now, unqualifiedly, that it was the head of the man whom he knew as Joaquin. So that matter rests.

Lieutenant Claudio met a befitting fate upon the gallows, being hanged for horse-stealing, down in Los Angeles County. And if the grimness of the joke may be pardoned, Mr. Dorsey still expresses himself in doubt whether or not the horse which Claudio was trying to steal was not the "splendid animal with gorgeous trappings" that dashing young robber promised him while immured in jail in Sonora.

MILITARY AND POLITICAL AFFAIRS. Several companies of volunteer troops, infantry and cavalry, were organized for service in the war, the history of whom is interesting. The first organized was the famous Tuolumne Rangers, who were recruited in Columbia and vicinity, and of whom many were well-known and respected citizens. The Rangers numbered at the time of their departure for service one hundred and nine men all told. These troops, which were cavalry, were enlisted for service on the Overland Route, but going to San Francisco in September, 1861, they were stationed for a time at Camp Alert, forming a part of Colonel P. Edward Conner's Third Infantry Regiment, of California Volunteers.

In the Fall of '61 recruiting offices were opened in Sonora, several companies, independent organizations were formed, the object of some of whom was to proceed to the theatre of warfare and engage in the defence of the Union, while others were simply Home Guards, whose object was to restrain the acts and expressions of disloyal people.

Captain Watson organized a company of Home Guards, who used the arms and equipments of the old Sonora Greys. Don Pedro Lepi formed a company of Mexican Home Guards,

Columbia Marble Company at the Columbia marble quarry. Marble was a desired building material used in expensive homes, banks, and other structures. Some stayed in the area while a great deal was sent to San Francisco to serve the needs of the rapidly growing population.

On Wednesday a large number of wild Indians, both men and women, passed through our town on their way to the Tuolumne River. Many of them were almost nude, having nothing but a shirt on or blanket wrapped around them; the men with their bows and arrows, the women with their long conical baskets slung over their backs, kept from falling by a strap passing over the tops of their heads. The women appeared to do all the drudgery, having their baskets, which hold about a bushel each, well filled with meat which they gather wherever they can, not scrupling to kill any one's horse or ox if they fail in finding elk or deer.

At Slater's ranch, within three miles of Sonora, two warriors of the party attempted to steal several horses kept by a Mexican. At their approach the Mexican posted himself behind a tree and while in this position, they fired three arrows at him, one of which took effect in the left arm, near the shoulder, passing clear through it. He then fired a pistol at them which had the effect to drive them off. A party of armed Americans started out in pursuit of the Indians Thursday morning, but they have returned without overtaking them.

On the same day two Frenchmen found the remains of an American a few miles from town, evidently murdered, with the head lying several rods from the body, the pockets and belt cut open as with a knife, and the body much mutilated and torn by the coyotes.

Enos Christman,
Friday, September 6, 1850

Logging train showing seven 16-foot logs. Part of the operation of the Westside Flume and Lumber Company.

The Mexican population preponderates in Sonora and its vicinity, and nearly every thing is stamped with their nationality. The gambling-tables are surrounded by them; and, dirty fellows as they are, they are very picturesque at a distance with their slouch hats and long serapes. The American population, between whom and the Mexicans a rooted hatred exists, call the latter "Greasers," which is scarcely a complimentary sobriquet, although the term "Greaser camp;" as applied to a Mexican encampment, is truthfully suggestive of the filth and squalor the passing traveler will observe there.

Frank Marryat, early 1850s

forty-eight in number, and an infantry company was formed at Jamestown, and another at Severance's Old Mill in the mountains.

The Sigel Guard, of Sonora, organized in April, 1862, were Home Guards.

"Tuolumne Home Guards," of Columbia, should not be omitted, who were organized in August, 1861, receiving uniforms and equipments from the Government, and fitting up for their exclusive use an armory in Nellis' building.

So much for the military organizations. In regard to the contents of newspapers, it is to be observed that they were almost wholly given up to the discussion of political subjects and to war news, and to vilifying their neighbors. Probably no more violent, incendiary utterances ever emanated from any sheet than those which appeared in the weekly newspapers of Sonora, during the war times. Insolent, overbearing and abusive to the last degree, it is quite remarkable that their language did not lead to more frequent displays of personal violence. Judging by the columns of these periodicals, their writers were selected mainly in accordance with their power to blackguard and recriminate; and whole pages were filled with the choicest specimens of shrewdly concealed insinuations, or open defiance and bullying, that the brain of any newspaper writer ever inspired.

DECADENCE OF THE SOUTHERN MINES. Towards the end of the fifties, the Southern Mines had diminished so greatly in their output of the precious metal that the population began to decrease alarmingly. The towns were in their decadence. Tumble-down houses, adobes falling to ruin in the rain; sidewalks rotted away; doors off of hinges, and windows the absence of whose lights indicated that the liver too was gone; all these signs showed the departed glory of the Mines, and gave even more painful promise of a yet deader epoch.

With the departure of the miners came dull times for the camps. The stores and saloons, no longer crowded with customers, put up their shutters and retired from a business no longer profitable. The professional gentlemen mostly withdrew from a country where there existed no demand for their services. The baker, the butcher, and the other tradesmen who ministered to the wants of an active population, sought in other and newer localities the golden harvest which had ceased in their former home.

Ditches and flumes were suffered to go to ruin, and all the thousand and one evidences of man's energy and perseverance gave token of the day of departed greatness. By the close of the next decade the resounding crash of the stamp mill had well nigh ceased, and now, in 1882, while one can not say that

Beardsley Flat trestle on the Middle Fork of the Stanislaus.

[Jamestown] has from a thousand to twelve hundred inhabitants. The second [Sonoranian Camp] is smaller, but has a floating population of from 2,000 to 3,000 people at least. In both of these settlements there are well stocked stores, restaurants, cafés, billiard halls, etc., and in the evening when these fine tents are lighted and thousands of people are circulating through the streets of these strange towns, it is hard for one to believe that he is in a wild and uncivilized country, surrounded by Indian tribes and at the foot of the Sierra Nevada wilderness.

Jacques Antoine Moerenhout, 1848

The "Tin Man", or tinsmith, displaying his tools and wares, 1850.

The chief town of the southern mines; and as, independently of my curiosity to inspect it, I wished to visit that section of the country, we started at four o'clock one evening in a small river boat called the "*Jenny Lind,*" bound to Stockton, a town situated on the San Joaquin River.

On starting from San Francisco for the mines, it was but natural to bid adieu to cleanliness and comfort for the time being; and having so fortified myself, I was better able to withstand the intolerable filth of the "*Jenny Lind.*" She has since "blown up," which is about the only thing that could have purified her.

    Frank Marryat, early 1850s

mining is entirely done—for yet many valuable quartz veins and much unprospected placer ground, and miles of concealed auriferous river-beds remain—yet gold extraction is comparatively at a painfully low ebb.

Victor Trabucco ran freight wagons for his brother's store. He'd haul freight to Merced, with many stops in the middle. Hauling the heavy loads uphill required him to disconnect the second wagon and return for it after the first was safely up the grade.

Chapter 4: Mariposa County — Mariposa, Coulterville, Hornitos, Yosemite and vicinity

[Mariposa County was one of the original counties of California, created at the time of statehood in 1850. While it began as the state's largest county, over time the territory that was once part of Mariposa was ceded to twelve other counties: Fresno, Inyo, Kern, Kings, Los Angeles, Madera, Merced, Mono, San Benito, San Bernardino, San Luis Obispo, and Tulare. Thus, Mariposa County is known as the "Mother of Counties."

The county's name came from Mariposa Creek, which was named by Spanish explorers in 1806, when they discovered thousands of butterflies ("mariposas" in Spanish) in the area.

During the Gold Rush large quantities of the glittery substance was found. Placer mining was used initially, but from lack of water in the area, hard rock mines quickly took over.

Soon after dinner we fell in with four or five broken-down-looking fellows on foot who were returning from the mines, and they gave us some rather discouraging accounts. They told us that they had been there some five or six months without being able to make anything, and that hundreds were there working for their board alone. This did not in the least abate our bright anticipations and we are determined to go and see for ourselves.

Enos Christman,
March 14, 1850

Mariposa Mine's stamp mill was water powered. It was the first hard rock mill in California since water was scarce and hydraulic and placer mining generally not viable options.

Got up about half past five this morning all having slept pretty good — there being no donkeys and very few fleas. We had to carry some along with us from the Flats for company sake. We don't get started till about seven o'clock. The Chinaman is to remain here until the stage passes — with his big two horse wagon it would be rather difficult to pass or get out of the way of a six horse stage. Ida and Mr. Stroby are on horseback this morning. Aggie and Mr. Sax, Jack and Addie, Doc and myself in buggies. We are driving along at full speed when the folks ahead call out stage. Doc is in a very bad place to turn out, but Mr. Stroby gets down and lifts the buggy around.

Tillie Daulton,
June 24th, 1880
en route to Yosemite

John C. Fremont had claim to a Mexican land grant but had to fight for his claim for many years. In 1855 the US Supreme Court finally ruled in his favor. As a result, the area was resurveyed, giving Fremont areas that already contained several productive mines.

The discovery of gold brought thousands of white men into the area. It wasn't long before hostilities with the Indians led to the Indian War.

In 1851, Major Savage led two Companies of men to an Indian stronghold in what is now called Yosemite Valley, the white man's discovery of Yosemite, Mariposa's real gold.

With no narrative history written in the 19th century, the stories are told exclusively through available newspaper articles, photos, diaries and journals.]

1863. DEATH OF COLORADO JACK. The Indian Desperado closed his career of crime on Saturday last. His whereabouts was discovered through his sending a message to his squaw by a Yaqui Indian named Poncho, who was traced to Jack's place of concealment in a gulch near Colorado. A party well armed immediately started for his den, which proved to be a small drift in the bank of the gulch. Upon their approach Jack came out and faced the enemy – drew a pistol and fired – then threw it away and fired one shot with a shot-gun. – A shot, followed by a whole volley from the party, "settled his hash." He died game. There is no doubt that he was lying around in that neighborhood for the purpose of getting even with some of the party who attempted his capture on Bear Creek. The community is rid of a very dangerous Wally.

FOUND DEAD. Saturday last — man named Peter Testor, was found dead about a mile above Merced Falls, yesterday afternoon. When the body was found, it was lying under a cliff of rocks, with a large stone, supposed to be at least 200 pounds weight, lying upon the breast, and the skull bone was mashed. It is supposed that the deceased was walking upon the edge of the cliff, and that the stone gave way, precipitating him to the bottom together with the rocks.

MYSTERIOUS MURDER. A Mexican came into town a day or two since and gave the following particulars in relation to the murder of his brother. He say that about the 2d of February, the two were working and camping together in the neighborhood of the Cunningham Toll Road, on Green's gulch — that his brother left very suddenly, that he thought nothing of it at first, but afterwards got uneasy and made search for him,

The Valley was originally tenanted by a small tribe of particularly unwashed aborigines of some five hundred persons. They eschewed the pursuit of large game, and lived chiefly on scenery and fish. One day, while one of these sheep-hearted braves was employed in trouting at Mirror lake he heard a sort of ursine chuckle behind him. Desisting in his search for a fresh bug amid his capillary bait-box, the Indian turned and beheld an enormous grizzly in the act of choking down his entire string of fish. Being entirely weaponless, the noble redman made haste to scramble to the top of a large bowlder, conveniently at hand. While engaged in frantically blowing his police-whistle from this vantage ground, the bear began to climb up also. As his enemy was swarming up the slippery granite, the Indian espied beside him a heavy, loose stone. This he dumped upon the rock-hugging head of the brute with such emphasis as to crack its skull between the two bowlders. The Indian then returned to his people, covered with perspiration and glory, and they, thunderstruck at the prowess of a brave who had slain a bear with his naked hands, at once dubbed him "Yo Semite"—that is, "The Great Grizzly." In course of time this deed became so vaunted among the coast Indians that the tribe referred to gradually adopted the appellation as a distinctive title.

Frank Harrison Gassaway, 1882

Mi Wuk Indians in their native dress. Early 1900s.

Courtesy Mariposa County Museum and History Center

The Princeton Mine used tanks to store water for processing gold and for the miners personal needs. Barefoot, these men cleaned the tanks.

I am celebrating my 15th birthday today. Tonight we're having a big family celebration! For my birthday, my mother gave me a fragrant pomander, rosebud sachet, and this beautiful journal. It's red with gold lining, and on the cover, in gold, it says "Journal". My mother told me that her 15th year was one of the best. I hope mine is, too.

I know tonight is really a special occasion because mother and my sisters made a juicy pink ham, home made bread thickly sliced, fresh butter, creamed potatoes and gravy. For dessert, we're having a chocolate cake.

Thinking back over my life so far, I realize that I have been through a lot.

In 1857, I was born at Benton Mills on the Merced River. My father's mine had failed so our family had moved there, where my father worked as an assayer. Only two years after we had settled in Benton Mills, a great storm came and broke the dam upstream from us. Everything we owned was washed away except the clothing on our backs. We stayed with close family friends in Bear Valley until our new home was built in Hells Hollow.

Julia Lois Jones,
November 10, 1872

but gave it up and concluded that he had got tired of the place and left. On Saturday last, his body was discovered near some China camps. It was in an advanced stage of decomposition; but from appearances it seems that foul play had been used. The hands were tied with a sash behind his body, and he was lying on his face. Such a length of time had elapsed that it would have been nearly impossible to detect the wounds if there were any on the person of the deceased. He had no money at the time and the motive for the commission of the crime is left to conjecture. It may be that he was killed by the Chinamen in retaliation for depredations committed by Mexicans on their persons and property, which have been of frequent occurrence.

ROBBERY AND MURDER OF CHINAMEN. On Friday night of last week a company of Chinamen engaged in mining near Mariposa 6 miles from this place, were attacked by a party of white men, and their camp robbed of all the money that could be found, which was $70, we understand. Not content with taking their money, the scoundrels assaulted the Chinamen with knives and six-shooters, killing one of them almost instantly, and injuring three others so that they died from the effects of their wounds, on the following night. Nothing definite has yet been obtained as to who the parties are that perpetrated this dastardly crime, and in fact, we have not heard of any steps being taken to discover the wretches. Outrages of this kind upon Chinamen, are getting to be quite too common in this locality, and it is quite time that something should be done to put a stop to them. If we have got officers whose duty it is to look into such matters, it might be well perhaps, to attend to it; if not, then the people had better take the law into their own hands, and adopt some plan whereby these robbers and murderers may be apprehended and punished.

ACCIDENT AT PRINCETON. An accident occurred at the mine in Princeton, on Tuesday morning last, which resulted fatally to one workman, and which another was seriously injured. They were in the mine engaged in propping up under the tunnel, when some of the timbers gave way [so the] rock fell upon, and buried them. As soon as the accident became known, men set to work, to extricate them, and succeeded in getting out Mr. Thomas Noel, who was considerably, though not fatally injured. The other, Mr. Henry Floto, they were unable to get out until his life was extinct.

A FATAL FERRY DISASTER. A Merced dispatch of May 23 says: News reached here this morning of the drowning of the Portuguese, Charles Lucas, at Murray's Ferry near Merced Falls, in this county, late on Friday afternoon last. A two-mule team, loaded with flour, driven by Mr. Gagliardo, a merchant of Hornitos, was being ferried across the river and when about midway the stream the mules took fright at something and commenced backing the wagon, while endeavoring to hold the

The Coulterville Hotel and stage to Yosemite.

We are all up early and feel quite refreshed from our sleep out in the open air last night. If the fleas did travel with their families making noted discoveries all over us. Well it is to be hoped we will leave the fleas (that portion of our party behind) and continue our journey. The Chinaman has already rung the bell (a tin pan for a substitute) twice so I suppose the best way to get rid of the breakfast is to store it away in a safe place by eating it.

Ida Daulton,
June 25, 1880

Coulterville in the late 1800s. The big white building is the hotel.

James D. Savage, a trader, who in 1849-50 was located in the mountains near the mouth of the South Fork of the Merced river, some fifteen miles below the Yosemite valley.

At this point, engaged in gold mining, he had employed a party of native Indians. Early in the season of 1850 his trading post and mining camp were attacked by a band of the Yosemite Indians. This tribe, or band, claimed the territory in that vicinity, and attempted to drive Savage off. Their real object, however, was plunder. They were considered treacherous and dangerous, and were very troublesome to the miners generally.

Savage and his Indian miners repulsed the attack and drove off the marauders, but from this occurrence he no longer deemed this location desirable.

Lafayette Houghton Bunnell, 1851

wagon on the boat was thrown into the water, the wagon and mules following after. Lucas rose to the surface and struck out for the shore, but the current being strong and the water icy cold, he sank and was drowned. One of the mules got loose from the wagon and swam ashore, while the wagon and other mule were washed down the river and over the dam at Nelson's flouring mill, a half mile below, the mule being drowned and the wagon and flour a total loss.

DEAD BODY FOUND. An inquest was held Sunday last on a body of a man found on a mountain about three miles from Mariposa near the ranch of D. C. Ashworth. Dr. Kavanaugh, the Coroner, informs us that from appearances, the man had been dead five or six weeks. Death was caused by a shot through the lower jaw and escaping through the crown of the head. From appearances, two or more balls had passed through the head, which was much lacerated. Appearances indicated that the deceased was shot while lying on his back. It was the opinion of the jury that he committed suicide.

SUICIDE. On Friday morning last, a man by the name of Al Cleaves jumped from the roof of Coulter's Hotel, in Coulterville, and killed himself. No particulars are given, but from the character of the man, it is probable that he was intoxicated at the time. He was the same man who had his feet frozen three or four years ago, and laid in the County Hospital for some time.

1864. HANGING AT AURORA. Four men named respectively Dailey, Buckley, Masterson and "Three Fingered Jack," were hung by a vigilance committee at Aurora on the 9th. They were accused of the murder of W. Reason Johnson.

A HIGH OLD TRAGEDY. A tragedy combining the elements of a sensation chapter in a "yaller givered" romance, occurred at an Indian fandango on the Upper Fresno last week. Two rival bucks of the Digger species fell out about an Aboriginal female of gentle blood, known among the dusky belles of that region by the name of "Sally." "Sally" had been playing the coquette, leading each of the enamored Walles to believe that he was the sole heir to the acorn and clover fed affection of this "forest maiden." They met at a fandango—a collision ensured, and a chunk of clod lead whizzed through the agonized heart of the unlucky "Injun." His body was burned on the following day. Mourning dwells in the lodges of the tribe of Chowchitta, and there is tar upon the face of his daughter "Sally."

FIRE. The house of S. N. Stranahan, near Jeffersonville, in Tuolumne county, was burned last Sunday night. A correspondent of the Stockton Independent, says there were sleeping in the house at the time Mr. Stranahan and wife, and Isaac Dann, wife and two children, Mr. Dann's wife and one child

The Fallen Monarch supports a stage with 16 people. Henry Washburn, was posed as the driver since he couldn't really drive a stagecoach.

At the base of El Capitan, is a stockyard, whose proprietors have suffered much from the depredations of some bears that descend nightly from the rocky ravines above. Their tracks show them to be three in number, one very large, and suspected by experts to be a grizzly. Already we have visited the pit, dug by the river-side, in which we propose to await the stealthy approach of the MIDNIGHT PORK-LIFTERS, And have superintended placing the bait — a leg of mutton and a pan of honey—just where it will appear to the best advantage in the silvery moonlight.

As we have just said, it is suspected that one of said bears is a grizzly. If, in next Saturday's edition, the startled reader of the Post finds this department decorated with reversed rules surrounding a touching obituary, he may conclude the supposition to have proved a certainty. The sorrowing public will then understand at once that the most gigantic intellect that ever illuminated Pacific Coast journalism is no more—has been stilled in the cold embrace of bears. We don't exactly weaken on our project, but yet it is a terrible thought that by the time these lines meet the reader's eye, the hand that writes them may be in a more or less advanced stage of digestion; that the cheek that hand now so pensively supports may be given to some baby bearling to cut its teeth upon; that—but we must stop; the bear idea, even, is too much for us.

Frank Harrison Gassaway, 1882

Suppertime at Standart's Mill.

When they gained the valley the Chief who was on the mountain asked Savage how [many] men he had lost who, after replying, asked them how many they had lost. He replied none of his men, only a few strangers. He then went on to apologize for not making a better fight saying that 300 of their warriors were away for the purpose of attacking Mariposa. The Americans took 4 horses from them & could hear the Mules bray in the next valley but they were not numerous enough to try & retake them.

Robert Eccleston,
February, 1851

were burned to death. Mr. Dann was lately tried for the Murder of McAlister, and acquitted. It is supposed that some friends of the latter fired the house in revenge.

INDIAN KILLED. An Indian was shot and killed at Green's Gulch last Monday night, by George Dobbin. It is supposed that the unfortunate aboriginal was in quest of plunder at the time, as quantities of amalgam had been missed for a number of nights. Upon the night in question, Mr. Dobbin was placed on watch, and seeing the Indian enter the mill, gave him three shots with a six-shooter, from which he died immediately.

FATAL SHOOTING AFFAIR AT PRINCETON. A young man by the name of Willis Harville got into a difficulty with a party of Mexicans who were celebrating St. Johns Day at Princeton, on Friday night last week. Some angry words passed, and threats of shooting. Harville, who was unarmed, started out of the house with another American, followed by the Mexican and some companions. Shortly afterwards a shot was heard, and Harville was seen running in the direction of town. This occurred about 3 o'clock on Saturday morning, and at daylight he was found lying in the street near the office of Frank Giltner, dead, being shot in the left side of the body, the ball probably going near the heart. Evidences of a short but violent struggle were to be seen around the spot where the unfortunate man fell. The Mexican fled, and at last accounts no trace of his whereabouts had been obtained by officers who had gone in pursuit.

FATAL CASUALTY. An unknown man was crushed to death, under one of Warren's heavy freight wagons loaded with 11,000 pounds of barley, on Wednesday last, between Bear Valley and the Pine Tree Vein. On the day previous he had fallen in with the teamster who was hauling the load, and accompanied him from near the Cow and Calf Ranch to the Valley, and thence started with him for Pine Tree. In making a short turn he ran up and threw the brake onto the hindmost wagon, when it capsized, during which time he suffered fearfully. He was a stout built man, sandy complexion, and roughly dressed. He was partially intoxicated from the time he fell in with the teamster up to the hour of the accident.

FATAL CASUALTY. Yesterday afternoon the remains of Mr. Robert Bradford were interred. His death resulted from injuries received while descending the Jacksonville hill, he being on his return from Stockton with his team. It occurred about noon on Monday. It is supposed that the lock chain gave way, causing the horses to run — the wagon tongue striking his remaining leg, (he having been a cripple for several years) and fracturing it — of which fact it seems that he must have been unconscious at the time. At the same time, the stage from Big Oak Flat was ascending the hill. Mr. Bradford seeing that a collision was inevitable, jumped from his seat in the saddle, and alighting on his newly broken leg, fell under the wagon wheel which passed over the body. One of the fore wheels breaking was the means of stopping the team, just in time to prevent a collision with the stage, which had several passengers who undoubtedly would have been injured had it occurred. One of Mr. Bradford's horses was killed and two crippled during the run. He lingered in agony

You won't believe what happened today. A man named John stole a lot of chickens. When he was accused, he kept denying it and felt insulted. Yet he had the chickens in his hands when he was arrested. He claimed that the owner was asleep so he was going to borrow them and tell the owner the next morning. John isn't very smart.

I wonder why he took them, probably for food. John was probably poor. I think if maybe he asked nicely, he would have been given one.

Julia Lois Jones,
August 28, 1873

John Gillmore and his freight wagon are entering Mariposa on Charles Street sometime after the 1866 fire.

F.T. Trabucco's store in Mt. Bullion.

> After traveling some four hours we at last come in sight of the Grand Yosemite Valley. We get a very good view from a place on the road called Inspiration Point. We turn and twist and seem as tho' we are going back from where we started but after all the twisting & turning we are at last passing thro' the grand and beautiful Valley of the Yosemite. Yes we are really here at last and hunting for a suitable place to camp. We are not very hard to please and at last stretch out our tent under three very large oaks and directly in front of the beautiful Yosemite Falls. Indeed it is grand & beautiful.
>
> Ida Daulton,
> June 24, 1880
> en route to Yosemite

from his injuries until about half past two A.M. Tuesday, when death relieved him of his sufferings.

FATAL CASUALTY. A fatal accident occurred at Hite's cove on Friday of last week, in the mine owned by John Hite. A man by the name of John Thomas, one of the miners, was engaged in tamping a blast, when from some cause unknown the charge ignited and prematurely exploded, instantly killing him.

1865. FATAL MINING ACCIDENT. A letter from Millerton gave an account of a fatal accident which occurred at the Knickerbocker Copper load at about six o'clock on Sunday evening, by which Mr. Henry Clendenen lost his life. It seems that he was at work in the bottom of the shaft, when a heavy oaken bucket used for hoisting rock was, by some means, detached from its fastenings and suddenly fell down the shaft, striking the unfortunate man on the head and instantly killing him.

LOVE AFFAIR. A difficulty grew out of a love affair at Knight's Ferry, on last Monday week, between William Rodman and Peter Gamble in which the former was killed and the latter badly wounded. Rodman made an assault on Gamble and shot him twice, when the latter succeeded in getting the pistol away from him, fired one shot and killed him.

FRANCISCO GONZALES was convicted of murder in the first degree. He was charged with the deliberate murder of Indian Tom, and the evidence was very clear. He met him in the street at Colorado, talked to him excitedly for a moment, and then seized him with one hand and inflicted nine stabs with the other, letting him fall dead from his grasp. He was defended by Dr.

Grandvoinet, who was appointed by the court, and who made an earnest, zealous defense, doing all that could be done in the case. It was too plain, however, and the jury found a verdict of guilty in half an hour. On being called upon to give any reason he had why sentence should not be pronounced, Gonzales had nothing to offer that was calculated to benefit his case. The court directed that he be taken to the county jail by the Sheriff, and kept in custody until the 26th day of January 1866, on which day between the hours of 1 A. M. and 4 P. M., he will be hanged by the neck until he is dead. He received the sentence without any indication of much feeling. He was further warned to put away all hope of escape from the penalty and to prepare for death.

KILLING OF CHRIS WILSON. It again becomes our painful duty to record the details of another homicide which occurred in this place last Saturday evening on Main street, in front of the Arcade Saloon — we allude to the shooting and killing of Chris C. Wilson by James H. Lawrence, senior editor of the *Mariposa Free Press*. We conceive it to be our duty as a journalist to publish the circumstances and particulars under which this homicide was committed, and in commenting upon the

Whistling Billy, the eight-ton Porter locomotive, was shipped around the Horn and came to Coulterville in 1897 by mule team. Purchased by the Merced Gold Mining Company for $3,500, Billy ran on thirty-inch gauge track and was capable of hauling fifteen ore cars, each weighing five tons when full. Its route ran from the Mary Harrison Mine to the forty stamp mill located at Black Creek. It was a steep and twisting climb, for which it earned the title, "Crookedest Railway in the World."

Dear Charlie,

Mr. Pike came into a country where Yankees abounded and where Yankees abound, there you find an atmosphere impregnated with a small quantity of freedom; I say small quantity of freedom, because 30 pieces of silver will work miraculous things nowadays. Wel, his slaves inhaled this atmosphere and it wrought wonderful changes upon them, for it is utterly impossible for a slave to associate with a Yankee and not catch the Spirit of Liberty as it is to jump into the water and not get wet. Therefore, his slaves, like Thomas Jefferson, thought, "all men were born free and equal" and consequently, took their departure and told not Mr. Pike which way they went. But the best part of the story is that the slaves thought the oxen ought to have their liberty, besides having a great attachment for them, as they had lived together and accordingly they deserted them not and all went on their way rejoicing, leaving poor Mr. Pike to bake his own beans and earn the money to buy them. Now Mr. Pike is exceedingly wrathful and goes about like a roaring lion with his head full of venom, swearing vengeance upon the Yankees, for he says they are beneath the lowest reptile that creeps on the face of the earth.

*Horace Snow,
August 19th, 1854,
from Agua Frio*

Rich Greeley's ox team pulling logs at Big Tree Station.

> The day was occupied in pressing animals, & by the members in revisiting their camps & finishing their preparations for a start. In the Evening the Companies paraded, & although numerically the smallest, the Mariposa Co. was the only company who were ready for instant service, both the other companies having in them men not only unarmed but otherwise not in readiness to march.
>
> Robert Eccleston,
> February 13, 1851

same shall endeavor to be faithful and impartial to all parties concerned. It appears for the evidence brought forth at the examination of Mr. Lawrence, which took place on Monday last before Justice Giltner, that the deceased had, just previous to the shooting, been quietly sitting and conversing with Mr. George Temple, at the saloon above mentioned. After conversing some time Wilson arose remarking that he would go to bed, and walked out to the end of the porch in front of the saloon. At this time, Mr. Lawrence was seen standing also in front of the saloon but some distance down the street, talking with one Peter Johnson. Soon after, Mr. Lawrence left Johnson and walked up street, when Mr. Wilson stepped out into the street in front of Lawrence and said, "Lawrence, you don't like me," or words to that effect. Lawrence then spoke to Wilson, and proposed to him to shake hands in friendship extending his hand, one witness says, with the index finger pointing to Wilson. The latter then said to Lawrence, "If you have anything against me take it out," or to that effect. Mr. Lawrence instantly jumped back some two or three steps, drawing his pistol at the time, cocked it and fired twice at Wilson the first shot taking effect in the left side, just below the heart, and going nearly through the body, which caused the death of Wilson, the second shot missed.

Wilson made no demonstration to assault Lawrence — the above being all that passed between them. Immediately after the first shot Wilson turned round towards the saloon and exclaimed, "Oh, I'm shot," or "I'm a shot man," and walked into the back room of the saloon, and Lawrence ran up the street towards his office. Only one of the many witnesses states that he saw a pistol in the hands of Wilson until after the firing on the part of Lawrence. Johnson stated that during the conversation Wilson had his right hand on his hip, and after the first shot he turned his attention to Wilson, and saw a pistol in his hand. Other witnesses state that immediately after the first shot Wilson turned round towards the saloon, with both hands placed near the wound, and they saw no pistol until he was assisted back to a chair, when a pistol was found on his person. Johnson stated also that the first intimation he had that a difficulty would take place, was when Lawrence jumped back and drew his pistol and fired.

The above are the facts of the case, and in the face of all this evidence, the Court saw fit to discharge the defendant from custody. No witness stated that Wilson made the slightest demonstration towards assaulting Lawrence —that he did not change his position when Lawrence jumped back and fired, or raise his hand until after he had received his fatal wound — he then turned away from Lawrence, who again fired at him and then ran away. It was permitted in evidence to show that the deceased had made threats against Lawrence just before the difficulty — but this was not made known to Lawrence. He had, however, been informed some time previous that the deceased had threatened him, and they had a difficulty at the time of the Democratic convention in July last.

Both parties are old citizens of this county. Mr. Wilson has for many years been engaged as a sawyer in the different saw-

> Today I heard something about Yosemite's roads being unfinished and all. John Conway, the champion road builder, returned from Yosemite last Monday. He's been working on the Big Oak Flat road and said that there are 4.5 miles of unfinished road and three miles where are only half finished. Work has to be suspended until next March because of the snow. I guess even a champion road builder can't overcome snow!
>
> Julia Lois Jones, December 9, 1873

Chute builders at Standart's Mill. Late 1800s.

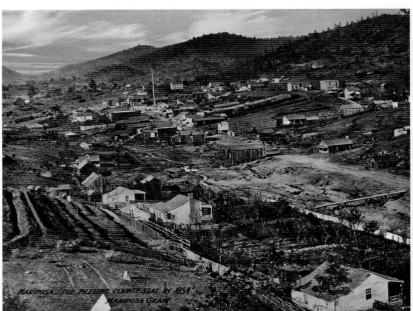
Mariposa in 1854.

A number of Frenchmen who came up in the steamer with us have left in a small whale boat for Merced City, near the Merced Mines.

We have concluded to store our trunk, take our tent and what clothes we can on our backs, and start on the morrow for Wood's Diggings. Before we came, we were informed that better accommodations were to be found here for going to the mines than at Stockton, but at the latter place persons offered to carry freight for us to Wood's Diggings for twenty dollars per cwt., and here we cannot get our goods taken up at any price, and we have not enough to load a whole train of mules, and if we had, it would cost thirty-five dollar per cwt. As we can carry no cooking utensils except a tin cup each, we have purchased and cooked three beef tongues at 37 1/2 cents apiece to take with us, and a few pounds of pilot bread at 20 cents per lb.

Enos Christman,
Monday March 11, 1850

mills in this neighborhood, and was well known as an industrious, hard working and useful citizen. —He was generally a temperate and very peaceable man, yet occasionally would permit his reason to be carried away by intoxicating drink, on which occasion he would sometimes become troublesome with those towards whom he entertained any dislike. On this occasion Wilson was in liquor — killed when intoxicated! While thus speaking of the faults of the deceased, we must say, as a true journalist, that the same thing is true, and to a much greater extent, of Mr. Lawrence. He is constantly armed, and within a very few weeks past has had many difficulties — made assaults upon inoffensive persons with a six shooter, invariably without just provocation. If Wilson was a dangerous and desperate man, Lawrence was the most dangerous, and the greatest desperado, and the rule of law that acquits Lawrence of the murder of Wilson, would have justified his being slain on numerous occasions during the past year. But we cannot justify Lawrence in this killing of Wilson, as did the Justice. We do not think or believe that he was acting in necessary self-defense, or even in self-defense at all, for Wilson had made no demonstration towards assaulting or injuring the person of Lawrence. We believe that the attack upon Wilson was unprovoked, and entirely unjustifiable.

FOUND DEAD. A Frenchman by the name of Durand, residing at French Camp, was found dead on Wednesday morning last, near his residence. He died from exposure and excessive use of liquor. Deceased was formerly a barkeeper at the old French restaurant, and was a competent business man, but latterly had become a habitual drunkard. His case is but one among thousands who owe their moral, intellectual and physical ruin to intemperance.

AN AFFRAY – TWO INDIANS KILLED. On Wednesday last another of those affrays which have been so frequent here of late years among the Indians, took place, in which two were instantly killed, and an old squaw severely stabbed. The circumstances are: An old Indian, well known in this community by the name of "Jim Torrey" in company with another Indian, started for the town of Colorado. When they reached what is known as the "Barley Field," they were met by other Indians, who were somewhat intoxicated, Torrey had some money in his possession, and they attempted to take it from him. In resisting he was knocked down and rocks thrown upon him until his head was mashed to a jelly. After disposing of "Torrey," they attacked his companion and literally cut him to pieces.

MURDER AT BUCHANAN HOLLOW. Last Monday an English miner by the name of Rogers was killed at the copper mines in Fresno county. The following is the evidence taken on Bolinger's examination before Justice Yarborough, of Millerton: Testimony for Prosecution — M. D. Green, sworn — Says that on last Monday between the hours of one and two o'clock I saw Mr. Bolinger and Mr. Rogers come out of Mr. Smith's saloon, in Buchanan Hallow, Fresno county from the appear-

This morning we got up about half past five & the Chinaman has breakfast, been hammering away on a tin pan for some time calling out second bell. After we ate our breakfast, the men folks got the horses up and saddled them — we soon were all ready to mount. We are going today up to the top of the Yosemite falls, the highest falls in the Valley. To look up at them, for we are camped right under, we thought the trail must be perpendicular. Some of the girls thought they couldn't ride over it at all, said they knew they would get dizzy and fall off — but the trail was much better than we expected to find. It is something like the wagon road up here winds back and forth.

Tillie Daulton,
June 26, 1880
en route to Yosemite

The Mariposa Tunnel Tree with a family riding through. This tree was so weakened by the cut through the center that it has now fallen.

The hoist operation at the Mariposa Mine around 1900.

While as a female I don't have the right to vote, I am always intrigued by political campaigns. This year there are two candidates running for Mariposa constable. One is W.W. Barnes, who is from Mariposa and works at the *Gazette* office. Jacob Lambert is the other candidate and is also from Mariposa. They both can speak and write English correctly. Those are two skills that are essential if you are running for office.

Julia Lois Jones,
September 1, 1873

ance of both parties they came up to have a fight. Mr. Rodgers had his coat off when he came up and Mr. Bolinger pulled his coat off after he came, Mr. Rodgers remarked to him to pull his arms off, Mr. Bolinger did not take his arms off but struck Mr. Rodgers with his fist they exchanged two or three blows then Bolinger stepped back and drew his six shooter and gave Rodgers a tap on the head with it. Rodgers then caught Bolinger or they clinched; they then stopped and talked with each other, Bolinger said to Rogers, "You hunt me do you" Rodgers said "no"; Bolinger then pushed him off at arms length and told him to go away; Rodgers then pulled out his knife with his left hand, it had a red scabbard on it; he then let go with his right hand with the intention of taking the scabbard off, or to change it from one hand to the other. Bolinger then made a lick at him with his six shooter; Rodgers rushed on him with a knife; about that time Bolinger fired his pistol; Rodger rushed at Bolinger; Bolinger backed about twenty feet; Rodgers cutting at him with his knife; then Bolinger fired the second shot; Bolinger then turned round and said "Boys, he has killed me." I was standing about forty or fifty steps off when the difficulty was going on, so that I could see it.

BLOODY AND FATAL AFFRAY. Last Monday evening a serious and fatal difficulty took place at Buchanan Hollow, between William Rogers and Frank M. Bolinger, in which the former was killed, and the latter severely wounded. The particulars, as far as we have been enabled to learn them, are that Rogers was engaged in playing a game of cards with H. F. Dodds, in L. H. P. Smith's house, when Bolinger came in and had some words with him, and finally slapped him in the face. The parties afterwards went out of doors, and Rogers offered to fight Bolinger a fair fight, but the latter drew his pistol (a dragoon six-shooter) and shot at Rogers but missed him. Rogers then sprang for his antagonist, caught hold of the pistol and at the same time drew his bowie knife. In drawing this the scabbard went with it, rendering it ineffective; he was therefore obliged to let go of the pistol and unsheathe the knife. While doing this, Bolinger shot him through the heart. Rogers succeeded in getting the scabbard off the knife, plunged it into Bolinger, and then fell dead. It was thought at first that Bolinger was mortally wounded, though it is now considered that he is not so badly hurt as was at first anticipated, and that he will recover.

LOWER AGUA FRIA DESTROYED BY FIRE. Yesterday morning, about 2 o'clock, the town of Lower Agua Fria was entirely consumed by fire. The town was built of the most combustible material, and when the fire commenced it spread with such rapidity that it was impossible to do anything. The fire first appeared in the Chinese Church, and was undoubtedly the work of an incendiary. About 75 buildings composed the town, all of which, excepting Mr. Leverone's house, were entirely destroyed.

1870. SHOCKING ACCIDENT. On Friday last, Frank Whitford, an employee of the Pine Tree Vein, in Bear Valley, was descending the ladder in the mine with powder and fuse, when, from some unknown cause, the powder exploded, mangling and mutilating him in a dreadful manner. Both eyes were put

The Whitlock Mine.

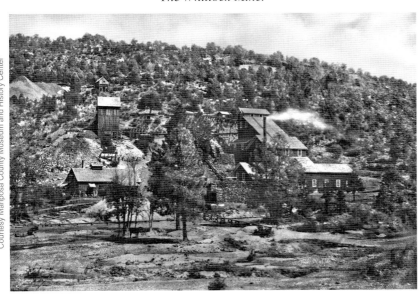

Col. Johnson & some other officers arrived about 8 o'clock last Evening. The prospects are now that we will be stationed, each company separately, while the Commissioners in Company with Mr. Savage & a group of Regulars proceed to make overtures of Peace. This will take, no doubt, 15 or 20 days. It is Major Savage's opinion that no treaty can be made with Indians or if made it will not be respected. Some Indians drove 13 Americans into Mariposa this morning.

Robert Eccleston,
February 14, 1851

Whistling Billy traveling to Coulterville in 1897 by mule team.

out, his nose blown off, one arm torn off below the elbow, and other portions of his body literally torn in shreds. His mangled remains were born to the surface of the ground, and notwithstanding the frightful nature of the injuries, the unfortunate man survived an hour and a half, had perfect consciousness of his condition, and dictated his will and gave directions about his affairs. No one knows with any certainty as to the cause of the explosion.

Whitford's duty was superintending the loading and firing of blasts, and at the time of the occurrence had attached to his person a number of cartridges, some fuses and caps. The powder used is a compound of giant powder and ordinary gun powder, and is called Hercules powder. It only burns slowly upon application of ordinary fire, but explodes by percussion. It is supposed that in descending one of the cartridges may have suddenly struck a rung of the ladder.

1871. Rev. L. B. Lockley Killed. On Last Friday evening, about nine o'clock a most distressing homicide occurred about one mile below Centerville, on King's river. The victim was the Rev. L. B. Lockley a local preacher.

A young man aged about seventeen years, named Coon, having formed an antipathy to a dog owned by Mr. Lockley, went on the night mentioned to his residence for the purpose of killing the animal. Mr Lockley's residence is situated on the bluff of what is known as the King's river bottom.

The young man was down in the bottom and made a noise evidently to attract the dog's attention. It had the desired effect,

> All of us girls want to be on horseback when there is any danger of meeting stages. The road seemed 22 miles instead of 11 which it was from Big Tree to the place where we are camping. I think from the grumbling about fleas, we have found another flea town.
>
> Agnes Daulton,
> June 24, 1880
> in Yosemite

and the dog went charging in that direction. It seems that Mr. Lockley also heard the noise, and went out doors and started in the direction taken by the animal. As the dog made his appearance on the edge of the bluff the young man, who, by the way, was armed with a shotgun, heavily charged with buckshot, leveled his weapon at the dog and discharged it killing the animal instantly. Mr. Lockley, at that time of the shooting had advanced just far enough to have his breast on a line with the dog, and three of the buckshot struck him in the breast, killing him almost instantly. The young man then ran off. An examination was made of the ground on the following morning and traces were discovered which led to the detection of the offender, who surrendered himself to the officers of the law.

FATAL ACCIDENT IN THE YOSEMITE VALLEY. On Saturday last, an Italian, named George Campi, fell from the platform at the head of the first flight of steps at the Vernal Fall, about thirty-five feet, and received several very severe bruises and a fracture of the skull, from the effects of which he died on the following morning. The deceased was the proprietor of the Italian's Restaurant, on Clay street, San Francisco. Several persons were ascending the steps at the time, and the deceased had just proffered his assistance to a lady in the party, who declined his

last night a party of Californians commenced gambling and drinking in a tent close by and kept up their infernal noise and revels until daylight this morning, then fought with knives and separated.

Enos Christman,
March 11, 1950

Sixteen year old Trixie Reynolds graces Standart's Camp. Based on the weapon, she may have been joining others for a hunting trip.

Townsfolk gather around Mr. Reeb, in the white apron, of Reeb's Butcher shop, one of the more calm establishments in Hornitos. Fights, shootings, stabbings, and gambling earned this town a reputation of being wild.

We started again last Evening a little before sunset intending to reach a Rancheria before morning which we were to surround & take. This was for the purpose of obtaining guides to the Large Rancheria where all the Indians this side of the Fresno nearly have united & are prepared for war. It is said there are 3000 warriors & the ground they are supposed to occupy is a natural fortification almost impregnable. We travelled fast for the first few miles, the road being good & the boys lively, but as usual some of the packs came slipping off & delaying the train. As we ascended the Mountain, the snow grew deeper, the road either sloppy or slippery which made it exceeding hard travellin.

Robert Eccleston,
Sunday, March 23rd, 1851

aid, whereupon he stepped backward, bowing, and not noticing his surroundings, fell over the edge of the cliff. The accident is solely attributable to his own carelessness.

CHILD BURNED TO DEATH. The children of this place [Coulterville] have been in the habit of having their little picnic parties in a vacant lot belonging to Mr. Francisco, a trader of this place, where they were allowed to use fire for the purpose of cooking their dinners, making tea, coffee, &c. Whilst thus engaged, a little girl near nine years old, daughter of Mr. Gazzola, a restaurant keeper was superintending the cooking, when her clothing caught fire and was nearly burned off before her condition was known; her little companions, child-like, all ran and hid themselves in fear.

An Italian laborer who was working near by was the first to come to her relief, and acting under the impulse of the moment caught her up and put her into a large tub of water that was near by, for the purpose of extinguishing the fire, which he accomplished, but greatly to the injury of the child. She was then taken to her father's house where everything was done that could be thought of to relieve her, but all in vain, her suffering being so great that all their efforts proved unavailing. She lingered until Friday evening at about half past eight o'clock, when death came to her relief. She was a beautiful little girl, the favorite of the town. Her death can only be attributed to the wanton carelessness of the parents of the children of this place in allowing them to use fire among so much combustible matter as is about these vacant lots.

1875. DEATH OF A GOOD CITIZEN. This week opened with the terrible news of a fratricide occurring on the Chowchilla, some eight or ten miles east of Mariposa, on Tuesday last, between two brothers, Charles and William Hart, wherein the former shot the latter with a rifle, the ball passing through the left arm just below the shoulder, and entering the body and lodging in the backbone, supposed to have cut the left lung. It occurred about five o'clock in the afternoon, and the wounded man died at three o'clock the following morning. Unfortunately no medical relief could be obtained before death ensued. On receipt of the news, which was quite late at night, Sheriff Mullery with Under-Sheriff Howard started for the scene, but no arrest was made until Thursday when officer Howard with a posse, came upon Hart, who was concealed in the rough and almost impenetrable bushes and rocks, a short distance from the cabin

I never realized how many people come to Mariposa. I suppose most of them are here to see Yosemite. There was a list of all the new arrivals in the newspaper. They come from all over the country and the world. Today, just some of the places are Boston, New Jersey, Texas, Ohio, New York, Chicago, Central America and England.

Every summer more and more people come to Yosemite. At this rate, in many years, there will be thousands coming!

Julia Lois Jones,
August 7, 1874

This breathtaking view from Glacier Point was enjoyed by many daredevils until the Park restricted access to this point. Half dome rests in its mighty splendor in the center of the photo.

Higman's Groceries in Mariposa.

Dear Charlie,

I am just as strick an observer of the Sabbath as I used to be. I never have worked an hour on the Sabbath in California, nor ever attended places of amusement or practiced visiting gambling houses. It is almost impossible to attend church on account of their scarcity and locality. The last meeting I attended was in a bar room. Verily, this seemed like bearding the lion in his den.

Drinking and swearing was the order, before meeting and after.

*Horace Snow,
April 5, 1854*

which he inhabited. When discovered he was carrying a gun, but when told to holdup his hands, he dropped it to the ground and surrendered without an offer of resistance.

1876. GOLD INGOT FOUND. Some boys in San Francisco, in examining some ashes taken from the mint and cast upon the vacant lot opposite, one of them, named Murphy, found a small bar of gold, with the impress of the mint upon it. The boy took it to his mother, and shortly after she was waited upon by several of the mint men, who demanded the ingot, which was valued at four thousand dollars, but she stoutly refused to give it up, and afterwards sold it. A loose way they have of doing business at the United States Mint.

SHOCKING DISASTER AT BENTON MILL TUNNEL, MERCED RIVER. On Wednesday evening last a messenger from Bear Valley rode into town with the intelligence that a fatal accident had occurred at the Benton Mill tunnel. The accident happened at half past five o'clock on the afternoon and was caused by the premature explosion of about forty pounds of No. 1 Hercules powder in the face of the main tunnel. A set of holes, 18 in number, had been loaded and were ready for explosion, when Mr. Etheridge Hunt, to whom the management of the battery was entrusted, attempted, as usual, before firing, to test it. If the connections are all perfect, this test current rings an alarm bell, and all hands clear away to places of safety in the cross drifts. It seems that on this occasion the bell failed to ring, indicating a break in the wire between the battery and the face. As customary in such cases Mr. Hunt took the battery up to the face in order to test the wires back from joint to joint, as that is deemed the most expeditious way of finding a break. The wires had been again connected with the battery, and it is supposed that Mr. Hunt, at this time, being in a state of slight confusion, as men are apt to be, when any thing goes wrong about Hercules powder, touched the wrong key, sending the current directly through the several exploders in the face, instead of back down the wires as intended.

A scene of carnage — in sickening horror the most desperate battle field, and too shocking to be minutely described. Six white men and a Chinaman were near the heading at the time, of whom but one, Mr. John Larid, survived, his injuries consisting chiefly of a broken leg, which the physician pronounced a simple fracture, from which with the kind nursing he is receiving, he will speedily recover.

1877. KILLED. At Hite's Cove Mine, a sad accident occurred by means of a boulder, weighing about two tons, sliding out of its natural bed, a distance of about two feet, and crushing a miner by the name of James Cook who unfortunately was at work close by preparing to timber up the rock that caused his death. The other laborers who were present soon extricated the unfortunate man from the perilous situation and found him so badly crushed about the hips and legs, that death was inevitable. They removed him from the mine to his cabin, where for about four hours he suffered the most intense agony, when death came to his relief.

This war has been going on in Georgetown. It broke out into a pure gunfight. People have been shooting at each other with such anger that no one knows where the bullets might be aimed. No one knew what the consequences might be later on. As I read the article, I saw them calling the Negroes savages. They explain how ignorant they are, but we are all the same so we must be ignorant savages, too.

Julia Lois Jones,
September 14, 1874

The Hornitos Hotel and guests in 1884.

The Hornitos Saloon in 1890 with Ralph Barcroft, Proprietor, in the first row on the left with his dog.

Miss Jennie Jenkins had a tragic day today. Poor thing fell off a horse. Miss Jenkins, who is about 17 years old, had just returned to town from a camp meeting in company with several other young ladies and gentlemen. While she was passing the Courthouse on her horse, a dog ran out and snapped at the horse's legs. The horse jumped back, flinging Miss Jenkins into the air and snapping her against the ground. Miss Jenkins hit her head and was picked up in an insensible condition. She was unconscious for an hour or two. Fortunately, she only had a few bruises and is doing quite well now.

Julia Lois Jones,
September 6, 1874

A SAD ACCIDENT. One of the saddest, and most lamentable accidents occurred near this place on Thursday last, at about 2 o'clock in the afternoon. The unfortunate man was at this time engaged with his team hauling flour from the Eden flouring mill, to Mariposa. The accident occurred in descending the hill, on the approach to the crossing of Mariposa creek, where Frank Lewis Wulbern's attention was attracted by the unusual noise in the direction of the hill and crossing of the creek above mentioned, and anticipating trouble or accident, he hastened forward and soon arrived at the scene of disaster, where was to be seen a complete wreck of the team, wagon, and the unfortunate man, who in some unaccountable manner had fallen, together with the saddle mule of the wagon, which must have stumbled and fell, at a moment when the team was going down the hill with considerable velocity; for both rear wheels of the wagon passed over the rider and mule. The wheels passed nearly square across the breast of Mr. Halterman, which was crushed to such an extent, that death was inevitable, and he expired in about three quarters of an hour after the sad occurrence.

1878. ANOTHER DIABOLICAL MURDER. Another cold blooded and cowardly murder was committed in this county. The victim was Jonas Thompson, an old and highly esteemed citizen, who resides on Striped Rock, a tributary of Chowchilla. Word was brought to town about eleven o'clock on Thursday of the shooting, by young Laird, who had stopped at Thompson's to get a drink; he says that when he rode up to the door, it was closed; but Thompson hearing him, called to him from the inside, and told him to come in; that when he opened the door he saw Thompson lying on the floor, and asked him if he was sick; Thompson replied that he was shot, and requested him to go for a doctor. Laird then went to Whitney's, some two or three miles distant, and sent him to Thompson's, and came on to town for a doctor. Doctor's Ward and Kavanaugh immediately repaired to the scene, and rendered the unfortunate man all the assistance that was possible; but it was soon apparent to the doctor's that the work of the assassin was complete.

Thompson told them [the doctors] that at about eight o'clock in the morning he had gone out into his garden and was stooping or kneeling by a small walnut tree, for the purpose of examining it, when he was shot in the back from a pile of rocks near by; that he walked to his house as quickly as possible for fear of another shot, went inside, took down his gun, and then pulled a mattress unto the floor and laid down on it, with his gun by his side. An examination of the wound showed that he had been shot in the back, the ball entering on the left side of the backbone, passing through the left lung, and coming out under the pelvic bone; thence it passed into the right thigh, from where it was extracted by the doctors. Thompson was perfectly rational until his death, and said that he did not know that he had a enemy in the world.

ACCIDENT AND DEATH. On Monday last a sad accident occurred at the Washington mine, by which a man named Charles

We were informed that a train of pack mules and teams were stopping for the night a few miles distant and would be along here on their way to the mines. We therefore concluded to wait until they came up, in the hope that we could get them to carry our baggage. A team arrived here about four Tuesday afternoon on its way to Mariposa Diggings. We agreed with the teamster, Mr. Cox, to carry our baggage for $50

Enos Christman,
March 14, 1850

The Howard family Indian camp in Mariposa, 1890.

Court officials stand in front of the home of the first Superior Court judge, John M. Corcoran, who is in the middle position.

> In the afternoon, we had some foot racing, jumping matches, &c. An Indian ran with one or two of our boys but got beaten. The chief here offers to send with us 50 warriors to fight against the Yoosemita's providing we give them the women as prisoners. Dis. 6 miles.'
>
> Robert Eccleston, February, 1851

Ebert was killed and another by the name Thomas Williams, was severely, though not fatally injured. From what we can learn, the accident was caused by the bucket, upon which the two men were returning to the surface from one of the lower levels, striking a timber when within one hundred feet of the top, and catching Ebert in some manner so that he was crushed to death instantly. Williams, who was with Ebert upon the bucket, was badly hurt, but it is thought by his physician that he will recover. It seems to us that some safer means for the transportation of men up and down deep shafts, than clinging to the outside of a bucket should be employed.

1879. HOMICIDE. In the vicinity of Indian Gulch, about six miles from Hornitos, a terrible homicide was committed by one Henry Ivy striking ' in the head with the handle of a pick, containing the eye of the broken pick only; and killing him almost instantly. The difficulty was about a mining claim which J. H. Malone had purchased last year at tax sale, and held a sheriff's deed of. It appears the deceased was availing himself of the mining law requiring a certain amount of annual expenditure upon mining claims, and had jumped the claim; and the claimant Malone, in company with Ivy, came up to the mine and presented to Royal a paper purporting to be some evidence of authority by which Malone held the claim. While Royal was reading this paper, Ivy picked up from behind, unobserved by Royal, the deadly weapon and struck the fatal blow which caused his death. A man by the name of Ferguson who resides near by, and Mr. Malone witnessed the tragedy, Ivy was in the employ of Malone. Ivy gave himself up and Malone was arrested for complicity.

HORRIBLE MASSACRE – THREE INDIANS KILLED – ONE HUNG – AND A SQUAW WOUNDED Never, since the organization of Mariposa county, or the existence of the *Gazette*, which is about 25 years old, has its editor ever been called upon to chronicle such a dastardly, infamous, and inhumane massacre; wherein several Indians were mercilessly slaughtered at a rancheria, while in their quiet slumbers early Sunday morning last about five miles below town; as the bloody deed we are at this writing attempting to give the public a description of. The first intelligence of the wholesale murder, was brought to town by two squaws, who were present and were probably here within a hour or two after the deed was committed. Notwithstanding the enormity of the outrage, there was a remarkable quietness pervading among the citizens; whispers could be heard from them, asking what is going to be done; no one knew or could find out. Some appeared dumbfounded, others stricken with terror and agonizing suspense. In fact, there was no movement made in an official manner towards investigating the scene of bloodshed. It was however, visited by several during the day, whose curiosity sought gratification at seeing a dead Indian or two, who had

> My father taught us all not to judge people by their color. That is why our household is in such an uproar. Ever since the colored war began and is mentioned in the Saturday paper, we all get angry.
>
> Julia Lois Jones,
> September 12, 1874

The L.M. Sain store in Coulterville in the early 1900s.

Courtesy Mariposa County Museum and History Center

The Magnolia Saloon in Coulterville.

Today about noon Major Savage started for the Yoosemita Camp with 57 men & an Indian Guide. These men were all mounted & took 4 or 5 days provision. They are going to the Rancheri whether they meet the Indians on the way or not. If the Indians have left it, they will burn it.

Robert Eccleston,
Thursday. March 27th, 1851

fallen by the relentless bullets fired from the rifles or pistols of the white men. It was, as described to us, a scene of carnage never before witnessed in this region of the country. There lay promiscuously upon the ground dead, three stalwart young Indian men, each shot through the head; close by was an old decrepit Indian about 70 years of age, who had been hung up by a rope till dead, and afterwards cut down, said to be the father of Willie Ross, convicted for the murder of Thompson, and sent to prison for life. The young Indians were known respectively by the names of Sam, Charlie and Amos.

Our informant gathered the following from Indian Jeff who had with another Indian Jack escaped from the assassins. Early in the morning, Sam, who occupied the cabin with his family, was awakened by a knock and call at the door. He responded to his name, and requested the outsider to wait till he put on his shoes and he would come out; as he opened the door he was seized and his hands tied behind him. At the same moment, the other Indians who were sleeping in another wig wan, were seized and likewise tied in the same manner, when all five were required to stand or sit down together with a guard over them, while the old Indian was being executed by hanging. Just at this moment a break was made, Sam ran into his own house where he was followed and killed. Jack and Jeff made good their escape. Charlie was shot in the forehead and in the neck. Amos in the eye and in the back. Sam in the head. A favorite old washerwomen about the town, was shot in the side of the face inflicting a severe wound, considered dangerous supposed to have been a accident although she says the gun was pointed right at her, which is evidently so, or she would not have been hit. On Monday following, a jury was summoned by Capt. J. W. Thomas J. P. acting coroner, and they proceeded to the locality, where the bodies of the Indians except Charlie, had lain undisturbed since the messenger of death had called them in.

ACCIDENT AND DEATH. Near Boot Jack Ranch, about six miles from Mariposa on the road leading to Big Tree Station, John Hoagland, a teamster and driver in the employ of Washburn & Bruce, was accidently thrown from the wagon, run over and killed. We have been unable to get the particulars, although a man named Ralph Williams was with him. From what we could learn it appears that Hoagland dropped one of his lines, and in attempting to jump out after it one or both of his feet caught in the lines remaining, and he fell in such a manner that the hind wheel of the wagon passed across his breast. He lived for some moments after the accident and talked quite freely with Mr. Williams, stating to him that he was going to die and expressed a desire for Mr. Williams to know something

An amazing thing has just occurred in Yosemite! A man named George Anderson has just accomplished a feat that seems as though it would be impossible. In the wide valley of wonder and beauty, there's a dome that seems as if it was sliced in half. And this October, George Anderson has climbed it and strung a cable so not only he alone may reach the top. Others had attempted the climb but never made it. When news got out about Anderson's accomplishment, the whole town was beyond amazed.

Only one other man since has climbed it since the cables were strung. Galen Clark, is the second man who has now been to the top. This will probably be a challenge that people will attempt for many years to come.

Julia Lois Jones,
October 16, 1875

Galen Clark in the Mariposa Grove of Big Trees. Clark, in awe of Yosemite's unique grandeur, helped get the Yosemite Grant enacted in 1864, creating the first state park. He was appointed "Guardian of Yosemite" in 1866 to oversee the Yosemite Grant from 1866 until 1880, and then again from 1889 until he died in 1910. Acting like a park superintendent today, he kept trails, roads, and bridges in good repair, protected the environment, and moved homesteaders to assure access to Yosemite's wonders.

Courtesy Mariposa County Museum and History Center

When water was in short supply, "washing" often occurred at a barrel of water. The young man at the right might have been getting a lesson.

The rain changed to snow last night & we had a sweet time of it standing guard. The snow continued all day without the intermission. Major Savage returned with his men about 4 o'clk, P.M. They found the Rancheris deserted, the only living object, except dogs, was old woman over 100 yrs old in a cave. On being asked where the others were, she told them to go look. Our boys not having provision sufficient & it snowing hard, were unable to pursue the Indians although from the sign they could not be far off, they, however, burnt over 5000 Bushels of acorns, & any quantity of old Baskets.

Robert Eccleston,
Saturday, March 29th, 1851

about his affairs in life; but Mr. Williams, not supposing he was so near his death from the fact of his lively expression at the moment, did not give but little heed to what he said about his business.

ACCIDENT AND DEATH. At Hornitos a sad accident occurred by the falling into a mining shaft twenty feet deep of a little boy, son of A. Campodonico, aged six years. He with a number of other children were playing in the vicinity of the shaft where it is supposed he attempted to look down and slipped in, receiving fatal injuries from which he died the next day. This is a hard blow upon Mr. and Mrs. Campodonico, it being the fourth son they have lost within the last few years, three of whom died with the scarlet fever.

DEATH FROM SNOW SLIDES. Several disastrous snow slides occurred during the recent storms, on the line of the Central Pacific Rail road. In one instance some thirty Chinamen were buried, seventeen of whom were taken out dead. In another, fifteen white men, three of whom were killed, and several badly bruised.

1880. DROWNED. Last Friday at Split Rock Ferry, Merced River, on the road leading from Bear Valley to Coulterville, the ferry-boat was swamped whereby the ferryman and a chinaman were drowned. The river was unusually high and swift, and by some accident or mismanagement the boat was allowed to attempt the crossing, square across, instead of throwing one end of the boat down, and taking an angle or quarterly position with the current, usually required to impel the boat on its course and for its safety. The white man drowned was Wm. Fullerton an old citizen. He was employed as ferryman. The chinaman Ah Kay, a well known gardener close to Bear Valley, was with his horse on his way peddling vegetables. The horse swam out, but the chinaman and ferryman disappeared in the swift turbulent stream below.

HOMICIDE. On Tuesday morning last our people were somewhat startled at news received, by a special courier from Cathey's Valley, that Paddy McCann, Jr. was shot and killed, and that, too, by a women, which doubly added to the interest of the unfortunate affray and anxiety for the particulars and just how it occurred. Officers comprising Justice Temple and Deputy Sheriff Skelton made haste to the scene of difficulty where they found as reported a corpse terribly mutilated from the contents of a shot-gun; and also the woman who committed the act, who proved to be the wife of Frank McCann, brother of the deceased. Frank was absent from home and his wife alone, when about 9 o'clock on Monday evening Paddy came along, as it is said, very much intoxicated, and made improper demands, accompanied with serious threats of shooting and taking her life if she did not yield to his requests. In the meantime she managed to get hold of a shot-gun, and rested reliably upon it

On Wednesday in Bear Valley a crazy crime occurred. Andrew Rocco, an Italian man, was under the influence of liquor. Rocco entered Mrs. Trabucco's store and said he was hungry and hadn't eaten for three days. Mrs. Trabucco gave him some supper. When Rocco was finished, he snatched Mrs. Trabucco's baby and hit Mrs. Trabucco over the head with a pick he was holding. John Baptiste, Mrs. Trabucco's son, happened to be in the kitchen. When he heard his mother scream, he came to her rescue. John grabbed the pick and hit Rocco over the head knocking him out. John then grabbed the baby and fled to the house and locked the door. While Rocco was attempting to force the door open, he encountered an old man. Rocco hit the old man on the lip and finger.

Julia Lois Jones,
January 9, 1878

Knowing the building housed a "mill," you might think all the logs mean a lumber mill. But this was really the stamp mill at the Mariposa Mine in about 1850. The logs were used to generate steam to run the stamps 24/7.

Courtesy Mariposa County Museum and History Center

By the 1880s, when this image of Mariposa was taken, the town had grown and was thriving. The Odd Fellows Hall and the Schlageter Hotel are visible.

Dear Charlie,

A Pacific Rail Road is all we want. When that is built Snow is coming home! I suppose we shall have to look to the Know-Nothing Party for this accomplishment, as they seem to be one that "Does Something."

*Horace Snow,
September 16, 1854,
from Agua Frio*

for her own protection. But Paddy wouldn't desist, as she appealed to him to do, whereupon the fatal trigger was pulled and the aggressor launched into eternity. She must be a woman of remarkable presence of mind, as well as extraordinary nerve, for immediately after the fatal shot, fully realizing the result, she started for her brother-in-law's some mile or so distant, and gave information of what she had done. Mr. House, with some others, immediately repaired to the spot and found her statement to be true. The body was found a short distance from the house in a terrible condition. It appears the clothing had taken fire from the effects of the shot-gun and burned one of the arms of deceased to a crisp. According to her statement, he was approaching her and was within six feet when the gun was fired, the contents of which entered his stomach. To all appearances the deceased fell without a struggle ever occurring afterwards.

HOMICIDE. Intelligence was received from Coulterville that a homicide had been committed on the outskirts of the county bordering Stanislaus. The killing occurred on the evening of Friday, the 13th, at Junction Station, in Mariposa county, at a French store and whiskey den within two or three hundred yards of the line dividing the counties. The parties to the deadly conflict were James H. McGrath, a stranger, and Julian Varain, a citizen of this county. The former was shot and killed by a shot gun in the hands of the latter. The stranger was in Coulterville on or about the 12th, the day before he was killed, where he represented he was from Bodie, where he had been engaged in business and had sold out a wood claim for $1,500, and was on his way to Modesto, where a check was waiting for him there amounting to $800. From thence he expected to proceed to Oakland. After leaving Coulterville on the 12th, as before stated, he brought up the same day in the evening at the aforementioned French Store, where he put up until the next day in the evening. During the day Varain appeared, who together with the stranger and several others, such as naturally do congregate about such places, occupied the day in talking, drinking, playing cards and other frivolous pastime, when it is supposed they all got pretty full, especially the stranger. As usual in a whiskey carousal something occurred by which the stranger became incensed at Varain, and according to the testimony called Varain hard names, and so far as words go abused Varain in the most aggravating manner. Varain seemingly to get out of the way, went to a cabin about 80 yards distant, where he remained with an apparent view to avoid the stranger. The cabin, unfortunately, was situated on the road leading to Modesto, for the stranger had about this time saddled up his horse and after making inquiries about which road led to Modesto, he proceeded as directed, and as he neared the cabin the first that attracted his attention was the report of a gun in the direction the stranger

One meal a day was all he could afford and sometimes none, but he was a very zealous advocate and patronizer of free lunches. At ten in the forenoon and nine in the evening the most fashionable drinking saloons furnished roast beef, pickled cabbage, crackers and cheese, etc., for their patrons, with the expectation that all will step up and take a drink before taking a bite, thus giving permanence to the custom, but Snow, with more sense than cents at the time, would walk in and carelessly peruse a newspaper or two till a right opportunity afforded and then he would pitch in with a good relish and in the same quite manner take his exit! thus saving his money and not troubling the proprietor.

Horace Snow, September 16th, 1854, from Agua Frio

When you consider all the lumber needed for structures and flumes, and the logs needed as mine timbers and fuel for the stamp mills, it's easy to understand why you see so many logging operations and hillsides stripped of their once luxurious forests.

Courtesy Mariposa County Museum and History Center

Men loading ore carts in the Princeton Mine.

We packed up early this morning & went to our Camp or rather the Commissary as we were out of provision. We passed the Camp of the Commissioners & Regulars on our way down. Our Camp is on the Road [to] the Fine Gold Gulch about 20 miles from it. The wood here is scarce being willow. We enjoyed the luxuries of bathing. We have just heard that 250 Indians which were coming in & who were escorted by Capt. Bolen & 18 men, escaped last night, having been turned back by 4 of the Chou Chilians, having come to them & told them false tales about the fate of the Indians already in our power.

Robert Eccleston,
Wed. April 2nd, 1851

had taken, and next was the prostrate form of the stranger upon the ground near to the cabin and the horse making off from its rider. The men had but a moment before had been the stranger's drinking companions started forthwith to the cabin and bloody scene where they found the stranger fatally shot and was dead. Upon the approach of the men Varain came out of the cabin and represented that he was observed by the stranger while passing, who appeared disposed to continue the bandy of words and quarrel that had just passed between them, and made signs of breaking in the window of the cabin, and drawing his six-shooter which he carried. Whereupon, Varain felt himself justifiable in resorting to extreme measures to defend himself, which evidently he did, either through fear, malice, or justifiable defense, which appears yet not to be fully ascertained.

SAD ACCIDENT. A very sad accident occurred at the South Hite Mine, situated in Hite's Cove, whereby a young man named John Jewell lost his life. Mr. Jewell was foreman of the mine, and in his anxiety to make the connection with the tunnel which was expected to be accomplished on last Saturday went down into the shaft on Wednesday in order to ascertain whether or not he could put men to work in sinking. He found the air so foul that he felt very dizzy when he returned to the surface, and so expressed himself to Mr. Widman, the Superintendent. He went into the shaft without Mr. Widman's knowledge or consent, and was censured by that gentleman for his imprudence. Mr. Widman had occasion to go down to the Hite Mine the next day, and in his absence Mr. Jewell, through his great anxiety to push the work ahead, again went down into the shaft, and on reaching the bottom sounded to the men working the upraise in the tunnel, and in coming up, and reaching within a few feet of the 200-foot level, where he had stationed one of his men, he exclaimed to him, "John, I am gone," and fell backwards off the ladder to the bottom, a distance of about 80 feet. Immediately after the accident means were resorted to recover the body by forcing fresh air down the shaft through hose, but this falling hot air was forced down by means of a fire built in a stove and a five-inch pipe connected with it. It took all night and up to ten o'clock next day to displace the foul air sufficiently to enable a man to go down. Mr. Clement, a young man made the attempt to recover the body and it was hauled to the surface.

The foreman of the celebrated Hite Mine, Mr. Joseph Sterns, had received orders to notify the men under him of the sad calamity that had befallen a brother miner in the neighboring mine, which was but a short distance off, and that they were at liberty to go to the rescue of the unfortunate man. As soon as possible the most efficient service available was rendered by the principal and working men of the Hite Mine. To recover the body from the bottom of a 300 foot shaft, 100 of which was

> This has been a very exciting Christmas. We got a family gift called a "phonograph", which plays music from sounds recorded on foil-wrapped cylinders. It's wonderful to listen to our favorite tunes on.
>
> Julia Lois Jones,
> December 25, 1878

The Princeton Mine shaft which decended below 1660 feet.

Probasco's team at Cold Springs Lumber.

About four o'clock we reached Capt. Hardie's Ferry where we crossed the San Joaquin, by unloading the wagon and taking the baggage across in a whale boat. The wagon had to be taken apart and crossed on a barge. The cattle were swam over. For this service our teamster paid half an ounce and as it would have cost us one dollar each, we concluded to lighten his expense if he included us in his family for the time being. We therefore paid the dollar apiece to him instead of the ferryman.

When in the middle of the stream, our camp kettle, in which our provisions for the journey were stored, took a notion to slip off the guide-pole upon which it was hanging, and to our utter horror we saw it going down the stream. It was soon rescued however, from the watery element, and our "bread and dinner" saved.

Enos Christman,
March 16, 1850

impenetrable with any degree of safety on account of the density of foul air, was a task that required bravery as well as great risk of life. It was, however, attempted by several, who were let down by ropes and returned to the surface in an insensible condition. Many were the suggestions and devices made and acted upon, none of which proved successful, until the following day when lime was thrown in and hot air introduced. Great credit is due to Mr. John R. Hite and his noble crew for the great interest manifested in this lamentable affair. Also that of Mr. Widman, the Superintendent of the works of the South Hite Company, for the exceeding interest manifested and zealousness on the part of his men, who so assiduously labored to recover the body of the unfortunate man who had unpremeditatingly launched himself into eternity.

1882. FATAL ACCIDENT. It becomes our melancholy and unwilling duty to chronicle the sad and untimely death of John Fagundas, a miner, who resided with his family on the Merced river near Red Bank, where he was employed by the Merced Mining and Hydraulic Co., which occurred about half past nine o'clock in the forenoon of Saturday last. He was accompanied to his work in the morning by Antone De Silva, the foreman of the works, where he left him engaged in removing rock, and pursuing his daily labor in the mine. Mr. De Silva, who had left him but a few minutes before, was surprised by an alarm given by some of the other men, hurried to the terrible scene that awaited him, where he found that a large boulder of many tons weight had rolled, and caught the unfortunate man underneath, crushing one leg and severely injuring the other; besides, another falling boulder had struck him on the back and hips, which is thought to be the immediate cause of his death. Owing to the unwieldiness of the enormous boulder, it required considerable time and hard labor before the unfortunate man could be extricated from the perilous situation. Dr. Adams, of Coulterville, was immediately dispatched for (a distance of about ten miles), and arrived at 1 o'clock P.M., who did all that could be done to relieve the sufferer from pain, but all human skill proved unavailing, and at 4 P.M. his agonies were over, and he passed away in death.

SAD ACCIDENT. About sundown, Higman's four-horse team and wagon, driven by Rafael Ruiz, a young man, was on its return from Merced loaded with goods, when nearing its point of destination for the night a most painful accident occurred which will result in the death of the young man, or he will be maimed for life. His last attempt was to drive into Higman's new barn which fronts on main street entering town, and either the seat of the wagon was too high, or the upper floor of the barn was too low, in either event, Rafael was caught between the two and probably forever ruined. He was relieved as speedily as possible from the painful position, and taken to Mrs. Contreras' where medical aid was forth with summoned. Upon examination by Dr. Turner, it was found his spine was probably broken in one or more places and that his limbs were paralyzed from the hips down. The accident is to be exceedingly regretted, as he was a worthy young man and highly esteemed by all who knew him, besides he was the chief dependence of an aged mother and two sisters, for support. At the present writing, Friday noon, he was still alive.

Rich Greeley's ox team at Big Tree Station.

Nothing interests visitors from abroad so much as these California jehus, and it is a sight to see some HELMET-HATTED, vail-enveloped English tourist convulsively clutching the siderail as the coach swerves at full canter around some dizzy mountain turn, listening the while with bated breath as the driver confidentially discourses of moving accidents by field and flood, intermingled with marginal notes as to the undesirability of snapping one's brake on a down-grade along the edge of a thousand-foot precipice. Stagemen have a saying that anybody can drive two horses; that it requires education to drive four, but that six-horse drivers, like poets, are born, not made. They tell a story of a party of Englishmen who chartered a special stage of the Oak Flat road, and who stood the reckless speed at which they were driven, until near the close of the day their nervous systems were completely exhausted. They then stopped the vehicle, and made up a purse of twenty dollars, which they offered the driver on condition he would proceed more slowly the rest of the way. The "whip" calmly pocketed the coin, walked his team around a short turn ahead in the road, and pulled up at the hotel. They had only about fifty yards further to go.

Twenty-three of the twenty-seven miles referred to are thus agreeably placed behind one, when suddenly the stage swings cut upon the brow of a mountain, the horses are stopped, and, pointing his whip forward into space, the driver ejaculates, "Inspiration Point!" This is the famous spot from which the first view of the Yosemite Valley is had, and the passengers crane forward and gaze with as much eagerness as if the PEARLY GATES OF THE HEREAFTER were themselves ajar.

Frank Harrison Gassaway, 1882

Stage travel seems a romantic notion in modern times. The reality was, however, that you got dirty, jostled, and hot for hours on end to reach your destination.

Facing the incomer, and always the most imposing and best-remembered feature of the "Yo," is El Capitan, a rounded pile of white, almost polished, granite, that lifts its conspicuous front three-quarters of a mile into the air, the whole as trim, straight and rigid as a militia-captain on parade. Vis-a-vis to this, and pouring its shifting, feathery flood from the brink of the opposite cliff, is the Bridal Veil Fall, or the fall of the

"SPIRIT OF THE EVIL WIND,"

As the Indians term it, on account of the mysterious gusts that upon the calmest days play with the creamy sheet, and turn it into endless capricious forms, as though the curious wind-spirits strove to steal a peep at the bride beneath.

Frank Harrison Gassaway, 1882

HOMICIDE AND SUICIDE NEAR HORNITOS. A Father-in-law Fires Three Shots at his Son-in-law and then Shoots Himself. At the residence of Joseph Spagnolia and family, at No. 9 Mine, about three miles above Hornitos occurred one of the most sanguinary scenes that has ever taken place in the county. Alvin Branson and his wife, who is sister to Mrs. Spagnolia were stopping there for the time being. By means of some difficulty naturally occurring between families, Branson had removed to Spagnolia's, as above stated. The cause of the desperate act by the father-in-law, if any other than insanity, are yet to be developed. At the time mentioned the two families were altogether in the house, when Wm. Simmons rode up on horseback, dismounted and went into the house, and immediately addressed himself to Mr. Branson, who, as we understand, was in a sitting position, and without giving Mr. Branson a moments warning, or time to gain his feet, he drew a navy six shooter, and fired, the bullet entering the body on the right side. Following the first shot Branson started to run out of the house, when the second shot was fired which took effect in Bransons right hand, the third shot missed him. After firing the third shot, Simmons two daughters seized him and again prevented him shooting. Just at this instant Dr. Corbett, who was at the mine visiting a patient, arrived, and immediately ran up and disarmed Simmons who instantly sprang upon his horse and started full speed for home. He was called upon to stop but paid no attention to the command. As soon as horses could be saddled Simmons was pursued by J. F. Thorn and John Mitchell, but before they arrived there he had shot the top of his head off with a double barreled shotgun. They found him sitting in a chair, the toe of his boot against the trigger, and the upper portion of his head blown away. At last accounts, Branson, whose wound is supposed fatal, was still alive.

1884. RICHARD B. THOMAS, COUNTY SURVEYOR, DROWNED. By F. H. Woodard, whose stage arrived here last Saturday afternoon, and who was himself, the first to discover the sad calamity was brought the sad news of the drowning of our County Surveyor, Richard B. Thomas, which occurred on Thursday, March 6th, at the crossing of Bear creek on the main road about one mile west of Andrew Zinkland's toll house and residence. Mr. Thomas left here early in the week to do some surveying in the lower portion of the county, and was on his return home, to Mariposa. Before arriving at the fatal spot, he was informed by some one at Slattery's tollhouse, that the late rain had swollen the waters of the creek to an unusual height, and it was enjoined upon him to be careful. In his eagerness to get home, Mr. Thomas pursued his way, and as results have shown, he attempted to cross the creek some 300 yards below the crossing. He stopped and recognizing the horse, he endeavored to drive him out of the creek by throwing stones and hallooing at him, but he appeared immovable from some cause, and as it was raining hard and getting late, Mr. Woodard hastened his retreat back to Slattery's for the night. After reciting what he had seen in regard to the horse, it was at once predicted by the people at Slatterys, what misfortune had befallen Mr.

Standart's carriage for cutting logs into lumber.

Courtesy Mariposa County Museum and History Center

We commenced our journey again early this morning and crossed the Merced River about 10 A.M. in a flat boat, for which four teams, ours among the number, paid $5 each. A team that had crossed just before us paid $10, but it was a regular trader. The reduction was made on account of our teams belonging to emigrants reaching the mines for the first time. The ferry is known as the New York Company's Ferry.

As soon as we crossed this river the worst part of our journey commenced, for then we entered the high hills bordering the Sierra Nevada, climbing high rugged precipices and crossing low swampy quagmires, in which we saw the bones and saddles of several mules that had been lost there. In ascending some of these steeps and crossing these swamps they had to hitch two teams to each wagon. Supper—a cup of tea, a piece of boiled beef, cold, and a hard cracker—is just over. We are encamped upon the side of a hill and near a small ravine in which we get our water, which is muddy. As we are but four or five miles from the first diggings, we hope tomorrow will put an end to our weary pilgrimage for a short time.

Enos Christman,
March 18, 1850

These young men take a moment to pose on the 2700 year old Grizzly Giant in Yosemite's Mariposa Grove. It is the oldest known sequoia tree. The tree is 100 feet around at the base with a diameter of 29 feet, and is 209 feet high, although it presently has a snag top and once was much higher.

Our original load of thirteen wayfarers mounted on a saddle-train of as many fly-footed, though melancholy-looking horses, and heading up the best trail in the valley in the direction of Glacier Point. Our procession was led by the best-known guide in the valley, named Pike, and whose individuality would merit a place here were it not for a feeling that Bret Harte owns the patent-right for all that description of character-writing on the coast.

Frank Harrison Gassaway, 1882

Thomas in attempting to cross Bear creek. Information of the probable accident was sent to the nearest neighbors, and early Saturday morning, several persons had collected at Slattery's who proceeded to the creek, about two miles distant. The horse was found in the water in the same position and place seen by Mr. Woodard the evening before, fastened to some of the gearing of the vehicle which had gone to pieces and was scattered along the creek. The body of Mr. Thomas was found about 100 yards below the crossings caught fast in some bushes, was taken out and upon examination one of his legs was found broken in two places and otherwise bruised. He must have endeavored to extricate himself from his overcoat as it was half-way off and hanging to one arm.

Fresno Flats (now Oakhurst) Post Office and Mary Dick's home at 425 B Street in 1900.

Chapter 5: Madera County — Oakhurst (Fresno Flats), Coarsegold, and vicinity

Fresno Flats is today [in the late 1800s] a tumble-down mountain camp near the head of the Fresno River in a farming, mining, lumber and stock raising country. The Yosemite road passed it and the head of the Madera flume is eight miles away. Discovered quartz outcroppings once promised a future never realized. T. J. Allen was postmaster and general merchant, R. T. Burford lawyer and Thurman & Dickinson lumber men there in 1876-78. Smaller camps in the hills to the south and east in the 80's were Michael's and Walker's ranches, Brown's store and Oro Fino.

FRESNO PRIOR TO COUNTY ORGANIZATION. During the summer of 1851, Coarse Gold Gulch became a prominent mining camp, and in the fall of that year an election for county

In the early days, every miner was a walking arsenal. Naturally, a popular amusement would be rifle and pistol practice, and tempted by the surroundings hunting and fishing. A game of cards called "rounce" was a prime favorite. Of course all the card and mechanical devices for gambling were at hand to tempt the unwary and reckless. And scrub mule and horse races had their attractions.

The Never Sweat Mine in Grub Gulch.

So we leave it to its downfall and go some 12 miles when we leave the new road and come into the Fresno Flat road. We then halt at another Station, the hotel post was opened for the first this Spring. Doc ordered three Lemonades one with a stick in it. Mr. Foster the gentleman in charge of the hotel brought them out with a straw in each one. Doc thinks this a little too much style and discards the straw. After leaving there we travel along on the old road with the exception of a mile or two of new grade all the way to the Flats. We pass several Ranches on our way from Foster's to the Flats a distance of 8 miles.

At the Flats there is another Stage Station. The place is not very large — it contains in the way of public houses — one hotel, two stores, two Saloons, one blacksmith shop and several dwellings. There is a splendid school house across the Fresno River from this place where they never fail to have a good school. There are quite a number of families living around from One mile to six or eight miles apart. The Flats is an old settled place, but the town part was started a few years ago. The first thing we come to when we get into the Flats was the town — we drive up to a Saloon and have a lemonade each, inquire about our party and ascertain that they are just across the Fresno (River) about half a mile from here behind Nichols hotel.

Tillie Daulton,
June 24th, 1880
en route to Yosemite

officers of Mariposa County was held. At this election there were polled at the Texas Flat Precinct over 150 votes. Jim Wade was elected member of the Assembly, and Capt. Bowling, Sheriff, whose opponent, Judge Rumsey, afterwards became County Judge of Monterey County. Wm. Faymonville and Jos. M. Kinsman acted as clerks of election at the Texas Flat Precinct; the polls were held at the store of Roney & Thornburg. Of those who voted then at that precinct, and who are (1880) still alive and in this county, may be named the following: Wm. Faymonville, Jos. M. Kinsman, Jas. H. Bethel, R. T. Burford, Wm. Abbie. There were also present, T. T. Strombeck (nicknamed Swede Bill), and J. P. Cohnore, neither of whom voted, not then being citizens; and Nap. Broughton and William Douglass, not now of this county. Stroinbeck afterward married Mimiellet, an excellent Indian girl, who bore him several children, the eldest of whom, blue-eyed, flaxen-haired Mary, is now the respected wife of Thomas Jones. A large vote was also polled at Savage's store.

COARSE GOLD GULCH IN 1851. By the first of October, 1851, the Indians having threatened another war, Coarse Gold Gulch was deserted, only four or five miners remaining, among whom was William Abbie; but before December many returned, among whom were C. P. Converse and T. C. Stallo, who opened a store about one and a half miles below Texas Flat, which was placed in the charge of Samuel H. P. Ross (nicknamed Alphabet Ross), who was afterward District Attorney of Merced County. Asa Johnson, with three negroes and a wench, Mary, also arrived about December and engaged in mining. In the summer of 1852, Johnson managed to kill a man named Thomas Larrabee; Johnson was tried and acquitted and finally left the county; what became of the negroes is not positively known; it was reported that Mary was murdered while on her way back to Texas, in company with another negro.

In the spring of 1852, Stallo & Converse discontinued their store on Coarse Gold Gulch, and the Walker brothers, Jas. N. and C. F., erected a store there, which they continued until 1859.

In 1852, John Letford and one Carson erected a store at the Fresno crossing but soon sold out to J. L. Hunt and J. R. Nichols, and Nichols soon after sold out his interest in the store, to James Roan.

MINING. The first quartz mill erected in the county was at Coarse Gold Gulch—a ten-stamp mill. Various and valuable mines are located within the county, and only await development to yield an immense treasure. One cause of delay in developing the mineral interests of this county is the lack of railroad transportation. This cause will soon be removed, as soon there will be built from Fresno a railroad direct to the mineral and timber region of the Sierras. Another and principal reason why capital is not used in developing the mineral resources of the county is, that better returns for money invested can be had

In 1863 the looting of Chinese stores and camps was resumed with at least eight known desperadoes in the gang. The China store at Andrew Johnson's place at Coarse Gold Gulch was robbed three times and patience had ceased to be a virtue. A company of about a dozen men organized and one dark night in the dead winter of 1864 it invaded the camp of the desperadoes. Whether warned or not of the coming, only one of the gang —Al Dixon— was caught that night and found a corpse hanging from a tree the next morning between Coarse Gold Gulch and the Fresno. The life of the brother John was interceded for and six of the gang left the country and were not again heard from. The eighth, James Raines, remained to weather it out and came in conflict with the provost marshal in the latter's prosecution of his duties. A squad from the fort was sent to arrest him. Raines appeared pistol in hand to resist arrest and himself was shot and wounded in the arm. After having convalesced at the fort, Raines was taken to Alcatraz and spent several months at hard labor on the rock. Following release, he moved with his family to Raines' Valley, east of Centerville. He and others took up cattle and hog stealing until the neighborhood decided that it had enough of this business and one fine morning Raines' carcass was found dangling from a tree in or near the valley that bears his name.

The Duncan freight team hauling goods into Yosemite about 1900.

Courtesy Fresno Flats Museum

This family, probably near Fish Camp, looks pretty settled in with their cow, canary, and horse.

"I'll never forget the time when the first woman came into camp. The miners heard she was coming, and they all quit work and marched four miles down the road to meet her. Several large arches were erected over the road, and a band of music led the march into town. The town was alive with miners when we got there, who came in from the hills to get a glimpse of the woman and participate in the celebration."

J.D. Peters, miner

from fruits, grapes, prunes, peaches, apricots, etc., which yield larger profit for money invested than do the great majority of gold mines.

REMEMBERED EARLIEST CAMPS. Among the best remembered earliest mining camps in the northeastern Fresno County region were Coarse Gold Gulch, discovered in the summer of 1850, Texas Flat, Grub Gulch, Hildreth, Fine Gold Gulch, Temperance Flat, Rootville the immediate predecessor of Millerton on the San Joaquin and one mile below the fort, "Soldier Bar" and "Cassady's Bar" on the bend of the river above the fort. The channel of the river with its small tributaries from the bridge at Hamptonville, below Millerton, was worked for forty miles up into the mountains. The Kings, which contributes to the wealth of the country as the provider of the water for irrigation and has its rise San Joaquin, has never witnessed any mining operations, though some placer mining was once upon a time conducted at or near what is now known as Piedra where the magnesite mine in an entire mountain is located.

Quartz locations on its banks have been made many times though no notable mine has been developed.

It is conceded that during the early mining period, as well as in subquent years and as late as the 70s and 80s the placers and the surface outcroppings were well worked over and exhausted. No portion of the county but has been prospected by the grub-stake miner. Discoveries are being made to this day and quartz mine locations are frequent occurrences. Even the old mining district boundary lines are adhered to as a reminder of the past. These locations prove to be little more than chance discoveries of pockets or vein outcroppings, raising great expectations with no realization save in a few exceptions. No systematic development of the mineral deposits has followed for self evident reasons in the too great risk of investment, cost of or lack of transportation and remoteness of the locations.

A marked map of the county would show it peppered in spots as remote and inaccessible as the upper precipitous gulches of the Kings River forks with mining locations and punctured with prospects holes and developing tunnel openings with their dumps. Late in the 70s there was sporadic effort at a development of quartz mines, but no rich or lasting ones resulted from the labor and money investments. Even the picturesque and extravagant names of the most notable of these have passed from memory. On the Madera side of the river in the drift gold gulches districts of earliest days several mills were erected, but the life of the enterprises was evanescent. In the end they were all money losers, encouraging though the first prospects. The names of them if recalled are reminders of wasted effort and misspent money. Not all were absolute failures, though all were

"Old Betsey," the steam locomotive, hauls her load of logs through the woods above Baptist Camp.

I think Fresno Flats is a very warm place, any way in the day time, but most always the nights are cool. Jack got tired waiting for us and started. We got off about half past ten. Mr. and Mrs. Nichols are very fine people. They have a large family of real nice lady like daughters — it would be a good place for a gentleman to go in pursuit of a wife. After leaving Mr. Nichols we went over to Phelp's farm. I had left several things there. I got out of the buggy and went in. Doc drove off up town and I thought very probably that would be the last I should see of him that day.

Tillie Daulton,
June 28th, 1880
en route to Yosemite

The Madera flume under construction in about 1881. This was a 54-mile flume that was in use from 1882 to 1923.

Recklessness in gambling was characteristic, with Converse a notable example of it. There was nothing that he would not risk the hazard of chance on. He would wager any stake on who could expectorate closest to a given mark. He and McCray laid a bet whose road was the longest from their respective ferries. Converse lost, and after the wager was paid it leaked out that the night before the surveyor's measuring chain had been shortened by several links. On another occasion, it is related, Converse was in a card game for high stakes—gold dust in buckskin sacks—at McCray's with cutthroat "greasers," and Converse was cleaned out. Undismayed, he excused himself, asked that the game be not halted, and on return reentered it, won back all he had lost, and more too. The buckskin with which he regained everything contained only sand that he had scooped up on the river bank during his temporary absence.

abandoned and are memories now. The number of them spells legion.

In Grub Gulch district was the Josephine, owned by an English syndicate fourteen miles northeast from Raymond, located in 1880; also Les Mines d'Or de Quartz Mountain, a Belgian corporation that sank, without returns, a fortune of the stockholders in erecting and locating a costly plant that has been idle for many years in charge of a watchman and given over to the bats and owls. The Raymond quarries have furnished granite for the state buildings at Sacramento, for miles upon miles of street curbing in San Francisco and after a period of comparative inactivity were drawn heavily upon for the rebuilding of the San Francisco public and other buildings after the great disaster, and the later Panama Exposition. The quarries at Academy in this county have and are furnishing granite rock for ornamental architecture and grave stones and monuments. In the inaccessible Minarets section, north of the San Joaquin there are said to be on the southern slope inexhaustible iron deposits in practically a mountain of almost pure metal, one of the known largest and richest iron ore deposits in the world.

The Kniepper copper mine, in the Big Dry Creek district, was later developed as the Fresno, and a first successful development of a copper ledge was that of the Ne Plus Ultra, on the Daulton ranch on the Madera side and it actually for a time sent mats to Swansea, Eng., for refining. It paid for a time but in the end petered out and another costly experiment was charged up to experience and corresponding loss.

LUMBER BUSINESS. The Madera Flume and Trading Company in 1878 became the property of E. McLaughlin, C. T. Ryland, and R. Roberts, of San Jose, who have two mills in the Sierra Nevada Mountains, about fifty-two miles east of Madera, which produce annually from 10,000,000 to 12,000,000 feet of lumber. It is of choice sugar and yellow pine and fir, and is brought to Madera in a 30-inch V flume, constructed as early as 1874, at a cost of $460,000, from surveys made by Mark Howell. This flume operates admirably and enables the company to deliver their lumber cheaply to the shipping point, where it goes long distances, even to the far southeast at El Paso. The company has also steam, saw, and planing-mill, sash and door factory, etc., which has a good local patronage.

The Flume Company cut during 1881, over 11,000,000 feet of lumber. Owning 5,000 acres of the choicest timber land in the Sierra. Nevadas, running three steam mills, in addition to their large factory, and giving employment from 100 to 200 men, the Madera Flume and Trading Company, under the local management of Mr. E. Roberts, will constitute an enterprize of which any county might justly feel proud.

Judge M. B. Lewis, an aged old gentleman yet living in this county, a Texan soldier under Sam Houston, and one of the Commisioners for the organization of the county, was in early days an Indian Agent on Fresno River, and was always the friend of the Indian. As agent he felt himself in some sort bound to protect them from wrong. On one occasion an Indian was arrested for some offense. On his trial he introduced through the Judge, who acted as his counsel, quite a number of his tribe, who swore to facts showing his complete innocence. Their testimony being in, and knowing how little weight Indian evidence received, the Judge solemnly arose and asked to be sworn. This done, he as solemnly stated to the court that he knew nothing personally of the facts, but that he did know these Indian witnesses, and knew them to be honest and credible witnesses, so that he would swear that what they swore to was true! Tradition does not inform us whether this ancient practice of our forefathers succeeded in its purpose or not in this instance.

Fish Camp life was always a great getaway for a family.

Courtesy Fresno Flats Museum

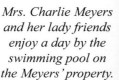The principal amusements indulged in by the miners in those days was rifle and pistol practice, and a game of cards called rounce, and sometimes an indifferent horse-race was gotten up; but Shannon took a new departure in the way of getting tip races. In the summer of 1856, Shannon and Jim Roan made up a foot-race between two squaws. Jeff trained a young squaw, known by the euphonious name of Mustang, and Roan trained another named Chutaluya. Quite an interest was manifested in this race, and considerable money was bet. On the day appointed for the race a great crowd assembled to witness the speed of the contestants, and when the squaws appeared upon the track, Mustang dressed in red, and the other in blue, a deafening cheer rent the air, and both the squaws looked eager for the fray, and when the word "go" was given, away they went, each doing her level best. The result was, Mustang came out a few feet ahead and was declared the winner, and Jeff won about $150 on the race. L. A. Holmes, then editor of the *Mariposa Gazette*, in commenting on the race, observed, that "if Roan had kept his squaw in as good training as Jeff kept his, the result of the race would have been different."

Mrs. Charlie Meyers and her lady friends enjoy a day by the swimming pool on the Meyers' property.

HOT SPRINGS. Mineral springs, both hot and cold, are found in this county. The Rogers Hot Springs are possessed of remarkable remedial properties, highly recommended for rheumatic, neuralgic and scrofulous complaints. On the upper San Joaquin, near the toll-house, are also remarkable springs, one of which boils up like a geyser, through a cone-like mound of cemented matter. Sulphur Springs, near Millerton, were purchased by a company incorporated in 1873. They are situated about three-quarters of a mile from the old court-house.

Bibliography

BOOKS AND JOURNALS

Thompson & West, History of Amador County, California, 1881

W.W. Elliott & Co., Calaveras County Illustrated and Described, 1885

B.F. Alley, A History of Tuolumne County, 1882

W.W. Elliott & Co., History of Fresno County, 1882

The Lewis Publishing Company, History of Fresno, Tulare, and Kern Counties, 1892

INDIVIDUALS.

BREWER, WILLIAM HENRY (1828-1910) was a professor of chemistry at Washington College in Pennsylvania when he joined the staff of California's first state geologist, Josiah Dwight Whitney, 1860-1864. On returning east, Brewer became Professor of Agriculture at Yale, a post he held for nearly forty years. *Up and down California* (1930) collects Brewer's letters and journal entries recording his work with Whitney's geological survey of California, chronicling not merely the survey's scientific work, but the social, agricultural, and economic life of the state from south to north as the survey's men passed along.

BUNNELL, LAFAYETTE HOUGHTON (1824-1903) was a member of the Mariposa Battalion that became the white discoverers of the Yosemite Valley in 1851 when they rode out in search of Native American tribal leaders involved in recent raids on American settlements. Dr. Bunnell later served as a surgeon in the Civil War. *Discovery of the Yosemite, and the Indian war of 1851 (1880)* contains his account of that event, beginning with the history of the battalion and the tribal unrest that inspired its creation. He goes on to chronicle the unit's march from its camp near Agua Fria into the mountains down the South Fork of the Merced River. Bunnell recalls his comrades' reactions to the natural grandeur they encountered in the Yosemite Valley as well as the trivia of camp life and encounters with the native tribes they were sent to pacify.

CLEMENS, SAMUEL LANGHORNE (1835-1910), better known as "Mark Twain," left Missouri in 1861 to work with his brother, the newly appointed Secretary of the Nevada Territory. Once settled in Nevada, Clemens fell victim to gold fever and went to the Humboldt mines. When prospecting lost its attractions, Clemens found work as a reporter in Virginia City. In 1864, Clemens moved to California and worked as a reporter in San Francisco. It was there that he began to establish a nationwide reputation as a humorist. *Roughing It* (1891), first published in 1872, is his account of his adventures in the Far West. He devotes twenty chapters to the overland journey by boat and stagecoach to Carson City, including several chapters on the Mormons. Next come chronicles of mining life and local politics and crime in Virginia City and San Francisco and even a junket to the Hawaiian Islands. The book closes with his return to San Francisco and his introduction to the lecture circuit. Regarding some of the story from the *Territorial Enterprise,* The Petrified Man, Twain writes for a monthly magazine, The Galaxy: "...I certainly did not desire to deceive anybody. I had not the remotest desire to play upon any one's confidence with a practical joke, for he is a pitiful creature indeed who will degrade the dignity of his humanity to the contriving of the witless inventions that go by that name. I purposely wrote the thing as absurdly and as extravagantly as it could be written, in order to be sure and not mislead..."

CHRISTMAN, ENOS (1828-1912), a West Chester, Pennsylvania, printer's apprentice, left for the gold fields in June 1849, returning in October 1852. *One man's gold* (1930) contains both sides of his correspondence with his fiancee and his former boss in West Chester and his journal of his experiences in the West. Highlights include his brief career as prospector on the Calaveras River and Mariposa diggings and his partnership in publication of the *Sonoma Herald* and life in that town, 1850-1852.

COLTON, WALTER (1797-1851) of Vermont had a career as clergyman and journalist before sailing to California as naval chaplain of the Congress. In July 1846, Commodore Stockton named him alcalde of Monterey, a post to which he was elected a few months later. He remained in California until 1849, using his time to found the state's first newspaper and building its first schoolhouse. *Three years in California* (1850) contains Colton's memoirs of that period, including descriptions of the U.S. military occupation of California, social life and customs of Monterey, discovery of gold and firsthand impressions of the Sonora mining camp in the Southern Mines, visits to Stockton and San José, John Charles Frémont, the Constitutional Convention of 1849, and California missions.

DAVIS, STEPHEN CHAPIN (1833-1856) and his brother left Nashua, New Hampshire, to act as agents for local merchants in Gold Rush California. Before he was done, young Davis crossed Panama four times in the period June 1850-May 1854. *California gold rush merchant* (1956) prints Davis's journal entries from the original in the Henry E. Huntington Library. Highlights include his Panama crossings; descriptions of Marysville, Long Bar, Coulterville, Stockton, and San Francisco; and a side trip to Oregon. His business interests included both general stores and a boardinghouse in mining camps.

DOBLE, JOHN was born in Indiana, and served in the war with Mexico in 1846. After returning to Indiana, he journeyed to California in 1851 via New York City and a steamer to Panama. On leaving the Sierra foothills he joined his brother at his iron works in San Francisco. Doble wrote a diary of his trip to California and of his daily life as a prospector during the gold rush.

EVANS, ALBERT S. (1831-1872) was a New Hampshire-born California journalist, serving as correspondent for the *New York Tribune* and *Chicago Tribune*. *À la California* (1873) is a volume of reminiscences and anecdotal history published after Evans's death at sea. He begins by taking his reader on a tour from the Sierra Morena through the San Andreas Valley, south to Pescadero and Santa Cruz, up the Napa Valley and Mount St. Helena. He offers several chapters on San Francisco, with special attention to the legends of the Barbary Coast and Chinatown and tales of miners in the Gold Rush.

GASSAWAY, FRANK HARRISON used the pseudonym "Derrick Dogg" for his numerous writings in the *San Francisco Evening Post*. *Summer saunterings* (1882) contains travel letters originally published in the Post. They report transportation routes, hotels and camping sites, natural wonders and manmade tourist attractions, and local lore in Santa Barbara, Santa Cruz, Monterey, San José, Napa, Sausalito, San Rafael, Santa Rosa, Yosemite, and other popular spots.

JOHNSON, THEODORE TAYLOR of New Jersey sailed to California in February 1849 and had returned home by the end of June. *Sights in the gold region* (1849) is the first published book to relate authentic personal experiences in the California gold fields. Johnson describes his voyage to California and Panama crossing and prospecting in the Culomma (now Coloma) Valley. He also writes of his return to San Francisco in the hope of finding work at the end of spring and his discouraged decision to take passage home,

again crossing the Isthmus at Chagres. Personal recollections are fleshed out with secondhand discussions of the state's history and culture.

JONES, JULIA LOIS (b. 1857) was born at Benton Mills (now known as Bagby) on the Merced River. Julia was an inquisitive, intelligent woman who became a teacher in 1877. She became superintendent of Schools in Mariposa in 1894. The insights into her life begin at age 15 and reflect her unique look at the times.

KIP, LEONARD (1826-1906), a young Albany lawyer, sailed for California in 1849. On his return east in 1850, Kip resumed the practice of law in Albany and published stories, articles, and novels. *California sketches* (1946) reprints accounts of his adventures that Kip sent home for newspaper publication and that were published as a pamphlet in 1850. The eight chapters describe his arrival in San Francisco, journey through Stockton to two months of gold-mining on the Mokelumne, and reasons for his abandonment of California.

LEEPER, DAVID (1832-1900) left South Bend, Indiana, for an overland trip to the California gold fields in February 1849. *The argonauts of forty-nine* (1894) details Leeper's journey west and his life in California, 1849-1854: prospecting at Redding's Diggings, Hangtown, and the Trinity River; lumbering around Eureka; and early Sacramento and Humboldt Bay. Leeper shows special interest in the Digger Indians, illustrating the book with sketches of tribal garb in his personal collection.

MANLY, WILLIAM LEWIS (1820-1903) and his family left Vermont in 1828, and he grew to manhood in Michigan and Wisconsin. On hearing the news of gold in California, Manly set off on horseback, joining an emigrant party in Missouri. *Death Valley in '49* (1894) contains Manly's account of that overland journey. Setting out too late in the year to risk a northern passage through the Sierras, the group takes the southern route to California, unluckily choosing an untried shortcut through the mountains. This fateful decision brings the party through Death Valley, and Manly describes their trek through the desert, as well as the experiences of the Illinois "Jayhawkers" and others who took the Death Valley route. Manly's memoirs continue with his trip north to prospecting near the Mariposa mines, a brief trip back east via the Isthmus, and his return to California and another try at prospecting on the North Fork of the Yuba at Downieville in 1851. He provides lively anecdotes of life in mining camps and of his visits to Stockton, Sacramento, and San Francisco.

MARRYAT, FRANK (1826-1855) left England for California via Panama with a manservant and three hunting dogs in 1850, hoping to find material for a book like his earlier *Borneo*. On his return to England in 1853, Marryat married and brought his bride back to California that same year. Yellow fever contracted on shipboard forced him to cut the trip short and return to England where he died two years later. *Mountains and molehills* (1855) is a sportsman-tourist's chronicle of California in the early 1850s: hunting, horse races, bear and bull fights. It also includes an Englishman's bemused comments on social life in San Francisco, Stockton, and the gold fields.

MOERENHOUT, JACQUES ANTOINE (1796-1879) was the French consul at Monterey in 1848. *The inside story of the gold rush* (1935) contains Moerenhout's official dispatches concerning the discovery of gold in California. He reports his trip to the goldfields above Sacramento in July 1848 as well as later developments in the Gold Rush, 1848-1850.

MCCOLLUM, WILLIAM S. DR. (1807/1808-1882) was born in Pennsylvania and grew up in Niagara County, New York. He went to California in 1849, returned to New York the following year and then paid a second visit to California as a physician for the Panama Railroad Company. *California as I saw it* (1960) reprints McCollum's 1850 book describing his first visit to the West: San Francisco in 1849, a journey to Stockton and the Southern Mines and to Sacramento and the Northern Mines, prospecting near Jacksonville, and medical practice in Stockton and San Francisco. After describing his return voyage east via Panama, McCollum closes with advice and reflections on the law of the mines, Native Americans, the life of women in California, etc. The book's appendix includes letters written from Panama by H.W. Hecox, McCollum's fellow passenger on the voyage to the Isthmus, February-March 1849. Hecox was so disheartened by his wait for passage to California that he returned to the United States without ever seeing the Pacific Ocean.

NORDHOFF, CHARLES (1830-1901) and his family came to America from Prussia when he was a boy and settled in Cincinnati, Ohio. Winning a reputation as a journalist and writer on the sea, Nordhoff was managing editor of the *New York Evening Post*, 1861-1871. He spent 1872-1873 travelling to California and Hawaii, and returned east to become the Washington correspondent of the *New York Herald*. He continued to visit California frequently and spent his last years in Coronado. *California: for health, pleasure and residence* (1873) was an extremely popular guidebook that persuaded many to settle in California. It opens with descriptions of the various routes available to the traveller to California and the visitor to Yosemite. Next come suggested points of interest; California agriculture (with hints to prospective settlers); and notes on the Southern California climate.

PIERCE, HIRAM DWIGHT (b. 1810) was a successful blacksmith in Troy, New York, when news arrived of gold discoveries in California. Leaving his wife and seven children behind, Pierce set out in March 1849, crossing the Isthmus to reach San Francisco. *A forty-niner speaks* (1930) prints the contents of notebooks kept by Pierce from the day he left Troy until his return in January 1851. He describes his journey west and work in the gold fields near Sacramento, the Stanislaus mines, and the Merced River at Washington Flat, until his return home via Panama. Pierce offers an excellent account of the details of a prospector's life and the organization of miners' camps as business companies and local government units.

PLAYER-FROWD, J.G. was an English visitor to California in the early 1870s. *Six Months in California* (1872) is a traveler's guide based on that visit, recounting stays in Omaha, Salt Lake City, the Sierras, Lake Tahoe, Sacramento, San Francisco, Calistoga, Stockton, and the Yosemite Valley. Player-Frowd discusses topics such as California climate, agriculture, mining, and lumbering.

ROOT, HORACE left his wife Eliza A. Root in Comanohe, Iowa, in 1849 to seek gold in California.

SCHAEFFER, LUTHER MELANCHTHON, A native of Frederick, Maryland, sailed around the Horn to California in 1849. He spent most of the next two-and-a-half years in the gold fields, mining on the Feather River, Deer Creek, Grass Valley (Centerville) and other Nevada County sites. *Sketches of travels in South America, Mexico and California* (1860) gives an excellent picture of the international, interracial community of miners, with comments on social patterns, creation of local government, vigilance committees, and legal disputes in this society. Schaeffer also describes visits to San Francisco and Sacramento, Mexico, and Panama before his return to the East in 1852.

SHAW, DAVID AUGUSTUS, left Marengo, Illinois, in 1850 for the overland trail to California, where he settled in Pasadena and was an active member of the local Society of Pioneers. *Eldorado* (1900) records Shaw's first stay in the West, 1850-1852, when he worked as a miner and rancher; his return to Illinois and second overland journey west, 1853, this time bringing a herd of horses; and a third round trip to the East, 1856, this time crossing at Panama. In California, Shaw worked as a miner and rancher.

SNOW, HORACE from Bridgewater, Massachussetts left New York Harbor by ship on September 5, 1853 and arrived in San Francisco on October 12, 1853. His travels took him by side-wheel steamer to Chagres, Panama and across the seventy-five mile Isthums by dugout canoe and mule. With little money, he walked to Mariposa County and joined his brother Hiram at Agua Frio who had, at age fifteen, sailed round the Horn in search of gold.

STEELE, JOHN, REV. (1832-1915) traveled overland from Wisconsin to California in 1850 and remained for three years. Returning east, he taught school, served in the Union Army, and became an Episcopal minister after the Civil War. *Echoes of the past about California* and *In camp and cabin* (1928) reprints works by John Bidwell and Steele published earlier. Bidwell's narrative was composed in 1889 and first published in 1890 in the *Century Magazine*. The version published here as "*Echoes of the past*," however, was based on a somewhat different version published in pamphlet form by the Chico, California Advertiser after Bidwell's death in 1900. This version does not include Bidwell's "*Journey to California*," the journal that he kept in 1841 and which was published in Missouri in 1843 or 1844. Steele's *In camp and cabin*, first published in 1901, recounts Steele's experiences mining in camps near Nevada City and the American River, with tales of trips to Feather River, Los Angeles, and an expedition to San Andres and camps on the Mokelumne, Calaveras, and Stanislaus Rivers. He provides numerous anecdotes of the people of the camps and their varied national and ethnic backgrounds with many tales of crime and lawlessness. He also discusses contrasting mining methods and gives special attention to Hispanic and Native American Californians whom he met.

STEPHENS, LORENZO DOW (b. 1827) was born in New Jersey and raised in Illinois, where he joined a party for California in 1849. *Life sketches of a jayhawker* (1916) begins with Stephens's overland journey west, including Brigham Young's sermons at the Tabernacle in Salt Lake. He describes prospecting on the Merced River, farming in the Santa Clara Valley, and cattle drives from San Bernardino and San Diego. His memoirs continue through the 1860s, including his part in the 1862 British Columbia gold rush.

TAYLOR, BAYARD (1825-1878) was already a well-established writer when he traveled to California as special correspondent for the *New York Tribune* in the summer of 1849. On his return to New York, Taylor established himself not only as one of America's great travel writers but as a true man of letters, producing distinguished novels and poems as well as nonfiction for the next quarter century. *Eldorado* (1850) consists of Taylor's rewritten dispatches to his paper. Volume 2 tells of the 1849 elections, horseback tours of the Sierras, gold camps on the Mokelumne River, analysis of the 1849 overland emigration, San Francisco social and cultural life, and a return to the East with stops in Guadalajara, Mazatlàn, Mexico City, Popcapeptel, and Vera Cruz. Thomas Butler King's official report on California, 22 March 1850, is printed as an appendix.

TWAIN, MARK, See Samuel Clemens

WOOD, HARVEY (1828-1895), a young clerk in a New Jersey store, joined the Kit Carson Association of would-be California miners that set out from New York in February 1849, sailing to Texas and crossing Mexico overland to find passage north to San Diego. Wood reached the Southern Mines in July 1849, spending the next seven years searching for gold on the Merced and Stanislaus Rivers. In 1856 he purchased an interest in Robinson's Ferry across the Stanislaus River, a business he maintained the rest of his life. *Personal recollections* (1955) reprints a memoir written in 1878 and first published in 1896. Wood describes his voyage to California and his experiences as a miner in modern Calaveras and Tuolumne Counties, 1849-1850.

WOODS, DANIEL B., of Philadelphia sailed to California in February 1849, crossing Mexico to San Blas, and arriving in San Francisco in June. *Sixteen months at the gold diggings* (1851) recounts those travels as well as his experiences as a prospector in the Northern Mines on the American River and at Hart's Bar and other camps in the southern mines before starting home in November, 1850. His book offers an exceptionally realistic picture of the drudgery of mining and the business side of miners' companies.

Index

A
Abbie, William 276
Adams & Company 172, 174, 197, 198, 213-215
Adams, Dr. 271
Addison, a man named 63
Agua Fria or Agua Frio 246, 251, 266, 267
Alabama House 65
Alcatraz 277
Alexander 54
Alexander, D. G. 156
Alger, Horatio 105
Algerine Camp 199
Allen, Brother Daniel 70
Allen, T. J. 275
Alpine County 51
Altaville 103, 110, 111
Alvarado, Governor Juan B. 81
Amador City 25, 28, 37, 50, 72, 75, 76, 80
Amador County 15-86
Amador Hotel 28
Amador Livery Stable 19
Amador Mine 73
Amador Reduction Works 85
American Exchange Hotel 31, 172, 218
American Flat 74
American Hill 30, 74
American Hotel 39
Angel, Mr. 112
Angels Brewery 126
Angels Camp 16, 103, 104, 107, 110-112, 115, 120, 121, 124, 126, 132, 133, 144, 137
Anna Welch, a bark 51
App Mine 206
Arcade Saloon 245
Argonaut Mine 23
Arkansas Creek 54
Arkansas Hotel 172
Armstrong 187
Arnett, Joe 133
Arnett, Susie 108
Arroyo Seco 76
Art Union 103
Ashloy 73
Ashton, Charles 218
Ashworth, D. C. 240
Askey 17, 38
Askey, A. 32
Astor House 31, 35
Astor, John Jacob 105
Atkins 154
Aurora 241
Avent, Captain 155

B
Bacon 213
Baker, Fletcher 81
Bald Mountain 178
Baldwin Hotel 112
Ballard 60
Balliol Mine 65, 68
Baptist Camp 279
Baptiste 211
Baptiste, John 265
Barclay, John S. 160
Barcroft, Ralph 258
Barden, Harry 111
Barlow, Mr. 70
Barnes 93
Barnes, W. W. 250
Barron, W. H. 172
Barry, Justice 178, 225
Barry, Major 191
Bart, Black *see also* Boles, Charles 105, 127, 128
Bassett, Charles 156, 158
Bastion, Leslie 101
Beal, C. R. 116
Beals 170
Beardsley Flat 233
Bear Valley 238, 243, 251, 256, 264, 265
Beebee 47, 57
Beecher, Henry Ward 105
Beiterman 51
Bella Union 117, 118
Belle Creole Baths 26
Bellow, J. 219
Belt, G. G. 184
Benard, General 168
Benjamin, Mr. 139
Bennett & Phillips 184
Benton Mills 238, 256
Beckman 55
Bergel 196
Bertine 197
Bethel, Jas. H. 276
Besancon, L. A. 194
Bessey 215
Bicknell, Thomas 39

Bidwell, John 105
Big Bar 154
Big Oak Flat 188, 218, 225, 243, 247
Big Tree and Carson Valley Toll Road 137
Big Trees 88, 90-96, 93, 99, 103-105, 114, 119, 133, 135, 137, 139, 143, 144
Big Tree Station 246, 263, 271
Birdsail's Store 71
Birmingham 57
Blakely, John 222
Boardman, John N. 59
Bodkin 47
Bolen, Capt. 268
Boles or Bolles, Charles *see also* Black Bart 105, 131
Bolinger, Frank M. 249, 250
Bolter, Richard 191
Bonanza Mine 143
Bond 166
Bonillos 155
Boot Jack Ranch 263
Boston Bakery 173
Bottle Spring 25
Boucher, Dr. M.K.
Boucher, Tom 63
Bowen, William 225
Bowman 57
Boynton, Charles 31, 33
Brack's Landing 90
Bradford 156
Bradford, Robert 243
Brandy and Sugar Hotel 31
Branson, Alvin 272
Brewer, William Henry 25, 70
Bridgeport 38
Briggs, E. M. 42
Broadway Hotel 55, 176
Broughton, Nap. 276
Browett 70
Brown 275
Brown, A. 138
Brown, Charles J. 214
Brown, Dr. 217
Brown, George 217, 218
Brown, H. N. 174, 229
Brown, Thomas 79
Brown claim 75
Brown's Flat 159, 170, 191
Bruce 263
Bruce, Robert 164

Brunner, A. A. 39
Brunton, Judge 199
Bryant 64
Buchanan 47
Buchanan Hollow 249, 250
Buchannan Mine 198
Buckley 241
Buena Vista 31, 42, 62, 81
Bull and bear fight 21
Bullock, Mr. 215
Bund, J. C. 135
Bunker Hill Mine 72
Bunnel 60
Bunnell and Coles Carpenters and Builders 145
Bunnell, Lafayette Houghton 240
Burce 107
Burden, C. H. 207
Burdick's Saloon 132
Burford, R. T. 275, 276
Burk, Pat 198
Burke 229
Burke, John 35
Burn's Ferry 164
Burson 103, 115
Burt 189
Burton, John 101
Butler & Talbot 52
Butterfield's Store 192
Byrne 64

C

Cabesut, J. M. 149
Calaveras County 16, 21, 32-34, 51, 75, 87-144
Calaveras Big Trees, *see* Big Trees
Calaveras Chronicle 97, 99, 107
Calaveras Citizen 116
Calaveras Grove 96
Calaveras Hotel 137
Calaveras Prospect 92, 112, 115, 116
Calaveras Weekly Citizen 131, 137
Calaveritas, Upper 132,
California Volunteers 231
Caminetti, Anthony 30
Campi, George 253
Campodonico, A. 264
Campo Seco 87, 91, 103, 109, 114, 115, 119, 138, 143, 147, 169, 210, 212
Campo Seco Copper Mine 119
Campo Seco Ditch and Mining Company 143

Candelaria 127
Cape Horn 134
Carder, Town Marshall 160
Cardinell, John A. 173
Cardinell's Theatre 175
Carr, Andrew J. 166
Carrington, Mr. 148
Carson, Alexander 154
Carson City 126
Carson Hill 101, 102
Carter 60, 74
Cassady's Bar 278
Cat Camp 115
Cathey's Valley 265
Cavagnaro, Henry A. 142
Cave City 91, 132
Cazneau, Tom 226
Cedarville 76
Centerville 277
Central Hill 115
Central Hill Mine 106
Central House 32, 55
Central Pacific Railroad 89, 92, 135, 137, 264
Chapline 64
Charleville, F. A. 58
Chatfield, A. F. 198
Chichizola Store 50
Childers, Moses 77, 78
Chili Camp 115
Chili Gulch 97, 99, 101
China Gulch 64
Chinese 95, 130, 138, 140, 147, 149, 150, 151, 160, 173-175, 179, 199, 201, 202, 218,
Chinese Camp 140, 147, 160, 199
Christman, Enos 147, 152, 162, 181, 205, 229, 230, 231, 235, 248, 253, 259, 270, 273
City Hotel 204
Clapboard Gulch 62
Clark, Galen 263
Clark, Terrence 184
Clark, W. H. 172
Clark, William O. 28
Claudio, Lieutenant 230
Cleaves, Al 240
Clement, Mr. 269
Clendenen, Henry 244
Clinton 37, 47
Clyde 57

Coarsegold (Course Gold) Coursegold 275-278
Cohen, Morris 100
Cohnore, P. 276
Cold Spring Ranch 136, 137
Cold Springs Lumber 270
Coffroth, James 194
Collier, Patrick 97
Collins 184
Colyer, Colonel 33, 34
Coloma 16, 27, 47, 170, 171
Colombo Saloon 38
Colorado 236, 244, 249
Colorado Jack 236
Colton, Walter 145, 159, 167, 186, 188
Columbia 145-148, 151, 154-176, 179, 181, 183, 185, 187, 191, 193, 194, 200, 206, 214, 215, 226, 228-232
Columbia Brewery and Syrup Manufactory 173
Columbia Fusiliers 164
Columbia Gulch 157, 165, 169, 191
Columbia Marble Company 231
Comanche 103, 104, 114, 115
Condit, J. H. 191
Conner, P. Edward 231
Connor, Constable 194
Contra Costa County 35
Contrares, Gregorio 169
Contreras, Mrs. 271
Converse C.P. 276, 277, 280
Cook 60, 134
Cook, Henry G. & Mrs. 90, 91
Cook, Jacob 60
Cook, James 257
Coon 103
Coopers, Col. 127
Copperopolis 55, 87, 92, 100, 102-104, 108-110, 128, 129, 135, 203
Corbett, Dr. 272
Corcoran, John M. 260
Corcoran, Thomas 118
Corwin 113
Cosner, Robert 28
Coulter's Hotel 240
Coulterville 235, 239, 240, 245, 252, 254, 261, 262, 264, 266, 267, 271
Cow and Calf Ranch 243

Cox 70
Cox, George W. 90
Coyado, Jose B. 144
Coyote Diggings 169
Coyote Joe 35, 84
Crail, J. H. 104
Creaner, Judge 195
Crockett 156
Crouch, John 47
Cruz, Antonio 182
Cunningham, Mr. 85, 86
Cunningham Ditch 46
Cunningham Toll Road 237
Cunningham, Tom 128
Curtis 60, 74
Curtis, J. 198
Curtis, W. F. 28
Cyane, USS 157

D

Daegener, Wm. 172
Dailey 241
Daley Claim 149
Dambacher, Fred 217
Dance, Joseph 168
Danielson, Daniel 113
Dann, Isaac 241, 242
Daulton, Ida 239, 244
Daulton ranch 280
Daulton, Tillie 236, 249, 276, 279
Davenport, Braxton 45
Davidson, Mr. 70
Davis 185
Davis, Jefferson 40
Davis, Leven 191, 192
Davis, Stephen Chapin 163, 173
Day 107
Dead Man's Creek 26
Deep Gulch 73, 74
DeHaven, Abe 63
Demorest, D.D. 111
Denig, Wm. M. 132
DeShamps, Jos. 102
Diamond Springs 25
Dick, Mary 275
Dickinson 275
Digger Indians 122, 174, 188
Diggs 81
Dillon 203
Divall's Camp 180
Divoll, J. G. 191
Dixon, Al 277
Dobbin, George 242

Dobin, Jeremiah 131
Doble, John 100, 111, 113, 135
Dodds, H. F. 250
Dodge, Mayor 198
Dodge Co. 183
Dog Ranch 136
Dolf 229
Domingo, Lizzie 140
Donald & Parsons 174
Don Pedro's Camp 187
Don Pedro reservoir 197
Dooley 203
Dorrington 133
Dorsey, Caleb 191, 223, 225
Dosh's Store 65
Double Springs 25, 33
Douglas Flat 113
Douglass, Joe 34
Douglass, William 276
Downs 63
Doyle, Ed 212
Drake, Eugene B. 216
Drytown 15, 17, 19, 31, 49, 50, 53, 55, 68, 70, 73, 76
Duncan & Gage 32
Duncan freight team 277
Dunham, Captain 32
Durand 248
Duval, Claude 127

E

Eagle Cottage 173
Eagle Restaurant 184
Eagle Shawmut Mine 227
Eagles Wings 98
Eastman, Isaac E. 50
Ebert, Charles 259, 260
Eccleston, Robert 242, 246, 251, 254, 260, 262, 264, 268
Eden flouring mill 258
Edmundson 184
Edwards, Mr. 210
El Capitan 272
El Dorado 27, 38, 55, 75, 77, 120
El Dorado Hotel 210
Elkins, A. 184
Elkins, J. 55
Elliott, Dr. 32
Elordi, Louis 184
Else 63
Emerson 54
Empire Market 145
Empire Mill 156

Epperson, Mr. Robert 99
Eproson, John 138
Evans 38, 51, 82
Evans, Albert S. 80, 141, 221
Evans, Edward 71
Everbeck, Charles 142
Examiner newspaper 109, 122, 123, 130
Experimental Gulch 170

F

Fagundas, John 270
Fairplay 76
Fallen Monarch 95, 241
Farley, Jim 56
Farmer's Exchange 86
Farnham, H. C. 56
Farnsworth, Major 155, 156
Father of the Forest 93, 96
Faymonville, Wm. 276
Fellinsbee, P. 60
Ferguson 261
Fiddletown 26, 27, 33, 55, 58, 63, 74, 75, 110
Fields, Dr. 173
Fine Gold Gulch 268, 278
Fish Camp 278, 281
Fish, J.B. 70, 107
Fish, J. T. 173
Fisher 203
Fisher, Eli 82
Fisher, Mr. 211
Fleming 173
Flint, Dr. 54
Floto, Henry 239
Ford, Mr. 116
Ford, William 180
Foreign Miners Tax 158, 159
Forest Home 54, 74
Fort Ann 54
Foster 64, 276
Fox, Dr. 28
Fox, Harry 55
Francis, Joe 219
Francisco, Mr. 254
Frazie, Alcalde 154
Frazier, James 153
Fremont, John C. 236
French Camp 15, 248
French Flat 74
Fresno 234, 241, 249, 254, 277
Fresno Copper Mine 280
Fresno Flats 275, 276, 279

Friedenburr water wheel 189
Fuller 178
Fullerton, Wm. 265
Funk Hill 128

G

Gagliardo, Mr. 239
Gale, George 94
Gamble, Peter 244
Garadella, George 112
Gardella Mortuary 112
Gardner, John 137
Garrat, Letinois L. building 142
Gassaway, Frank Harrison 237, 241, 271, 272, 274
Gazette newspaper 168-171, 173, 214
Gazzola, Mr. 254
Gebhardt, Judge L.P. 43
Georgia Claim 59
Ghirardelli's chocolate shop 198
Gillette, Dr. 211
Gillmore, John 243
Giltner, Frank 242
Giltner, Justice 246
Gischel 173
Gitchell 116
Glacier Point 255, 274
Globe Hotel 77
Glover, Mr. 70
Gold Cliff Mine 124
Golden Gate Mine 162, 164, 176, 219
Gold Hill 195
Gold Springs 169, 190
Gonzales, Francisco 244
Goodrich, Boz. 69
Goodwin 56
Goodwin, Dr. 67
Goodwins 44
Gopher Flat 68
Gore, Mr. 194
Gould, G.E. 69
Grady, Patrick 97
Grain Mine 115
Grandvoinet, Dr. 244
Grant House 61
Grant, Ulysses S. 105
Grass Valley 22, 102
Gravel Range Mine 150
Greeley, Rich 246, 271
Green 59, 61
Green, Charles 18, 79
Green claim 64
Green & Holden 183

Green Flat Diggings 178, 180
Green, Alonzo 204
Green, M. D. 249
Green's Gulch 242
Green Springs 172
Gridley, Captain 210
Griffith 212, 213
Griswold, Mr. 39, 54
Griswold, Martin Van Buren 39
Grove 189
Groveland 218
Grub Gulch 276, 278, 280
Guerin, Denny 226
Guy, Mrs. 107

H

Haggle, J. E. 120
Hale's Mill 182
Half Dome 255
Halsted 64
Halterman, Mr. 258
Hammond, Wm. 197, 198
Hamptonville 278
Handford, Levi 69
Handford store 81
Hardie's Ferry 270
Harding's Hotel 70
Harlow, Sylvester 184
Harnett 35
Harroll, Nathan and Jasper J. 143
Hart, Charles and William 255
Harte, Bret 23
Harville, Willis 242
Haskell, Daniel 45
Haskins 130
Hatch 169
Hawes, B. F. 119
Hawkins Bar 186, 187
Hawkinsville 187
Hayes 164
Hayes, Ellec 62
Hayes, Thomas 20
Hayward 113
Hayward Mine 68
Hedden 173
Helltown 74
Hendricks, Lee 82
Hendrickson, Mr. 143
Herschner, Dr. 29
Heslep, Joseph 212
Hetch Hetchy Valley Railroad 209
Hick 81
Hicks' Ranch 66

Hicks, William 77, 78
Higman 271
Higman's Groceries 256
Hildeubrand 173
Hildreth 278
Hildreth, Thaddeus 154
Hill, Jim 147, 210
Hiniker, Henry 150
Hipkins, Dick 59
Hite, John 244
Hite, John R. 270
Hite Mine 268, 269
Hoagland, John 263
Hobert 113
Hochmouth, Andrew 173
Hoerchner Building 108
Hofer, Louis 219
Hogtown 74
Holden, Joshua 189
Holden's Hotel 202
Holmes, A. J. 64
Hoopers 56
Hornitos 135, 239, 254, 257, 258, 260, 264, 272,
Hot Springs 88, 281
Hotel de France 199
Houghtaling, A. J. 44
House, Mr. 266
Howard Family Indian Camp 259
Howard, Under Sheriff 255
Hubble building 32
Hudson's Bay Company 15
Humbug Gulch 61
Hume 130
Hunt, Ethenridge 256
Hunt, J. L. 277
Hunt, Steven 51
Hunter 216
Huntington, J. M. 199
Husband, Bruce 32
Hussey 170
Hutchings 92
Hutchins, J. M. 100
Hutchinson, Mann & Co. 35
Huxley 63

I

Iba, Fred 34
Ice Trail 206
Imbrie 212
Independent newspaper 116
Independent Saloon 104
Independent Twelve Company 118

Indian Diggings 75, 76, 100
Indian Gulch 27, 60, 62, 260
Indian Jeff 262
Indian Tom 77
Ingalls 38
Inyo County 235
Ione 15, 17, 19, 21, 24, 30, 39, 40, 42, 43, 54, 61, 63, 69, 76, 77, 79, 80, 82, 84, 85, 86
Ione & Eastern Railroad 19
Ione Hotel 30
Ione Stage 136
Isgrigg 215
Ives, Dr. 72
Ivy, Henry 260

J
Jackass 103
Jackass Gulch 147
Jackson 15, 19, 22-25, 29-55, 60-62, 6-68, 71, 73, 76-82
Jackson Brewery 29
Jackson, Colonel 31
Jacksonville 154, 184, 186
Jacksonville Damming Company 184
James, Mr. 89, 211
Jamestown 145, 147, 154, 171, 180, 192, 201, 226, 232, 233
Janori, Patricio 182
Jeffersonville 241
Jenkins, Jennie 258
Jennie Lind 103
Jenny Lind, a river boat 234
Jesus, Gabino 178
Jewell 218
Jewell, John 268
Joaquin Murietta 15, 18, 31, 170, 171, 223, 224, 227, 228
John Ep's Saloon 138
Johnson 134
Johnson, Andrew 277
Johnson, Asa 276
Johnson, Capt. 163
Johnson, Peter 246
Johnson, Theodore Taylor 68
Johnson, W. Reason 241
Johnston, E. M. 45
Johnston family 47, 82
Johnstons, Jim and Jack 75
Jones 69
Jones, Henry 48, 62
Jones, Henry W. 64

Jones, Julia Lois 238, 243, 247, 250, 255, 257, 258, 261, 263, 265, 269
Jones, Thomas 175, 276
Jones, William 154
Jonnings, William 55
Jose, Mr. 210
Jumping Frog of Calaveras County 126
Junction Station 266

K
Kavanaugh, Dr. 240
Kees 144
Keiger 185
Keller, David 142
Kelley 60
Kelly's Feed Stable 213
Kelsey, Dr. 60
Kelty & Co. 172
Kemp, J.C. 58
Kendall brothers 45
Kendall, Drs. 217
Kennebec Hill 156
Kennedy Mine 48, 49
Kenny 45
Kern County 235
Kerr, Dave 82
Ketchum, Judge 207, 208
Keystone Mine 37, 72, 73
Kilham, Horace 39
Kincaid Flat 196
Kinsman, Jos. M. 276
Kip, Leonard 87, 101, 108, 117, 120, 121, 132, 134
King, Captain John 57
Kings County 235
Kirkland, a bark 134
Kittering 199
Knickerbocker Copper load 244
Kniepper Copper Mine 280
Knight, Samuel N. 22
Knight Foundry 22, 45, 53, 66
Knight's Ferry 244
Koehler, Henry 80
Kohlburg & Co. 118
Krupps Ranch 167
Kutchethll, Henry 42

L
Labetoure 192
Lager Beer Company 216
LaGrange Ferry 197
Lamb 134

Lane, James 204
Lane Mine 112
Larid, John 257
Late, Geo. 134, 135
Latimer's Gulch 95
Lawrence, James H. 245, 246
Leary, John 173, 190, 228
Lepi, Don Pedro 231
Lerty, Moore 48
Lesaw, William 73
Letford, James 155
Letford, John 277
Leverone, Mr. 251
Levinsky 32
Lewis, Joe 63
Lewis, Wash. 63
Lightner Mine 120
Lincoln & Mahoney mills 68
Lincoln Mine 70
Linoberg, E. 183, 198
Lipton, Thomas 105
Livermore's Ranche 157
Lloyd, Chancey R. & Mrs. 119, 120
Loafer Hill 75
Lockley, L. B. 252
Los Angeles 164, 172, 230, 235
Louisiana Hotel 39
Louisiana House 38, 51, 82
Love, Harry 230
Love, Martin 45
Loveridge, A. C. 46
Lower Rancheria 73, 77
Lucas, Charles 239
Ludgate, Robert 78
Ludwig, Albert 20
Lutter, Captain 187
Lyons 222
Lyons Lake Dam 186
Lytton's Exchange 194

M
Madame Pantaloon 45, 47
Madeira, Colonel 63
Madera County 235
Madera flume 275, 280
Madera Flume and Trading Company 281
Magnolia Saloon 262
Mahoney 68
Mahoney Hall 55, 57
Malone, J. H. 260
Mammoth Grove Hotel 90
Mann, Henry 35, 36

Manning, Dr. 212
Mansur 67
Mariposa 102, 171, 229, 235-274
Mariposa Free Press 245
Mariposa Mine 236, 250, 265
Mariposa Tunnel Tree 249
Marryat, Frank 93, 94, 96, 122, 146, 151, 156, 179, 180, 192, 202, 207, 208, 219, 224, 232, 234
Marsh, Dr. 35
Marsh, Mr. 102
Marshall 173
Marshall, Edward and Tom 194
Martell 19, 79
Martha's Saloon 160
Martin 81
Martin, J. P. 77
Martinez 157, 165, 178, 224
Martinez, Doña 165
Martinez, Donna 157
Martinez, Pablo 177
Marvin 180
Marvin, J. G. 177
Marvin, Judge 178
Mary Harrison Mine 245
Marysville 39
Mason 64
Masonic Hall 198
Masterson 241
Matteson, T. J. 105, 107, 137
Matthewson 37
Maynard, Si 67
McAlister 65, 242
McAlpin, Mr. 179
McAvoy Company 187
McBirnie, Mr. 212
McCann, Frank and Paddy 265
McCathy 185, 215
McCauley 222
McCauley, Edward and Tom 166
McCollum, William S. 95, 105, 107, 119
McConnell 128
McCray 280
McDowell 60
McFadden, Barney 101
McFarland, J. F. 226
McFarlane, Marshal 197
McGrath, James H. 266
McIntyre, Mrs. 70
McIntyre, E.B. 69
McKay's sawmill 125

McLaughlin, E. 281
McLellan, Robert 70
McLeod 203
McLeod, William 45
McRae 225
McRae's store 226
McSorley, Jack 101
Means, Major 148
Meek 144
Mehen 168
Mehen, Peter 179, 183, 193
Merced City 248, 271
Merced County 235
Merced Falls 237, 238
Merced Gold Mining Company 245
Merced Mines 248
Merced Mining and Hydraulic Co. 270
Messer 65, 66
Methodist Episcopal Conference 107
Metropolitan Hotel 118, 119
Mexican Home Guards 231
Meyer, Mrs. Charlie 22
Michael 275
Michigan Log Buggy 114
Miller, Joaquin 23, 24
Millerton 244, 249, 278, 282
Mills 60
Mills, D.O. 56, 168, 172, 213
Mills, James & Co. 172
Milton 92, 1-2-105, 108, 128, 135, 137-139, 188, 203, 226
Mimiellet 276
Mineral Springs 56
Miner's Ditch Company 117
Miner's Tax 158, 159
Mitchell, John 272
Mitchell, W.H. 73
Mitchler's Hotel 104, 105
Miwok Indians 140, 237
Modesto 267
Moerenhout, Jacques Antoine 76, 78, 80, 82, 129, 233
Mokelumne and Campo Seco Canal and Mining Company 114
Mokelumne Hill 15, 17, 19, 29, 32, 36-38, 44, 55, 70, 79, 87, 103, 107, 108, 112, 114-118, 131, 136, 143, 144, 154, 171
Molina, Ruiz 178
Mono County 235
Monterey 50

Monteverde, Louis 84
Montezuma 205
Moore 112, 113, 184
Moran, Tom 130, 139
Moquelome Indians 78
Morgan, Dr. 61
Morgan Gold Mine 133
Morgan, Harrison 190
Morgan, J. P. 105
Morgan's Camp 187, 190
Morgan gold mine 133
Mormon Gulch 147, 159
Mormon Island 77
Morris, Mr. 183
Morrows 136
Morse, Harry 128, 130
Moser, S. S. 143
Mother of the Forest 94
Moulton, Dick 69
Mountain Echo 111
Mountain Spring Home 54
Mount Ophir 171
Mt. Bullion 244
Mudge, Theo. 33
Mud Springs 25, 38
Muletown 82, 83, 85
Mullan, Marshal 190
Mullery, Sheriff 255
Murder's Gulch 53
Murietta, Joaquin 15, 18, 31, 170, 171, 223, 224, 227, 228
Murphy 256
Murphy Canal 144
Murphy, Martin 103
Murphy, Morris 132
Murphy's 16, 44, 76, 87, 92, 103-107, 112, 118, 119, 132, 140, 142, 144, 171
Murray's Ferry 239
Murphy's Hotel 105
Murray, Mr. 205
Murray, Walter 159
Mushet 42

N
National Hotel 31, 32, 39, 78, 82
National House 38, 42
Natural Bridges 88, 91, 139
Nellis 232
Nelson, Waterman H. 32
Nevada Narrow-Gauge Railroad 80
Never Sweat Mine 276
Newby 178

Index

New England Water Company 171
Newcom, Daniel 130
Newman, S. 107
New York Company's Ferry 273
Nicholas, Peter 194
Nichols, J. R. 277, 279
Nimms, Warren 81
Noel, Thomas 239
Nordhoff, Charles 209
Northern Belle Mine 64
Number 9 Mine 272

O

O'Brien's Store 149, 199
O'Neil's Bar 132
Oaf 63
Oakhurst 275
Oakland 19, 24, 267
Oakland Times 24
Ochoa, Dionisio 178
Odd Fellows 108, 118
Odenheimer, William 173
Ohio Hill 47
Old Betsey 279
Old Goliah 98
Old Gulch 132
Oleta, *see also* Fiddletown 30, 42, 58, 74, 75, 110
Onita Ranch 115
Oro Fino 275
Osborn's Store 132

P

Pacheco Shaft 101
Pacific Rail Road 266
Page, Bacon & Co. 213
Page's Ranch 169
Palmer, George 172
Palmer, Dick 38
Palmer, R.W. 31
Palmer Stable 82
Papac, John 31
Parker, Lola 82
Parker, Ray 82
Parker, Sam 82
Parks, Edward 136
Parou, Adolf 200
Parrot, John 194, 195
Parrott's Ferry 166
Patterson, Dan 195
Patterson family 78
Paulk brothers 134
Peek, Frank W. 108
Pelton, Lester Allan 22

Penn Mining Company 87, 91, 109
Pen Stock plan 106
People's Accommodation & Express Company 203
Percival 49
Perkins 50
Perkins, William 198
Perry 93
Perry, John 105
Peter 168
Peters, J. D. 278
Petticoat Mine 144
Peyton, Mr. 163
Phelps, Dr. 45
Phelps Farm 279
Phillips 184
Phillips, Constable 212, 213
Phoenix Livery Stable 119
Phoenix reservoirs 196
Pike, Mr. 245, 274
Pierce, Hiram Dwight 77, 79, 81, 83, 85, 86, 127, 130
Pilkinton 50
Pinecrest Lodge 216
Pine Grove 60, 77
Pine Log 194
Pine Peak 115
Pine Tree Vein 243, 251
Pioneer Livery Stable 134
Pioneer's Cabin 95, 96
Pioneer Society 20
Pitt, Dr. 84
Placer Hotel 216, 217
Placerville 16, 119
Player-Frowd, J.G. 73, 204
Pluto's Chimney 95
Plymouth 15, 52, 55-57, 67
Podesta 27
Poer 222
Pokerville (*see also*, Plymouth, Puckerville) 56
Poole 57
Poole, Sam 215
Poompoomatee 74
Pioneer's Cabin 95, 96
Pope's Emporium 60
Pope, Captain Robert 117
Porter Engine or Locomotive 223, 245
Potter, H.E. 67
Poverty Ridge 115
Preston Castle 63

Princeton 239, 242
Princeton Mine 238, 268, 269
Probasco's team 270
Prospect Rock 69
Puckett, Captain 206, 207
Purtham 54

Q

Q dwelling house 65
Q Ranch 79
Quartz Mountain 73, 206

R

Radcliff, Charles M. 198
Radcliffe 180
Raddatz, John 20
Raggio, Dave 120
Rail Road Flat 137, 144
Raines, James 277
Ralph, F. J. 217
Ralph, Frank 207, 210
Ralph Blacksmith Shop 211
Ralph's Chinese Camp stable 199
Ramirez, Mariana & Jesus 149
Randall, Deputy 212, 213
Randall 195
Rattlesnake Gulch 53
Redmond, Dick 112
Red Mountain Bar 187
Reeb, Mr. 254
Reed, Colonel 192
Reed, D. B. 91
Reed, Myron 111
Reed, Silas 73
Reno 131
Reynolds & Company 183, 197
Reynolds' Ferry 203
Renolds, Trixie 253
Rhodman, William 244
Rice 69
Rice's blacksmith shop 71
Richards, Captain 63
Richardson 55, 212
Richardson, A. G. 198
Rickey, Father 86
Roan, James 277
Roberts, R. 281
Robinson, Edward 78
Robinson, Henry 195
Robinson, R. A. 172
Robinson's Ferry 193, 195, 230
Rocco, Andrew 265
Rodgers, William 249, 250
Rochette, (Frenchy) 158

Rocker, P 173
Roctersino, Johanna 120
Rodersino, Johanna & Phillipini 120, 121
Rogers' Camp 187
Robers' Hot Springs 282
Rolleri, Olivia 137
Roney 276
Rood, Silas 73
Root, Horace 197, 220
Rootville 278
Ross, Samuel H. P. 276
Rosasco Ranch 194
Rose 174
Rounds, Mr. 194
Ruiz, Rafael 271
Rumsey, Judge 276
Rural Press 114
Russel Hill 61
Ryland, C. T. 281

S

Sacramento 19, 24, 31, 32, 34, 46, 50, 52, 55, 58, 60, 61, 69, 76, 78, 79, 107, 131-134, 142, 168, 171, 172, 197, 217
Said, E. 144
Sain, L.M. 261
Salcido 116
Saloschen, Alexander 191, 192
Salt Spring Valley Reservoir 106
Sampson, Harvey Myron 147
Sampson, Jeremiah 147
San Andreas 40, 87, 92, 103, 104, 107, 111, 116-120, 131-133, 140-144, 170, 171
San Benito County 235
San Bernardino County 235
Sanderson & Co. 184
San Francisco 17, 20, 24, 28, 32, 35, 49, 61, 92, 95, 100, 102-104, 107, 109, 113, 124, 128, 130-136, 142, 147, 155, 157, 171, 177, 189, 196, 197, 201, 215-217, 227, 231, 234, 253, 256
Sanguinetti 38
Santiago Flat 166, 170
Santiago Hill 154
San Joaquin and Sierra Nevada Railroad 89, 115, 119, 133, 137, 142
San Joaquin County 16, 60, 128, 135
San José 100

San José Mission 78
San Luis Obispo County 235
Savage, James 188
Savage, Major 236, 264
Savage, Mr. 174
Savage's store 276
Saw Mill Flat 184, 194, 224, 225, 228
Sawyer Act 97
Schaeffer, Luther Melanchthon 177, 187
Schlageter Hotel 266
Scott, Constable 66
Scribner, Mr. 112
Sears and Wenzel's blacksmith 198
Seaton, D.W. 28
Seaton Mine 28
Severance's Old Mill 232
Sharp, Elder 85, 86
Shaw, David Augustus 74, 176
Shawmut Mine 227, 228
Shaw's Flat 163, 166, 169, 180, 182, 183, 204, 216, 220,
Sheep Ranch 90, 92, 102, 103, 120, 124
Sheldon 96, 226
Sheldon, John 226
Shields, Doctor 33
Shine & Co. 203
Shipmen, Major 56, 63
Shirt-tail 61, 74
Shultis 63
Sickle Shaft 113
Sigel Guard of Sonora 232
Silva, Antone De 270
Simmon 152
Simmons, Wm. 272
Simpson 57
Simpson, Frank 150
Siniac 129
Sisson, C. H. 203
Skelton, Deputy Sheriff 265
Slate Gulch 73
Slater 49
Slater's ranch 231
Sloan 32
Smiley, Jim 124, 125
Smith 249
Smith, John H. 160
Smith, L. H. P 250
Smith's Cabin 92, 98
Snelling's ranch 67
Snow, George W. 182

Snow, Horace 245, 256, 266, 267
Sober, Dr. 20
Soher 44
Soldier Bar 278
Soldier's Gulch 5, 60-64
Solomon 195
Solomon, Sheriff 213
Sonora 17, 19, 79, 103, 128, 145-149, 152-164, 168, 171-184, 188, 190, 191, 193-232
Sonora Grays 164
Sonora Herald 152, 159, 176, 190, 205, 209, 220, 225
Sonora Railroad Depot 201
Sonorita Gulch 153
Sotrr 173
Soulsbyville 172, 222
South Grove of Big Trees 92, 96
South Spring Hill 72
Spagnolia, Joseph 272
Sparks, John G. 173
Spaulding, Mr. 29, 49,
Spaulding, N.W. 19, 37, 48
Spencer 63
Sperry 93
Sperry, James L. 90, 105
Sperry's 94, 121
Sperry and Perry 93, 105
Split Rock Ferry 264
Springfield 157, 170, 215
Spring Hill mill 73
Squaw Gulch 32, 47
Stallo, T. C. 276, 277
St. Charles Restaurant 173
St. James Church 145
Standart Lumber Company Railroad 205, 242, 247, 253, 273
Stanislaus Flour 142
Starkey brothers 66
State Journal 132
Steele, Rev. John 41, 116, 131, 148, 171, 184, 189
Steinberger, J. 198
Steinmetz's restaurant 185
Stephens, Lorenzo Dow 21
Stephenson, George 150
Sterns, Joseph 269
Stranahan, S. N. 241
Stevens 32
Steven's Bar 187
Stevenson 15, 43, 58, 63
Steward, M. M. 184

Stewart 69
Stewart A. L. 83
Stewart, Major 184
Stewart Mine 83
Stockier 32
Stockton 15, 16, 21, 24, 60, 79, 80, 92, 102, 105, 118, 131, 132, 134, 135, 137, 142, 152, 157, 171, 177, 183, 184, 192, 196, 203, 215, 217, 227, 234
Stockton-Murphys Stage 118
Stockton Narrow Gauge Railroad 79
Stoddard, Thomas 196
Stoddart, Captain 158
Stone, A. W. 128
Stone, Charles 81
Stone, H. 173
Stone's Blacksmith shop 110
Stony Point & Company 188
Story 63
Story & Co. 64
Stothers, John E. 183
Stowell, Bod. 60
Stowell, Rod 54, 60
Stowers, Captain 49, 60, 74
Strafford, a bark 51
Stranahan, S. N. 241
Street & Co. 184
Stroby, Mr. 236
Strombeck, T. T. 276
Stuart, Sheriff 161
Sucker Hill 75
Suckertown 74
Sullivan 156
Sullivan & Mehen 183
Sullivan, Major 198
Sullivan's Gulch 169
Sulphur Springs 282
Summerville 196
Summit Pass 168, 170
Sutherland, Billy 18
Sutherland, Jack 18
Sutter, General 67, 78
Sutter Creek 15, 19, 20, 31, 32, 41, 43, 45, 52, 53, 57, 58, 60, 64, 67, 68, 71, 72, 76, 78, 81, 84, 97, 136
Sutter Creek & Sacramento Stage 52
Sutter Creek Brewery 20
Sutter Creek Methodist Church 64
Swain, C.W. 43
Swett's Bar 187, 188
Sydney Ducks 151

T

Table Mountain 88, 90, 195, 216
Taney & Bertine 197
Taylor, Bayard 150, 157, 165, 211, 223
Taylor, T. R. 173
Telegraph City 103, 136
Tellier, Louis 15, 31, 34
Temperance Flat 278
Temple, George 246
Testor, Peter 237
Texas Camp 186
Texas Flat 276, 278
Thacker, Johnny 131
Thayer, J. 191
Theall, H.W. 210
Thomas, Mr. 50
Thomas, Richard B. 273
Thompson 112, 113
Thompson, Jonas 258
Thompson, Judge 19
Thorn, Ben K. 128
Thorn, J. F. 272
Thorn, Sheriff 90
Thornley, John 172
Three Fingered Jack 241
Thrornburg 276
Thurman 275
Tibbetts, Frank 70
Tienda Mexicana 183
Tiger Claim 153
Tim's Springs 166
Todd & Co. 197
Tormey, Captain 198
Tovey, Mike 120
Trabucco, F.T., Victor & family 235, 244, 265
Tracy, Captain 211
Tragedy Springs 25, 70
Trapper Smith's Cabin 92
Tripp, W. O. 184
Tucker 69
Tucker, J.A. 73
Tulare County 235
Tuleburgh 16
Tunnel Hill 18, 38, 45
Tuolumne County 16
Tuolumne County Water Company 168, 205
Tuolumne Home Guards 232
Tuolumne Hydraulic Association 205, 206
Tuolumne Rangers 231
Tuolumne Water Company 172, 215
Tupper 49
Turner 225
Turner, Dr. 271
Turner, Helmer 35
Turner, John 63
Tuttle 180
Tuttle, Judge 147, 172, 198
Tuttletown 129, 147, 190, 226
Twain, Mark 103, 105, 126, 128, 133
Tyndal 63

U

Union Company 118
Union Construction Company 223
Union Copper Mines 100
Union Ditch Company 111, 144
Union Hotel 58, 102, 112
United States Hotel 33, 45, 213, 226
Unkles 60
Upper Calaveritas 132, 143
Utica 112, 115, 121, 132

V

Valencia 130
Vallecito 91, 103, 135, 137, 139
Valley Springs 87, 90, 92, 103, 115, 133, 134, 137
Valmaseda, Donna Josefa 157
Vanarsdall, W. G. 172
Vanciel, Charlie 138
Varain, Julian 266, 267
Verplank 222
Vigilance Committee 195
Virginia's Company 216
Vogan, John 18, 79
Volcano 15-17, 20, 25, 31, 35, 38, 48, 50, 51, 54, 56, 58, 59, 61, 63, 64, 76, 82, 84
Vyse, Deputy Sheriff 172
Vyse, W. 198

W

Wadsworth, Captain 158
Wahn, Ah See 95
Walker, Jas. N and C. F. 275, 277
Walker, John 154
Wallace 222
Wallace, Fred 62
Wallace, Richard 190
Warren 242
Warren, USS 157
Washburn & Bruce 263

Washburn, Henry 241
Washburn, J. F. 118
Washington Company 189-192
Washington Hose Company 196
Washington Mine 259
Washoe 51, 108, 133
Watson, Captain 231
Webb House 130
Weber, Captain 16
Weber party 76
Webster, Dan 124
Welch Claim 62
Wells, Fargo & Company 45, 62, 102, 111, 120, 124, 127, 128, 131-133, 136, 160, 171, 174, 203, 213, 214
West, Ike 62, 63
West Point 103, 137, 139
Westside Flume and Lumber Company 232
West Side Lumber 152
Wheaton Company 193
Wheeler, James T. 69, 73
Whisker Bill 127
Whistling Billy 252
White, D. C. 32
White Sulphur Springs 56
Whitford, Frank 251, 252
Whitlock, C. M.
Whitlock Mine 251
Whitney 69
Widman, Mr. 268
Wildman's store 81
Williams, J. C. 28, 57
Williams, Ralph 263
Williams, Thomas 260
Willow Creek 117, 120
Willow Springs 55
Willson 73
Wilson, Chris C. 245, 248
Wind Hill 54
Winters brothers 78
Wirthington, Leonard 142
Withrow, Bill 127
Wolfling's slaughter-house 210
Woodard, F. H. 273
Wood, Harvey 89, 98, 118, 193, 227, 228
Wood's Creek 185, 216
Wood's Diggings 248
Woods, Daniel B. 149, 153, 158
Woolsey, George 62
Woolsey's store 40
Work, George 178
Work, Sheriff 172, 180
Worley, Dan 52
Wright, Joseph 73
Wulbern, Frank Lewis 258

Y

Yancy 82
Yaney 197
Yankee Claim 54
Yankee Hill 54, 155, 170, 214
Yarborough, Justice 249
Yates, Squire 49
Ybarra, Pedro 191
Yeager, Doctor 62
Yellowjacket, Captain 140
Yeomet 47, 57
Yerba, Teodosia 81
Yorktown 155, 199
Yosemite (sometimes Yo Semite) 28, 92, 119, 135, 139, 150, 218, 225, 235, 236, 239, 240, 244, 249, 252, 253, 265, 263, 264, 271, 274-279
Yo Semite House Hotel 224
Young, Brigham 51
Young America Saloon 32, 42

Z

Zinkland, Andrew 273

More "Golden" Books

The "Golden History" Book series focuses on the life and times in Northern and Central California and Northern Nevada in the 19th century. It is distinctive because it brings together the unique observations and viewpoints of dozens of people who were in a particular area at a particular time-frame in history.

The Golden Corridor paved the way for a more in-depth look at various California and Nevada communities. We made some exciting "finds" in creating these first three books, and there is much more to discover, preserve and share. Through today's technology, information that could only be obtained looking through huge historical texts in vast research libraries is now accessible to everyone. And we'll bring it to you.

More *"Golden History"* books are in the works. They will be even more informative and more fun for readers like you. They will include more photographic treasures and information from the archives of dozens of smaller historical societies and private collections. And, we're working with the community of historians, historical parks and friends, to discover even more new sources of information.

Over the next couple of years you'll be able to visit many places and see many scenes that few have experienced. Here are some titles and estimated release dates:

The Golden Hub - Sacramento	Summer 2008
The Golden Gate - San Francisco	Summer 2009

To pre-order copies of any of these books, or for bulk orders for schools or other organizations, please contact us at:

19th Century Books / Electric Canvas
1001 Art Road
Pilot Hill, CA 95664
916.933.4490

If you'd like to receive an e-mail announcement when new titles are released, please contact: Jody@19thCentury.us

Thank you for your interest in our rich history. We hope you've enjoyed *The Golden Highway* and will enjoy more of our books in the future.

Does your family have 19th century photos, journals, letters or other documents you'd like to share and preserve?

Let us help you archive your originals electronically. You will receive a copy of all your materials on CD, and you decide if you'd like to retain the originals or entrust them to your local historical society, the Library of Congress, or some other institution for safekeeping.

Please share your family's history. It'll provide one more piece to the complex puzzle that represents our rich culture and background.

Contact us today for details.
Jody@19thCentury.us or
916.933.4490